About This Book

The Big Book of Antique Furniture offers a comprehensive view of English and Continental, Colonial Revival and Victorian furniture, with up-to-date pricing. It is a compilation of three books written by David P. Lindquist and Caroline C. Warren: *English & Continental Furniture*, *Colonial Revival Furniture*, and *Victorian Furniture*.

W9-BUI-484

About the Authors

David P. Lindquist is a well-known antiques dealer and world-class authority on antique furniture. He is the owner with Elizabeth Lindquist Mann of Whitehall at the Villa Antiques and Fine Art in Chapel Hill, North Carolina, and participates in major antiques shows throughout the country.

Lindquist served the National Association of Dealers in Antiques, Inc., in various capacities, including president. He is an accredited senior appraiser in the American Society of Appraisers since 1981. He lectures and writes extensively on antique furniture, silver, and identifying fakes and reproductions.

Caroline C. Warren, a writer and research librarian, was publications manager for Whitehall at the Villa.

David P. Lindquist

Dedication

To our parents
Chester and Ruth Lindquist
and
David and Rebecca Warren

———————◆———————

For Paul,
who has to live with all this old stuff

The Big Book of Antique Furniture

Table of Contents

English & Continental

Colonial Revival

Victorian

ENGLISH &
CONTINENTAL

FURNITURE

WITH PRICES

CONTENTS

ACKNOWLEDGMENTS

A book of this scope would be impossible without the help of many people. We would like especially to thank all of the auction houses and antiques dealers who generously loaned us photographs. Our thanks go to Marisa Capaldi of Frank H. Boos Gallery, Bloomfield Hills, Michigan; Rita Bucheit, Ltd. of Chicago; Pamela Tapp at Butterfield & Butterfield of Los Angeles and San Francisco; Leighton Adair Butts of Tryon, North Carolina; Mary Lou Strallindorf at Christie's of New York City; Barbara Clare of Edenton, North Carolina; Dunning's Auction Service, Inc. of Elgin, Illinois; Leslie Lynch Clinton at Freeman/Fine Arts of Philadelphia; Morton Goldberg Auction Galleries of New Orleans; Grace Yeomans at Grogan & Company of Boston; Whitney McCune at Leslie Hindman Auctioneers of Chicago; Clarence Pico at Litchfield Auction Gallery of Litchfield, Connecticut; James D. Julia, Inc. of Fairfield, Maine; Cynthia Tashjian and Ann Trodella at Skinner, Inc. of Boston; Sotheby's of New York City; Weschler's of Washington, D.C.; and Wolf's Fine Arts Auctioneers of Cleveland, Ohio.

We are grateful to the Sloan Art Library at the University of North Carolina at Chapel Hill for the use of their fine collection of materials about the decorative arts and the history of furniture.

Finally, we would like to thank the editors at Wallace-Homestead for their patience and suggestions for improving the book and this series.

INTRODUCTION

English and Continental furniture constitutes the most widely collected area of antiques in the U.S. Chippendale, Regency, Biedermeier, Louis XV—the period and artisans' names alone conjure up for most Americans the romance of English and Continental furniture. With its fascinating history, beautiful woods, and superb craftsmanship, Americans have coveted European furniture for generations. And, as antique European furniture has become more widely available in America, many in the antiques business have noticed the obvious need for a reliable guide.

A browse through the average bookstore or library reveals many wonderful books on the history of English and Continental furniture, but for the most part, they simply are not relevant to what is actually for sale on the American market. They describe the masterpieces of furniture that one finds only in museums or in elite private collections. There are also price guides to European furniture that feature more affordable pieces, but almost all of these guides reflect the market for these antiques in England. The market in America is a very different thing—with availability, demand, and prices varying dramatically. This book specifically sets out to address the value of antique European furniture on the American market. And even if you are traveling to England or the Continent to buy antiques, this is the price guide you should use to understand what the pieces will be worth once you bring them home.

English and Continental Furniture with Prices serves as a practical guide to the kinds of pieces that you see every day in good shops and auction houses in America. These are not museum-quality pieces. These are *good*-quality pieces that often have repairs, some minor, some major. With more than 400 black and white photographs, as well as an informative color section, we cover the major styles and forms of European furniture. And, although it is often said that a picture is worth a thousand words, in the world of antiques, pictures seldom tell the whole story. The pictures are indispensable in helping you learn styles and forms, but they rarely tell you much about the condition of the piece—an aspect that is crucial to value.

Repaired breaks, replaced chair legs or table tops rarely show up in a photograph, but they dramatically affect the value. It is unusual to find a piece of antique furniture that has not been repaired in some way. After all, it has seen many generations of use. It is also possible for any piece to have been altered from its original state. As often as we can, we specify the condition of the piece photographed and explain how that affects the value. Also, in the introduction to each furniture form, we discuss the kinds of repairs you should expect to find and how those repairs will affect the price. Some repairs are more problematic than others, and we will alert you to those.

This book covers antique European furniture from the Renaissance to the early twentieth century. Out of this huge span of work, the most popular on the American market today is eighteenth-century furniture—considered by many to represent the greatest flowering of the decorative arts. True to the American market, our book has many photographs of eighteenth-century furniture and later copies of those styles. We also give lots of tips on distinguishing original period antiques from later copies, and what to look for in a good-quality reproduction. The market is rife with nineteenth- and early twentieth-century copies, so it is important to understand how to distinguish the antique from the reproduction, and to also understand the place of both in the market. If you are on a budget, a good copy can be a sensible investment. When the original period antique is too expensive, reproductions become more desirable. The important thing is to know what you are buying and to pay accordingly. Throughout the book we alert you to forms that are copied frequently and tell how to spot them.

As an introduction to forms and prices for English and Continental furniture, the first part of the book provides the background you will need to understand prices on today's market. You will learn what aspects to consider when thinking about the value of antique furniture— quality, rarity, condition or originality, provenance, and usefulness in today's lifestyle. You will learn how to look for the genuine signs of age and wear on antique furniture. We also provide an overview of the history of European furniture, covering all the styles that one finds on the market today. Knowledge of the evolution of these styles is one tool that is essential to distinguishing genuine antiques from copies that bring together incongruous stylistic details in one piece.

Following these introductory chapters, we have divided the book into two parts: English Furniture Forms and Continental Furniture Forms. Each part is organized by usage—seating, tables, etc.— with introductions that cover common construction techniques, evolution of forms, common wear and repairs, fakes, and alterations. We have tried to include all the popular forms of furniture, as well as a sampling of the major styles, ranging from fine urban pieces to provincial work. Each photograph is accompanied by a description, including style, age, whatever repairs we are aware of, comments about style and desirability of the form, and the price range. These prices are our judgment as to *retail* values in a shop. What an individual might receive—what an auction might bring—are *not* aspects of these value estimates.

The subject of English and Continental furniture is complex, covering numerous centuries, styles and makers. Obviously, one book will not make you an expert. However, we have tried to make this book a practical guide for Americans buying English and Continental antique furniture. As any antiques dealer will tell you, there is no substitute for years of hands-on experience with antique furniture. But wherever possible, we share with you the practical knowledge built up over many years of experience in buying, selling and appraising antiques. Read this book carefully. Take it with you on your antiquing expeditions for reference. Ask questions of antiques dealers. We hope this book will add to your confidence and pleasure in collecting antiques.

1

Antique Furniture: What it is, What it's Worth

How the Antiques Market Works

Invariably, the first question about an antique concerns its current value. That may seem like a simple concern, but the answer depends on more than just the age and condition of the piece. Traditionally, antiques have a variety of value levels, depending on the purchaser's position in the sales hierarchy. Items are first purchased from an individual by a "picker" or a dealer. That picker then sells the item for a profit to a shop dealer. Perhaps that shop dealer then sells the item to a dealer with a larger and more prestigious shop or to a dealer from another part of the country who has a stronger market. That dealer might well sell the item to yet another dealer or perhaps to the ultimate customer.

Now, is the value of the antique the $100 that the original owner got for it or is its true value the $1,000 that the final purchaser paid for it? Is there a value in between that is the true value of the antique?

We would argue that it is very difficult to think in terms of any stabilization of value which does not look at ultimate retail price. What the item can be sold for in the strongest possible market is its value. That does not mean that everybody who sells an object will get that price for it. Clearly the above scenario is typical of the life of an antique—it is passed from hand to hand until it finally reaches its ultimate home. It is not unusual to watch a particular object be sold by three or four different dealers at an antiques show in the space of two or three days' time and to finally see the object taken off the floor by a retail purchaser. That final purchase, that ultimate placement of the object, is the value of the item in today's market.

Value ranges in this book reflect this ultimate retail price, and any other interpretation of these values is invalid. These ranges of value might well be used by an appraiser ascertaining fair market or replacement value. The ranges in this book may guide the individual purchasing an object. Or they may assist a dealer in valuing inventory. The prices are shop or show prices, not wholesale prices.

How do we go about understanding what this ultimate value is likely to be? How do we cope with the different levels in the market?

Antiques as an Investment

If antiques have value, then part of their value must be based on their utility as an investment. If we're smart, we seek to turn our cash into long-term investments, which will appreciate in value. We invest in our homes, in the objects with which we furnish our homes, in jewelry, in art, etc. All of these investments plus stocks, bonds, savings accounts, and so forth are designed to cushion our future against any possible setbacks. Historically, antiques are viewed as a good investment because given time they go steadily upward in value.

It is a mistake, however, to view them as part of a short-term investment portfolio. An investment portfolio demands liquidity, and antiques are not liquid. It requires great effort to sell them, and it is seldom the case that the individual owner will receive the highest possible price for the piece. In fact, the individual who owns an antique is most likely to sell it at its lowest wholesale value. Even if one consigns it to auction, chances are about 80 to 20 that the item will be bought by a dealer, which means it was bought at wholesale! Antiques are, therefore, an investment in lifestyle and an opportunity to pass on the heritage of past generations to future generations. They provide long-term accrual of value. They may, with a lot of luck, provide long-term cushioning against future reverses.

For antiques to have this long-term investment potential, they must be purchased for the right price, and they must be purchased with the understanding of what they actually are. By this I mean the purchaser must know what it is he or she has bought, know its relative value, and know that it is "real"—i.e., that it is a period (eighteenth-century) Chippendale chair rather than a nineteenth- or twentieth-century copy. *Or* if it's a reproduction, pay accordingly. This means that purchases of antiques and fine art should include a guarantee.

Guarantees come in many forms. Antiques shops and antiques show dealers regularly provide a guarantee in the form of a detailed bill of sale. Some auction houses make an attempt to provide some general guarantee as to the authenticity of what they sell. However, the rule of all auction houses is *caveat emptor*—buyer beware. Individuals must be their own guarantors when they go to an auction or an estate sale, or when they purchase from a flea market. Many buyers are indeed experts and can be their own guarantor. In this case, one has a chance at bargains. After all, the reward of spending huge amounts of time and effort seeking a bargain is the finding of one. Just make sure it *is* a bargain.

Determining Value

Assuming that the item in question is *real* (the genuine article), then what is it that determines its value? There are five major components of value. The first is quality of design and of craftsmanship. The second is condition. The third is rarity. The fourth, provenance. And the fifth is utility and appearance in the context of today's lifestyle.

Quality

Quality of design is of the utmost importance. It speaks to the original merit of the piece as an object of both utility and of pleasing style and design. An ugly antique has little value. A beautiful object, whether antique or modern, has far more value than a similar object that is ugly. And of equal importance is quality of craftsmanship. A poorly made piece quickly shows the ravages of time. A piece beautifully crafted of the highest quality materials to the highest standards of workmanship lasts for hundreds of years.

Let's look at two examples. Figures 1-1 and 1-2 show two transitional-period Hepplewhite-Sheraton Pembroke tables, c. 1780–1800. The larger, flat-front table is made of solid flame mahogany, while the smaller, bowed version is made of very finely grained mahogany with no flame. We tend to value flame wood over wood with no figure. However, the former must be handled with care. We also tend to think that solid wood is somehow better than veneer. It isn't. The solid flame piece is now seriously cracked and split (Fig. 1-3) due to the inherent weakness of solid flame wood, which is why it should be used as veneer only and not in solid form. Thus, what seemed easy to the cabinet-maker—avoiding the extra steps involved

Fig. 1-2 Hepplewhite-Sheraton Pembroke table, c. 1780–1800. Finely grained mahogany, bowed front, oval top.

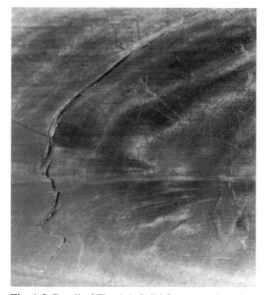

Fig. 1-3 Detail of Fig. 1-1. Solid flame wood cracked and split.

in the use of veneer—has in this case failed the test of time.

Furthermore, the larger example (Fig. 1-1) is *all* solid mahogany, with no inlays. The smaller is veneered on the apron and has original satinwood line inlays and edging on the legs, adding interest.

Fig. 1-1 Hepplewhite-Sheraton Pembroke table, c. 1780–1800. Solid flame mahogany (cracked and split), flat front.

The shapes of the two Pembrokes, of course, have nothing to do with craftsmanship, but clearly the small oval one has finer styling. Note also that the end apron and drawer front bow in concert with the oval top—another nice touch. The size of the smaller Pembroke is also a desirable attribute. All of these features put the smaller Pembroke head and shoulders above the other solid flame Pembroke in terms of style and construction. How do these differences affect value in two pieces made around the same date? Flawed construction techniques and a lower grade of style give the flame Pembroke a value of about $2,400, while the smaller veneered piece has a value of about $6,500.

Condition

When determining value, condition is of enormous importance. When we talk about condition, we mean the retention of original elements, plus the addition of patination and oxidation. We do not want major losses or alterations. We revere the antique which is most original, both in its components and in its surfaces. We like to find the signs of softening, of darkening, of highlighting, of oxidation and patination. It is these aspects which give antiques their unique beauty when compared to fine reproductions.

In Fig. 1-4 we see an eighteenth-century English mahogany knife box that has been changed into a decanter box. Cursory examination would not reveal this, as the conversion appears to date from 1830 or so. The alteration becomes apparent from a side view which shows the grain pattern is *vertical* on the lower part of the box but *slants* on the lid. No eighteenth-century cabinetmaker would have done that! The grain would have lined up perfectly between the bottom and the lid. While this box has value for utility and value as social history—it documents what happened to knife boxes when they were replaced by silver-drawers in sideboards—it does not have any value based on origi-

Fig. 1-4 Eighteenth-century English mahogany knife box converted c. 1830 into decanter box.

nality. The value of the made-up decanter box? $1,200. The value of an original knife box—$2,200. The value of an original decanter box of equal age and design quality—$2,200.

Rarity

Rarity is another important aspect of value and can be considered from several points of view. How limited was production when the object was first made? How broad is the current market for the object? How intense is the interest in such an object? Rarity as it affects value is thus created not only by the number of items made originally, but also by the breadth of current demand. Let's take an example. The size of a slant-front desk helps determine its value. If we think a 36-inch-wide desk is rarer than a 42-inch-wide desk, we would assume the former is far more desirable and far more expensive. Yet the truth is that more of the narrower desks were made originally than the wider ones. Because we prefer the narrower ones, families tend to keep them and sell off the less-desirable wider examples. Thus it is not *original* rarity that makes a narrow

Fig. 1-5 Sheraton-style writing table. Clearly based on drawings in Sheraton's design book. **$30,000–50,000.**

slant front desk valuable today. It is rather the breadth of the current market, the enormous demand for such pieces, and the lack of examples coming to market that create value.

Provenance

Provenance, the history of a piece, is of great importance in determining value. There are several factors that comprise provenance, and each of them influences the value. Is the maker or the designer of the piece known? Is the history of ownership of the piece known? Is there a history of the selling of the object, that is, are the dealers who have sold the object known? All of these types of history are part of the concept of provenance. The owner, per se, need not have been an important person, but a known owner can document the age of a piece and add authenticity.

The photo showing the writing table (c. 1795) (Fig. 1-5) is shown with a photo of the drawings by Thomas Sheraton,

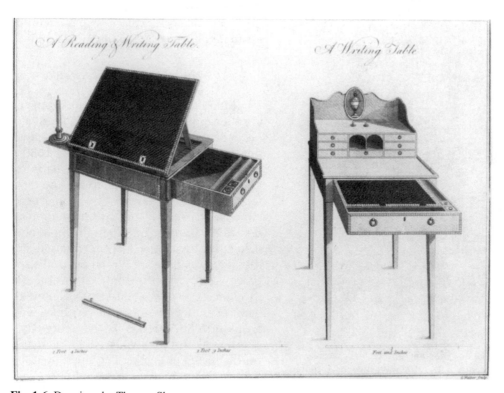

Fig. 1-6 Drawings by Thomas Sheraton.

c. 1792 (Fig. 1-6) from which this particular example clearly derived. This does not mean that this table was made by Thomas Sheraton. In fact, we think he never made a piece in his life (he only designed them). However, it is clear that the maker used Sheraton's design book to develop this piece. And we know from a thorough examination that the piece was made near the publication date of Sheraton's book. Thus it has far more value than a more poorly designed, more poorly executed example with no real antecedents other than a cabinetmaker's effort to copy the work of the other cabinetmakers of his day.

In recent years, we sold a c. 1795 English secrétaire-bookcase (shown in Fig.

Fig. 1-8 Detail of label on Fig. 1-7. *Courtesy K. G. & A. Freeman, Surrey, England.*

1-7) which bore the label of a cabinetmaker in Sarum. The label had a wonderful drawing of a chair, Pembroke table, chest of drawers, and "Norton, Cabinet-Maker and Upholsterer, Sarum" (see Fig. 1-8). This was a beautiful Sheraton-design piece of tall, slender proportions. It had a fine, faded color and a very good old, and possibly original, finish. The label certainly added to its value, which I would estimate between $25,000 and $35,000.

Current Usefulness

Finally, of course, utility and appearance for today's lifestyle are important aspects of value. Fig. 1-9 shows a rare and fine yew wood livery cupboard, c. 1680–1720. Such pieces were used in halls of manor houses for servants' livery and also for riding gear—they are also called tack cupboards. Yew is the rarest and most desirable wood in English antiques collecting. Even the feet are original on this piece, as they are turned of solid yew (not worm-prone walnut). Its value is $15,000–20,000. Fig. 1-10 shows an eighteenth-century linen press of ordinary design worth $6,500–8,500. The livery cupboard will probably be bought by a sophisticated collector. The linen press is a nice example—not extraordinary, yet highly sought after. The cupboard is a

Fig. 1-7 Sheraton-design secrétaire-bookcase, c. 1795. Mahogany with satinwood interior. Original label, well-proportioned, fine color. *Courtesy K. G. & A. Freeman, Surrey, England.* **$35,000–55,000.**

Fig. 1-9 Yew wood livery cupboard, c. 1680–1720. Double raised panel doors above five drawers. Substantially original turnip feet, replaced crown molding. **$30,000–35,000.**

brilliant example taken to the highest level that one could imagine for that time period. Why isn't it ten or twenty times more valuable than the press? Because its use is limited in today's home. It is too shallow for an entertainment center and too wide for most modern walls. The linen press, on the other hand, has found a place in the family rooms, drawing rooms, and bedrooms of American homes as a place to hide the television, the stereo system, or the bar, or as a place to put clothing—its original purpose. Thus, utility and appearance have a significant impact on value.

The other side of this connection between lifestyle and value is that if an antique does not fit into modern lifestyles, it is often altered to meet a current need. This has always been the case and continues to occur today. Pieces that were built for large homes with high ceilings are often cut down to fit in today's smaller rooms. Chests, secretaries, sideboards are

all commonly cut down. How does this affect value? It ruins any value that would be associated with originality of condition. A chest of drawers cut down from a large Victorian chest will no longer have its value as an antique. It is left only with a value as an attractive and useful piece of furniture.

Throughout this book, as we discuss specific examples, we will highlight those aspects that add value and those that detract. In a particular form (chest of drawers, for example), we will examine what construction techniques are most sound and, hence, most valuable; what repairs are almost inevitable and thus have minimal impact on value; what woods are most in demand; and what sizes are most desirable. Knowing what is considered most desirable can also help identify what tempts counterfeiters, and can keep you

Fig. 1-10 Irish Chippendale linen press, c. 1760–170. Mahogany primary wood, oak secondary. Raised panel doors above three drawers. Original bracket feet, partial set of interior sliding trays. Short (6'4") height suggest early date. **$8,000–12,000.**

alert to possible problems when you find that highly desirable piece.

The Ultimate Criterion

There is one key that is foremost in understanding the value of an antique in today's marketplace: "How valuable (expensive) was the piece when it was originally made?"

Furniture was purchased during the eighteenth and nineteenth centuries much as an automobile is today. One signed a contract to buy a chest of drawers from a cabinetmaker. Then the additions to the chest were listed, and the cost of each was noted (Fig. 1-11). And so we might well have a chest costing $2, locks for each of the five drawers running an additional dollar, inlay work to the drawer corners (a dollar), inlay and banding on the top, and so on. Finally, the sum of money for the elaborated piece would be considerably more than the basic unit price.

It is important to examine all of the original elements of the antique, come to an understanding of how those would have impacted the value of the antique in the eighteenth or nineteenth century, and determine where that particular object stands in relation to other similar objects made at the same time. Then we can judge its value in the eighteenth century. From that, its current value can be extrapolated.

Valuing Reproductions

Since so many pieces we see on the market today are not period antiques but later reproductions, how do we assign value to those reproductions? Good-quality reproductions were made in England and on the Continent throughout the nineteenth century and are still being made today. We value them in much the same way we do the originals. We will find a broad range of quality in reproductions—some are quite good, and we will eagerly purchase them. Others we will avoid. We look at style and how faithful the copy is to the original in terms of proportions and details. We look at construction techniques—quality of timber and materials used, amount of handwork evident, types of joints used (seeking the stronger mortise-and-tenon and avoiding dowels, for example), and the quality of details like carving. We also consider the rarity and the desirability of the period antique prototype. If a certain style or form is extremely rare or desirable, it is likely to be priced out of our range, and thus we will be forced to consider a good-quality nineteenth-century reproduction.

Is originality of condition important in old reproductions? Not to the extent that it is in period antiques. However, even old reproductions are altered to meet a new need, and value is affected—sometimes for the better. Take for example a c. 1890 Edwardian sideboard that

	Mohogany £ s d	Wallnut £ s d	Jurnyman £ s d
Cloaths-Presses			
Cloathe Press in two parts upper Part about 4 feet Square in the front the Doors hung with Rule Joints and Sliding Shelves with 3 Drawres in the Lower part in Side work of Red Ceder	15: 0:0	11: 0:0	3:10:0
Do inside work not Red Ceder	13:10:0	9:10:0	3:10:0
Do in one part without Drawers inside work of Red Ceder	12: 0:0	8: 0:0	2:10:0
Do inside work not Red Ceder	10:10:0	7:10:0	2:10:0
Do with tow Drawers inside blow and Pins above with Doors hung in the Common way . .	8:10:0	6: 0:0	2: 0:0
Do of Pine		4: 0:0	1:10:0
N.B. Add to any of the Presses with a Pitch Pediment, Dentils fret & Shield	6: 0:0	5: 0:0	2: 0:0
Do with out Dentils fret or Shield	3:10:0	2:10:0	1: 2:6

Fig. 1-11 Original list of options for "cloaths-presses."

began life as a rather ugly piece with two central drawers. We bought the sideboard, had the lower drawer replaced with a gracefully shaped apron, added cross banding, and actually increased the value. Before alteration, the functional but unappealing piece would have gone for $1,500. After improvements, the piece will sell for $3,500. No longer in its original state, it has lost its value as an antique, but it is a more desirable piece after the alterations. Let's compare this scenario with the same situation using a period piece. An eighteenth-century sideboard of not entirely successful proportions—if original and pristine—might fetch $18,000. If altered by adding cross banding and making the apron more graceful, the value would be slashed to about $8,500. Obviously, tampering with a period antique will drastically lower its value—when the alterations are unmasked. With a reproduction, originality of condition does not carry the same premium. In fact, value can even be increased with alterations.

What Happens to Old Wood

While virtually no statement can be made about furniture construction that does not have a few known exceptions, there are nevertheless some generalities that should always be kept in mind. The following points will apply to all antique furniture, and they can often quickly "clue you in" to a problem piece. These absolutes all relate to what happens to wood over time. Every single piece of wood that goes into making furniture is subject to certain natural effects over time—to softening of edges, to wear, shrinkage, and oxidation and patination. Once you understand these basic properties of wood, you will be better prepared to spot fakes, repairs, and even the actual antique!

Absolute #1: Soft Touch

All exterior edges on antique furniture are soft to the touch. Whenever you see a piece that you like and that looks right in terms of style, the next step in your examination should be to close your eyes, let your fingers do the walking, and feel every edge—all around the feet, all up and down the back, all the edges. They should all be soft. If you find an area that is sharp to the touch, take a look at it. It will lead you to an old repair, a restoration, etc. Air erodes wood over time—just the gentle flow of air for 200 years erodes all the edges of an antique. It is easy to use your sense of touch to uncover replaced feet on a chest of drawers or a large case piece. The edges will be noticeably sharper than those of the original feet. But don't go at it willy-nilly or you will get splinters galore!

Absolute #2: Signs of Wear

All antiques show obvious signs of wear. And these signs should be in places that make sense. Any piece of furniture with movable parts should show evidence of these parts having moved and scraped and worn down over the years. For example, on a Pembroke table the butterfly supports should have scraped the undersides of the flaps over the years. You should see exposed, lighter wood where the supports have rubbed. You should also find extra grime—or patination—where generations of hands have touched the underside of the table flap, raising and lowering it. Fig. 1-12 shows both of these manifestations on the underside of a Pembroke table. You

Fig. 1-12 Underside of a Pembroke table showing scrapes from butterfly supports and markings left by years of handling.

Fig. 1-13 Table bottom with sewing-bird scars.

can see the grimy patination along the edge of the table at the bottom of the photograph. You should find the same kinds of wear and patination on gateleg and drop-leaf tables. Some of the other signs of everyday use include sewing-bird scars (little round indented marks about ¼ inch in diameter) that one often finds on the undersides of antique tea tables or work tables (see Fig. 1-13). Ladies used these sewing birds to clamp their needlework to the table. These little signs, if one looks closely enough, will reveal glimpses of everyday life long ago.

Normal use should have resulted in worn drawer runners (with probable restoration of runners or runner edges) and scarred drawer bottoms. We expect wear on hardware on drawer fronts. In fact, we seldom see original hardware because it doesn't stand up to wear. It's worth remembering, however, that on false drawers, hardware should be original, as it obviously was never used. On doors to breakfronts, secretaries, on a *buffet à deux corps,* you may well be able to trace the arc made by the swing of the upper door on the lower part of the piece.

On seating furniture, expect to find worn legs (chairs may even have lost several inches); stretchers should show

where feet, mops, etc. would normally rub. If you sit down in a chair with stretchers, put your feet where the wear is. Is it comfortable, natural, normal for you to put your feet where the wear is? If not, the wear has probably been faked. Do the same with stretchers on big tables. It is common to find English Jacobean tables with brand-new massive stretchers with worn down areas in the strangest spots, indicating obviously faked wear. If a chair has a carved back splat and carved arms, you should find a gentle wearing away of the carving where head and hands have rested. If the piece is upholstered, and you can see the frame at all, it should be riddled with holes from earlier sets of upholstery tacks.

Remember, no wear, no antique—but the wear needs to make sense. Fakers do try to add "wear" to their "antiques." However, faked wear is often uniform or random—two things that natural wear never is. You must think about how a piece would have been used and find the wear in the right places.

Absolute #3: All Wood Shrinks

Whether it is a ⅛-inch piece of inlay or a 36-inch-wide board, wood shrinks *across the grain* from the day it is cut into a board, and it continues to expand and contract, interacting with the air's moisture. You will find evidence of shrinkage on *all* antiques. And wood does not shrink uniformly—it shrinks across the grain. This point can be seen in many an eighteenth-century tea-table top. A 200-year-old tea-table top will no longer be perfectly round. It will have shrunk about ½ inch across the grain.

You should expect to find shrinkage on the backs of antique case furniture. For example, on the back of a chest of drawers, one will often find gaps between the boards where they have either split or moved apart in their frames. These cracks in the backs of English furniture were often taped to keep out the coal dust which resulted from the prevalent system of heating homes with coal. You will often find splits at nails in the backs where the weakened board easily split as it shrunk. Drawer bottoms will show major shrinkage or gaps where the board pulled out of the groove at the front of the drawer, pulled away from the back, or split apart. Look inside a chest of drawers, you will often find splits in the drawer bottoms. Fig. 1-14 shows a drawer that was made of deal and has a typical split. You will sometimes find these splits repaired with a spline, which is not a problem. What *is* a problem is to find no signs of shrinkage on a supposed antique. You may find a split in the leaf of a drop-leaf table repaired with a butterfly patch on the underside. This is the sort of shrinkage and appropriate repair that we expect to find.

If a piece used frame-and-panel construction, the panels should show some movement if they have been around since the eighteenth century. In this type of con-

Fig. 1-14 Deal drawer showing typical splits in bottom.

struction, grooves in the frame hold the panels loosely to allow movement without causing splits. You can often see evidence of movement due to shrinkage when the unfinished edge of the panel comes away from the frame and is exposed—revealing patination that is different from the finished panel. Again, this is a good sign of age.

Even pieces of inlay shrink with time, and later inlays may be unmasked by finding little or no shrinkage. Inlays are nothing more than the addition of various elements into the surface of another substance. While one occasionally finds inlays of ivory, bone, pewter, copper, silver, brass, and gold, most inlays we encounter are made of wood, and we can expect to find shrinkage. (Ivory and bone may be cracked; the alloys have often popped out of the surrounding wood.)

In old inlay, you can see signs of cracking and shrinkage in each small piece of wood creating the inlay, whether it is a multipiece fan or a narrow line inlay. These cracks and gaps, left as the inlay shrunk away from the surrounding wood, will be filled over the years by dirt, wax, and other surface treatments. Not only can you see the signs of shrinkage, you can feel them. Let your fingers do the walking—you will feel ridges, gaps, and bumps on all areas of antique inlay. It takes a very long time for these flaws to develop to the point where they can be seen and felt—their presence is a strong sign of originality.

Finally, don't just examine the inlays; examine the surface around the inlays. If you find a crack in the structure of a piece, the inlay over it should *also* be cracked or damaged. When shrinkage tears the body of an antique, it tears the inlays as well. Fig. 1-15 shows where the veneering cracked on an eighteenth-century table apron. Notice that the stringing also cracked. That's the way it should happen. Obviously, intact inlays over cracks were put there *after* the cracks occurred.

Fig. 1-15 Cracked veneering and stringing on eighteenth-century apron.

Absolute #4: Patination and Oxidation

All finished wood surfaces develop patina and oxidize over time (and all unfinished wood surfaces oxidize, depending on their level of exposure to air). Oxidation is the interaction of wood with oxygen—the "rusting" of wood. All wood oxidizes when exposed to air. It darkens, and the pores of the wood fill with dust particles and so forth. This natural darkening of the backs, drawer bottoms, etc., cannot be duplicated mechanically. Furthermore, any disturbance to oxidized surfaces leaves telltale light-colored areas that *never* again match the surrounding areas. And it is perhaps the most valuable tool you have in your arsenal of defenses against difficult-to-spot restorations, repair work, or even fakery, because you cannot undo a disturbance to oxidation. If the surface is scratched, and light wood suddenly shows up, it cannot be successfully darkened. If a foot comes off a chest of drawers and has to be put back on, the pattern of oxidation that is disturbed in that process cannot be undone. It will be there, and in 200 years there will still be contrast, because the whole time after that repair has taken place, even as the light area begins to darken, the already-dark area also continues to darken—so the contrast in oxidation patterns remains.

Glue blocks and their associated patterns of oxidation can provide important information as to how long adjoining pieces have actually been together—and thus, how original the piece is. You will find glue blocks in a number of places: where crown moldings were attached to case pieces, on the undersides of tables where the top meets the undercarriage, adding strength to bracket feet, and in the corners of chair frames. The point is not that all the glue blocks need to be original. In fact, it can be reassuring if a glue block is missing and you can see the silhouette (the shadow) of the missing glue block on *all* adjacent pieces of wood. The area where the missing glue block used to be will be lighter, since it was not exposed to air as long as the glue block covered it.

We recently examined a linen press, and by looking at the glue blocks, we were able to determine that the crown molding was original to the piece. Several glue blocks were missing, leaving behind lighter areas that had not been exposed to the air. There was even one that must have let go very early in the life of the piece, because the oxidation was almost perfect. Just below the glue block was a perfect silhouette of where the glue block protected that corner all those years—a shadow line, proving that this glue block was always in juxtaposition to this molding, because it too had a corresponding shadow line.

Patination and oxidation are basic to evaluating an antique. Undisturbed antique surfaces will be beautifully patinated on the finished surfaces. Patination refers to the rich, dark, rather crusty finish created by the build-up of waxes, dirt, and constant rubbing of the surface by oily hands and cleaning. It cannot be duplicated mechanically. It is that gorgeous dirt that gives furniture contrasts of light and dark. Grime will collect around anything that protrudes—a cuff of a leg, hardware on a drawer front, or carving. Grime will collect in the crevices, so that you get highlights on the higher areas, which can easily be seen on antique carving. The wax and grime settle into crevices, darkening, while the dust cloth rubs the high areas keeping them light and polished. Feet scuffing chair legs over the years will leave lots of little nicks and indentations, which will darken with accumulated grime.

Sadly, we find very few original finishes, and thus, not the accumulation of patina that we love so much. In America, up until about 1960 or 1970, the reigning idea was that you made the antique look like it did the day it was made. All that dirt and grime—the beautiful patination—was stripped off. Many antique shops now French polish everything, using a technique that involves scraping down the old surface, thus removing patination and hiding new work. The end result is a hard, shiny finish that does not mellow with age. So unfortunately, we may not see as much patination as we would wish, but when we do find it, it can be a good sign of true age.

These are basic rules that affect all antique furniture. You don't have to be an expert in furniture construction to put these rules to use as you examine antiques on your own. If you feel for soft edges, look for shrinkage and signs of appropriate wear, and examine patterns of oxidation and patination, you will be well on your way to unlocking the secrets of antique furniture.

2

A History of European Style

Major trends in England and on the Continent from the Renaissance up through the early twentieth century will be covered in this chapter. We will focus primarily on style periods and the construction techniques that shaped those styles in England, France, and Germany. Other areas on the Continent, though interesting in themselves, are less central to the evolution of European style. The furniture of Spain and Italy, for example, had the most influence during the Renaissance, after which time French styles were copied, although subtle interpretations were added. The Scandinavian countries followed the German styles (and the Germans, like everyone else, were *greatly* influenced by eighteenth-century French styles). In all of these countries, it is important to note that the centers of culture—the royal courts of Europe and the great urban centers like Paris, Rome, and London—produced furniture that was more sophisticated, more costly, and better made than furniture made outside these centers for ordinary people. Provincial furniture lagged far behind in style and in construction techniques.

The focus of this book is the English and Continental styles available on the American market today. As such, this is not an academic book covering every stylistic nuance in Europe's long history, whether or not we ever see such things in American shops. For example, we do not commonly see actual Renaissance pieces for sale in America. We do, however, see many *copies* of Renaissance styles. So it is important to know something about the period being copied.

By the same token, we do not provide equal coverage to every country on the Continent—again, reflecting what is on the American market. For example, Spanish and Italian designs from the Renaissance are about all that is on the market from those countries, except for Spanish and Italian versions of eighteenth-century rococo styles. Coverage is limited to the periods when these countries had the most influence on European design and to the design periods that appeal to the American market.

Chronology of Furniture Styles

Date	English Monarchs and Styles	French and French Influence	Germany, Austria, and Germanic Influence
1558–1603	Elizabeth I: Elizabethan	Renaissance	Renaissance
1603–1625	James I: Jacobean		
1625–1649	Charles I: Carolean	Baroque / Louis XIII (1610–43)	Baroque
1649–1660	Commonwealth: Cromwellian	Louis XIV (1643–1715)	
1660–1685	Charles II: Restoration		
1685–1688	James II: Restoration		
1688–1694	William & Mary: William & Mary		
1694–1702	William III: William & Mary		
1702–1714	Anne: Queen Anne		
1714–1727	George I: Early Georgian	Régence (1715–23)	
1727–1760	George II: Mid Georgian	Louis XV (1723–74)	Rococo
1760–1811	George III: Late Georgian	Louis XVI (1774–93)	Neoclassical
		Directoire (1793–99)	
		Empire (1799–1815)	
1811–1820	George III: Regency	Restauration (1815–30)	Empire
1820–1830	George IV: Regency		Biedermeier (1815–48)
1837–1901	William IV 1830–1837 / Victoria: Victorian	Louis Philippe (1830–48) / Second Empire (1848–70)	Historicism and Revival (1830–80)
1901–1910	Edward VII: Edwardian	Third Empire (1871–1940)	Jugendstil (1880–1920)

1550–1600: The Renaissance and Elizabethan Era

Continental Features

Italy set the style standard for the rest of Europe during this period. Drawing on classical sources, particularly the classical orders of columns, the Italian courts produced monumental furniture that was richly embellished with carving, inlay, and painting. Renaissance furniture was not based on ancient furniture *forms,* but adapted classical *motifs,* which were added onto current forms. Decorative motifs of the Renaissance included scrollwork, arabesque designs, garlands of flowers and fruit, fantastic and mythological creatures, grotesque masks, putti, and more. In fact, the volume of decoration tended to overwhelm the furniture. On fine pieces, carving could be almost as impressive as the stone sculpture of the

Renaissance. Even more opulent were the pieces of furniture that were gilded as well.

Another popular form of decoration was intarsia—a method of inlaying bone or ivory in geometric patterns into a dark wood such as ebony or walnut. Inlays using other materials were also introduced during the sixteenth century, especially the technique of *pietra dura,* which created inlays of marble and semiprecious stones, primarily in table tops, but also in magnificent cabinets-on-stands.

There are a number of furniture forms from the Renaissance that we still see today. The *cassone* (a chest) was probably the most ubiquitous piece of Italian furniture in the sixteenth century. In its highest form, it was covered with carving (see Fig. 2-1). The *cassapanca,* which evolved out of the *cassone,* is a bench with back and arms, using the *cassone* as a base (the seat also being a lid). The *credenza* was another popular form; it corresponds roughly to the modern buffet incorporating architectural motifs in its massive size. Most Renaissance pieces were mas-

sive, as were the center tables, which had trestle bases. Most armchairs were rectilinear in design and were upholstered in leather or velvet. There were also X-chairs (Savonarola), one of the few forms revived from classical times (see Fig. 2-2). These chairs were not common, however. Simple stools were more prevalent.

The influence of the Italian Renaissance gradually spread to France, with walnut, which was ideal for carving, replacing oak as the favorite wood. French Renaissance furniture included classical columns and other architectural motifs, along with fantastic animals and the whole horde of Renaissance figures. Particularly French forms include the *dressoir,* or buffet, an imposing piece found in several variations, all having an enclosed base with cabinets, and sometimes stepped-back shelves (open or with doors) above. The draw-leaf table also dates from this era in France. Its top extended by means of slides, and it usually had a frieze below the top and box stretchers.

Spanish furniture also followed Italian Renaissance styles and under Charles

Fig 2-1 Italian Renaissance walnut and parcel gilt *cassone,* from Rome or Florence, with carved putti and horse-drawn carriages in high relief. On paw feet. Resting on separate, modern plinth. 34" high x 66" long x 22 1/2" deep. *Courtesy Skinner, Inc. Bolton, Mass.* **$12,000–18,000.**

Fig. 2-2 Italian Renaissance Savonarola armchair with scroll arms and X-shaped curule frame, upholstered in scarlet cut velvet. *Courtesy Christie's New York.* **$6,000–9,000.**

writing cabinet on a stand. The upper part has a fall front enclosing a multitude of small drawers and compartments. These pieces often show a Moorish influence, with geometric inlays and bases with arcades.

Different regions in Germany had distinct furniture styles. There was a stylistic split between north and south that continued through the centuries, the north being allied with the Low Countries and England, and the south with Italy and France. The influence of the Italian Renaissance was felt first in southern Germany, which adopted Renaissance styles by about 1550, especially around Nuremberg. In southern Germany, large ornamental cupboards, credenzas, and chests were popular. The cabinet cupboard (a

Fig. 2-3 One of a pair of Spanish baroque carved walnut armchairs from the seventeenth century. Nail-studded rectangular backs and seats, slightly scrolled arms on square supports, raised on square legs joined by stretchers. With restorations. Popular in the Southwest because of their Spanish Colonial appearance. *Courtesy Butterfield & Butterfield, San Francisco.* **$3,600–4,800** the pair.

V and Philip II, the arts flourished in Spain. As in Italy, chairs tended to be simple, with cushions and stools used for familiar acquaintances and chairs reserved for honored guests. The hip-joint chair (X-chair), known as *sillon de cadera,* was made in walnut, beech, or orange wood. There were also simple rectangular-backed chairs with leather or velvet hung from the back stiles. If the upholstery was attached, large decorative nail heads were used. The legs were joined by low side and back stretchers and a high wide stretcher on the front (see Fig. 2-3). These chairs are sometimes known as monk's chairs—they were used in monastaries and elsewhere. They were exported to Italy, France, England, and the Netherlands, no doubt influencing chair design in those countries.

The *vargueño,* another important Spanish form from the Renaissance, is a cabinet top on a close-in base) was inspired by similar pieces from sixteenth-century Italy. The German cabinetmakers helped lead the way in improvements in joinery techniques, such as mitred corners and wave molding.

Northern Germany was influenced by the Netherlands, which was, in turn, influenced by Spain during the Renaissance. In northern Germany, as in England, oak was the principal wood used, while southern Germany furniture makers tended to use more fir and pine.

English Features

In England this era is known as the Elizabethan period. Politically cut off from the Continent, England was slow to embrace the Italian Renaissance designs. English design has often been conservative, and this was true of the English interpretation of Renaissance styles, which took a less elaborate form than on the Continent. Pieces were massive and ponderous, as they were elsewhere, but the carving did not approach the virtuosity of the high-relief work in Italy and France. Walnut, perfect for carving, was not readily available in England for another 100 years, when trees planted by Queen Elizabeth reached maturity. In England, oak was still the principal wood, and this fact greatly influenced design, since oak is tremendously strong but does not carve as well as other woods. Oak furniture was functional and largely rectilinear, rather than curved. There was decorative carving, but usually not in high relief. Common forms were limited to joint stools, wooden-backed chairs, settles, heavy cupboards (the court cupboard or aumbry), coffers, chests (with lift lids and no drawers), and tester bedsteads with solid, full-height headboards and tall posts hung with draperies. There were also long sturdy tables with trestle bases or box-stretcher bases (we now call these refectory tables).

Market Report

We should note that very little from this period is on the American market today. Only occasionally do we see pieces dating from the Renaissance (or at least including some Renaissance parts). We are more likely to see *copies* of Renaissance pieces, most of which date from the nineteenth and early twentieth centuries. Lack of appropriate wear and modern construction techniques (including machine-tool marks) usually give these piece away.

Construction Details

In Italy and France, walnut was widely used, as it was well suited to the exhuberant high-relief carving of the Renaissance. Where oak was the principal wood (in England and northern Germany), joiners produced simple, sturdy, functional pieces. Joiners knew many methods of joining wood by this time, and the mortise-and-tenon joint was common (Fig. 2-4). The frame-and-panel construc-

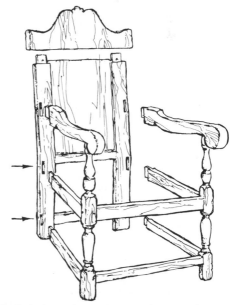

Fig. 2-4 A mortise-and-tenon joint was widely used on chairs and other furniture from the Renaissance up to the Industrial Age.

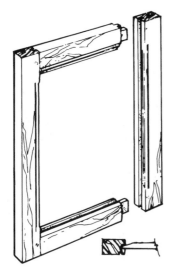
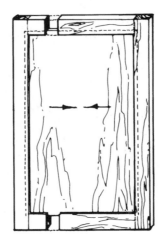

Fig. 2-5 Rectangular frames constructed with a mortise-and-tenon joint. Left to right: frame ready to receive panel in its grooves; panel nesting in the frame; fielded panel.

tion was widely used, with framing members joined at right angles by mortise-and-tenon joints (Fig. 2-5). The frames carried the weight of the piece, while the panels rested loosely in grooves in the frames. This practice allowed the wood to shrink and move without splitting. Its use was limited to rectilinear forms. No glue was used, but pegs added strength to the joint. These pegs were squarish, never perfectly round as modern pegs are.

Among the more sophisticated joiners, the mitred corner (Fig. 2-6) allowed more subtle concealment of the necessary mortise-and-tenon joint, and it was an improvement over the simple square-butted

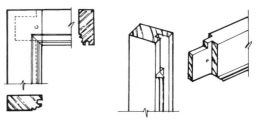

Fig. 2-6 Mitred mortise-and-tenon joints. The mitre is made only on the interior corner.

mortise-and-tenon joint. The mitred corner allowed for curved moldings and a more decorative effect. It made possible the boldly curving moldings of the baroque era, soon to follow.

1600–1650: Baroque

Features

By the end of the sixteenth century, the baroque style began to evolve in Italy, at first marked by the use of Renaissance motifs in exaggerated proportions. In this phase, Renaissance architectural motifs took on a dramatic, overdone effect. Large scrolls, reversing scrolls, broken pediments, deep moldings, twist turnings—all

these created a sense of restless movement in furniture. High-style baroque furniture was dramatic and formal.

Wall pieces were important, including console tables and mirrors, tall cabinets, and similar pieces. This early stage of baroque style first appeared in Italy as a sort of overgrowth of the Italian Renaissance. It was embraced by the rest of the Continent and by England a little later in the seventeenth century, and there were various interpretations and embellishments.

Chairs during the baroque period had curving crests, arms, and stretchers, and energetic turnings on the legs. A Portuguese chair style that embodied most of these features became very influential during the seventeenth century. It was exported to Spain and France and, eventually, became very popular in England as well. The tall-backed chair had an embossed leather seat and back, metal finials, and an arched crest which was echoed by a wide, high decorative front stretcher often graced with ˆinterlaced scrolls. (Fig. 2-7 shows a nineteenth-century interpretation of this seminal style.)

Spiral and bulbous turnings were also

Fig. 2-7 Two of a set of six Portuguese baroque-style walnut side chairs (nineteenth-century copies). Arched and canted backrests upholstered with tooled leather set with large-headed nails and surmounted by leaf-cast finials above similar seats. On block-and-ball turned legs ending in paint-brush feet joined by pierced scroll-carved front stretcher and ball-and-ring turned side stretchers. Wear to leather, worming to frames, rear feet restored. *Courtesy Butterfield & Butterfield, San Francisco.* **$8,000–12,000.** *A pair* of armchairs would be worth nearly as much! Most are used for accent, not for dining.

found on Spanish and Portuguese furniture during this period. These features made their way to the Netherlands and England in the last part of the seventeenth century.

The Netherlands achieved its greatest impact in the decorative arts during the seventeenth century, with Dutch baroque design maturing around 1640–1660 and then spreading to England, Germany, and the rest of Europe. Dutch domestic furniture, along with the palace furniture of seventeenth-century Italy, had a strong influence on baroque furniture design as a whole. Still using the frame-and-panel construction, large-scale pieces such as cupboards made a dramatic impact, with oversized cornices or pediments and large bases, and with architectural accents decorating the wide panels. Modified from the Renaissance elements, columns were twisted and molded panels created a sense of movement and contrast of high and low planes, light and dark areas. In many cases, the panels were further decorated with high-relief carving.

Italian baroque styles moved into southern Germany around 1620, particularly in cabinetmaking centers like Augsburg, where skilled craftsmen used mitred corners and elaborate moldings to great decorative advantage. In northern Germany, architectural features were an important part of the overall design, and the same was true in the Netherlands.

During this period English furniture was strongly influenced by the ornate furniture of Holland and France. Tables reflected the baroque taste for the massive, with heavy, bulbous legs and box stretchers. There were also draw-leaf tables, with tops extending on either end. Chairs were similar to Continental forms—high backs with arched crest rails, twist-turned legs, scrolls and carving.

In France lathe-turning became a popular means of decorating uprights and legs for tables and chairs. Turned pieces were also split and applied to flat surfaces.

Construction Details

Lathe-turning became more widely practiced in the seventeenth century. Frame-and-panel construction was still dominant, although skilled cabinetmakers used mitred corners to allow the frame-and-panel construction to be accented by dramatic, curving baroque moldings. Turnings were somewhat slimmer and decoration consisted of applied spindle turnings, along with some applied moldings. Oak and walnut were common. Dovetailed construction was in use to a limited extent.

1650–1715: Later Baroque, Restoration, Louis XIV

English Features

The seventeenth century was a period of rapid change in the English monarchy, as well as in furniture styles, types of pieces, and so on. The period from about 1680 to 1730—often called The Age of Walnut—is characterized by elaborate turnings, exuberant carving, and extravagant fabrics (Fig. 2-8). Walnut was dominant in this era, but this is not to say that oak was completely abandoned. Oak was still used for many provincial pieces all through the seventeenth and eighteenth centuries.

In 1660, Charles II returned from exile in France and Holland bringing with him the latest ideas from the Continent. It is quite possible that the great London fire of 1666 also encouraged the development of Continental-inspired baroque furniture in England—there was certainly a strong demand for new furniture!

Innovations in forms included lowboys (dressing tables or side tables) and many other types of tables, including the gateleg. New multicase pieces also emerged in the late seventeenth century, for example, the slant-front secretary/bookcase, highboy, and the cabinet-on-stand (the cabinet often opening to reveal drawers). The chest of drawers took the basic form that we recognize today (it became taller and had more than one drawer, unlike the earlier chests that had lift lids and perhaps a single drawer).

All of these case pieces were veneered, with accents in cross banding and feathering (or herringbone pattern). The finest pieces were covered in burl veneer. Especially prized was oyster veneer, made of circular-patterned pieces cut from wal-

Fig. 2-8 William and Mary carved walnut and caned armchair, c. 1690 crown-and-scroll-carved crest above caned back and seat. On scrolled legs joined by stretchers. *Courtesy Leslie Hindman Auctioneers, Chicago, Ill.* **$4,500–6,500.**

not or laburnum wood and laid down in a repetitive pattern. In short, the art of veneering opened up a whole new world of decorative possibility based on making the most of the figure of the wood itself. The result was very different from the carving that had characterized Renaissance decoration.

More innovation in construction and style came as a result of trade with India and the Orient, by way of the Dutch and Portuguese. Caning, an Indian technique, proved to be lightweight and inexpensive (and scorned by the wealthy). It is found on many chairs from this period. Lacquer from the Orient (along with porcelain) arrived in Holland around the end of the century, and soon became fashionable in England. The cabriole leg, which also appeared in Holland near the end of the century, probably originated in China but was most fully developed in England later in the eighteenth century.

Continental Features

The period from 1643–1715—called The Age of Louis XIV (The Sun King)— brought dramatic change to France and ended the domination of Italian designs. Native genius flowered and created a uniquely French ethos. Many Italian craftsmen were employed by the crown until the Gobelins factory, founded in 1662, provided a distinctly French style, as seen at Versailles. During this period, interior decorators reigned. The *maîtres ornemanistes,* in consort with the architects, set up elaborate plans for cohesively designed interiors which created a whole new world for the decorative arts. Furniture became an integral part of the architectural and decorative scheme, and indeed, at the court, furniture had strictly prescribed uses and placements. The idea of symmetry played an important role in the overall placement of pieces, and in each individual component as well. The effect was formal and magnificent in the extreme.

One of the great cabinetmakers of this period was André Charles Boulle (1642–1732). Among his many creations was the intricate style of veneered marquetry using tortoiseshell and brass in elaborate, scrolling arabesque designs. Marquetry using exotic wood veneers quickly became one of the hallmarks of fine French furniture and boullework, as this technique is called, has been popular ever since. Other advances included elaborate gilt-bronze (ormolu) mounts, which developed partly from the necessity to protect marquetry, veneer, and lacquer, which were all fragile. Louis XIV was responsible for a great deal of the innovation, as he maintained an opulent lifestyle, supported the arts, and generally stimulated French supremacy in every aspect of ostentatious living.

New furniture forms of great importance emerged in France, especially the commode (chest of drawers), which appeared by the end of this period, but also armoires (wardrobes), desks such as simple writing tables or elaborate *bureaux plats,* and more table designs, including elegant console (or wall) tables with only two legs at the front. Much finer, more diverse seating became available with the wider use of *fauteuils* (open armchairs), which had previously been reserved only for the king (see Fig 2-9).

By the seventeenth century, special areas of expertise had been established for furniture makers in France. *Ébénistes* worked with exotic woods (ebony being one) in veneer form. They produced the marquetry and veneered creations that were the glory of France from the time of Louis XIV through the reign on Louis XVI. The *menuisiers,* on the other hand, made seating furniture, tables, armoires, and buffets out of solid native woods, such as walnut, ash, cherry, and other fruitwoods. *Ébénistes* made luxurious furniture primarily in urban areas, while the furniture of the *menuisiers* was more in demand in the provinces, although a major area of Paris had hundreds of family-run furniture making shops in this tradition. Over the years, the *ébénistes* tended to be more innovative

Fig. 2-9 Late Louis XIV to early Régence (c. 1720) walnut *fauteuil à la reine,* rectangular padded back and seat on incurved legs headed by acanthus and bell flowers and joined by a curving X-shaped stretcher, upholstered in needlework. The Régence influence is seen in the curving arms and legs, without curves, the piece would be at typical Louis XIV *fauteuil. Courtesy Christie's New York.* **$8,000– 12,000.**

and open to foreign influence. In fact, during the eighteenth century, the best cabinetmakers all around Europe sought to join the ranks of the Parisian *ébénistes.* The *menuisiers,* in contrast, were more closely tied to traditions passed down from father to son, and shunned outside influences.

The Louis XIV style marked a very exciting period in the history of French furniture. *However,* we see very little actual Louis XIV furniture on the market today—lots of copies, but very little dating from the period.

During the reign of Louis XIV, some French craftsmen went to Germany to work for the German princes, taking French designs with them. By the second half of the seventeenth century, the baroque period had arrived in Germany, through the influence of Italy, France, and Holland. Forms and decoration were similar to the countries already discussed. German craftsmen excelled in making monumental baroque cabinets of frame-and-panel construction, accented with moldings and architectural elements. In southern Germany, elaborate carving further enhanced these pieces, especially in places like Nuremberg, Augsburg, and Frankfort. Walnut was the wood of choice in Germanic-influenced countries. By the beginning of the eighteenth century, the cabriole leg appeared in Germany, and the rococo style of France would soon follow.

Construction Details

A major construction change which took place during this period was the use of dovetailing (Fig. 2-10) as the joint of preference, replacing framed construction for case pieces. The early dovetails were fairly large and crude, but the technique was refined over the course of the eighteenth century, when cabinetmakers began to take pride in the small size of their dovetails. The use of dovetails resulted in flush, or flat, surfaces, with no variations in depth as there had been between the frame and panel when other construction methods were used. On this flat surface,

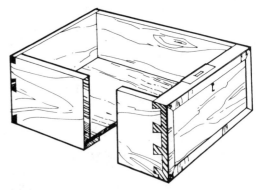

Fig. 2-10 Dovetailed joints provide a flat surface suitable for veneering.

cabinetmakers began to use veneer (thin sheets of wood glued on to the base wood) to decorate, rather than relying on the lights and shadows of framed construction. Early veneer was quite thick (about ⅛″) when compared to modern, machine-sawn veneer. Veneer allowed use of cross-grain, a feature not generally used with solid wood as it lacks strength. Moldings during this period were often veneered cross-grain for contrast. Hand in hand with veneering came the practice of marquetry (floral inlay in veneer form), which was wildly popular in this era and continued to be a vital form of decoration on later rococo furniture.

Oak and walnut were the woods of preference (the latter on the Continent only until about 1680). In England, where walnut was relatively scarce, the art of veneering allowed walnut to be used to its best advantage. It was veneered onto pine or oak and only used in solid form for legs or shaped pieces.

Lathe-turning with treadle lathes was introduced into England and the Continent from the Netherlands, making intricately turned walnut legs and uprights possible.

1715–1730: Queen Anne, Baroque, Régence

English Features

In England, the Age of Walnut reached its greatest heights in the Queen Anne style, which actually included her reign (1702–1714) and the early years of the reign of George I (1714–1727).

A truly English style, which emerged after a century of strong Continental influence, the furniture of the Queen Anne period is known for its elegant simplicity achieved by a beauty of line. Design depended more on the lines of the form and less on added decoration, although tasteful carving added interest. The busy marquetry (floral inlay) and parquetry (geometric inlay) that had been so popular during the Restoration were no longer in fashion.

This era was not marked by new forms, but by a maturing of style into more richly carved and molded pieces, including the ball-and-claw foot (often mistakenly attributed to Chippendale, but actually found as early as the reign of Queen Anne). Queen Anne chairs displayed an overall unity of design, with the graceful curves of the cabriole leg echoed in the comfortable spoon (cyma-curved) backs, the curving stiles, and the rounded seats. The beautiful lines were often embellished with carving on the knees, feet, back splat, and crest rail. The lowboy or dressing table was another favored form during this period, with cabriole legs and gracefully shaped apron (Fig. 2-11). The rather busy William and Mary gateleg table gave way to the drop-leaf table, which was simpler in line and construction, losing its stretchers, as the cabriole leg had.

Continental Features

In France, the Régence period heralded the coming reign of Louis XV, which would bring vast changes in style and form. France was ruled by the regent Phillippe d'Orleans from 1715–1723, until Louis XV came of age. In furniture forms, the Régence (or French Regency) lasted from 1700 to 1730 and showed a transition from the rectilinear and symmetrical to the curvacious, asymmetrical Louis XV style of 1730 to 1765 (the rococo

Fig. 2-11 Queen Anne walnut lowboy, c. 1710–1730, with well-formed cabriole legs ending in pad feet. Banded drawers (no herringbone inlay). Replaced hardware. *Courtesy Whitehall at the Villa, Chapel Hill, N.C.* **$8,000–12,000.**

style). Régence furniture displayed more grace and lightheartedness than the furniture of the formal Louis XIV era.

This hybrid form of Louis XIV and Louis XV elements made its greatest departure from the past in seating furniture and tables, both of which became lighter, with few or no stretchers to connect the legs. The *fauteuil,* in particular, took the form we admire today, with a lower back than in the Louis XIV period, curved (cabriole) legs, and arms widely spaced to accommodate ladies' dresses. The four-legged *bureau plat* replaced the massive

seventeenth-century *bureau* with eight legs. Walnut remained the wood of choice, although beech was most often used for chairs. In the provinces, oak continued to be used by the *menuisiers.*

In Germany, high baroque ruled indigneous style, although French stylistic influence was spreading throughout the Germanic areas and would blossom even more during the reign of Louis XV. The court of Frederick I was furnished with Louis XIV furniture, and other palaces followed suit. Domestic furniture, however, lagged behind.

Construction Details

Construction reached a point of great sophistication and remained at this level until the early nineteenth century, when machines slowly began replacing handwork as a more efficient means of carving, turning, sawing, planing, and sanding.

Nailed construction was found only in country pieces from this era. Panel construction was also found, although mainly on country pieces—rarely on urban pieces in England or on the Continent, except in some instances for doors. Other allowances were made for the shrinkage of wood. For example, in the construction of chests of drawers, cabinetmakers used drawer stops, leaving a gap between the back of the drawer and the back of the piece. Shrinkage would close that gap over the years without doing damage to the piece (this technique is explained in depth in Chapter 6).

Walnut continued to be the favored wood.

1730–1775: Georgian, Louis XV, Rococo

English Features

In England, the period of George II (1727–1760) and the early reign of George III (1760–1811) was known as the Age of Mahogany. Mahogany was first imported into England in the 1720s, and cabinetmakers soon discovered that its properties were markedly different from walnut. Because of its strength and beauty of figure, mahogany is equally suited for use in solid and in veneer forms. Consequently, cabinetmakers made less use of veneer than they had during the walnut period. Nor were marquetry and inlay used as frequently. Whereas walnut was accented in cross banding, the same strategy did not work with mahogany. Instead, drawers might be lipped or cockbeaded for accent. Carving dominated decoration, as mahogany is an even better wood for carving than walnut (which splinters more easily) or oak. Acanthus leaves, paterae (inlaid geometric designs on round or oval disks), and other motifs were carved into pieces, along with the traditional shells and leaves.

Thomas Chippendale published his influencial *Gentleman and Cabinetmaker's Director* in 1754, with updated editions in 1755 and 1762. Chippendale's rococo designs were dependent on the properties of mahogany and featured brilliant carving. His *Director* indulged the fad for "Gothick" designs and encouraged the chinoiserie craze with carvings featuring fanciful Chinese figures, pagodas, and geometric patterns.

Although Chippendale's book did not include anything that we would recognize as a dining table, such tables did exist in England by that time, along with matching sets of dining chairs (Fig. 2-12). Aside from this important development, not many new forms emerged, but lovely adaptations and progressions occurred, such as movable corner cabinets (not built-in pieces); chests-on-chests as opposed to highboys, which never really "took" in England; and kneehole desks, which evolved from a combination of the lowboy and chest.

By the 1760s, the move in England to neoclassicism was evident in the designs of the Adam brothers. These designs drew directly from Piranesi's etchings of classical Roman architecture, whose swags and drapery were popular motifs on the Adams' light, elegant designs. Adam designs were especially noted on formal wall furniture, such as console tables and sideboards flanked by pairs of urns on pedestals.

Fig. 2-12 Two of a set of six George III c. 1760–1770 mahogany dining chairs, each with shaped crest rail centering a foliate canopy above a carved and pierced splat. Padded seat, on square legs joined by stretchers. Replacements. One chair of a later date. *Courtesy Christie's New York.* **$12,000–18,000** the set.

Continental Features

It was during this era, under the reign of Louis XV, that the greatest flowering of artistic French furniture spread its influence throughout the western world—from Russia to Sweden to Italy. Through the influence of its monarch, Paris became the center of the western world in the decorative arts. During the reign of Louis XV, the royalty of Europe ordered its beautiful rococo furnishings from Paris. The most talented of Europe's cabinetmakers frequently emigrated to Paris, adding to the international character of rococo design (famous examples being Oeben, Riesener, Wolf, Roentgen, and Weisweiler from Germany; and Mewesen from Scandanavia).

Forms and styles both evolved enormously during this extraordinary period.

Comfort, not grandeur, was most valued in furniture. The general ambiance was curvilinear, as seen in cabriole legs and curving chair backs. Decoration involved asymmetrical, naturalistic carving, and gilding of solid woods like walnut or beech. The techniques of lacquering, veneering, parquetry, and marquetry were taken to their greatest heights, accompanied by extensive (sometimes excessive) use of bronze mounts to protect delicate corners and edges.

Not every piece reflected the asymmetry of the rococo, but most did. The sense of fluid movement was in some cases compounded by the use of fantastic geometrical inlays (parquetry) creating optical illusions of shifting focus. Louis XV marquetry, on the other hand, found its most characteristic expression in naturalism, dominant themes being animals (especially monkeys), cherubs, floral sprays, rockery, and fanciful Indian and Chinese motifs.

Furniture was no longer stuck in a fixed architectural scheme, but became more movable in order to form relaxed groupings conductive to comfort and conversation. Old forms evolved and completely new ones emerged. The height of seats dropped three to five inches as the lifestyle at court and in fine homes became more casual. Stretchers disappeared, as legs were rather short, curved, and graceful. New chair forms included the *bergère* (an armchair with the arms closed in to the seat; Fig. 2-13); the *fauteuil* (open armchair) with old style straight back (*à la reine*), now joined by a concave-backed variation designated as

Fig. 2-13 Louis XV painted bergère, c. 1750, marked by *maître* Jean-Baptiste Tilliard (1685–1766). Molded crest and seat rail carved with a scroll-framed cabochon flanked by trailing leaves. Cabriole legs headed by an acanthus leaf. Loose cushion. *Courtesy Grogan & Company, Boston.* **$15,000–20,000.**

en cabriolet. The *marquise*—a loveseat—was new, as was the *duchesse* or *chaise longue* and the *duchesse brisé* (with leg rest detachable to form a large ottoman). The range of table types grew enormously, including games tables of various types, work tables, reading tables, dressing tables, and writing tables (sometimes combined into one piece). Desk forms were quite innovative: the *bureau plat* was joined by the *secrétaire en pente* (slant front on legs) and the *secrétaire à abattant* (with a large drop front over a set of drawers or cupboards).

In Germany, the rococo style was dominant from 1730–1760 (or by some accounts, as late as 1790), reaching the south first and then spreading northward. During this time commerce with France was extensive. While German states—supported by princes and various rulers—made great advances in porcelain, furniture was dominated by French tastes. Style, function, and forms all mimicked the French fashion. In fact, most great palaces of the time were furnished with imports from Paris. The German rococo of court life was most noted for its opulent fantasy worlds created by a seamless union of interiors and furniture. Away from the German courts, from the Régence period onwards, regional cabinetmakers displayed a love of the bombe shape—especially evident in the commodes and secretaries of southern Germany.

By about the second quarter of the eighteenth century, Italian design had come under the influence of the French rococo movement, which now dominated the whole of Europe. Italian *ebanistas* made luxury furniture in the same manner as the French, with marquetry and exotic woods. The Italian rococo style was somewhat exaggerated, with commodes, for example, having a markedly bombe form and an overabundance of ornamentation. The Italian commode is noted for its pronounced bombe, top-heavy form. Towards the end of the eighteenth century, Louis XVI designs were copied throughout Italy, with the exception of Venice, which held on to the fanciful, rococo pieces (often lacquered) which seemed to suit it so well. One sometimes finds that Italian furniture is not made to the same standards of construction as French furniture, more attention having been given to the decoration, less to the unseen interiors and backs.

During the eighteenth century, Spanish furniture design was also dominated by French ideas—especially rococo designs—and also by Queen Anne and early Georgian styles from England.

Construction Details

Little changed during this era except for improvements in tools and equipment that allowed greater precision. The groundwork for construction techniques needed in rococo furniture had already been laid during the seventeenth century. Furniture makers quickly learned how to achieve the curving forms that marked the best eighteenth-century design.

1775–1800: Late Georgian, Louis XVI, Directoire, Neoclassical

During this last quarter of the eighteenth century, style and forms were once again in great flux. A sense of grace, elegance, and restraint captured the stylistic imagination of furniture designers. There was a renewed interest in the classical orders of columns—the design concepts and motifs of ancient Greece and Rome—and these new interests determined style in England and on the Continent.

English Features

In England, it was still the Age of Mahogany, but mahogany furniture became enhanced by the use of elegant, light satinwood in veneer and solid forms. Veneers and inlay were as important—indeed, more important—than carving.

The late Georgian period was dominated by the neoclassical movement, popularized through the design books of Hepplewhite (1788–1794), Sheraton (1791), and others. Rectilinear design replaced curvilinear; symmetry replaced asymmetry. The cabriole leg was replaced by a tapered, straight or turned leg. The more dramatic the taper, the better the piece. Fig. 2-14 shows a popular Hepplewhite

Fig. 2-14 Hepplewhite solid mahogany flip-top tea table, c. 1780, veneered apron inlaid with stringing, cuffing, and paterae. This form was also very popular in America. *Courtesy Whitehall at the Villa, Chapel Hill, N.C.* **$3,600–4,800.**

form featuring characteristic tapering legs and inlay.

Innovative forms included many pieces for the newly important dining room: serving boards with few or no drawers early in the period, banquet tables that added console ends to the traditional drop-leaf table, and pedestal-form tables. Sideboards with drawers and cupboards superseded serving boards around 1780. Fig. 2-15 shows a Sheraton sideboard from this period.

Continental Features

In France, this period saw a short transition combining the rococo with the neoclassical, the latter being strongly associated with the Louis XVI (1774–1793) and Directoire (1793–1799) styles. The move to classicism was evident in France as early as 1750—well ahead of England.

This trend was due to a number of events, the most significant being the 1748 publication of information about the discoveries at Herculaneum and Pompeii. Ornamentation from the classical world became more and more popular, so that by 1765 France had fully embraced the neoclassical movement. Parquetry (inlay in geometric patterns) became more prevalent than marquetry. Cabinetmakers began using brass accents on furniture—on galleries, for example—with increasing regularity, and porcelain plaques were added to furniture for the first time.

Not only did styles become more rectilinear, making dramatic visual differences, but also many new forms emerged in this important period. Dining tables (borrowed from the English) appeared at this time, usually oval-shaped with leaves. Vitrines (small glass display cabinets) were created to display rare objects in this age of collectors, and the free-

Fig. 2-15 Sheraton sideboard, c. 1795, with exceptional-quality carving and well-turned legs. In a fine state of preservation. *Courtesy Whitehall at the Villa, Chapel Hill, N.C.* **$18,000–24,000.**

standing bookcase (*bibliothèque*) evolved from the armoire. Also new were round *bouillotte* tables, fern or plant tables (*jardinières* or *tables à fleurs*), the cylinder rolltop desk (*bureau à cylindre*), and corner cabinets (*encoignures*), en suite with commodes. The *secrétaire à abattant* (fall-front secretary) was well suited to this rectilinear style and was a favorite form of the neoclassical period.

Generally, the overall style was more restrained than Louis XV. Chair legs tended to be straight or turned and tapered, with spiral or fluted carving (Fig. 2-16). Other carving tended to repeat a single motif, producing an overall effect quite different from that of the Louis XV flowers and other objects arranged in more relaxed, asymmetrical patterns. Ormolu was not as overwhelming as during the Louis XV period.

The end of the French monarchy naturally brought tremendous change in fur-

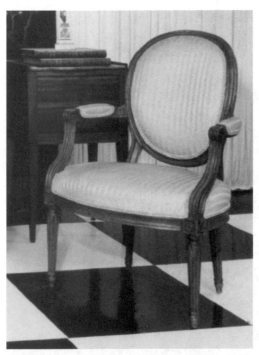

Fig. 2-16 Louis XVI *fauteuil en cabriolet*, c. 1780, with turned, fluted legs. Walnut. *Courtesy Whitehall at the Villa, Chapel Hill, N.C.* **$3,000–4,200.**

niture design, as the expensive additions of marquetry and bronze mounts were abandoned. The old distinctions between the *ébénistes* and *menuisiers* broke down as the luxurious furniture made for the French court became unacceptable—the opulence of extensive marquetry and ormolu of *ébénisterie* were no longer appropriate.

With the Directoire period (1793–1799), comfort was sacrificed to the straight lines that came to dominate furniture, with very little ormolu enhancing the simple lines. Decorations drew from the ancient world, especially Greece, with the Greek key being a popular motif, along with the classical egg-and-dart pattern and paterae. Egypt became another source of inspiration after the Egyptian campaign of 1798; the sphinx appeared on furniture as chair arms and legs, along with other symbolic animals such as the swan, serpent, and griffon. Charles Percier and Pierre Fontaine designed a room for Madame Récamier, including the famous daybed modeled after a Grecian couch with rolled-over arms. The récamier, as we call it now, is a very stylish-looking piece of furniture, but not especially comfortable, as is true of most furniture from this period. Percier and Fontaine's book, *Recueil de Décoration Intérieure* (1802), became the source for much of the Empire design.

In Germany, neoclassicism was dominant in urban areas, but the cabinetmakers in the countryside often continued to produce rococo furniture. From the 1770s on, Germany was influenced by both England and France. It should be noted that German-born cabinetmakers living in Paris, like Roentgen, Reisener, Georges Jacob, and Weissweiler, created some of the finest neoclassical furniture.

Neoclassical designs flourished in Sweden and Denmark as well. The Swedish King Gustav III (1771–1792), an ardent Francophile, had his craftsmen execute French neoclassical designs for his court.

Copenhagen was also the site of sophisticated interpretations of neoclassical furniture.

Italy also took up Louis XVI and English neoclassical styles, and indeed, joined the prevailing European trend of the nineteenth century as Empire gave way to eclecticism.

1800–1830: Empire, Regency, Restauration, Biedermeier

English Features

In England, mahogany remained the preferred wood, but exotic woods gained wide use—among them rosewood, satinwood, ebony, coromandel, and padouk. This period marked the ultimate in classical influence, as the styles of Greece, Rome, and Egypt left furniture encrusted with lions, winged creatures, sphinxes, and so on, as well as with columns of every type. The influence of China and India (virtually synonymous in the English mind of the time) also affected every aspect of the decorative arts. Brighton Pavilion in England, built by the Prince Regent (later George IV), typified this stylistic period at its most extravagant.

Fig. 2-17 Two of a set of six early nineteenth-century English Regency brass-inlaid rosewood and grained dining chairs. The set consists of two arm and four side chairs, each with curved back centering a stylized brass-inlaid panel within a scrolled and gadrooned frame. Caned seats. Sabre legs. Regency furniture is a classic example of the way the tastes of the buying public change. Ten years ago there was hardly any interest in Regency furniture, today it's popular. *Courtesy Christie's New York.* **$6,000–9,000** the set of 6.

A-35

From the Regency period came several new forms, including the Klismos chair, based on an ancient Greek form (Fig. 2-17). Other new forms included the Greek-style sofa with scrolled-over arms, the Carlton House writing table, and the circular dining table on pedestal. Mahogany and rosewood were the principal woods, and brass was used as an inexpensive inlay material. Many Regency forms came directly from the ancient world, with slight modifications. Thomas Hope's book, *Household Furniture and Interior Design* (1807), was full of close copies of ancient Egyptian, Greek, and Roman furniture. Hope's designs were further popularized by George Smith's book, *A Collection of Designs for Household Furniture and Interior Decoration* (1808).

Continental Features

In France, the opening years of the nineteenth century were dominated by the Empire style (1799–1815), which continued the Directoire trends of rejecting the luxurious monarchical styles. A middle class emerged with the distribution of wealth which resulted from the revolution, commerce expanded, and the industrial age began.

The stylistic essence of the Empire period was twofold: rectilinearity became even more important than in the Louis XVI style, and the structure of an object became the dominant decorative characteristic (as opposed to the extravagant use of applied decorative devices and fabrics which previously suppressed the visual impact of a piece's structure). Very little ornamentation was used and then on mainly plain surfaces. Fig. 2-18 shows a good example of this style.

Comfortable seating was impossible to find, given the new popularity of tightly upholstered seats and backs. The scale of pieces was quite grand, dominated by hard lines and heavy shapes. Furniture was made for effect, not for comfort, in

Fig. 2-18 Empire mahogany dressing cabinet with ormolu mounts, c. 1810. Marble top above frieze fitted with two short drawers, on caryatid stiles in front of an adjustable mirrored panel. Base fitted with similar inset marble top over three short drawers on gilt paw feet. 42" high x 20" wide x 15" deep. *Courtesy Christie's New York.* **$3,000–4,500.**

sharp contrast to the best French furniture of the eighteenth century.

Military themes, such as spears and helmets, were vital to the expression of Napoleon's rule. Napoleon' domination of this era is seen in motifs such as the laurel wreath around his initial and the Napoleonic bee, which replaced the *fleur-de-lys* that had been associated with the monarchy.

The variety of forms actually *decreased* dramatically during the Directoire-Empire period; it is another example of the rejection of the excesses of

When producing Colonial Revival furniture, these machines could not duplicate the fine work or hand carving of early American craftsmen. Machines could produce only adaptations. The marks left from machine carving on lower-end pieces is one of the easy ways to spot Colonial Revival furniture. Large companies did have their own carvers, and on better pieces the carving was sometimes done by hand, but some pieces were contracted out to specialty carving works in Grand Rapids. Even when the carving was done by hand, however, it was not as deep or crisp as eighteenth-century carving. Anyone familiar with good eighteenth-century carving can easily spot most Colonial Revival–era carving.

After 1900 the finishing process was done by machine and often the hand-rubbing was eliminated. By the 1910s furniture was being spray finished, a process that offered great potential savings to furniture manufacturers. With a spray gun, two men could finish twenty-four chairs in an hour. With the brush-and-dip method, one man could finish only four chairs in an hour.[18] Hand-rubbing between each coat of finish added to the cost, and of course the number of coats increased the cost as well. On pieces that are beautifully and carefully finished, the finishing process can easily account for half of the final cost. The method of finishing is one important aspect of quality that collectors today look for. Not surprisingly, hand-finishing will always be more highly valued than machine-finishing.

In 1895, George Gay of Berkey and Gay described a furniture industry that manufactured two classes of furniture— low-end furniture for the general public and high-end furniture that was made to order and combined old traditional methods with new machine methods.[19] At the turn of the century, Grand Rapids produced large quantities of low-end furniture, but its manufacturers also produced high-quality pieces that still required a great deal of hand work.

Not only did the Grand Rapids furniture companies make efficient use of the available technology at the end of the nineteenth century, but they also understood the art of promotion. Grand Rapids had always marketed itself aggressively, and the semiannual Furniture Market was an essential marketing tool. Beyond that, the major companies advertised in the most important national magazines. For instance, Berkey and Gay advertized in *The Saturday Evening Post*. At the turn of the century, Grand Rapids also founded several trade journals, including *The Furniture Manufacturer, The Stylist, Furniture Record,* and *Good Furniture and Decoration*.

By the 1890s Grand Rapids had begun to promote itself as a "style center." Companies hired furniture designers who had been trained in London, New York, and Chicago and began producing copies of period pieces and furniture in the Arts and Crafts style. The Phoenix Furniture Company employed the services of David W. Kendall, who was a major designer of period furniture from 1895 to 1910. In his search for authentic period designs, he traveled to England to study examples.[20] Around the turn of the century, Grand Rapids became the home of the College of Furniture Designing, headed by Arthur Kirkpatrick, who designed for Berkey and Gay. Students could take classes at the school or through correspondence courses.

In addition to the three major Grand Rapids companies at the turn of the century, several other large companies were founded in the nineteenth century in

18. Ransom, *The City Built on Wood,* 61.
19. Edward S. Cooke, "The Boston Furniture Industry in 1880," *Old Time New England* 70 (Winter 1980): 85.
20. Ransom, *The City Built on Wood,* 27.

and walnut, used in solid and veneer forms, with ebonized woods as accents.

Biedermeier style celebrated domestic life, not the grand life of the courts. The furniture was comfortable and has modern appeal because of its geometric simplicity. This was a style marked by large curving surfaces rather than fussy ornament. Scrolls, columns, pediments, and lyre shapes were not merely decorative but were incorporated into the structure of the piece. The repetitive, small motifs of the true neoclassical period (such as Louis XVI in France) were no longer found.

Characteristic Biedermeier pieces included the *secrétaire à abattant,* work tables (especially with globe-shaped tops), and side chairs with decorative, shaped backs inspired by Prince of Wales plumes (Fig. 2-19).

By 1835 or 1840, the purity of the style was degraded as Historicism and Rococo Revival spread into this area from England and France. Renaissance, Turkish, Oriental styles, etc. were all revived, just as in England.

It is important to remember that Biedermeier, Regency, and Empire styles saw major revivals in 1895, 1910, and 1920–1930. With both original pieces and copies dominated by mechanization, scale and subtle advances in technology must be used to differentiate pieces spanning almost 100 years.

Construction Details

Paneled construction, always used for doors, made another appearance on

Fig. 2-19 Biedermeier ash armchair with stylized Prince-of-Wales-plume back and tapered legs, c. 1825. *Courtesy Christie's New York.* **$2,500–3,500.**

the sides of pieces. During this period, the panels were flat, not raised, on the exterior sides. Machines were becoming ever more important with sawing, planing, and sanding often machine-powered, as was more technical work such as the cutting of veneers. The Bramah lock was patented during this era and can be recognized by its characteristic round shape standing out slightly from the drawer front.

1830–1910: Mechanization

Victorian and Edwardian England

For the mighty industrialized Empire of Great Britain, basking in the halcyon days of Victoria's long reign (1837–1901), this was an era of mechanization leading design, and, unfortunately, occasionally triumphing *over* design. What we note here is true of all of Europe: the thrust of the period is "perfection" expressed by mechanization removing the imperfect hand of man from as many processes as possible. Manufacturers tried new technologies and new materials with great enthusiasm. Papier-mâché chairs and tables (Fig. 2-20) date from this period. Wire, horn, and iron were other new materials used for rustic or outdoor furniture. Spring upholstery was a huge success.

The styles of the period consist of one revival after another, from Gothic to Louis XV to Sheraton to Renaissance to japonisme to Turkish. Every new rage of the room designers—often architects—set the factories of the day into high gear producing the latest style. The continually growing middle classes readily snapped up these products as mechanization improved their lifestyle. After mid-century, Sheraton Revival and Hepplewhite Revival pieces were much in demand. The collector looking for period Sheraton and Hepplewhite furniture needs to be aware that these revivals produced a great deal of furniture during the Victorian era.

It is only through knowledge of early styles and construction that one distinguishes all of the revival-era pieces from the original prototypes. In general, the "imperfection" of the master craftsman has been replaced by mechanical "perfection." In an age that worshipped progress, most felt that machines could do anything better (certainly faster and usually cheaper) than by hand.

The Great World Exhibition of London in 1851 confirmed the bias of the Victorian age. What was presented did *not* demonstrate excellent design, but the latest in technology and novel materials. Design consisted of a plethora of debased revival forms. Not everyone was pleased with what was displayed at the Exhibition. Reform-minded designers turned their focus to revitalizing craftsmanship and simple forms.

With the publication of his book, *Hints on Household Taste* in 1868, Charles Eastlake sought to popularize designs that were inspired by medieval England. Eastlake's furniture was designed to be useful rather than ostentatious. It was simple, rectilinear, and decorated with shallow carving in geometric patterns. It was intended for a wide market, and in fact was well suited to machine production, which meant that it could be manufactured inexpensively enough to be affordable. Eastlake's designs were a practical alternative to busy, curvaceous Victorian forms.

On the other hand, there were design-

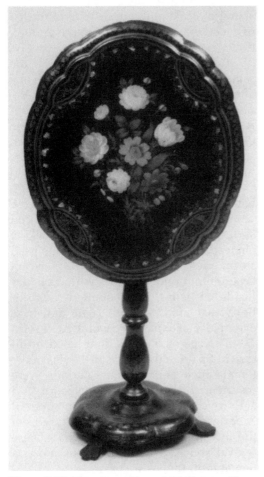

Figure 2-20 Victorian papier-mâché tilt-top table, c. 1850–1875, shaped oval top painted with floral bouquet surrounded by gilt highlights and abalone inlay. On turned support ending in dished base. Needs minor edge repairs. 27" high × 26" wide × 21" deep. *Courtesy Leslie Hindman Auctioneers, Chicago, Ill.* **$600–800** as is. **$1,800–2,400** restored.

ers whose furniture was beautifully planned, but because old-fashioned construction techniques were required, ownership was out of reach to all but a few. The Arts and Crafts movement of the late nineteenth century was inspired by English medieval designs, as Eastlake design had been, but William Morris and his colleagues also placed a high value on the role of the artisan, as opposed to mechanized processes. Arts and Crafts furniture sought to use medieval forms and some of the simple techniques from that era. For example, these designers returned to oak, and avoided the use of veneer. Construction on these pieces is straightforward, and in fact, framing, joints, and pegs draw attention to themselves and become part of the decorative aspect of the piece.

Encouraged by Oscar Wilde, Edward William Godwin (1833–1886) created furniture that was inspired by Japanese prints. The Aesthetic Movement did not actually copy Japanese furniture forms, but the decoration was indebted to Japanese motifs. Like Arts and Crafts furniture, it was simple and rectilinear in form. However, it was not as robust in design, nor did it require the skills of an artisan. Godwin often used inexpensive ebonized wood in designs that were easily imitated and adapted to mass production.

At the beginning of the twentieth century, the Edwardian period continued the Victorian tradition of producing inexpensive furniture for the mass market. Edwardian taste ran to revivals, especially of Adam, Hepplewhite, and Sheraton styles. These revival pieces can be distinguished from the originals by wood which is not of the highest quality, spindly proportions, and painted decoration rather than inlays.

Louis Philippe, Second Empire, Third Republic, and Revivals on the Continent

In France, as in England, the nineteenth century was a time of stylistic re-vivals based on the eighteenth-century monarchical fashions, especially Louis XV and XVI, and Empire Revival (strongly degraded by Restauration influences). This period is usually divided into the following styles: Louis Philippe (1830–1848), Second Empire (1848–1870), and Third Republic (1871–1940).

All of the many furniture forms created during the previous 200 years were revived again and again throughout this period. Styles came and went, influenced by social upheaval and interior design concepts. The major characteristic of most of these revival pieces was the downsizing of scale and simplifying of design to meet the exigencies of mass production.

German design was subject to the same influences. Revivals followed one after the other, but the Renaissance Revival was especially popular at mid-century. Historicism and Rococo Revival predominated from 1840 to 1860, when all sorts of decorative styles broke loose, as they had in England and France.

In Austria, Michael Thonet's steam-bent beechwood furniture exemplified the wonderful marriage of mass production and style. His side chairs and rocking chairs are especially famous. Thonet used steam to curve veneer and solid pieces of beech into rounded shapes with curlicues inside curlicues. His technique was initially patented around 1840 and was eventually patented in several countries.

The age of revivals dominated furniture in Spain and Italy, as the styles of the Renaissance and baroque periods were resurrected in the late nineteenth and early twentieth centuries. On the current American market, the only furniture from the Iberian peninsula that sells are these revival styles, which tend to be most in demand on the West coast.

As the twentieth century approached, reform was brewing on the Continent, just as in England. Various terms were used to describe the prevailing styles: Jugendstil (1880–1920) in Germany and Austria, and Art Nouveau in France and Belgium—

borrowing from Siegfried Bing's Paris shop, "L'Art Nouveau." In Italy, the movement was called the *stile floreale.*

Art Nouveau furniture is marked by the rhythmically repetitive use of natural motifs, such as vines and tendrils (Fig. 2-21). This is a sensuous style full of fluid lines, and to create furniture required all the skills accumulated by generations of *ébénistes* and *menuisiers,* skills that had not been forgotten in nineteenth-century France. Two prominent manufacturers were located in Nancy, in southern France. During the 1880s, Emile Gallé manufactured glassware and furniture there. Louis Majorelle took over his family's furniture factory in Nancy and used it to provide Art Nouveau designs, which sold well and widely.

Clearly, nothing can be said of the mid-nineteenth or early twentieth centuries that holds true for long. Curvilinear and rectilinear forms alternated in popularity—sometimes produced simultaneously. Furniture forms were stagnant, except for modifications to accomodate new inventions such as telephones and phonographs. Machines were occasionally replaced by the hand work of craftsmen in some of these stylistic movements, but on the whole, the expanding market and rising labor costs meant that the home furnishings market was dependent on machines. No other production methods could meet the need. Chippendale had customers for a chair or two per day. In 1900, the Thonet factory filled orders for 4,000 chairs a day. A "Chippendale-style" chair today may be made in runs or 10,000, 50,000, or even 100,000.

Fig. 2-21 Two of a set of six c. 1900 French Art Nouveau carved walnut dining chairs (two arm and four side chairs). Each with whiplash-carved crest rail over padded backs above elaborate pierced foliate tendrils and scrollwork. Foliate-carved cabriole legs. *Courtesy Butterfield & Butterfield, San Francisco.* **$2,500–3,500.**

Construction Details

Naturally, the coming of machines influenced the construction of mass-produced furniture. The circular saw had been invented towards the end of the eighteenth century. However, the steam-powered circular saw was not in widespread use until 1830–1850. Machines were invented to accomplish many things traditionally done by hand, but not all were immediately successful unless used on a mass scale. In smaller shops, the array of new machines was simply not affordable. Machine dovetailing, for example, was not widespread until the twentieth century. After about 1830, the mortise-and-tenon joint was often replaced by the use of dowels, which were easily made with machines but did not produce as strong a joint.

Construction was further debased in the Victorian era by the use of timber that was not of as fine a quality as that used in the eighteenth century. Less expensive timbers were stained to look like mahogany and other fine woods. French polishing (a varnish over wood) was used more and more in England to hide a multitude of sins. It also prohibits the accumulation of natural patina that we now cherish on antiques.

PART ONE

English Furniture Forms

3

Seating Furniture

More than any other furniture form, chairs are subject to multiple demands. Their form must change quickly to respond to current fashion (they need to accommodate the latest styles of dress, such as voluminous skirts or, in the Elizabethan period, ruff collars), and they must be attractive. They must cater to comfort to some extent and, on top of all these things, they must be sturdy enough to hold a person's weight and to sustain being moved around carelessly, tilted back, and so on. Thus, antique chairs rarely survive without some repairs, and complete original sets are rare indeed (these are usually assembled, sometimes with new copies rounding out a set). Given the fact that chairs have to be so carefully constructed, it makes sense that the chair maker established himself as a distinct tradesman among furniture makers by the mid-seventeenth century.

Sixteenth- and Seventeenth-Century Chairs

Early chairs from the sixteenth and early seventeenth centuries were in the form of a box with an attached panelled back. The lid of the box (or the seat) would often lift so the base could be used for storage. Legs, as opposed to the box base, did not develop on chairs until the seventeenth century. More plentiful than chairs were joint stools, generally joined by low stretchers. On early oak chairs, the construction was very simple, with no rake or angle to the back legs. These oak chairs were devoid of curves; right angles were joined using the mortise-and-tenon joint and pegs. Backs were sometimes paneled. As the back and rear legs became somewhat angled back, a more comfortable chair resulted. Other forms dating from the early seventeenth century included the Farthingale chair (named after the large hoop skirts that it could accommodate, it was a simple, straight-back chair with upholstered seat and back, and no arms). There was also the X-chair, which originated in Italy and Spain, and was derived from an ancient form.

When Charles II returned to England from exile in 1660, he brought with him ideas about the design of chairs and other furniture. With the importation of Continental techniques and the wood of choice—walnut—new features appeared. Flemish scrolls, twist turning for legs and uprights, and crest rails that were elaborately pierced and carved created a baroque exuberance. Caning was introduced by way of the Dutch trade with India, and caned seats and backs became a popular feature during the Restoration.

Time and again, we will say that mortise-and-tenon joints are one of the hallmarks of antique furniture construction, but these late seventeenth-century chairs are an exception. They actually used dowels, which resulted in a weaker joint. This poor construction technique, combined with very high chair backs and legs that were not always raked back adequately (they fell over easily) made for a form that was more decorative than sturdy and has not withstood the test of time as well as chairs from other periods.

The wing chair dates from the second half of the seventeenth century (when it was known as an easy chair), and it developed further in the William and Mary, Queen Anne, and Chippendale periods. At their best, wing chairs offer true comfort and style, and thus their perennial appeal. We may first be drawn to a chair because of its upholstery, which may be beautiful (but is rarely very old). However, the value of a chair is in the construction and design of the frame. If you have a chance to examine the frame of a wing chair, you will see that it is made up of several different types of wood. A soft wood like beech would be used for areas requiring upholstery tacks (harder woods split more easily). On an antique wing chair, this area should be absolutely riddled with holes from multiple sets of upholstery tacks.

The part of the leg that shows should be walnut or mahogany, and once under the upholstery, this primary wood should be spliced into the secondary wood. This construction technique does not indicate a repaired leg—it is standard on antique wing chairs (see page 58). The exposed legs and feet should exhibit fine carving or good, simple lines. One expects to find wear, and repairs are common. In terms of form, the best wing chairs have dynamic lines that are visually exciting from any angle.

Eighteenth-Century Chairs

By about 1700, England was beginning to develop a style of graceful curves and simple lines. Building on influences from Holland, the Queen Anne style evolved into the first uniquely English design. The cabriole leg was basic to the design and represented a significant change from seventeenth century styles. The curve of the cabriole leg was repeated in the cyma curve of the back, the curving crest rail, and rounded seat. All came together to create a style of balanced curves and restrained ornament. An important departure from seventeenth-century chair design was the lack of stretchers with cabriole legs. (Seventeenth-century chairs usually had highly decorative stretchers that called attention to themselves.) On Queen Anne chairs, the cabriole legs often ended in the ball-and-claw foot (a design motif borrowed from the Orient), a pad foot, or a stylized hoof. The finest Queen Anne chairs were veneered in figured walnut and had delicate, carved ornaments on the knees and crest rail.

Construction improved with the use of mortise-and-tenon joints instead of dowels; dowels on eighteenth-century style chairs indicate a later copy. Fig. 3-1 shows an inexpensive twentieth-century chair using dowel construction.

There are several construction changes for eighteenth-century chairs that help one distinguish copies from originals. Throughout the eighteenth century, on quality chairs with backsplats (from Queen Anne onwards), the backsplat fits into a "shoe" which then attaches to the seat rail (Fig. 3-2). This is called a detached or two-part shoe. It is a detail is rarely found on nineteenth- and twentieth-century copies of Queen Anne and Chippendale chairs. These later chairs have a splat that fits directly into the seat rail, called an integral shoe (page 55).

Another feature that we expect to find on eighteenth-century chairs with backsplats is silhouetting. That is, when viewed from the rear, you will notice that the curving design of the splat has a beveled or chamfered edge. This makes the design stand out more clearly when

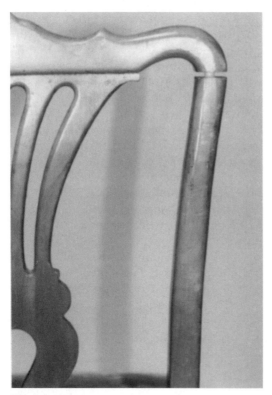

Fig. 3-1 Dowel construction on an inexpensive twentieth-century chair.

Fig. 3-2 Backsplat illustrating detached or two-part shoe.

viewed from an angle. If a splat is not silhouetted, the design tends to look fuzzy or muddy when viewed from an angle (note silhouetted and unsilhouetted splats on Figs. 3-3, and 3-8, versus 3-11).

When looking at eighteenth-century chairs, it is common to find a simple, uncarved chair that has been "improved" at a later date by the addition of carving. Period legs were planned in advance to include enough extra wood for deep carving, and period carving will stand proud or leap off the line of the leg. Carving that has been added to an old leg will be shallow and will not stand proud. Also, later carving, even when original, tends not to be as deep, crisp, or vital as good eighteenth-century work (Figs. 3-7 and 3-10 illustrate the comparison).

Around 1720, the importation of mahogany from the West Indies brought the

Fig. 3-3 The Splat of the George II chair (Fig. 3-4) is silhouetted, as are the backs of all good eighteenth-century chairs. This mean that the edge is bias cut or in-cut to clarify the line of the design when viewed from the front. Even from an angle, the line of the back splat design is exceedingly clear because of this silhouetting.

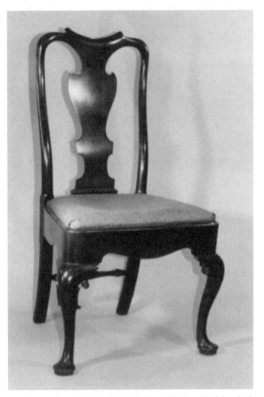

Fig. 3-4 George II, c. 1730 "Red Walnut" side chair with boldly shaped cabriole legs, pad feet, rear turned stretcher, shaped apron, and a bold splat well-contoured with the entire back. Slip seat. Crest with turning reflected from the C-scroll of the front leg. 21 1/4" wide × 38 1/2" high × 16 3/4" deep. *Courtesy Whitehall on the Villa, Chapel Hill, N.C.* **$7,500–9,000** pair. **$2,500–3,500** single. **$50,000–75,000** set of 6.

the Queen Anne period, the crest rail and the rear stiles meeting almost at right angles rather than forming the continuous curve of stile to crest rail on Queen Anne chairs. The cabriole leg is found on many chairs, but so is the straight leg (or Marlborough leg) with stretchers.

It is important to note that straight legs joined by straight (not turned) stretchers have a mortise-and-tenon joint, and the stretcher is flush with the side of the leg, not centered (Fig. 3-5). This is because when the mortise-and-tenon joint is executed by hand, it is easier to line it up accurately using the side of the leg as a guide. When machine doweling replaced the mortise-and-tenon joint in the nineteenth century, stretchers lined up with the center of the leg. On a Chippendale-style chair, this centered stretcher will indicate a later copy.

next important change to English furniture design. Not only did mahogany have a density and strength that made it perfect for structural pieces, but it also lent itself well to carving and also could be found with stunning flame figuring which was used to great advantage on large flat surfaces. Mahogany soon dominated furniture making, the way walnut had in the early years of the eighteenth century, leading to more elaborate carving, which was so much a part of the rococo styles of mid-century.

The back splats and stiles of Chippendale chairs are more vertical than those of

Fig. 3-5 Flush stretcher on an eighteenth century chair.

Fig. 3-6 One of a pair of c. 1760 carved mahogany armchairs after designs by Thomas Chippendale. Boldly carved and broadly well-proportioned. Shaped stretchers. Such fine pairs are very rare and highly collectible. *Private collection.* **$45,000–75,000** the pair.

Fig. 3-8 Detail of chair in Fig. 3-6, showing a variation on the detached shoe and a silhouetted back splat, both of which we expect to find on a good eighteenth-century chair.

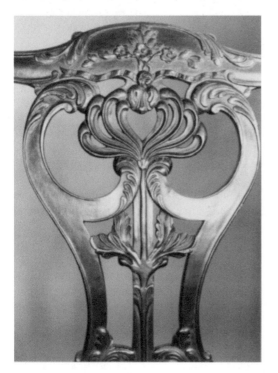

Fig. 3-7 Detail of the carved back splat of chair in Fig. 3-6. Note the depth and crispness of the carving. This is the kind of carving you will find on an eighteenth-century chair. You will not find the same quality on a nineteenth-century copy.

Fig. 3-9 One of a set of eight c. 1880 mahogany Chippendale-style dining chairs (2 arm, 6 sides). Well-carved backs and good cabriole legs (good for nineteenth-century copies, but not as brilliantly and deeply carved as the eighteenth-century chair in Fig. 3-6). *Photo courtesy Whitehall on the Villa, Chapel Hill, N.C.* **$12,000–18,000** set of 8.

Fig. 3-10 Detail showing the carving on the back splat of the chair in Fig. 3-9. When compared with the carving on the eighteenth-century chair in Fig. 3-6, it is easy to see the difference between eighteenth- and nineteenth-century carving. The eighteenth-century carving has more depth and energy.

The rococo style of Chippendale was at its height at mid-century, when it was joined by an abundance of exotic design ideas—Gothic and Chinese being the most prevalent. Gothic arches can be found in the back splats of chairs, and Chinese fret carving decorates legs and seat railings.

Around 1760, the neoclassical designs of Robert Adam began to have an impact on English furniture. Adam chairs were made of a soft wood, such as beech, which was carved and gilded. The legs were characteristically tapered and turned or fluted. Classical motifs abounded, including husks, honeysuckle (anthemion), sheaves of wheat, paterae, and urns. The lyre form was also incorporated in backs of chairs. Oval-backed

chairs were a popular Adam form, even in France during that time. Their concave shape (also called compound curvature) posed technical problems for the chair maker, requiring more timber, as well as considerable labor and expertise.

Hepplewhite's first pattern book was published in 1788. His designs for chairs featured concave shaping for the backs, with arms often set high on the stiles. The shield-back chair presented the same kinds of difficulties as the oval back—the complex, compound shaping required a high degree of accuracy and expertise. The design had to be well-planned so that it would hold up visually in the round. Decorations include floral garlands, sprays and medallions, and the Prince of

Fig. 3-11 Detail of back of chair in Fig. 3-8 showing integral shoe construction, no silhouetting.

Wales plumes, painted in natural colors or grisaille (monochromatic, usually gray, painting which simulates sculptured relief).

Sheraton's designs, published in the early 1790s, continued the late eighteenth-century trend in Neoclassicism. Sheraton's chair backs tended to be rectilinear, so they were much easier and less expensive to make than Adam and Hepplewhite chairs.

Windsor chairs had their own development apart from the major style currents of the eighteenth century. Dating from the end of the seventeenth century, these chairs existed alongside the formal chairs of the eighteenth century. With seats made of elm, bent pieces of ash or yew, legs and spindles of beech, the mixed woods were often unified with a coat of paint. Windors with Gothic design elements are among the most coveted.

However, it is worth noting that although we Americans so often think anything English is better than our own work, in truth, it was in America that Windsors reached their most satisfying expression.

Nineteenth-Century Chairs

The Regency style of the years 1800–1820 was very eclectic, exotic, and fanciful in the extreme. Regency chairs borrowed motifs from the Romans, Greeks, Egyptians, Gothic, and Chinese, and even include some Arabic influence. It was another classical revival, but even more so than the Adam style, in that it actually sought to revive classical forms for furniture (based on paintings and vases that had been recently excavated) and not just classical motifs. One of the principal designers was Thomas Hope, who created mahogany and rosewood chairs based on the ancient Greek Klismos chair, with sabre legs, arms set high on the rear stiles, the top rail swept backwards and forming a continuous curve with the rear legs. George Smith's *A Collection of Designs for Household Furniture and Interior Decoration* (c. 1808) popularized Hope's designs and added the symbolic use of animals, warriors, winged figures, etc. Not surprisingly, the Regency style at the time was called "Grecian."

Regency design continued up to mid-century, when its eclectic nature was given unbridled license by the Victorians. Revivals abounded, including Gothic, Elizabethan, Turkish, and French styles. The English were even buying French-made reproductions of Louis XV furniture by this time. The Victorian "naturalistic" style drew on Louis XV and naturalistic carving, and included the balloon-back chair and many upholstered armchairs. After the invention of spring upholstery in the 1830s, upholstery reigned supreme, and the Victorians created some very comfortable chairs.

Apart from the Revival styles of the Victorians, the Arts and Crafts movement (which occurred toward the end of the century) created some simple and sturdy chair forms. The Morris chair (named after William Morris) is a perennial favorite, with its straight upholstered back that can be raised and lowered at an angle for comfort.

Signs of Age

One final note about antique chairs: it's a good idea to test out the wear by sitting in the chair. The wear should be greatest where your feet touch the stretchers, where your hand rests, where your head leans against the back, where brooms or vacuum cleaners might have bumped legs and stretchers. If the wear is in odd places that do not correspond to human anatomy and to daily usage, it has probably been faked.

Sofas and Settees

The designs for sofas and settees follow that of chairs from the Renaissance up to the present. Today's collector is usually seeking comfort or visual impact in a sofa. Settees and sofas from the Regency period with caned backs and painted decoration are currently a popular choice because of their stylishness.

Pair of 1650–1675 Charles II oak side chairs, each back with caned panel, turned stiles, and scrollwork, the caned seat on turned and scrolled legs with scrolled front stretcher, joined by turned stretchers. *Courtesy Christie's New York.* **$2,400–3,600** the set.

Mid-eighteenth-century George II walnut corner armchair. Curved back continuing to scrolled arms, above tow pierced beaker backs, drop-in seat, on cabriole legs joined by stretchers, with central claw-and-ball foot. *Courtesy Christie's New York.* **$8,000–12,000.**

Irish Chippendale carved mahogany library armchair with antique needlepoint upholstery, c. 1760. Shaped arms, carved frieze. Acanthus-carved cabriole legs ending in paw feet. *Courtesy Morton Goldberg Auction Galleries, New Orleans.* **$18,000–25,000** if real. **$6,000–9,000** if a nineteenth-century copy.

George III gilt wood armchair, c. 1780–1800, with oval back and seat upholstered in silk. Molded frame surmounted by a floral spray, downswept padded arms on turned tapering fluted legs (redecorated). English furniture in the French taste is a slow seller. *Courtesy Christie's New York.* **$5,000–7,000.**

George III mahogany library armchair, c. 1780–1800, serpentine padded back and seat upholstered in suede. On square chamfered legs joined by stretchers. *Courtesy Christie's New York.* **$8,000–12,000.**

George III mahogany armchair, c. 1780. A country piece—rather simple but neat, with straight legs, stretcher base, well-formed arms, simple back splat and crest rail. *Courtesy Whitehall on the Villa, Chapel Hill, N.C.* **$1,800–2,400.**

One of a set of six c. 1795 Sheraton-Regency design, George III period mahogany side chairs, raised on turned legs with leaf-carved and oval-inlaid crest rail. *Courtesy Whitehall on the Villa, Chapel Hill, N.C.* **$4,500–6,500** for six. **$375–475** single.

Pair of c. 1810 Regency ebonized and parcel gilt armchairs. Caned seats and transverses. Sabre legs. 35" high × 23" wide × 19" deep. *Courtesy Skinner, Inc. Boston.* **$6,500–8,500** the pair.

One of a pair of c. 1810 Regency black-and-gold painted armchairs. Each with curved back and splat decorated with Greek key and center lion's mask, the seat now with a loose cushion. On ring-turned sabre legs. Decoration restored; partly rerailed. *Courtesy Christie's New York.* **$6,000–9,000** the pair.

Queen Anne style side chair, 1880–1890. Well-formed factory-made reproduction of solid mahogany. Good form overall. Very good rear uprights. The chair seat is a little narrow across the front. 17 1/4" wide × 17" deep × 40 1/2" high. *Courtesy Whitehall at the Villa, Chapel Hill, N.C.* **$400–600** single. **$800–1,200** pair. **$4,800–7,500** set of 6. **$8,000–12,000** set of 8. The shoe of this chair and rear rail are a single board, called an integral shoe. The vast majority of nineteenth-century chairs were so constructed. Queen Anne, Chippendale and Hepplewhite *period* chairs, on the other hand, had a two-piece construction (called a detached shoe) on 95% or more of chairs made in the eighteenth century. Also note the lack of silhouetting on the back. This lack of attention to the finer details of construction is typical of nineteenth- and twentieth-century copies. It saved time, and time is money.

Pair of c. 1890 Queen Anne style fruitwood (unusual) side chairs with shell-carved knees, cabriole legs, and pad feet. Shaped aprons. Well-formed backs. *Courtesy Whitehall at the Villa, Chapel Hill, N.C.* **$1,200–1,800** the pair.

Chippendale-style solid mahogany carved ladder-back saddle-seat side chair, c. 1930, with straight, molded front legs and stretcher base. A pure copy of the best quality. *Courtesy Whitehall at the Villa, Chapel Hill, N.C.* **$400–600** single. **$3,600–$4,800** for 6. **$6,500–8,500** for 8 (without armchairs).

A-56

Pair of Chippendale-style mahogany c. 1920 armchairs with pierced, scrolling splats, molded stiles, straight legs. Ears are too exaggerated. *Courtesy Wolf's Fine Arts Auctioneers, Cleveland, Ohio.* **$2,400–3,600** the pair.

Left: Pair of curved mahogany side chairs in the early George III taste. Late nineteenth to early twentieth century. **$2,500–3,500** the pair. Right: Two of a set of eight George III style c. 1890 carved mahogany dining chairs in the Chippendale taste. **$8,000–12,000** set of 6, without armchairs. *Courtesy Butterfield & Butterfield, San Francisco.*

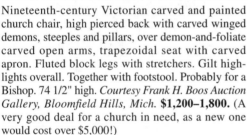

Nineteenth-century Victorian carved and painted church chair, high pierced back with carved winged demons, steeples and pillars, over demon-and-foliate carved open arms, trapezoidal seat with carved apron. Fluted block legs with stretchers. Gilt highlights overall. Together with footstool. Probably for a Bishop. 74 1/2" high. *Courtesy Frank H. Boos Auction Gallery, Bloomfield Hills, Mich.* **$1,200–1,800.** (A very good deal for a church in need, as a new one would cost over $5,000!)

George III Chippendale-design mahogany wing chair, c. 1760–1780. Very desirable turned, conical arm supports. Boldly formed wings and well-shaped crest rail Shown cut open to reveal eighteenth-century construction techniques: the mahogany rear legs splice into the secondary wood of the back (so as not to waste good mahogany on a part that would not be seen). The rear legs have a bold sweep making the chair visually interesting from all angles. The frame is completely constructed of mortise-and-tenon joints. *Courtesy Whitehall at the Villa, Chapel Hill, N.C.* **$6,000–9,000.**

Blind fret-carved Chippendale-design George III wing chair or easy chair, c. 1760. Diminutive proportions for a woman. These often had a commode in the seat and were used in bedrooms, especially for the elderly. *Courtesy Whitehall at the Villa, Chapel Hill, N.C.* **$3,000–4,500.**

Late nineteenth-century George II style walnut wing armchair. Great style and quality. *Courtesy Butterfield & Butterfield, San Francisco.* **$3,000–4,500.**

George III mahogany camelback sofa, in the Hepplewhite taste, c. 1780. 72" long. Provenance: Kenneth Hammitt Antiques. *Courtesy Skinner, Inc., Bolton, Mass.* **$10,000–15,000.**

George III Chippendale-style mahogany sofa, mid to late nineteenth-century. Acorn-and-leaf carved knees and arm supports. Ball-and-claw feet. Camelback. Down cushion (a big price plus). *Courtesy Whitehall at the Villa, Chapel Hill, N.C.* **$4,000–6,000.**

Sheraton Revival mahogany settee with serpentine seat rail (shell inlaid), c. 1860. Drapery inlaid crest rail. Fluted, turned arms and legs. *Courtesy Whitehall at the Villa, Chapel Hill, N.C.* **$2,000–3,000.**

George II c. 1750 red walnut double-chair-back settee. Transitional in style with a balloon seat, cabriole legs, but a more Chippendale-influenced back and arms, indicating an almost precise date of 1750. Typical of period examples is the extreme width of each "chair back." Nicely out-swept arms are again typical of the eighteenth century. Slip seat. *Courtesy Whitehall at the Villa, Chapel Hill, N.C.* **$8,000–12,000.**

Triple-chair-back Hepplewhite-style settee, c. 1890. Mahogany, shield back with Prince of Wales plumes carving. *Courtesy Whitehall at the Villa, Chapel Hill, N.C.* **$2,400–3,600.**

Edwardian, c. 1910 Sheraton- or Adam-style satinwood armchair. Well-painted decoration. Good carving and turning. *Courtesy Leslie Hindman Auctioneers, Chicago, Ill.* **$2,400–3,600.**

Edwardian, c. 1910 Sheraton- or Adam-style satinwood double-chair-back settee with painted decoration. This furniture has been very much the rage since the late 1980s. *Courtesy Leslie Hindman Auctioneers, Chicago, Ill.* **$3,500–5,000.**

George III style yew and elm wood "Gothick" Windsor armchair, the arched back with three pierced splats, saddle-shaped seat, and cabriole legs ending in pad feet. *Courtesy Grogan & Company, Boston.* This sold for $880 at auction. The estimate was $200–300. Late-nineteenth to early-twentieth century. If it was an eighteenth-century piece, the price would be **$6,000–9,000.**

Windsor armchair of dark ash and oak, c. 1830, with turned legs and pierced splat. *Courtesy Whitehall at the Villa, Chapel Hill, N.C.* $900–1,200. If yew wood, **$2,500–3,500.**

Pair of c. 1800 ash, elm, and mixed-wood Windsor armchairs from the Yorkshire era. Decent turnings and very good seats for English Windsor. Nice arm supports. *Courtesy Whitehall at the Villa, Chapel Hill, N.C.* **$3,000–4,500** the pair. **$1,000–$1,500** single.

Two of a matched set of eight elm and yew wood Windsor armchairs, each with an arched back filled with spindles and a central pierced splat over scrolling arms and a shaped saddle seat on turned legs joined by stretchers. "Matched" here obviously does not mean "identical." "Assembled" or "harlequin" are other terms you will find to describe sets that are similar but did not start life together. Some members of such sets may be modern, some antique. © 1991 Sotheby's. Values based on differing assumptions are as follows: c. 1830, elm: **$1,000–1,500**; one c. 1830, yew: **$2,500–3,500**; one modern, yew **$25,000–35,000**; eight modern, elm: **$4,000–6,000**; eight modern, yew: **$6,500–9,500**.

Two similar Windsor stools, c. 1830–1860, of ash, elm, and other woods. *Courtesy Whitehall at the Villa, Chapel Hill, N.C. Left:* **$375–475**. *Right:* **$300–375**.

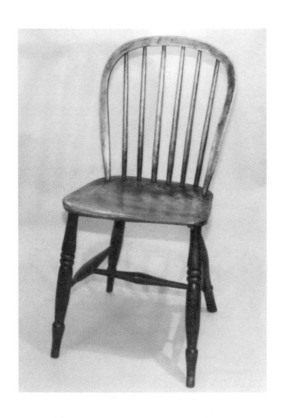

Yorkshire bow back Windsor side chair of elm, ash, etc., with turned legs, c. 1800–1830. This style is timeless; reproductions abound. Check them carefully. *Courtesy Whitehall at the Villa, Chapel Hill, N.C.* **$300–450** single. **$700–950** pair. **$4,800–6,000** set of six.

Ash, oak, and elm Windsor tavern armchair with round, molded seat and turned legs, c. 1860. *Private collection.* **$600–900**.

George III mahogany bench raised on tapered legs with stretcher base, c. 1790. Beaded top edge. Late rollers. Genuine benches of the eighteenth century are rare. More often than not they were made out of chairs or are Victorian copies. Examine with care. *Courtesy Whitehall at the Villa, Chapel Hill, N.C.* **$1,800–2,500.**

High back Windsor bow back armchair of ash and elm. Mid-nineteenth century. *Courtesy Whitehall at the Villa, Chapel Hill, N.C.* **$1,000–1,500.**

Pair of c. 1860 walnut footstools with Tunbridge- and line-inlaid decoration on original white porcelain feet. Later hand-worked needlepoint to copy the Tunbridge inlay (*Tunbridge* refers to the geometric inlay popular during the Victorian era). *Courtesy Whitehall at the Villa, Chapel Hill, N.C.* **$800–1,200.**

4

Tables

Throughout history, English furniture abounds with numerous ingenious table forms. There were tables for every function and occasion, and various types of tables are included in the listings in this book.

Trays-on-Stands

Most trays on the market date from the Regency or Victorian eras. The trays were made of tole, wood, or papier-mâché, and the stands are always of recent date. There are wonderful makers of custom stands in England or stands can be made stateside once the tray has been imported.

Edwardian trays of wood were often elaborately inlaid and were made of either mahogany or satinwood. They frequently look like the rarer Georgian trays but are readily identified by two characteristics: First, the gallery of an eighteenth-century tray has three strips of laminated wood running crosswise to each other. This creates great strength and durability, especially in the bending process. Edwardian galleries, on the other hand, are constructed of one piece of wood. The second characteristic involves inlaid pieces only. On antique trays, the inlays will have shrunk and moved, while Edwardian examples will show only minor shrinkage or none at all.

The more experienced buyer will find two more differences. Eighteenth-century trays of *mahogany* will be far heavier than Edwardian ones. The inlay styles of the eighteenth century were more elegant, restrained, and well-balanced when compared to the frequent flamboyance of the Victorian and Edwardian examples.

Drop-leaf Tables

The drop-leaf table was the dining table form for the seventeenth and most of the eighteenth centuries. Interestingly enough, Chippendale had no designs for dining tables in his *Director*. During the Chippendale era and until the latter part of the eighteenth century, drop-leaf or draw-leaf tables were most often used for that purpose. Frequently, two or three identical drop-leaf tables were joined, creating a banquet table. Since they were used as dining room furniture, they were never veneered and seldom inlaid.

CONSTRUCTION

Eighteenth-century drop-leaf tables used the rule joint with hinges underneath to join the leaves to the table top. The swing legs were joined to the undercarriage with a five-knuckle wooden hinge. The undercarriage is usually of oak or pine, while the top, leaves, and legs are most often walnut or mahogany. The leaves and the table top were each made up of a single board. One good clue to the age of a drop-leaf table is the weight of the leaves. On a good eighteenth-century table, the leaves will be *heavy*.

COMMON ALTERATIONS

The top may have been replaced or simply reset on its undercarriage. An originally plain apron may have been given a new graceful shape. Oval-shaped drop-leaf tables are more desirable on the market today, so leaves that were originally rectangular were frequently rebuilt and made oval. There are several clues to alert you to reshaped tables: Sharp edges will indicate new work and a leaf constructed out of two boards rather than one should raise suspicion. If the table started out life with leaves constructed of two boards each (this sometimes did happen), it is important to realize how the joint would have been made in the eighteenth century. When a cabinetmaker planned the table, he knew in advance how wide the leaves would be. If he did not have a single board wide enough, he would have taken two *unfinished* boards and glued them together (adding double mortise-and-tenon connectors as well). He would then have taken the newly enlarged boards and finished them as if they were a single. As a result, there will be no detectable difference when running your fingers across the joint.

On the other hand, if a finished rectangular leaf was being enlarged preparatory to cutting it into an oval shape, an entirely different sequence of events took place. Two already finished boards were laid on a very flat, smooth surface and glued together so that the outer side was perfectly smooth. As no two antique boards are ever identical in thickness, the rough line created on the back of the joint was sanded down until it was completely smooth. The result of this process is a shallowed area, which can be easily detected by running your hand across the joint. This is a signal that the table in question was originally rectangular, not the more desirable oval shape.

This same shallowing will alert you to any finished boards joined at a later date and may expose a false round tea table, a false banquet table top, a false breakfast table top, etc. Always check such joints when they appear unexpectedly.

SIGNS OF AGE

Look for patination under the leaves where they would have been handled often. Also look for swing marks where the supporting leg scraped the underside of the leaf every time the table was opened or closed. Due to shrinkage, leaves may not lie perfectly flat, but may splay out slightly. This is not easily repairable, and although this is a good indication of age, it detracts from the value of the piece if the problem is severe. Look for splits in the leaves, which may be acceptably repaired on the underside with butterfly patches.

Games Tables
(Fold-top Tables)

CONSTRUCTION

From the Queen Anne period on, fold-top tables have been popular. The fold-top table can take several forms, the best having a double or even (rarest of all) a triple top (one top designed for games, one for tea). Support mechanisms of two types are found on these tables: swing leg (or legs) and concertina action. The most common arrangement is one rear leg that swings out 45 degrees on a five-knuckled joint. Of greater sophistication, rarity, and cost (both then and now) is the table with two rear legs, each swinging 45 degrees. This is a desirable feature because it means that no one sitting at the table straddles a leg. This, of course, is found *only* on games tables, as it would be an unneeded extra expense on a tea table.

Concertina-action tables were made from about 1730 onwards. They feature a mechanism that doubles back on itself, the apron folding out accordion (i.e. concertina) style to create a finished apron on all four sides. Such tables are rarer and more costly by far than even double-gated tables. Again, they were only used on games tables.

Games tables come in several shapes: the basic rectangular top that opens to a square, a demilune shape that opens to a circle, D-shape, etc. Serpentine fronts, candlestick corners, and money wells are especially desirable features. Games tables originally had baize tops which usually need to be replaced, either with new baize or with leather. This replacement does not affect the value.

Most of these tables were walnut until about 1730, and then mahogany was used. After 1775, satinwood and rosewood examples were made, usually for games only, as the pedestal tea table enjoyed immense popularity after 1760.

COPIES

The Edwardians copied these game and tea tables in vast quantities. On Edwardian tables, the edges will be sharper and there will be less shrinkage. In terms of proportions, Edwardian pieces are daintier, more delicate (or as we would say, less robust).

Pembroke Tables

CONSTRUCTION

A Pembroke table is a form of small drop-leaf table in which the leaves are supported by hinged bracket supports rather than swing legs. They can have one or two drawers or none at all. Eighteenth-century Pembrokes will have two brackets for each leaf, and each hinge consists of five intermeshed wood knuckles. Nineteenth-century examples will usually have only a single centered bracket and frequently only three knuckles. Pembroke tables were made in all periods from 1750 onwards, and they may incorporate carving, inlay, or exotic shapes (serpentine leaves, bow ends, and so forth).

Bow-end tables made around 1770 or later were constructed with blocks or bricks of deal or other secondary wood over which veneer was applied. A solid mahogany curved end indicates either a later piece or one made about 1750–1765.

Pieces constructed between 1750 and 1830 will generally have very thin, elegant dovetails in the front of drawers (where they would be seen) and fewer, wider ones at the rear of the drawer. Machine dovetails indicate post-1870 pieces. Tiny dovetails in drawers of solid mahogany with mahogany sides are indicative of English Sheraton Revival and Edwardian furniture, from 1860–1910.

In order of importance, Pembrokes are graded for quality on the basis of size, form, number of drawers, and decorative visual aspects (including veneering and inlay). The smaller the table, the more valuable and desirable. Tables with bow ends or shaped leaves are preferred. A high-quality oval-topped piece, will have an apron that conforms to the top. Country examples often have no drawers, simple examples only one drawer, and more sophisticated pieces have a false drawer that exactly mirrors the real one or two real drawers.

English country examples were usually made of solid woods, such as mahogany, oak, cherry, maple, or walnut, urban examples were veneered onto solid mahogany, and flame-veneered pieces of great beauty reflect the highest level of the form. Design may be further enhanced by inlay, carving or features such as boxwood edging on legs and around real and false drawers or apron inlay. Remember, the more original the inlay, the greater the value; inlay added later (and recognized as such) lowers the value.

As with all antique furniture, signs of shrinkage must be discernible. Also note if there are patterns of oxidation on the underside of the table. Look for wear, especially where the brackets should scrape the underside of the leaves. The edges may have sewing-bird marks—small round dents made by the clamp of the screw-on sewing bird used by ladies of the eighteenth and nineteenth centuries. Sewing-bird marks may also be found on candlestands and round tea tables, as well as on work (sewing) table leaves. They are a reassuring sign of age. You might also find the scoring lines used by the cabinetmaker to plan hinge location.

On an eighteenth-century Pembroke, you should find shrinkage on drawer bottoms and on any inlay. Shrinkage may cause the leaves to fly outward or gap outward slightly. This happens when the cabinetmaker failed to make his center board wide enough to allow for shrinkage, and there is no truly satisfactory repair, as a spline to widen the board is ugly and replacing the center board destroys antique value.

REPAIRS AND ALTERATIONS

Examine the legs with care to make sure that they have not been extended (also called "tipped out"). Examine the line of the grain to see that it emerges below any inlaid cuffs or overlaid trim. Check the top to see if it is original. Tops are often replaced because of splaying or damage caused by inappropriate use. You may find a marriage between an old top and a base that were not originally together.

By turning the table upside down, you can check for marriage problems. There should be no "screw holes to nowhere." Also, look at the oxidation pattern. Where the drawer covers the top, the color should be lighter since it has had less exposure to air. The cross member below the drawer should leave a light-colored area on the drawer bottom. English country tables—and even many city pieces—will have very dark oxidation as a result of coal burning heat. The drawer is another likely replacement part. The oxidation patterns should be consistent, and there should be matching wear patterns on the drawer edges and table runners.

Add-ins and add-ons, such as inlay, carving, casters, and hardware, should be examined for originality. Do you feel shrinkage in the inlay? Can you see minute gaps between the inlay and the table surface? Are the casters leather (pre-1780), brass (post-1780), or ceramic (post-1860)? And, of course, are there holes from other hardware?

Sofa Tables

Sofa tables, which evolved from the design for Pembroke tables, were popular during the early years of the nineteenth century. Like Pembrokes, they have two leaves supported by hinged wooden brackets. They are usually about five feet long and can be placed before or behind the sofa. They usually have two drawers and rest on decorative supports (often lyre-shaped) that are joined by a turned stretcher. The two side supports end in outswept feet. Another standard design for the base consisted of a central support ending in four paw feet.

Tilt-top Tea Tables

CONSTRUCTION

This Chippendale form is very popular today, and thus, it is often faked or "improved." During the eighteenth century, these tables were always made of solid mahogany (not walnut) and were never veneered. The base of the table was made up of four pieces: the shaft and three legs, each dovetailed into the base of the shaft (usually with a wrought-iron bracket added for extra strength). The top is one solid piece of wood. On eighteenth-century tables, the top must show shrinkage across the grain—a difference of about one-half inch. Expect eighteenth-century tilt-tops to be very heavy as only the finest, densest Santa Domingo, Cuban, or Honduran mahoganies were used in their construction. Nineteenth-century copies are 30 to 50 percent lighter in weight!

There are very few tilt-top tables on the market today that are still in their original condition. Most have been "improved" by the addition of Victorian carving to the shaft and legs. Later carving can be spotted easily as it does *not* stand up off the line of the leg and it is *not* as deep or crisp as good eighteenth-century carving. Piecrust tops are especially desirable and so were often added to an earlier plain piece. An eighteenth-century piecrust edge was planned ahead and was carved out of a table top thick enough to accommodate it. On later additions, the molding for the crust was glued onto the original round table top and then carved. You will be able to see where they were joined. Sometimes the crust was carved out of the existing wood at a later date, in which case the result is a thin table top. This method often leads to problems since the dishing out of the table top can cause the screw that attached the top to the shaft to be uncovered. Patching here is an obvious sign of tampering.

Eighteenth-century "bird-cage" tilt-top tea tables are frequently found, very popular, and sometimes authentic. These feature a structure of two square blocks joined by four short, simply turned posts (about 3 to 3 ½ inches high), the blocks pierced by the shaft of the base, the shaft pierced by a rectangular hole. A wedge of wood was inserted into the latter hole—the key which stabilizes the table, yet allows it to turn about 345 degrees. The usual tilt mechanism joined the top block to the table top. Bird-cage tables bring a 25 to 50 percent premium, all other characteristics being equal.

VARIATIONS

There are several closely related styles, including supper tables, candle tables, and wine tables. All are of the same general form, but with differences in carving and scale.

Supper tables have a carved top dished in eight rings plus a large center ring to hold plates and a serving piece for the casual meal served in the parlor. Most date from the nineteenth century, some were created out of simpler eighteenth-century tables and some were made new around the 1860s.

Candle tables or candlestands are judged by the same criteria used to value tea tables: Look at the quality of carving and wood and for proportional balance between legs and top. The diameter is about three-quarters that of the tea table.

Wine tables are low (22-inch) candlestands or "miniature" tea tables. They were very rare in the eighteenth century. Fake candle and wine tables are often made by combining antique tray tops with antique fire screen bases—very tricky! Also, many post-1860s examples are found.

Lowboys or Dressing Tables

Lowboys date from the William and Mary period, and the form reached its peak during the Queen Anne period, when it featured three drawers and was raised on cabriole legs. Early William and Mary lowboys had stretchers, giving the form a heaviness. From the Queen Anne period onwards, stretchers disappeared. The late Georgian period found mostly simple, straight, or tapered legs, and the form went rather sterile. There were exceptions in the late Georgian period: high rococo pieces still on cabriole legs with whorl or ball-and-claw feet, often with brilliantly carved carcasses and superb, fine gilt brasses. These are very rare and sell for vast sums of money. The successor to the lowboy was the dressing table (kneehole form) which appeared about 1750.

Lowboy tops were constructed of no more than two boards (anything more is a replacement or a later table). Molded tops are more desirable than plain ones. Drawer construction is consistent with other case pieces of the same period. On veneered pieces, the drawer liners and carcass will be of oak or oak and deal combined.

Dutch lowboys, made for the English market during the seventeenth and eighteenth centuries were generally more elaborate. Many Victorian lowboys were made in England and also imported from Portugal and Spain.

Rent and Drum Tables

These round tables were made in various sizes, and have frieze drawers and pedestal bases. Along the frieze, real drawers alternate with false ones. Rent tables have the alphabet inlaid on the drawers and are larger than drum tables. Both styles first appeared in the mid-eighteenth century and were popular well into the nineteenth century. The style of the support will help date the piece: eighteenth-century pieces tend to have a plain, gun-barrel shaft. Nineteenth-century shafts tend to have more turnings and a heavier feel. Rent or drum tables can be found in all sizes from about three feet in diameter to four and a half feet.

Pedestal Tables

In the nineteenth century, pedestal tables became the preferred form for dining tables. The design was such that the top rested on a central support rather than four corner legs, thus providing more leg room.

Pedestal tables serve many functions and are found in a wide range of sizes. Many have short drop leaves and are breakfast tables or overgrown Pembrokes. Others are grouped in sets of two or more to create a banquet table which has many advantages over the drop-leaf varieties. Most pedestal banquet tables lack an apron, thus providing lots of leg room. They can be clustered in groups of two, three, four, five, six, or more to create giant tables. On banquet tables, three legs are preferred for end pedestals and four legs for center pedestals (if there are any). Downswept legs are preferred over spider legs.

The tops of these dining tables were always solid, never veneered, since veneer can be damaged by hot dishes and spills. Each leaf was made from a single board, and the edges were either plain or reeded, but the treatment of the pedestal and the edge should always be consistent. Sometimes reeding was added to enhance the value of a plain table. Check for roughness, which would indicate new reeding. Victorian interpretations abound and, generally, they are heavier and more bulbous. Victorian copies, however, can be quite faithful to original forms. Late nineteenth- and twentieth-century copies, as well as fakes, were very faithful to eighteenth-century forms!

Since many things can happen to pedestal tables over the years, they are probably the least original of all antiques found in the market place today, and values vary radically, depending on the level of originality. Leaves may have been lost, or tables split apart—the ends and center sections becoming separated. (This is true of drop-leaf banquet tables as well as pedestal forms!) To get them back up to banquet size, cabinetmakers now add old leaves from other tables, create extra pedestals with old wood tops, etc. Examine expensive tables (above $15,000) with great care. Use your fingers to explore edges—some may be sharper than others, indicating newer work. Measure the shrinkage of pedestals with calliphers—have they all shrunk or are some pedestals later in date? Examine the undersides of table tops for scars of old attachments, filled holes to nowhere, and old hinge scars, all clues to an enhanced table. Remember, most of these tables are enhanced and enlarged, which is acceptable. Just pay a price based on the alterations, not the price of an original, untouched table.

Refectory Tables

These are the long, heavy oak tables which were used for meals in manor house great halls. The tables, large enough to seat all those who lived in and around the house, tended to be narrow, as people sat along one side of a U-shaped arrangement. The legs on more interesting tables have bolection molding, which was achieved by building up the legs with wood prior to the execution of elaborate bulbous turning and carving. The legs were generally joined by stretchers that were flush with the floor, so that people could prop up their feet to avoid the cold stone or dirt floors.

SIGNS OF AGE

Naturally, tables dating from the seventeenth or even the sixteenth century have been subjected to heavy use. You should certainly find evidence of heavy wear on the stretchers, nicks and scrapes on the legs and the top, rot and disintegration or repair to leg bottoms and stretchers. Also look for heavy patination underneath the top (under the overhang) where generations of fingers would have handled the table.

REPAIRS AND ALTERATIONS

Upon close examination, refectory tables often turn out to be marriages—a new top (often made up of old floor boards) added to an old bottom. There are many late nineteenth-century and early twentieth-century copies on the market today (and more being made every day!). The counterfeits are usually wider than the originals and often have fairly obvious faked wear.

Be extremely suspicious of a refectory table that lacks extensive repairs—it surely is a later model. Most repairs, even serious ones, will not reduce value by much, as few such period tables exist and all have had heavy use (and probably abusive use, judging by the history of those rough times).

A good early Victorian green papier-mâché tray, gloriously painted and probably from the Clay factory. Gilding and painting of this quality are rare. On a modern faux bamboo stand of a rather mediocre quality, especially compared to the superb tray. Old repairs to edges at three points. *Courtesy Whitehall at the Villa, Chapel Hill, N.C.* **$3,500–4,500.**

Papier-mâché tray, c. 1820–1830, with gilt decoration and faux malachite painted "jewels." Custom-made stand, coffee-table height. *Courtesy Whitehall at the Villa, Chapel Hill, N.C.* **$2,800–3,800.**

Left: Table created of two c. 1900 lacquered Oriental trays in a turned mahogany stand of perhaps 1930s vintage. **$1,400–1,800.** Center: Anglo-European three-tier side table or etagere, c. 1870. Burl walnut with ebonizing. Gilt brass trim and gallery. **$1,800–2,400.** Right: c. 1830 small Victorian papier-mâché tray of cartouche shape, green with original decoration, in a new custom stand. **$600–900** tray alone. **$2,200–2,800** as shown. *Courtesy Whitehall at the Villa, Chapel Hill, N.C.*

Mahogany gun box, c. 1820–1860, brass corners, bindings, and recessed ring handle. These originally had a leather or canvas cover to protect the wood. On a modern stand. *Courtesy Whitehall at the Villa, Chapel Hill, N.C.* **$2,800–3,600.**

Oval George III mahogany butler's tray, c. 1790, original brass handles. The bent gallery was always made of three pieces of wood laminated together and running cross grain for strength. Now on a custom-made mahogany stand. *Courtesy Whitehall at the Villa, Chapel Hill, N.C.* **$2,800–3,600.**

Tunbridge-fitted travel box, c. 1860, brass inlay. Now on a mahogany stand. Adding a custom-made stand greatly increases the value and salability of a period box. *Courtesy Whitehall at the Villa, Chapel Hill, N.C.* **$2,200–2,800.**

A rare large field or ship's apothecary chest, c. 1820–1860. Solid mahogany, with original brass hardware. Many original bottles. Secret drawers behind the front drawer. Mounted on a custom-made mahogany stand. *Courtesy Whitehall at the Villa, Chapel Hill, N.C.* **$3,000–4,500.**

Nineteenth-century kettle stand in the George III style. Mahogany, with tea-cup slide and open brackets. Such stands, made to hold a samovar or other tea urn, are rare from any period. *Courtesy Whitehall at the Villa, Chapel Hill, N.C.* **$1,200–1,800.** An eighteenth-century example in this same design would sell for **$3,000–4,500.**

Custom-made mahogany wine table, c. 1920, George III Chippendale style. Dish top, fluted, turned and carved shaft. Fully carved legs end in ball-and-claw feet. *Courtesy Whitehall at the Villa, Chapel Hill, N.C.* **$800–1,500.** When real (period pieces are rare and often faked), **$6,000–12,000.**

George III commode or bedside table, c. 1780, Chippendale taste. All original except for converting the toilet section to a drawer. The side opening is quite unusual. Normally, the false-front drawer on this example would be the real commode drawer. Well-scalloped gallery top. *Courtesy Whitehall at the Villa, N.C.* **$3,000–4,000.** Prices have steadily skyrocketed in recent years, from an average of $1,200 in the late 1980s to $2,400 in the early 1990s, to $3,600 in the late 1990s.

George III mahogany three-tier washstand, c. 1790, with central drawer. Scalloped apron. The solid top is a replacement. The original had a hole to hold the wash bowl. *Courtesy Whitehall at the Villa, Chapel Hill, N.C.* **$1,000–1,500.**

Early nineteenth-century George III mahogany three-tier dumbwaiter. Each graduated circular platform with spindle gallery, on columnar stem and foliate-carved cabriole legs with ball-and-claw feet on casters. 45" high × 22" diameter. *Courtesy Christie's New York.* **$4,000–6,000.**

Set of c. 1810–1820 George III mahogany quartetto tables. Each graduated rectangular top with a shallow galleried border, raised on simulated bamboo-turned and blocked double standards terminating in a rectangular plinth above ringed feet. One age split to largest table top. Such nests of tables date as early as 1770 or 1780. *Most* date between 1890 and 1930! Purchasing this type of furniture demands extreme caution as pieces are often misrepresented (knowingly or unknowingly!). 30" high × 20" wide. *Courtesy Butterfield & Butterfield, Los Angeles.* **$4,000–6,000.**

Georgian mahogany corner or handkerchief table with gateleg support for the drop leaf, c. 1730–1760. Straight turned legs with pad feet. *Courtesy Whitehall at the Villa, Chapel Hill, N.C.* **$5,000–7,500.**

George III c. 1750 mahogany triple-top games and tea table (shown open for tea). Top opens again to a baize-lined games surface. Concealed locking well. Turned legs ending in pad feet. *Courtesy Whitehall at the Villa, Chapel Hill, N.C.* **$6,000–9,000.**

Georgian mahogany corner or handkerchief table, c. 1730–1760, in-cut corners and concealed storage well (not found on the previous example). *Courtesy Whitehall at the Villa, Chapel Hill, N.C.* **$6,000–9,000.**

George III tea table, c. 1780. A simple example of the related games/tea table—smaller than preceding example, lacks triple top and locking storage compartment. *Courtesy Whitehall at the Villa, Chapel Hill, N.C.* **$4,000–6,000.**

Regency rosewood and satinwood inlaid card table, early nineteenth century. Top with rounded corners over a conforming frieze, raised on square, tapering legs. 29" high × 18" deep. *Courtesy Grogan & Company, Boston.* **$8,000–12,000.**

George I inlaid walnut concertina-action games table, c. 1720. The burled walnut veneered top within narrow feather-banded and cross-banded borders, opening to reveal a baize-lined interior with shallow dished circular outset corners and oval counter wells, raised on slender molded cabriole supports ending in pad feet. 28 1/2" high × 32 3/4" long. *Courtesy Butterfield & Butterfield, San Francisco.* **$8,000–12,000.**

George III mahogany concertina-action games table with molded legs, c. 1760. *Private collection.* **$12,000–18,000.**

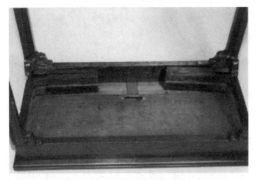

Concertina mechanism on above table: the sides of the table fold outward on a metal hinge to give a finished apron all around. The board with the finger hole is the "locking" board which slides forward to lock the table in the open position. Examine color, oxidation patterns, etc. very carefully on these tables which are much more valuable than swing-leg games tables and thus often faked.

Early George III mahogany games table, c. 1760, baize lined, in the manner of and possible from the workshop of Thomas Chippendale. The table has perfect proportions, and the attention to design details in a rather simple serpentine form is amazing. The serpentine repeats on the sides and in the curve when the legs meet the apron. Fine mahogany veneers over solid mahogany secondary wood. Solid mahogany rear apron and gate, with deal appearing only behind this one band. Molded straight legs. Good provenance. *Courtesy Whitehall at the Villa, Chapel Hill, N.C.* **$15,000–25,000.**

Sheraton Pembroke table of mahogany, c. 1795, straight tapered legs ending in original brass cuffs and rollers. Inlay along bottom of apron. One real and one fake drawer. A little large at 29" long to command the highest price. *Courtesy Whitehall at the Villa, Chapel Hill, N.C.* **$2,400–3,800.**

Simple oval mahogany Pembroke, c. 1780. No drawers. Thick top. A provincial piece, but shows good design in the relationship of the top of the body. *Courtesy Butterfield & Butterfield, San Francisco.* **$2,500–3,500.**

George IV mahogany sofa table, c. 1830, side leaves and two drawers. Flame veneers. *Courtesy Whitehall at the Villa, Chapel Hill, N.C.* **$8,000–12,000.**

William IV rosewood sofa table with gilt-tooled leather inset top, frieze drawer, c. 1845. On ring-turned leaf-carved trestle supports joined by a stretcher, which is raised on outward-sweeping legs on scroll-and-foliate cast feet. Stains on leather, minor losses to molding, as expected. *Courtesy Butterfield & Butterfield, San Francisco.* **$3,000–5,000.**

Mahogany Georgian tilt-top tea table, c. 1760, shaped, dished top; birdcage tilting mechanism; gun-barrel shaft; bold, triform legs. Note the simplicity of the turnings of the birdcage supports—a very simple design found consistently on English examples, even when the table shaft is far more elaborate. On American examples, the table shaft and bird-cage supports will almost always be mirror images of each other. Note the extravagant use of wood in this simple base—typical eighteenth-century quality. It's a miracle some Victorian or twentieth-century faker didn't "improve" the piece by elaborately carving the knees and feet! **$4,500–6,000. $2,500–3,500** *if* "improved."

Eighteenth-century Irish supper table with *later* elaborately carved top and base. Mahogany swirl urn, carved knees, ball-and-claw feet. Note the bird-cage tilting mechanism. As with tea tables, on Anglo-Irish examples the four supports in the bird cage are simply turned in gun-barrel form, no matter how elaborate the shaft. On American pieces, the four supports are usually mirror images of the shaft. *Private collection.* **$3,500–4,800.**

The legs and top of the table in the preceding photograph were carved in the nineteenth century (and not preplanned), thus a too-thin top and the recessed feeling of the leg carvings.

Bird-cage, tilt-top tea table, c. 1760–1780, carved, shaped edge (reshaped and later carved!). This table was originally round and was "improved" in the nineteenth century. Down-carved edges did not exist in the eighteenth century. The base and the swirl urn are original. *Private collection.* **$2,500–3,500.**

George III style c. 1860 mahogany piecrust tilt-top set on baluster and three down-curved legs with foliate-carved knees on ball-and-claw feet. These are usually made from eighteenth-century parts and are often misrepresented as period and original. Beware! *Courtesy of Leslie Hindman Auctioneers, Chicago, Ill.* **$2,500–3,500. $7,500–12,000 when real.**

George III mahogany tea table, c. 1750, circular molded piecrust top tilting and revolving above a tapering ring-turned and acanthus-carved standard on cabriole legs with leaf-carved knees on ball-and-claw feet. Note that the carving is of a later date. 27 1/2" high × 29 3/4" diameter. This *was* a fine, plain table until about 1860, when the top was reshaped, recarved, and dished out. The shaft and knees were then carved, as were those flat feet! Period carving, in contrast, is deep and brisk, jumping off the line of the piece. All of this carving sinks down into the piece. *Courtesy Butterfield & Butterfield, Los Angeles.* **$2,000–3,500.**

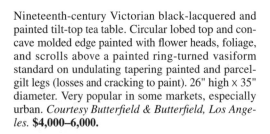

Nineteenth-century Victorian black-lacquered and painted tilt-top tea table. Circular lobed top and concave molded edge painted with flower heads, foliage, and scrolls above a painted ring-turned vasiform standard on undulating tapering painted and parcel-gilt legs (losses and cracking to paint). 26" high × 35" diameter. Very popular in some markets, especially urban. *Courtesy Butterfield & Butterfield, Los Angeles.* **$4,000–6,000.**

Japanned William and Mary style c. 1680 and c. 1860 lowboy. Altered and created from a period piece. *Courtesy Whitehall at the Villa, Chapel Hill, N.C.* **$4,500–6,000.**

George III mahogany dressing table or lowboy on straight legs with scalloped apron, c. 1780. Possibly original hardware. Oak secondary wood. *Courtesy Whitehall at the Villa, Chapel Hill, N.C.* **$4,000–6,000.**

Walnut, herringbone-inlaid Queen Anne style lowboy, c. 1900. Carved knees. Cabriole legs. *Courtesy Whitehall at the Villa, Chapel Hill, N.C.* **$2,400–3,600.**

George III mahogany harlequin-action dressing table, late eighteenth century, rectangular shape with a hinged divided top opening to a leather-lined writing surface, raised on a ratchet support and fitted with a mechanical rising superstructure, with small drawers, the frieze with a fitted drawer, above a pair of concave tambour doors. On straight legs ending in brass feet with casters. 31" high × 25 1/2" wide × 21" deep. © 1991 Sotheby's Inc. **$8,000–12,000.**

George II gun-barrel shaft breakfast table, c. 1800, solid mahogany (two highly figured book-matched boards). Reeded legs and edge. *Courtesy Whitehall at the Villa, Chapel Hill, N.C.* **$7,000–10,000.**

Regency mahogany drum table, c. 1810. Circular top with inset gilt-tooled brown leather surface above a frieze containing four drawers alternating with four simulated drawers, raised on a turned standard with four cabriole legs ending in brass paw feet with casters. Stamped "Gillow." The name "Gillow" has been associated with furniture making since the 1730s. The British firm was based in Lancaster and also had a location in London. They made furniture that was plain and unpretentious, but made to very high standards. 30 1/2" high × 47" diameter. *Courtesy Grogan & Company, Boston.* **$10,000–16,000.**

Regency mahogany breakfast table, c. 1825, reeded edge and rounded corners, turned vasiform standard and four outswept reeded legs ending in brass casters. 28" high × 60" long × 39" wide. The top seems unusually thin and narrow, possibly replaced. *Courtesy Grogan & Company, Boston.* **$5,000–7,000.**

A boldly turned shaft on a single board c. 1820 Regency-period breakfast table. Tilt-top, reeded legs with square-toed casters. *Courtesy Whitehall at the Villa, Chapel Hill, N.C.* **$7,000–9,000.**

Georgian mahogany dining table, c. 1830. Top with reeded edge and rounded ends raised on two baluster-turned pedestals, each with four reeded outswept legs with brass casters. 28"high × 53" wide × 88" long. *Courtesy Grogan & Company, Boston.* **$10,000–15,000** as is. **$18,000–24,000** with more leaves to seat 12.

Gillows & Waring signed mahogany double-pedestal banquet table, c. 1900, two leaves (not shown). Cross-banded top. Leaf carved legs. *Private collection.* **$5,000–7,500.**

George III mahogany Hepplewhite-design, c. 1780, tapered straight leg drop-leaf dining table. Swing-leg support for leaves. Added casters. Well-figured single board for the top. The rounded edges may be original, but need careful inspection. Rounded edges are often faked on large drop-leaf tables. *Courtesy Whitehall at the Villa, Chapel Hill, N.C.* **$1,800– 2,800** depending on size and condition.

Mahogany banquet table, c. 1830–1850, four pedestals and three additional leaves (not shown). These tables were usually altered, married, improved, inlaid at a later date, etc. This particular example had large humps at the tops of the legs where they met the pedestals—*very* Victorian. Some time in its history, it was "improved" by removing the humps so that it could be mistaken for an earlier example. The gadrooned urns probably made a simultaneous appearance. *Courtesy Whitehall at the Villa, Chapel Hill, N.C.* **$12,000–18,000.**

Fine-quality solid mahogany double-pedestal banquet table, c. 1900, two leaves (shown here). Gun-barrel shafts. Seats 12. *Courtesy Whitehall at the Villa, Chapel Hill, N.C.* **$8,000–12,000.**

Early Georgian provincial oak and fruitwood gateleg table. First-quarter eighteenth century. Oval top hinging above an end drawer and raised on slender ring-and-baluster-turned and blocked supports joined by molded tied stretchers and ending in ovoid feet. Old repairs, feet replaced. 28 1/2" high × 4'7" long, when open. *Courtesy Butterfield & Butterfield, San Francisco.* **$3,000–5,000** in the U.S. **$5,000–8,000** in the U.K.!

Drop-leaf table, American or English (you have to examine the secondary wood). Both countries produced thousands of tables identical to this from 1750–1790. Three-board top. Straight legs. Very heavy to lift due to the dense, early mahogany used. Found in sizes seating from 6 to 10. *Courtesy Whitehall at the Villa, Chapel Hill, N.C.* **$2,400–3,600.**

George III c. 1750 oval mahogany drop-leaf on turned legs with pad feet. Seats six. *Courtesy Whitehall at the Villa, Chapel Hill, N.C.* **$4,500–6,500.**

Jacobean-style c. 1920 oak refectory table with rectangular top over stylized floral-carved frieze raised on bulbous turned legs joined by wide stretchers. Note the faked wear on the stretchers—they look like a child's race-car track! 30" high × 67" long × 31" deep. *Courtesy Wolf's Fine Arts Auctioneers, Cleveland, Ohio.* **$4,000–6,000.**

Jacobean carved oak refectory table. First quarter seventeenth century. Plank top, leaf-carved apron, six ribbed and leaf-carved bulbous legs conjoined by box stretcher. 31" high × 102" wide 33" deep. *Courtesy Freeman/ Fine Arts, Philadelphia.* **$12,000–18,000** in the U.S.

5

Sideboards and Cellarettes

Sideboards as we know them today did not come into being until about 1780, with the advent of the Hepplewhite-Sheraton eras. Before that, in the Adam era (c. 1760), serving tables, usually in pairs, were used in fine dining rooms. One of the characteristics of serving boards is that they do not have any drawers, as cutlery was stored elsewhere. Period serving tables, either singly or in pairs, are a great rarity. The number of fake serving tables and modern reproductions (post-1880) is relatively small. However, to establish value, it is still imperative to determine the level of originality (whether any alterations have been made to a period piece) and to decide whether the piece is a nineteenth-century, or even a twentieth-century, copy.

Serving Tables and Sideboards

CONSTRUCTION

By the 1770s and 1780s, more and more sideboards were taking the place of serving boards. These pieces are found in great numbers on the American market. When looking at a serving table or a sideboard, begin by noting the quality of details, which should speak of typical eighteenth-century craftsmanship. The mahogany should be superb with rich grain patterns. Beading and fluting enhance the value of the piece.

By the Hepplewhite period, the classic sideboard design was the same in England and America. This particular form has remained popular since its inception—timeless in its grace and line, yet subject to many subtle variations. One aspect that has remained constant is that the legs all extend from the top to the floor, beginning their taper only at the base of the carcass. The legs were attached into the carcass with double mortise-and-tenon joints. All period English sideboards had deep drawers on either side of the central section, never cabinets. (American sideboards, by the way, had side cabinets rather consistently, even in the eighteenth century.) If the piece has been altered, the sides of the door front may still reveal where dovetailed joints were cut off and not fully covered over with a new strip of molding. Also, the interior bottom will be newer than the rest of the bottom of the piece—another example of what oxidation patterns can tell us.

COPIES

There are many c. 1890 Edwardian copies of Hepplewhite and Sheraton sideboards on the American market. Sideboards from this period have minimal value as antiques, so "prettying them up" can make them more desirable (it cannot ruin antique value, since they really don't possess it). We bought this rather mediocre Edwardian sideboard in England (Fig. 5-1) and had cross banding added to the side cabinets, and had one of the central drawers taken out and replaced by a pretty, shaped apron (Fig. 5-2). These changes did not make this piece more valuable. They did, however, make the piece more salable. It may go for as high as $3,600, clearly labeled as an altered Edwardian sideboard. Now, if you think you are dealing with an eighteenth-century sideboard and you suspect alterations, you had better get out your flashlight and get down on your hands and knees and thoroughly inspect the piece. Alterations will definitely affect the value—and many, many eighteenth-century sideboards have been altered over the years.

COMMON ALTERATIONS

Changing drawer configuration (removing a lower central drawer) is common on eighteenth-century boards, as th arched center fetches *far* more mone than the less-graceful, two-drawer centra configuration. This greatly reduces valu *if* discovered. Take a flashlight and examine the open area for signs of runners having been removed (evidenced by oxidation differences, filled nail holes, or a veneered interior to hide alterations). Exactly what was done to the Edwardian piece just discussed was and is frequently done to period pieces. Such a change will devalue a period board by up to 75%!

Inlays have frequently been added to eighteenth-century sideboards, and that practice continues today. Examine all inlays carefully. You should find shrinkage in every piece. Also, banding and large paterae will ripple over time, as the wood underneath shrinks at a different rate and in a different direction than the inlays. Added inlays—when discovered—greatly reduce value of a period piece.

Downsizing (the reduction of the size of a period piece) is frequent and devastating to value. Most frequently, sideboards

Fig. 5-1 Edwardian sideboard as purchased in England. Additions pictured in Fig. 5-2 make is a more salable piece.

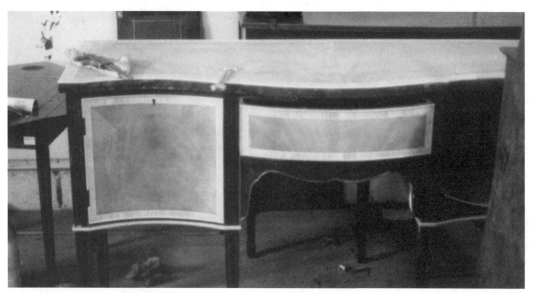

Fig. 5-2 Edwardian sideboard in Fig. 5-1 with added cross banding and replacement of central drawer with shaped apron.

have been made more shallow. Period sideboards are 26 to 36 inches deep—very large for dining rooms in the smaller homes of the twentieth century. To make them more salable, dealers sometimes reduce their depth, which also reduces their value by 25% to 50%. To spot this, look at oxidation patterns and look for sharp, new edges. Unless width has also been altered (look for this as well), such pieces usually look wrong—too wide for their depth.

REPAIRS

Some repairs are quite acceptable, some are not. A repaired broken leg, rebuilt drawer runners, split tops now pulled tight, split sides now repaired, plus the usual veneer patches and repairs are all acceptable and have little or no impact on value. Well-executed, minor repairs actually enhance value over the unrepaired state.

Replaced legs are frequent, and unacceptable, reducing value to utilitarian and decorative only (that is, comparable in price to a modern reproduction of similar style and quality). Heavy legs, turned legs,

and broken legs have often been replaced. Expensive sideboards (over $15,000) should be examined carefully, as the leg should extend to the top, the grain matching all the way up. This is very easily examined on the back legs.

Drawers replaced by doors (using the original drawer front) reduce value by at least 25%. The removal of cellarette dividers, or their replacement, reduces value by only 10% or so.

One final note: There were no period Queen Anne or Chippendale sideboards. Any now found on the market are fakes that will fool only those who are unfamiliar with design history.

Cellarettes (Wine Coolers)

CONSTRUCTION

Most eighteenth-century and early nineteenth-century sideboards have a cellarette drawer, often lead lined, frequently with drain plugs. Free-standing cellarettes and wine coolers were also made and have long been popular. (Wine coolers have lead liners which hold ice to cool.) Cellarettes and wine coolers made about

1750 have three- or four-leg stands, frequently include brass banding, and were always constructed of fine mahogany. Beginning at the end of the eighteenth century, floor and cabinet examples were made to match the sideboards. The coffer style sat under the arched center of the sideboard. The cabinet types matched the ends of the sideboards and stood slightly to each side of the board.

These pieces are used in myriad ways today, from bottle storage in the cellarettes, as originally designed, to coffee tables, end tables, etc. made from the coolers. Seldom do wine coolers land in the modern dining room, as they are heavy, awkward to empty, and unnecessary due to modern cooling devices (refrigerators!). They do find lots of other homes, however.

REPAIRS AND RESTORATIONS

The most problematic area with the cellarette or cooler on a stand is the stand. Legs were often broken, one or more legs replaced, all legs replaced, or the stand is a total replacement. Footed examples often have had at least one foot replaced. These areas of likely damage should be examined first because the very nature of usage often leads to destruction—stresses due to excessive weight, frequent moving across floors, and being tipped over to drain (in the case of coolers).

The next most frequently damaged areas are hinges and tops. Lids may have been thrown back and knocked off, and are, in fact, often replaced, having been shattered irreparably in an accident or through misuse.

Cellarettes are frequently redivided into shapes more useful for modern bottles (as opposed to early blown decanters and bottles). This certainly lowers value by 25% or so. Coolers often have the lead lining patched or strengthened (not adverse to value) or a new lining inserted (devalue by 10%). A cooler without its liner is worth 25% less than a complete example.

Watch out for created cellarettes. Frequently coolers are refitted as cellarettes, the more useful configuration for today's lifestyle. Such refitted coolers are only worth decorative and utilitarian value, they have no collectible value. Thus, they sell for one-quarter to one-half the price of a genuine, original, and complete example. Fake cellarettes are frequently created from large, early storage boxes, cartridge chests, document boxes, and so forth. They can be unmasked through careful examination of fittings, stand, feet, etc.— all of which will have been added to "create" the cellarette or cooler.

STYLE POINTS

Like all antiques, there are good and bad cellarettes and coolers. Some are awkward, some are quite ugly, some are splendid. Proportion is always the primary key to this form, as it is to all antique furniture. Beyond that, prized examples are those made from very fine mahogany or satinwood. Inlays and carving should enhance the overall effect, and *must* be original to the piece or they *detract* from value! Finally, the finest examples should have hardware and mounts of superior quality.

Page 103, lower left, shows a particularly fine example of a Regency period (c. 1805–1815) wine cooler with all of the most desirable characteristics. It is built of fine Santa Domingo or Cuban mahogany with flame mahogany veneers on the panels and top (*very* desirable). Carving is used to great effect; the feet are strong and realistic; and the tapered, stop-fluted pilasters are elegant (and fiendishly difficult for the carver, as the tapering leaves no room for error). Exterior and interior parts are original—hinges, liner, and all.

Its glories, however, are its design and mounts. The sarcophogus form is perfectly proportioned and every detail is harmoniously balanced. The mounts of gilt brass and gilt bronze, probably by Matthew Boulton, are simply superb. The motif of the lid banding is repeated on the rings in the lions' mouths, and the cast lions are incredibly realistic and detailed. And note the carved feet on the cooler are lion's feet, creating a conceptual whole from top to bottom.

A large (over 7' long) c. 1790 George III mahogany sideboard with pierced brackets, long, tapered legs, and well-inlaid and veneered case. Three central drawers, two side drawers. *Courtesy Whitehall at the Villa, Chapel Hill, N.C.* **$12,000–18,000.**

Georgian mahogany sideboard, c. 1790, large central drawer flanked by two deep drawers inlaid to appear as four drawers. Well inlaid. *Courtesy Whitehall at the Villa, Chapel Hill, N.C.* **$15,000–25,000.**

D-shaped George III mahogany sideboard, c. 1800. A restrained example with straight-grained veneers. Tapered legs with raised cuffs. Replaced pulls. Side cabinets. Line inlays on the legs. Warping. *Courtesy Whitehall at the Villa, Chapel Hill, N.C.* **$8,000–12,000.**

A desirably small late eighteenth-century mahogany sideboard with serpentine shape, cross bandings, and inlays. Cracks in the top. *Courtesy Whitehall at the Villa, Chapel Hill, N.C.* **$15,000–25,000.**

George III c. 1800 inlaid mahogany sideboard. Shaped top with later or altered brass gallery, central frieze drawer flanked by cupboard door inlaid to simulate two drawers and similarly inlaid cellarette drawer, all raised on ring-turned and reeded tapering legs. Brass galleries or wine rails are found on eighteenth-century pieces, but they were taller, as they held a curtain to prevent splashing of rare and costly wallpapers in great mansion. 36" high x 71"long x 29 3/4" deep. **$8,000–12,000.** Also shown are two typical c. 1780 knife boxes, one with shell-inlaid top. These are usually altered on the inside and turned into letter boxes, decanter boxes, etc. Pairs are worth *triple* the value of singles. Left: warped, altered interior. **$400–600.** Right: original interior. **$1,200–1,800.** Good pairs are at least $7,500—fine pairs are over $12,000! *Courtesy Grogan & Company, Boston.*

Edwardian (or late Victorian) mahogany sideboard with satinwood banding, side cabinets, tall wine rail. The shallow depth (22") and use of cabinets are dead giveaways as to the age of the piece. You don't even need to examine it, as it can't be antique! *Courtesy Whitehall at the Villa, Chapel Hill, N.C.* **$4,500–6,500.**

A small c. 1820–1830 sideboard with stepped-back shelf for decanters, etc. Called a brandy board in England, we would call it a server or serving board. Turned and reeded pilaster legs. Mahogany and flame mahogany veneers. Scrolled gallery. Central bottle cabinet. Flanked by four small drawers. *Courtesy Whitehall at the Villa, Chapel Hill, N.C.* **$5,000–7,500.**

A good "Sheraton Revival" c. 1860 mahogany sideboard with spade feet. Fiddle grain with dark mahogany banding. Cabinet sides. *Courtesy Whitehall at the Villa, Chapel Hill, N.C.* **$5,000–7,000.**

George III c. 1785 mahogany bowfront sideboard. With bowed rectangular top over conforming case. Central drawer flanked by two drawers and cellarette drawer. Spade feet. 35" high × 59" wide × 27 1/2" deep. The original auction catalog misidentified this as late nineteenth century. Only the *inlays* are late. The very deep *dimensions* are pure eighteenth century, and the use of drawers instead of side cabinets is also indicative of eighteenth-century work. The added inlays do reduced the value, however. *Courtesy Leslie Hindman Auctioneers, Chicago, Ill.* **$8,000– 12,000. $15,000–22,000**, if pure.

Large, elegant George III sideboard with drawers and cupboards. Note the incorrect position of the center legs— they don't continue through to the top. This piece was modified, perhaps from an even larger piece. *Private collection.* **$6,000–9,000.**

Scottish mahogany stepped-back sideboard, c. 1830, sliding dish storage in back, two small, one large, and two deep drawers. Great use of choice mahogany and mahogany veneers. *Courtesy Whitehall at the Villa, Chapel Hill, N.C.* **$8,000–12,000.**

Edwardian c. 1900 inlaid and penwork-decorated mahogany sideboard in the Neoclassical taste. Maple cross-banded top with recessed central portion, boxwood stringing on the edges and dart-and-line inlaid border above a concave-fronted frieze drawer inlaid with ribbon-tied swags of husks and flanked by simulated fluted end drawers over end cupboards, decorated in penwork with classically robed maidens representing summer and music. Left-hand cupboard enclosing three fitted drawers. Plinth base. 33" high × 6'9" long. *Courtesy Butterfield & Butterfield, Los Angeles.* **$10,000–15,000.**

Pair of c. 1825–1835 William IV mahogany wine coolers, urn-shaped with egg-and-dart borders and gadrooned bodies. Original lead liners and later removable copper liners. Over 2' in diameter. *Courtesy Whitehall at the Villa, Chapel Hill, N.C.* **$15,000–25,000** the pair. These were purchased for $19,800 by a London dealer at a New York City sale. In London they may sell for $50,000 or more!

A tea poy, a rare form of tea caddy. The very large tea caddy (four or more caddies and two or more sugar bowls) in the form of a table. Some tea poys look like sewing tables, others are more "boxlike," as in this example, which is rosewood, c. 1820, with gilt and brass mounts. *Courtesy Whitehall at the Villa, Chapel Hill, N.C.* **$4,000–6,000.**

One of a pair of wine coolers (rarely found but originally a frequent occurence—inheritors split them up). A fully developed example of c. 1815 Regency furniture in solid mahogany with flame veneers. Carved solid-mahogany lion's-paw feet. Original lead liners (to slow down ice melt and to prevent leaking). Bronze lion's-head mounts and banding, identical motif on ring and banding. Tapered, fluted pilasters capped with carved rosettes. Good provenance. 20" high × 30" long × 17 1/2" deep. *Courtesy Whitehall at the Villa, Chapel Hill, N.C.* **$30,000–35,000.**

George III brass-mounted mahogany octagonal wine cooler on stand, c. 1760–1770. Stand with slightly splayed square tapering supports ending in brass cappings. Lacking fitted interior. 29" high × 17 1/2" diameter. The style of the legs is later (c. 1790) than the cooler, indicating a possible marriage or leg replacement. *Courtesy Butterfield & Butterfield, Los Angeles.* **$5,000–7,000.**

A very good c. 1760–1770 George III mahogany cellarette with caddy (i.e., flat, coffered) top, molded
edges, cross-banded top, original stand with scalloping and leather casters. Original interior. Such a
level of originality is rare in these pieces, which saw
hard use by often less-than-sober hands. *Courtesy
Whitehall at the Villa, Chapel Hill, N.C.* **$6,000–
9,000.**

"George III mahogany drings stand, c. 1790," with
hinged molded top and single blind-frieze drawer
above two cupboard doors and three drawers, all
raised on square legs, casters. Actually an old
washstand (c. 1790) with multiple alterations, including removal of potty (middle drawer in base)
and addition lf solid shelf and casters. 34 1/2" high ×
30" wide × 21" deep. *Courtesy Grogan & Company,
Boston.* **$2,400–3,600.**

6

Case Furniture: Chests, Chests-on-chests, Linen Presses, Highboys

Case furniture encompasses all forms of furniture made on the principle of a box. The boxes may or may not contain other elements, such as doors, drawers, linen slides, and shelves. Stacked boxes constitute multicase furniture (such as secretaries, linen presses, chests-on-chests).

Case furniture was made over a long period of time and several different construction methods were used. Initially, pieces were made with stiles and rails with floating panels for sides, a nailed or paneled top, nailed bottoms and backs, and mortise-and-tenon construction elsewhere. With the advent of dovetailing in the late seventeenth century, the construction of case pieces changed. The chest of drawers was created, and secretaries, highboys, and other multipart case pieces followed around 1680.

Construction of Single-part Case Furniture

Cabinetmakers have continually sought ways to counteract the natural effects of shrinkage on wood. With time, wood shrinks across the grain and leads to splitting if the wood is held in place too tightly. As the old frame-and-panel form of construction was abandoned toward the end of the seventeenth century, re-placed by dovetailed carcasses, shrinkage again became a problem. With the new dovetailed carcasses, the sides (with vertical grain) would shrink front to back while the drawers (with the wood grain running back to front) would not shrink in depth, only in "height." Thus, the sides lose some depth over the years, while the drawers do not. The drawers will actually be expelled slightly by the shrinking carcass. Cabinetmakers were forced to develop new techniques to deal with the problem of unsightly, gaping drawers, as by 1730 this was an obvious defect. To counter it, cabinetmakers began leaving a gap at the back behind the drawers and using "stops" placed on the drawer runners or nailed to the drawer dividers near the front.

However, word of this solution did not reach everyone at the same time. As late as 1780–1800, provincial cabinetmakers still made chests whose drawers stopped at the back of the chest. Furthermore, it is important to realize that just because a chest has drawer stops does not necessarily mean it was made after 1730 (when drawer stops generally came into use). Many pre-1730 chests of drawers were, of course, altered to eliminate unsightly gaps by shortening the drawer sides and reattaching the drawer backs. Look for such signs if you suspect you have a pre-1730 chest. Gaping drawers are a good sign of age (fakers never leave gaping drawers), but you must rely on other visual clues to date the piece.

Virtually all English chests will have dust covers between the drawers (as do some American chests made by English-trained makers, while Continental chests do not). These dust covers made their appearance around 1700.

In drawer construction, the use of quarter-molding on the inside of the drawer sides can be found on pieces with superior construction that were made as early as 1770. The same is true of the use of control supports to divide large drawer bottoms into two sections, reducing sag problems. This is particularly true of fine London pieces. Linen presses, chests-on-chests, secretary bases, and large chests all have centrally reinforced drawer bottoms after 1770 or 1780, when cabinet-makers began responding to the needs of their clients. When it was noticed that large, loaded drawer bottoms sagged after a few years, techniques were quickly developed to improve the situation and by 1830 were used by even the most humble cabinetmakers in Britain.

We will generally find bracket feet (or ogee bracket feet) on eighteenth-century chests of drawers made after 1720. The bracket foot, a decorative piece applied to the skirt, hides the load-bearing foot, which is a glue block or a corner block. There is no weight on the bracket feet if the piece is properly constructed and the block will not be worn down unless it became unglued or suffered from worm or water damage. If such wear occurred, the block gradually lost its ability to hold the weight of the piece, and slowly the weight transferred to the decorative bracket foot. Then if the piece was shoved around, the bracket feet broke off. One replaced foot on an antique only marginally affects value. If all the feet are replaced, however, the piece loses 25% of its value, so such alterations are a very important consideration. It is also the reason cabinetmakers

use great skill to make replacements difficult to detect.

On really fine case pieces, you will sometimes find a glue block that is made up of stacked wood, with the grain pattern in each piece of wood running against the other, as with laminated wood. The opposing grain patterns create a more stable support. This is called a stacked block, and it is found only rarely and on only the finest pieces. If you find it, you are dealing with a piece made by a highly skilled cabinetmaker working for a wealthy patron, because it was an expensive technique. You will not see this often, but when you do, you are probably looking at a piece made to exacting standards and worthy of serious consideration.

Spotting Fakes and Alterations: Anatomy of an English Chest

The vast majority of "eighteenth-century" chests of drawers on the market today in shops and auctions are either old or recent fakes. They may be large pieces made small, the elements all being antique but cut down and made into a more salable form. They may be new creations with old elements thrown in to trick the buyer. They may be cleaned up Victorian chests made in England in the nineteenth century but in an eighteenth-century style. And finally, the chest you want may be authentic. How can you tell what is right and what is wrong?

We begin by examining a typical "English Hepplewhite-style nineteenth-century mahogany bachelor's chest," the type of piece commonly seen in every area of the country where English antiques are sold (Fig. 6-1). The moment you see this piece, your knowledge of style and form should set off alarms—this piece looks wrong! Bachelor chests were *always* smaller versions of large chests, i.e., the proportions and number of drawers remained constant, but the piece as a whole

Fig. 6-1 All-too-typical English Hepplewhite-style nineteenth-century mahogany bachelor's chest with significant problems.

was smaller. What we expect in a chest is either four graduated drawers or two short over three graduated drawers (and in Scottish chests, three small over three graduated drawers). In this piece, however, the drawers are all the same size, not graduated. Furthermore, there are only three drawers. No cabinetmaker of the eighteenth or nineteenth centuries would have created this abomination.

When we look at the side of this purported bachelor's chest, we discover that it is deal with mahogany stain (English white pine easily recognized by the myriad small knots and soft grayed color). It *should* have mahogany sides. After 1715, no English chest was made with a deal side; they were veneered with walnut into the 1730s, then made of solid or veneered mahogany. Again, the elements are wrong. In this instance, the explanation, judging from the many scars, is that these sides were originally mahogany-veneered but were stripped.

When we examine the back of this piece we see that it has been sprayed with black paint to fake oxidation—this is an obvious bit of tampering that is easy to spot. Next we look at the bottom of one of the drawers. Here we use our knowledge of both construction technique and tools. We notice a lap board down the center with grooves, with the drawer bottom constructed of two panels of wood attached in the middle and at the sides, front and back. This technique was *only* used for very large drawers, never for small drawers. Clearly, this was a large drawer cut down. We also notice little white streaks, nicks, and grooves on the drawer bottoms—joiner marks. The joiner was commonly used for planing after 1835–1840, but not in the Hepplewhite period. We also find sweeping circular-saw marks—another late-1830s invention. Clearly, the piece shows style and form inconsistencies and also exhibits many construction inconsistencies. The piece was once much larger and could not have been made earlier than the 1830s.

Looking at the interior of the front of one of the drawers, we see that besides the present modern reproduction brass, there is a large round hole where a wide wooden shaft came through. There are *no other* holes. Again, we know from the history of furniture styles that wooden pulls with large wooden shafts did not come into use until the 1830s and remained popular until the 1860s. The latest original element on this chest is the hole. So again, the piece must date from the 1830s or later.

Finally, look at Fig. 6-2, showing the bottom of the chest. Had you not been immediately suspicious after first glancing at the piece, you might have "let your fingers do the walking" on the base molding and feet—and sliced your fingers. This is sharp, new wood! And those feet were laminated. These are not, however, the famous laminated work of John Henry Belter. These were cut with a band saw from sheets of plywood! Here oxidation has also been faked—this time by spraying on a light coat of mahogany stain.

Fig. 6-2 Bottom of chest in Fig. 6-1 shoing new wood and plywood feet.

The verdict: this piece is a modern English fake created from an 1830s or later large chest of ugly proportions. If the price is fair ($500 or so) and you know what it is, buy it if it meets your needs. But please don't buy it for $400 to $600 under the assumption that you "stole" a period Hepplewhite bachelor's chest.

Marriages in Multipart Case Furniture

As the name implies, multipart case furniture is made up of several parts. The chest-on-chest, linen press, and highboy are examples of multipart case furniture. These pieces are most valuable when all the parts were made by the same hand (or in the same workshop) at the same time. Married case pieces certainly have value, but all things being equal, they have less value than the totally original piece. So it is important to know how to spot marriages, which are common.

When looking at any multipart piece to determine whether or not all the pieces started out life together, first look at the overall proportions and style. Is the treatment of moldings throughout the piece consistent? Look at the moldings on the top, around the middle, on the base. They should all be of the same style. Veneers should match throughout.

Look at the back of the piece. The color and size of the boards should be consistent. The same wood and same construction techniques should have been used top and bottom. The only exception to this rule is on display pieces and secretaries with glazed upper sections. The upper part may show a more sophisticated construction than the base, since the back of the top will be visible through the glazing. On a glazed secretary, for example, the base may have a nailed-on back while the top may have frame-and-panel construction. In this case, the difference in back treatment does not indicate a marriage. While looking at the back of the piece, examine the patterns of oxidation, which should be consistent throughout. By the way, the backs of chests, chests-on-chests, linen presses, and highboys can be surprisingly unfinished. All of these pieces were meant to stand against a wall, with the backs unseen. Eighteenth-century cabinetmakers wasted little time on these areas and, as a result, tool marks are often visible.

Pull out the drawers and see if the dovetails are consistent from drawer to drawer and from top to bottom. Of course, the carcasses will also be dovetailed. The dovetails of the carcass will be wider than those of the drawers, but dovetails throughout the carcass should be by the same hand. There is little evidence to support the concept of two or three sections of a multipart piece ever having been constructed by two or three craftsmen, even in large shops. When you find inconsistencies, you most likely have a marriage on your hands.

Finally, one must examine how the separate parts fit together. If top and bottom are attached by screws, there *must* be the same exact number of lined-up holes between the two pieces secured with the screws. Extra holes mean marriage.

Replaced feet are common (as on chests of drawers), and they can be detected by feeling for sharp edges and examining oxidation patterns. Some veneer loss and patching should be expected and does not affect the value if the repair has been well executed. It is common to find splits in drawer bottoms, as well as replaced drawer runners.

Chests-on-chests

This form dates from the Queen Anne period of the early eighteenth century. As the century progressed, the chest-on-chest was found in solid mahogany and then in mahogany veneers. You should keep in mind all of the rules previously discussed when examining a chest-on-chest to spot

marriages. Desirable features include flame veneers, canted and carved corners, carved bracket feet, cross-banded drawer fronts, and good cornice treatment. Of course, all of these features can be added to an originally plain piece. Be on the lookout for shallow, added carving or applied carving, reveneered pieces, and new cornices. On chests-on-chests and linen presses, the crown molding was attached directly to the top until about 1770. After that it was held in place by glue blocks.

Linen Presses

Generally introduced around 1750, Georgian linen presses were usually made of mahogany. Victorian linen presses, however, were often veneered in satinwood or walnut. Most of the linen presses we see on the market today are fairly simple in design, unless made for a very grand house. After all, they were originally intended for use in the bedroom and were not formal pieces.

Construction Points and Repairs

Feet and molding have often been repaired. Doors are prone to warping and splitting. Check for marriages using the guidelines given above. Linen presses on the market today have frequently had their interior altered to turn the piece into an entertainment center. This kind of conversion has little effect on value since it makes the pieces so useful in solving one of the problems of modern life—hiding the TV, VCR, and music equipment.

Highboys

Highboys or tallboys were found in two forms in England: a very tall, single-part chest with six to eight drawers or a two-part piece, with the lower case resting on rather tall legs. The American highboy derives from the latter form, and as may be readily seen in the listings, the English examples were generally a failure aesthetically—they were too squat, too wide, too short. In addition, the English didn't take to the form, so few were made. They do not appear to have been made as graceful matched sets—highboy and lowboy—as they were in America. Their value is minimal compared to fine chests-on-chests or linen presses, or even good chests of drawers. Poor design simply never sells well.

Queen Anne walnut chest, "c. 1780," original geometric-veneered top, on bun feet. A simple example with wide side facings and replaced feet. The photo shows little wear or veneer repair. This piece is almost certainly a later rework of an 1830s piece. 35" x 37" x 22". *Courtesy Morton Goldberg Auction Galleries, New Orleans.* **$4,500–6,500** if c. 1700. **$2,500–3,600** if reworked.

Late seventeenth-century William and Mary etched ivory and parcel ebonized carved oak and walnut chest of drawers. Rectangular top with a molded edge above double-panel sides and fitted with two frieze drawers over three double-fronted long drawers, with geometric cushion fronts or inset paneled fronts inlaid with etched ivory lozenges, divided and flanked by split-baluster ebonized moldings, on baluster ebonized moldings. 37" high x 40" long. Built or cut into two separate cases—an early "Townhouse chest." *Courtesy Butterfield & Butterfield, San Francisco.* **$10,000–15,000.**

c. 1760 raised-panel mule or dowry chest on bracket feet with two drawers. Replaced pulls (Victorian). Lacks one drawer bottom. *Private collection.* **$3,600–4,800.**

Georgian c. 1760 mahogany caddy-top four-drawer chest with later oval brasses. Original bracket feet. Four-drawer chests are less common in England than are two-over-three, or so-called five-drawer chests. Also unusual is the caddy form—a molded edge with no lip or overhang, which resembles the tea caddies of the same period. *Courtesy Whitehall at the Villa, Chapel Hill, N.C.* **$5,000–7,000.**

Chest by Gillows of Lancaster (stamped Gillows). The Gillows family were British furniture makers in Lancaster and London beginning in the early 1800s. By the end of the eighteenth century, they were furnishing some of England's finest houses. From the 1790s on, their furniture was often stamped, as this piece is. This practice was not adopted by other furniture makers until Victorian times. *Courtesy Whitehall at the Villa, Chapel Hill, N.C.* **$4,000–6,000.**

George III c. 1765 mahogany serpentine-front chest of drawers. Molded top above a case containing a slide over four graduated drawers flanked by canted corners with Chinese blind-fret carving, raised on bracket feet. 21" high × 35 1/2" wide × 22" deep. *Courtesy Grogan & Company, Boston.* **$10,000–15,000.**

Mahogany five-drawer chest with veneers over deal (pine), c. 1830–1860. Hardware is new and hides large round original holes (which were wooden pulls). Also the heavy rounded molding on top is indicative of post-1830 design. Finally, the feet are "funny"—too sharp and angular for an earlier piece. *Courtesy Whitehall at the Villa, Chapel Hill, N.C.* **$2,800–3,600.**

An interesting c. 1770 Chippendale bachelor's chest with fluted partial quarter-columns, ogee bracket feet, and nice proportions. Partially original hardware. Rich mahogany. 42" × 20" × 32 1/4" high. *Courtesy Whitehall at the Villa, Chapel Hill, N.C.* **$4,500–6,500.**

Hepplewhite mahogany chest of drawers, early nineteenth century. Line-inlaid top over pullout slide above three graduated drawers, on bracket feet. This is a classic "re-do" cut down from a larger four or five drawer chest! 33" high × 28 1/2" wide × 19" deep. *Courtesy Leslie Hindman Auctioneers, Chicago, Ill.* **$2,400–3,200.**

Bowfront, c. 1860 Georgian-style inlaid mahogany chest with bowed top above conforming case, two over three drawers. Satinwood inlay, bracket feet. Nice use of solid mahogany and mahogany veneers. Very faithful to eighteenth-century prototypes. 36" high × 44 1/2" wide × 23 1/2" deep. *Courtesy Leslie Hindman Auctioneers, Chicago, Ill.* **$2,800–3,800.**

George III c. 1765 mahogany commode in the French taste. This is a rare form directly related to many Chippendale and Hepplewhite designs. The top drawer has a writing surface and had (now lacking) fittings for a lady's or gentleman's needs—boxes, jars, brushes, etc. *Courtesy Whitehall at the Villa, Chapel Hill, N.C.* **$15,000–25,000.**

This form could also be shown in the section on desks, as it is known in America as a "butler's desk" and in England as a secrétaire. This early nineteenth-century example is well veneered and elegantly outlined with box or satinwood. Original hardware. Either the lower escutcheons are later or the upper drawer has had the escutcheon replaced *and* has had the large diamond inlay added to hide extensive damage around the keyhole (perhaps from a lost key or from a break-in). *Courtesy Whitehall at the Villa, Chapel Hill, N.C.* **$5,000–6,500.**

Four-door c. 1800–1830 late Georgian mahogany storage cabinet. Plinth base. 60" wide x 14" deep x 36" high. *Private collection.* **$4,000–6,000.**

A-113

A pseudo-Wellington chest, c. 1840, solid mahogany with mahogany veneers. The top five drawers are fake and actually comprise a door which opens to reveal an area which is now a bar-fitting but which originally held a safe. Elaborate door lock marked "Chubb & Son, Makers to Her Majesty." Lower drawers work. Original feet, which are heavy to support the original safe. Wellington chests with all working drawers, with or without a single side-lock mechanism, sell for this price and upwards! 21" × 21" × 42" high. *Courtesy Whitehall at the Villa, Chapel Hill, N.C.* **$3,600–4,800.**

Edwardian c. 1900 double-door side cabinet or dwarf's wardrobe, satinwood with elegant painted decoration. Note: Dwarf's furniture and children's furniture are both found with surprising frequency. A piece such as this could be either. A tiny sideboard cabinet, on the other hand, would almost certainly have been made for a dwarf. 49" high × 38" wide × 15" deep. *Courtesy Leslie Hindman Auctioneers, Chicago, Ill.* **$2,400–3,600.**

This tall eighteenth-century Chippendale-design chest divides into two parts at the molded waist to make it easier to carry up narrow, winding staircases. Thus the name "townhouse chest." An interesting and always popular form which is found only accasionally. Mahogany and mahogany veneers. Oak and deal secondary. *Courtesy Whitehall at the Villa, Chapel Hill, N.C.* **$4,500–6,500.**

George III c. 1780 mahogany chest-on-chest in two parts. Upper section with flat molded cornice above three thumb-molded aligned drawers and three graduated drawers. The lower section with pullout brushing slide above three thumb-molded graduated drawers raised on bracket feet. Feet and mid-molding of a later period. 42 1/2" wide × 22 1/4" deep × 76" high. *Courtesy Weschler's, Washington, DC.* **$6,500–9,500.**

Eighteenth-century George II c. 1750 walnut chest-on-chest. Projecting molded cornice over three aligned over three graduated drawers above lower case with three graduated drawers having reeded chamfered corners, on bracket feet; elements of reconstruction. 71" high × 41" wide × 21" deep. *Courtesy Leslie Hindman Auctioneers, Chicago, Ill.* **$12,000–18,000.**

A bold, wide c. 1820 Regency mahogany and mahogany veneered linen press with original sliding trays. French splay feet. Recessed pilasters. Pulls are original. Key escutcheons are Dutch-influenced replacements and overly elaborate for most English pieces. *Courtesy Whitehall at the Villa, Chapel Hill, N.C.* **$7,000–10,000.**

Regency to William XV linen press with highly figured mahogany, c. 1820–1830. Original wood pulls. Beaded border. French splay feet. Original sliding interior trays. *Courtesy Whitehall at the Villa, Chapel Hill, N.C.* **$7,000–9,000.**

A superb-quality *Victorian* wardrobe, c. 1860–1880, in the Georgian style. Solid mahogany, even the paneled back! Beautifully cross-banded drawers. Select veneers over the solid mahogany. Good carved details. Fine brasses. Bermuda cedar drawer liners. Original throughout. *Courtesy Whitehall at the Villa, Chapel Hill, N.C.* **$5,000–7,000.**

Shelves throughout the upper section for storage establish this as a late George III linen press. Hangers were not used until the Victorian period. Most wardrobe pieces are Victorian or Edwardian in an early style. Careful examination is required. To be eighteenth century, the piece *must* have had shelves or sliding trays originally, even though often later replaced with a rod for those "new fangled" hangers. This example is mahogany and mahogany veneers. As usual, the back is deal (pine) and the drawer liners are oak (sometimes they are found in deal). *Courtesy Whitehall at the Villa, Chapel Hill, N.C.* **$4,500–5,500.** The low price is due to the fact that it is less desirable for modern use as it is too shallow for a TV, etc.

Simple but stately flame mahogany veneered linen press, c. 1790. Because of scarcity, presses are now being created. An unusual one such as this with a flat top to chest section (no molding) makes one look with great care. Alarm bells should ring! This example is okay. Note how the veneers used on the drawer fronts were also used on the crown molding. *Courtesy Whitehall at the Villa, Chapel Hill, N.C.* **$6,000–9,000.**

A large, well-proportioned c. 1770 George III mahogany linen press with original bracket feet and replaced brasses. Note the obvious scars above the top edge of the brasses. Why not go back to bail and rosette brasses? (The original as shown by the scars.) The reason: If you note the bottom right in particular, an old hole and discoloration from a large wooden knob is hidden by this the *third* set of pulls! The mahogany has excellent figuring and is solid, indicating possibly a Scottish piece. Raised panel doors. Three hinges on the heavy doors—typical eighteenth-century construction. *Courtesy Whitehall at the Villa, Chapel Hill, N.C.* **$7,000–10,000.**

Late seventeenth- to early eighteenth-century English William and Mary japanned highboy. Top has three aligned over three graduated drawers. Lower section has central drawer flanked by two deep drawers, with arched and shaped apron. Turned, tapering legs joined by flat stretcher on bun feet. Overall gilt chinoiserie decoration (worn). 62" high × 44" high × 24" deep. *Courtesy Leslie Hindman Auctioneers, Chicago, Ill.* **$5,000–7,000** if the base is later (as it appears to be from crispness). **$10,000–15,000** if original.

Late Georgian to Regency linen press of tall, stately proportions on simple, carved bracket feet. Applied moldings on the doors. Sliding tray interior is complete. Typical two-over-two base configuration. (A common source for those "rare" low chests of two-over-two drawers is often found in shops and auction houses—a new top added!) *Courtesy Whitehall at the Villa, Chapel Hill, N.C.* **$6,000–9,000.**

English George II walnut highboy or tallboy. This is a marriage or has been reveneered (note different drawer fronts, top and bottom). The top and bottom proportions are what we expect from English highboys (not as elegant or well-proportioned as American ones). *Courtesy Whitehall at the Villa, Chapel Hill, N.C.* **$5,000–7,500.**

Early eighteenth-century William and Mary inlaid burl walnut chest-on-stand. In two parts, the upper section with cavetto-molded cornice above a divided top drawer and three graduated long drawers, each inset with foliate and floral marquetry on dark-stained reserves. The lower section with three similar short drawers, raised on spiral-turned legs joined by an X-form stretcher on ball feet. Restorations and minor losses. 5' high x 40" wide. A classically Engligh highboy—short and stubby. *Courtest Butter-field & Butterfield, Los Angeles.* **$8,000–12,000.**

English Chippendale linen
press, c. 1760. Impressive proportions. Solid mahogany.
Courtesy Whitehall at the Villa,
Chapel Hill, N.C. **$8,000–**
12,000.

7

Writing Furniture: Desks and Secretaries

Slant-front Desks

CONSTRUCTION

The slant-front desk (called a *bureau* in England) developed from the seventeenth-century desk-on-stand. In the early part of the eighteenth century, the Queen Anne slant-front desk was made in two separate parts: the slant-lid section and the base with drawers. At this date, even when it was made as a unit, the form retained the moldings that had been used to hide the joining of the two parts. These moldings had generally disappeared by the end of the Queen Anne period, when bun feet gave way to bracket feet, and walnut veneer gave way to solid mahogany. Oak pieces were also made throughout the eighteenth century. These are usually more rustic in design and generally sell for less than walnut or mahogany desks.

It is worth noting that, although one often finds chests of drawers that have shaped carcasses (serpentine or bowed), slant-front desks in England almost always had a simple front.

One of the special charms of the slant-front desk is the treatment of the interior. Secret compartments, valanced cubby holes, carving and inlay, all increase the appeal.

REPAIRS

As on any case piece, check for replaced feet (early bun feet will almost always be replaced). Slant lids are likely to have splits or warping. Check for replaced drawers (dovetails should be consistent, with finer dovetails in the front of the drawer, and larger ones in the back). Drawer handles are almost always replacements.

Pedestal Desks

Pedestal desks date from the Chippendale era, and designs for them are found in his *Director*. However, many that we see on the market today are from the mid-nineteenth century and the Edwardian era and are usually mahogany veneered. These desks were constructed of three parts: two pedestals (with drawers and plinth bases) and a top (with three frieze drawers). A partner's desk included drawers on one side of the pedestal, cabinets on the other. The pedestals and top should have a convincing fit. If not, the piece may be a marriage. Leather tops are almost always replacements and this does not affect value.

Secretaries

Secretaries evolved alongside slant-front desks, starting at the end of the seventeenth century. During the Queen Anne period, secretaries were constructed in three sections: bookcase, slant front with concealed storage well, and base (chest of drawers). Decorative moldings were used to disguise the points where the three sections were put together. Queen Anne secretaries were veneered in walnut and had bun feet. The bookcase doors were often mirrored, with candle slides in front of the mirrors.

On secretaries of this age, a host of alterations and problems are common. Bun feet are rarely original since they were usually made of solid walnut, which is especially susceptible to worm damage. They may have replacement bun feet or bracket feet (which we associated with a slightly later style period). The bookcase doors may have been altered by removing the mirrors and adding wood panels or glazing.

Secretaries from the Georgian era have several differences in terms of style and construction. After the Queen Anne period, they were made in two parts rather than in three separate pieces. Georgian secretaries do not have the extra moldings or the storage wells found on Queen Anne pieces. They were made of mahogany, with glazed bookcase doors and often with cockbeaded drawer fronts. If the upper section was glazed, the back, which is visible through the glazing, has paneled construction. The base, on the other hand, might have a plain, nailed-on back since it would not be seen. The more sophisticated pieces have detached crown moldings to allow for the effects of shrinkage.

Secretaries on the market today are often marriages. To determine if this is the case, use all the guidelines for multipart case pieces discussed in the previous chapter. In particular, be aware of how the sections fit together. The top of the desk section should not be finished, for example, since it would have been covered by a bookcase. A finished desk top indicates a marriage.

Edwardian painted satinwood lady's writing desk, early twentieth century. Serpentine structure with four ivory-handled drawers over a gilt-tooled leather-inset writin surface. Frieze with one long drawer flanked by short drawers decorated with floral garlands and bellflower swags, all raised on square tapering legs ending in spade feet. A very hot seller even in today's generally depressed, ho-hum market. 37" high × 39" wide × 19" deep. *Courtesy Grogan & Company, Boston.* **$2,500–3,500.**

An original c. 1810 Georgian mahogany desk-on-stand with cross-banded top, brass gallery, reading rails, cuffs, and rollers. Fake drawer front in stand. Fitted interior with drawers and cubby holes. Check these carefully, as the stands are often later (see next photo). *Courtesy Whitehall at the Villa, Chapel Hill, N.C.* **$3,500–4,800.**

Georgian c. 1780 mahogany writing desk with top well for ink, etc., and lift-up writing surface fitted with drawers, on a *modern* stand. Originally such pieces were more frequently *counter-top* desks in a shop. Original side carrying handles. *Courtesy Whitehall at the Villa, Chapel Hill, N.C.* **$1,800–2,800.**

Solid mahogany sides and figured veneer drawer fronts, c. 1770. The piece is quite simple. The feet a little awkward, but original. Mostly original hardware. Very simple interior. *Courtesy Whitehall at the Villa, Chapel Hill, N.C.* **$4,000–6,000.**

George III c. 1760–1770 mahogany kneehole desk with ogee bracket feet, small kneehole drawer, cabinet, fitted top drawer, and original pulls. If this piece has a serious flaw, it is in the design. A far more preferable style has smaller feet placed on the inner corners as well as on the outer corners. *Courtesy Whitehall at the Villa, Chapel Hill, N.C.* **$4,500–6,500.**

Queen Anne oak slant-front desk with fitted interior, c. 1710–1730; case with two candle drawers above two short drawers flanking one long and two short drawers below. Bracket feet. A sophisticated country piece, it also has a "hidden" well below the interior surface. Reading well. Simple fitted interior. 40" high x 36" wide x 40" deep. *Courtesy Grogan & Company, Boston.* **$4,000–6,000.**

George III c. 1770 kneehole desk with large kneehole drawer and small cupboard. Fitted top drawer. Blind fretwork. Original feet. Replaced pulls. Note how much more successful the use of four feet on the front is than the ogee-footed example above. *Courtesy Whitehall at the Villa, Chapel Hill, N.C.* **$6,000–8,000.**

Unusual country kneehole desk with slanted surface (hinged at top), reading rail, simple fitted interior, plinth base, and paneled sides, c. 1800. Scars of various old sets of hardware are evident. Oak or ash and deal (pine). The plinth base is an evloution from the original. *Courtesy Whitehall at the Villa, Chapel Hill, N.C.* **$2,500–3,500.**

In the U.S., we call this a slant-front desk; in England it is called a bureau. c. 1770 solid mahogany desk with cockbeaded drawers, ogee bracket feet (original); simple but attractive interior with secret compartment. The boxed area with the prospect door, the small interior drawers, all slide out to reveal a set of hidden drawers at the back. Replaced pulls. Note the obvious plugged holes on the drawers where there were once bail-and-rosette handles. The bat wings use only one original hole and also serve to conceal a large hole where 1830s wood pulls were once added. Note the split sides—very typical of all eighteenth-century solid-side case furniture. Be suspicious if you don't find splits. *Courtesy Whitehall at the Villa, Chapel Hill, N.C.* **$4,800–7,500.**

Edwardian c. 1910 inlaid mahogany modified Carlton House style desk. Shaped leather-inset top with raised curved bank of drawers and galleried shelf inlaid with floral and musical trophies and swags above central drawer flanked by banks of four graduated drawers on plinths. 48" high × 58" wide × 28" deep. *Courtesy Leslie Hindman Auctioneers, Chicago, Ill.* **$5,000–7,500.**

Georgian c. 1800 mahogany architect's desk. Adjustable top with removable ledge over a sliding secretary drawer with green baize-lined sliding writing surface over alphabet-inlaid filing compartments. Lower section with three short drawers flanking a central recessed cupboard. Sides fitted with brass bail handles. Possibly made by Gillows; hardware and construction are typical of that shop. 37 1/2" high × 49 1/2" long × 27" deep. *Courtesy Grogan & Company, Boston.* **$10,000–15,000.**

George III c. 1790 inlaid mahogany writing table with inset gilt-tooled green leather writing surface over three drawers flanked by probably later conch shell inlaid paterae and raised on reeded square tapering legs terminating in brass casters. 29 1/2" high × 62" wide × 35" deep. *Courtesy Grogan & Company, Boston.* **$6,500–9,500.**

French Louis XV ormolu-mounted tulipwood *bibliothéque*, third quarter eighteenth century. Rectangular-molded rouge royal marble top over a case fitted with doors enclosing shelves, raised on cabriole legs ending in sabots. 47 3/4" high x 30 3/4" long x 13 1/2" deep. *Skinner, Inc., Bolton, Mass.* **$18,000–25,000.**

Austrian neoclassical brass-inlaid fall-front *secretaire à abattant* c. 1810. Rectangular outset molded cornice above a frieze drawer inlaid with female caryatids, birds, and scrolling foliage over an inlaid fall-front depicting a muse seated in a chariot drawn by goats attended by dancing maids and putti, enclosing a fitted interior, over three inlaid long drawers flanked by inlaid pilasters and sides; raised on bold turned toupie feet. Revarnished; inlay repaired. 5' 8" high x 41 1/2" wide. *Courtesy Butterfield & Butterfield, Los Angeles.* **$18,000–24,000.**

Right: Late seventeenth-century William and Mary oyster-veneered yew wood and walnut chest of drawers. Rectangular top centering a compass within strapwork borders above two short and three long drawers, each with compass inlay, on bun feet. Note that this chest has original yew wood turnip or bun feet. Walnut feet *never* survive due to their susceptibility to worms. 33 1/2" high x 38" wide x 23 1/2" deep. **$35,000–45,000.** Left: William and Mary burl walnut marquetry chest of drawers. Rectangular-molded top above four long drawers on later bun feet, the whole decorated with oyster-veneered and geometric panels. 38" high x 40" wide x 25" deep. **$16,000–24,000.** *Courtesy of Christie's New York.*

A c. 1800 George III gilt-metal-mounted hare wood and marquetry console table. The shaped cross-banded top centering a pastoral trophy within foliate branches, the paneled frieze with floral scrolls, on square tapering partitioned legs applied with husk swags and joined by a conforming platform stretcher. Restorations to the feet. Relates closely to a commode pattern published by A. Hepplewhite & Co. in *The Cabinet-Maker's London Book of Prices 1788.* This is a fine piece with strong design background. *Courtesy of Christie's New York.* **$20,000–35,000.**

Walnut buffet c. 1780. Fine quality with shell-carved apron and doors. Iron hardware. Central candle drawer. Stop-fluted central panel. Molded, shaped apron. *Courtesy of Whitehall at the Villa Antiques and Fine Art, Chapel Hill, N.C.* **$10,000–14,000.**

English pine library or hunting-lodge table of octagonal form c. 1830. Gothic revival apron. Depicted, one on each foot, are a fox, a hound, a deer, and a boar. *Courtesy Whitehall at the Villa Antiuqes and Fine Art, Chapel Hill. N.C.* **$12,000–18,000.**

English Regency c. 1810-1825 rosewood chiffonier with brass grill work. Plinth base. Superstructure supported by simple ionic columns, coordinated with the base columns. 44" wide x 18 1/2" deep x 64" high. *Courtesy Leighton Adair Butts, Tyron, N.C.* **$5,000–7,000.**

Sheraton Revival c. 1860 flame mahogany veneered partner's desk with replaced leather top. A very strange example—*only* the center drawer is attached to the top and the pedestals have four drawers each rather than three. Note that the way the top was attached has caused some warping at each side, which can be eliminated by screwing the pedestals to the top. *Courtesy Whitehall at the Villa, Chapel Hill, N.C.* **$6,000–9,000.**

George III c. 1820 mahogany and oak secondary wood double-pedestal partner's desk, rectangular molded top with a gilt-tooled leather-inset writing surface, above a frieze fitted with three drawers on each side, each pedestal support fitted with three drawers opposed by a cupboard door and raised on a molded plinth. Original pulls (note the faded color and missing pull). © *1991 by Sotheby's, Inc.* **$10,000–15,000.**

Nineteenth-century George III style mahogany partner's desk with side cabinets. Molded, carved, paneled doors. Gouge and paterae carved edge. *Courtesy Whitehall at the Villa, Chapel Hill, N.C.* **$12,000–18,000.**

Victorian Georgian-style double-pedestal or executive desk with finished front, c. 1860. Molded edge plinth base. Bail-and-rosette pulls. Raised panel drawers–the Victorian give away! Fluted pilasters. Replaced gold-tooled leather writing surface. *Courtesy Whitehall at the Villa, Chapel Hill, N.C.* **$8,000–12,000.**

An unusual William IV c. 1830 double-pedestal desk with three drawers. Leather-inset center panel. Mahogany gallery, mahogany and flame mahogany case. Whorl feet. *Courtesy Whitehall at the Villa, Chapel Hill, N.C.* **$7,000–9,000.**

Simple George III c. 1780 mahogany secretary with replaced feet and a married top. Highly figured doors, simple grain on the base. Replaced hardware, simple interior. About 95% of all secretaries found on the market today are "married"—the top and base of separate origins, often the top of later date. This is totally acceptable as long as the buyer knows it and pays the appropriate price. One key to look for: If the base has a top board made of mahogany (or whatever primary wood constitutes the piece), the it is a marriage. A primary wood was *never* used as the top board if a secretary was planned. *Courtesy Whitehall at the Villa, Chapel Hill, N.C.* **$9,000–12,000.**

Glazed-door secretary, c. 1780, simple but good design. Straight-grained mahogany with a little flame veneer at the crown. Dentil molding. Marriage. Paneled back construction (always found on a secretary that originally had glazing on the doors). Note the left doors-locks imbedded in the door, top and bottom. Also, barely discernible are holes on the four interior corners of the doors. At some fashionable point, (c. 1795–1825), there were pleated curtains on these doors to hide the interior and add elegance to the piece. It is always encouraging to find these early signs of evolving taste as substantiation of age. *Courtesy Whitehall at the Villa, Chapel Hill, N.C.* **$12,000–15,000.**

George III c. 1780 mahogany secretary with simple Gothic glazed doors. *Not* a marriage. Original feet and escutcheons. Replaced pulls. Note the fine timber used throughout, from top to bottom. The shape and quality are totally consistent. *Courtesy Whitehall at the Villa, Chapel Hill, N.C.* **$12,500–18,500.**

Married late eighteenth-century bureau bookcase. The top is substantially later than the base. Mahogany. Diamond glazing. *Courtesy Whitehall at the Villa, Chapel Hill, N.C.* **$8,000–12,000.**

Left: George III mahogany blind-door secretary with raised panels and candle slides, c. 1770. Highly suspicious. Why candle-slides with no mirrored doors to reflect and intensify the light? Also, this appears to have a c. 1780 or later detached cornice. Early pieces had the cornice attached to the sides of the top of the bookcase. **$12,500–18,500** if original. **$10,000–15,000** if married. Right: Mirrored blind-door George III secretary with ogee bracket feet, c. 1770. Open bat-wing brasses (replaced). Fine wood. note that the drawers are solid with rounded edge, not cockbeaded as they generally were by 1780. Many blind-door examples were glazed later. Watch for this old trick. A dead giveaway is a back of vertical or horizontal boards instead of an elegantly paneled back. If the maker planned glazed doors, he planned a pleasing back that showed his skill (or the back may be a replacement). **$12,500–18,500.** *Courtesy formerly Coles & Company, Charleston, S.C.*

George III mahogany secretary bookcase, c. 1780. Molded cornice over a blind fretwork frieze and a pair of octagonally mullioned glazed cabinet doors revealing shelves, the lower section with a slant front opening to reveal a fitted interior with leather writing surface, over four graduated cockbeaded drawers and raised on bracket feet. Note that the banding on the slant-front lid has the keyhole partially in and partially out of the banding—a sure sign the banding was added later. A marriage—and a tight fit—no nice molding between base and top. Short feet, cut down or, more likely, replacements. 81" high × 36" wide × 19 1/2" deep. *Courtesy Grogan & Company, Boston.* **$9,000–12,000.**

George III mahogany secretary bookcase, c. 1800. Molded cornice over lancet-mullioned glazed cabinet doors revealing three shelves, fitted secrétaire section over three cockbeaded drawers. 76 3/4" high × 35 1/2" wide × 18" deep. *Courtesy Grogan & Company, Boston.* **$6,000–9,000.**

Gothic Revival mahogany secretary bookcase, c. 1840. Crenelated cornice over a pair of arch-mullioned cabinet doors alternating with engaged trifid pilasters. Lower section carved with Gothic tracery and having a secretary drawer mounted with lion's-head loose-ring handles opening to reveal a fitted interior with ivory-handled drawers flanking an arched kneehole with trifid pilaster stiles. 105" high × 50" wide × 18" deep. Probably real and period (i.e., c. 1830–1840. *Courtesy Grogan & Company, Boston.* Sold for **$29,700** against a $5,000–7,000 estimate!

8

Display Pieces, Bookcases, Breakfronts

Corner Cupboards

During the first half of the eighteenth century, corner cupboards generally looked like the paneled rooms in which they were situated. They used the same carving motifs and proportions that were found in the walls. The fronts were bowed or flat with chamfered corners. After mid-century, as wallpaper replaced paneling, corner cupboards were no longer strictly limited by wall-paneling design and proportions. Corner cupboards were then made as movable pieces, not built into the room. Bases were no longer limited to the plinth style, and were often made with bracket feet and a lighter overall appearance. They were generally made in two separate parts that were screwed together. Although these later corner cupboards were freestanding, they were backed with unfinished wood. Not surprisingly, a common alteration is the addition of a back to a built-in cupboard, making it freestanding and salable. Careful examination of the construction of the back can usually reveal if the piece started out life as a built-in piece. There were also barrel-backed corner cupboards, generally dating from the second half of the eighteenth century. Unless the piece was made of mahogany or walnut, it was generally painted on the interior and exterior, but almost without exception, the paint will

have been stripped off long ago, exposing the wood (which is usually pine). You should be able to find traces of the original paint.

Small hanging corner cupboards with bowed fronts or flat fronts with chamfered corners were also made. They may have double doors or a single door, glazed or solid, but never veneered.

There are many reproductions dating from the nineteenth and twentieth centuries. Generally these used wood of a lower quality. In fact, some Victorian copies that were painted were made up of different types of wood.

Bookcases and Display Cabinets

As with corner cupboards, bookcases and display cabinets of the first half of the eighteenth century were massive and incorporated architectural motifs even though they were freestanding. They were often made in a breakfront style: lower cabinet sections and upper sections with movable shelves and glazed doors or doors with crisscrossed wire mesh. On fine pieces, the edges of the shelf fronts are veneered in mahogany and the top and bottom sections are joined by screws. There are many examples of bookcases in

Chippendale's *Director,* and the form seems to have become even more popular as the century progressed. By the time of Hepplewhite and Sheraton, designs for bookcases were less dominated by heavy architectural motifs. The upper shelves were enclosed with glazed doors that have glazing bars inlaid with stringing or cross-banding. The glazing bars were laid out in geometrical or curved patterns, holding separately cut panes of glass. During the Regency period, a new form was intro-duced: the revolving bookcase. Display cabinets proliferated in the nineteenth century.

Many bookcases and display cabinets that we see on the market today have been cut down from larger ones to suit today's smaller rooms and lower ceiling heights. You can check patterns of oxidation and patination for signs of downsizing. Also, the vast majority of breakfronts encountered have been created from large Victorian or Edwardian breakfront wardrobes.

George III hanging corner cabinet with glazed door and shaped shelves, c. 1760–1780. Note the thinness of the shelves, which adds to the delicacy of the piece. Narrow. Blind-fretwork cornice. Good, strong (yet not overpowering) base molding. *Courtesy Whitehall at the Villa, Chapel Hill, N.C.* **$4,000–6,000.**

George III inlaid oak hanging corner cupboard, c. 1775. With flat dentilated cornice and a fluted frieze above a panel door inlaid with a six-pointed star, opening to view a shaped shelf, flanked by canted, recessed-panel sides, all on a flush base. The stained pine top and base are of a later period. With additions removed, this would sell very well. 27" wide x 15 3/4" deep x 36 3/4" high. *Courtesy Wescgler's, Washington, DC.* **$2,400–3,600** if improved.

Naturalistically carved bamboo vitrine cabinet with "roots" for feet, c. 1860. Ebonized and gilded. *Courtesy Whitehall at the Villa, Chapel Hill, N.C.* **$6,000–9,000.**

Late George III style mahogany corner cupboard c. 1820. Projecting molded cornice above pair of mullioned glazed doors and pair of cupboard doors. Shaped apron and bracket feet. Awkward veneering pattern (which you would not find on a period eighteenth-century piece). 80" high x 40" wide x 27" deep. *Courtesy Leslie Hindman Auctioneers, Chicago, Ill.* **$6,000–9,000.**

An unusual Victorian nineteenth-century brass-mounted mahogany double-sided standing bookshelf, in two parts. The upper section with graduated tiers raised on turned supports inset with brass spindles, the lower section with a leather-inset slide with hinged flaps on both sides centering a kneehole, the sides similarly fitted. 5'1" high x 27 1/4" wide x 18 1/4" deep. © *1991 Sotheby's, Inc.* **$18,000–24,000.**

Nineteenth-century stepped-back open pine one-piece bookcase over a case of three drawers. New feet. The top possibly altered from a blind door cabinet which had lost its doors. Original hardware is campaign or shop-fixture style. *Courtesy Whitehall at the Villa, Chapel Hill, N.C.* **$1,500–2,500.**

Late eighteenth-century fluted pilaster George III mahogany and mahogany veneered two-part corner cupboard. Replaced feet. Dentil molding (perhaps it had more molding originally). *Courtesy Whitehall at the Villa, Chapel Hill, N.C.* **$6,000–9,000.**

Late eighteenth-century George III architectural pine corner cupboard. Dentil-molded cornice over arched niche with fluted molding above pair of paneled cupboard doors, on molded base. 95" high x 52" wide x 17" deep. *Courtesy Leslie Hindman Auctioneers, Chicago, Ill.* **$8,000–12,000.**

Eighteenth-century architectural corner cupboard, originally a built-in. Robust carving and great moldings. Originally painted. *Private collection.* **$8,500–12,500.**

George III c. 1820 inlaid mahogany breakfront bookcase, the overhanging cornice above four glazed doors, the projecting lower part with a cross-banded waist above a secretary drawer opening to an interior fitted with small drawers and pigeonholes over three cockbeaded long drawers, all of coromandel wood. The sides fitted with a pair of drawers over cupboards, raised on a conforming plinth base. Some alterations. 7'1" high × 6'5" wide × 21" deep. © *Sotheby's, Inc.* **$18,000–24,000.**

Aesthetic Movement painted and ebonized buffet, c. 1870. In two parts: the superstructure with galleried shelf over a covered frieze decorated in gilt with birds in a marsh setting, over a rectangular mirror plate flanked by painted small cupboards over open shelves, decorated with portraits and birds in flight. The canted lower section with two frieze drawers over a pair of cupboard doors painted with medieval figures, flanked by leaded-glass cupboards enclosing a shelf, raised on turned feet. The six figures represent Morning, Night, Music, Chess, Billiards, and Whist. 7'5" high x 5'11" wide. *Courtesy Butterfield & Butterfield, Los Angeles.* **$6,000–9,000.**

Mahogany breakfront, c. 1795–1810. The piece appears somewhat out of proportion and when taken apart and carefully examined, it becomes apparent that the side sections have been made narrower at some point. Satinwood desk interior. *Courtesy Whitehall at the Villa, Chapel Hill, N.C.* **$12,000–18,000.**

Hepplewhite-style inlaid mahogany breakfront from the late-nineteenth century. With projecting molded cornice over inlaid frieze and four mullioned glazed doors. The lower section with six small drawers and four cabinet doors. Bracket feet. 97" high x 84" wide x 22" deep. *Courtesy Leslie Hindman Auctioneers, Chicago, Ill.* **$12,000–18,000.**

George III mahogany china cabinet, c. 1780. These are *almost* always made from period linen presses with the top moved back and glazed. Check them very carefully. It's a very tricky change as the new shelves fit in the old grooves of the press! *Courtesy Whitehall at the Villa, Chapel Hill, N.C.* **$7,000– 10,000.**

George III mahogany breakfront, c. 1780–1800. A fine example of "neat and plain" eighteenth-century design. Raised panel construction on the back, top and bottom, Adjustable shelves. Writing drawer with three graduated drawers below. This piece represents the best qualities of Georgian design and construction. *Courtesy Whitehall at the Villa, Chapel Hill, N.C.* **$25,000–45,000.**

An elegant c. 1830 mahogany four-door bookcase. Note the Bramah locks (the round integral brass keyholes identify this type of lock) which were inverted around 1815. Fine-quality timber. This probably had solid doors originally. While the back of the center section is floating panel construction, it appears that the sides are not. This may indicate a narrowing of the sides at some point. Very desirable as a display piece and highly unusual, thus a good value no matter what has been done to it. *Courtesy Whitehall at the Villa, Chapel Hill, N.C.* **$12,000–18,000.**

An elegant c. 1830 painted Regency glazed- and paneled-door breakfront bookcase. Pine with paint restored. Adjustable shelves. This is a very decorative piece with a green (soft and dark) background. *Courtesy Whitehall at the Villa, Chapel Hill, N.C.* **$18,000–24,000.**

Regency/William IV style pine breakfront bookcase with flat, paneled pilasters, c. 1830. The upper doors were almost certainly blind like the base when this piece was made. Originally false grained to look like mahogany. *Courtesy Whitehall at the Villa, Chapel Hill, N.C.* **$8,000–12,000.**

Triple-serpentine front glazed door bookcase of inlaid walnut. Late nineteenth century. Originally a large Victorian triple-section wardrobe which was cut apart, had added glass, and a shelf made between the two sections. *Courtesy Whitehall at the Villa, Chapel Hill, N.C.* **$10,000–15,000.**

Queen Anne/George I c. 1710–1730 oak Welsh dresser with bold well-shaped cabriole legs, most attractive friezes to the base and rack, the three drawers and two cupboards in the rack cross banded in mahogany. 6'6" wide x 6'7" high x 19" deep. *Courtesy Whitehall at the Villa, Chapel Hill, N.C.* **$25,000–35,000.**

Nineteenth-century Queen Anne/George I style oak pewter Welsh cupboard with geometric paneled doors and drawers. Very good style. *Private collection.* **$4,500–6,500.**

Late nineteenth-century English oak dresser with two shelves. Rich color. Spice cabinets, turned legs, raised-panel drawers, scalloped sides. 7' high × 44 3/4" wide × 22" deep. *Courtesy Whitehall at the Villa, Chapel Hill, N.C.* **$3,600–4,500.**

Queen Anne oak dresser and rack with cabriole legs and carved knees, c. 1750. Three drawers with original brasses. Deep moldings. Rack with scalloped frieze. 7' wide x 6'10" high x 20" deep. *Courtesy Whitehall at the Villa, Chapel Hill, N.C.* **$25,000–35,000.**

PART TWO

Continental Furniture Forms

9

Seating Furniture

Sixteenth and Seventeenth Centuries

Until the seventeenth century, seating furniture was sparse and fairly simple. Stools filled the daily need, with armchairs, which tended to be rectilinear in form, generally being reserved for guests of honor or formal situations. For example, the monk's chair of sixteenth-century Spain (in modern times called a *sillon frailero*) was of simple, collapsible construction. Leather was hung on the back or attached using nails with oversized decorative heads. Monks' chairs had low stretchers on the sides and back, and a high, wide stretcher in front. There were also hip-joint chairs (called Dante chairs in Italy) and X-chairs (called Savonarola chairs in Italy). Spanish chairs were upholstered in Cordovan leather or, as in Italy, with velvet accented with oversized decorative nail heads.

As the seventeenth century progressed, the forms and numbers of chairs increased. Chairs from the baroque era were formal and were basically rectilinear in design, with high backs and stretchers connecting the legs. This was the century of elaborately turned legs—bobbin-turned, twist-turned, etc. The Flemish scroll was also incorporated in legs as well as arms, uprights, and even in the backs of chairs. Holland and Germany also produced chairs with these general characteristics. Portuguese chairs from the early seventeenth century displayed especially elaborate turnings.

During the reign of Louis XIV in France, chairs had high upholstered backs, scrolling wooden arms, and stretchers (necessary to support their massive size). They were magnificent to look at, but not as comfortable or as conducive to casual conversation (or as movable) as chairs were to become in the eighteenth century. Chairs were made by the *menuisiers,* who worked in native solid woods, preferably beech, especially if the chair was to be painted or gilded. Upholstery was grand and expensive. In fact, it might easily have been the most expensive aspect of chair making.

Eighteenth and Nineteenth Centuries

Beginning in the transitional period of the Régence, chair design began to change. As the century progressed, many new chair forms appeared, most in the service of comfort and conversation, not the grand ceremony that reigned supreme at the court of Louis XIV. On *fauteuils* (armchairs), the arms moved further back from the seat rail to make room for the ladies' full skirts. By the time of Louis XV, chairs took on an almost completely fluid line, with the curving legs moving in an unbroken line into the seat rail, and that in turn melting into the arms and crest rail. Stretchers, which might detract from this harmonious design, were almost never found on eighteenth-century French chairs beginning with the time of Louis XV.

During the formative reigns of Louis XV and XVI, many types of chairs were developed. During the reign of Louis XIV, the *fauteuil* had been reserved for the King, but from the Régence on, the *fauteuil* developed many variations and was used by anyone who could afford one. The list below gives the names of the most common French chair types from the eighteenth century:

chaise: side chair

fauteuil: armchair

fauteuil en cabriolet: concave chair back (with arms going out to accommodate wide skirts)

fauteuil à la reine: flat chair back

bergère: enclosed and upholstered sides and loose seat cushion

marquise: bergère for two (also called a tête-à-tête)

duchesse: chaise longue

duchesse brisé: with separate leg rest

tabouret de pied: footstool

canapé sofa: all upholstered (no wood visible)

canapé settee: wood visible

ottomane: oval-backed sofa with back curving into arms curving into seat rail

Chairs made in France used the mortise-and-tenon joint, except during periods of curving lines (such as the Régence and Louis XV) when dowels and pegs were used (sometimes double or even triple dowels, for extra strength). Glue was rarely used. Makers of chairs often did their own carving rather than contracting it out, as might have been done on a larger piece. *Menuisiers* did their own caning if the chair was to have a loose cushion as well. Upholsterers were the main vendors of *menuiserie* furniture, including chairs.

By the eighteenth century, Italy had become more of a follower than a leader in decorative arts. Italian craftsman produced richly carved and gilded armchairs in the French rococo style. Spanish chairs of the eighteenth century were influenced by French and English designs, but those with cabriole legs differed from English chairs in that they were generally joined by stretchers. The Spanish and Italian interpretations of rococo tended to be somewhat exaggerated. For example, seats were higher on Spanish chairs and the length of Italian sofas was extraordinary.

German chair design was strongly influenced by French rococo tastes. The Régence style began to blossom around 1720, when German chairs were being made with curved underframes and legs.

With the Louis XVI style in France, straight lines were again emphasized; chair legs no longer melted into the seat rail in one continuous line but were clearly structural elements, obviously supporting the weight of the chair. Legs were round or square-sectioned, tapered at the foot, often with fluting (straight or spiraled), and headed by a square block with carved decoration. Chair backs were sometimes *en cabriolet,* rectangular, with the arms (with arm pads) coming down to the front of the seat rail and going directly onto the legs (a change from Régence and Louis XV). The backs of side chairs (*chaises*) often had pierced designs. Both side and armchairs were generally painted or gilded.

By about 1770, Germany was joining the return of classicism represented by Louis XVI design. By the end of the eighteenth century, the influence of Hepplewhite and Sheraton on German domestic chairs was visible. Italy was a little more reluctant to embrace the straight lines of

Louis XVI and continued to make seating furniture with more of the Rococo curves.

The comfort index for chairs peaked at Louis XV, declined somewhat during Louis XVI, and lost out to grand effect during the Empire period. During the Directoire-Empire period, there was not a soft cushion in sight. One finds chairs with the straight lines of Louis XVI, but with new design motifs dominating the furniture. Symbolic animals—rams' heads, eagles' heads, or lions' heads— were worked into the armrests and supports, which were often some form of small column. Rear sabre legs became common during this period, inspired by the ancient Greek Klismos chair. Another common Empire chair inspired by ancient forms had a transverse across the top of the back of the chair, with the transverse curving slightly inward and having painted or inlaid decoration. One comfortable chair from the Directoire period was the gondola chair, whose back sloped down into half-arms which sloped into the seat.

While French furniture styles were reacting with severity to the plush comforts of pre-revolutionary France, a more accommodating design philosophy was evolving in Germany and Austria. Biedermeier furniture, an Austrio-German development from 1815–1848, was designed for comfort rather than grandeur. Biedermeier chairs have graceful curving backs and supports and are decorative and truly inviting.

Michael Thonet's famous bentwood chairs came out of the Biedermeier period. His highly curved wood was achieved through steam bending rather than by carving, a process patented in 1842. He used strips of veneer and solid wood (bentwood). His firm expanded throughout the nineteenth century, and in 1900 the Thonet factory made 4,000 pieces a day and employed 6,000 workmen.

The many Revival styles that swamped the Continent and England during the second half of the nineteenth century brought back a host of chair styles— and exotic styles too, like Turkish chairs. Upholstery dominated most chair forms after the invention of spring upholstery around the 1830s.

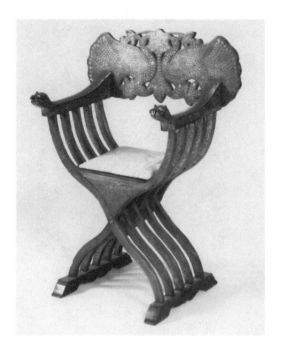

One of a pair of Iberian brass-inlaid walnut Savonarola armchairs. Each with a pierced back carved with peacocks. Straight arms ending in snarling animal masks above curule supports and ending in trestle feet. Inlaid throughout with scrolling foliage. This style of chair first originated in the Renaissance period and has been extensively copied. *Courtesy Christie's New York.* **$1,800–2,400** the pair.

Pair of nineteenth-century Spanish baroque-style walnut armchairs. Each with slightly canted stiles headed by carved foliate scrolls, embroidered velvet back over flat scroll-carved arms on foliate-carved supports. Velvet upholstered seat with fringe above square legs joined by compartmented cabochon-and-scroll-carved stretchers. *Courtesy Butterfield & Butterfield, Los Angeles.* **$3,000–4,500** the pair.

One of a pair of Spanish baroque walnut armchairs. Each with rectangular padded back with ribbed finials, the rectangular padded seat on square legs joined by a pierced geometric stretcher, upholstered in stitched velvet centered by a crest and coronet. *Courtesy Christie's New York.* **$3,500–4,500** the pair.

One of a pair of seventeenth-century Italian baroque parcel-gilt walnut armchairs. Each with padded rectangular back surmounted by foliate-carved finials, the padded seat on baluster-turned legs joined by stretchers, upholstered in green velvet. *Courtesy Christie's New York.* **$4,500–6,500** the pair.

French Louis XV style c. 1900 fruitwood ladder-back dining chair. Shell-carved top rail. Examples found on the market today almost always date from at least 1900, seldom earlier. *Courtesy Whitehall at the Villa, Chapel Hill, N.C.* **$400–600.**

Pair of Italian baroque walnut armchairs dating from the first half of the eighteenth century. Each with arched and upholstered back above scrolled arms on spiral-carved supports. Raised on spiral-carved stretchers resting on compressed-ball feet. Worming to frame, repair to arm supports. *Courtesy Butterfield & Butterfield, San Francisco.* **$4,000–6,000** the pair.

Mid-nineteenth-century country French cherry *fauteuil.* Turned uprights, rush seat, modified cabriole legs, shell carving. From Normandy or Brittany. These chairs are seldom found dating from this early a period. The softness of edges, depth of color, quality of carving all assist in dating such early examples. *Courtesy Whitehall at the Villa, Chapel Hill, N.C.* **$800–1,200** single. **$1,800–2,400** the pair.

A-158

Régence beechwood and caned *fauteuil* with rectangular caned back, c. 1720. Acanthus-carved scroll arms and serpentine caned seat within a lozenge-incised scallop-carved frame, in cabriole legs joined by an X-shaped stretcher, ending in scroll toes. *Courtesy Christie's New York.* **$2,800–3,600** single. **$6,000–9,000** the pair.

Late nineteenth-century Régence-style carved walnut, caned-seat *fauteuil* with interlaced stretcher. Like many Revival pieces, this one has narrower proportions and flatter carving than a period piece. See the preceding c. 1720 *fauteuil* for comparison. *Courtesy Whitehall at the Villa, Chapel Hill, N.C.* **$900–1,200.**

Two of a set of five mid-eighteenth-century Louis XV French provincial beechwood and caned *chaises,* each with cartouche-shaped back and seat within a flower-carved molded frame, on cabriole legs (with restorations). *Courtesy Christie's New York.* **$3,500–4,500** set of five.

French walnut Louis XVI style side chair with caned back and seat, c. 1870. Turned a fluted legs. *Courtesy Whitehall at the Villa, Chapel Hill, N.C.* **$600–900** single. **$2,400–3,600** 4 side chairs. **$3,000–4,500** for a pair of armchairs.

Set of eight mid-eighteenth-century Louis XV beechwood *chaise à la reine*. Cartouche-shaped upholstered backs above serpentine seat rails. Floral-carved cabriole legs. One chair with damage. 40" high. An original set of eight is very, very rare. *Courtesy Skinner, Inc., Bolton, Mass.* **$18,000–24,000** set of eight.

Pair of Louis XV/XVI gray-painted *chaises en cabriolet*. Third quarter eighteenth century. One bearing traces of G. Jacob signature; each with molded cartouche-shaped back and oval seat upholstered in velvet and raised on cabriole legs ending in ball feet. Marked by Georges Jacob, who became a *maître* in 1765. This chair and the ones in the previous photograph illustrate perfectly the difference between *an cabriolet* (concave-backed) and *à la reine* (flat-backed) chairs. *Courtesy Grogan & Company, Boston.* **$8,000–12,000** the pair.

Pair of Louis XV *fauteuils à la reine*, third quarter eighteenth-century. Each with molded cartouche-shaped back, padded arms, serpentine apron, and cabriole legs ending in scrolled feet; painted, with highlights. Upholstered in satin. Marked Nicholas Heurtaut, made a *maître* in 1755. *Courtesy Grogan & Company, Boston.* **$12,000–18,000** the pair.

Eighteenth-century French carved walnut *fauteuil à la reine*. Molded crest rail, upholstered cartouche-shaped back and armrests, shaped skirt and cabriole legs. *Courtesy Grogan & Company, Boston.* **$3,000–5,000** single, **$8,000–12,000** the pair.

Pair of Louis XV style, c. 1900, carved painted *bergères* with cabriole legs, finger carving and floral crest. Down cushions. *Courtesy Whitehall at the Villa, Chapel Hill, N.C.* **$2,500–3,600** the pair.

One of a pair of late nineteenth-century walnut Louis XVI style *fauteuils,* very well carved. **$4,000–6,000** the pair. One of a pair of c. 1870 oval Louis XVI style gild wood footstools. Well carved. **$1,200–1,600** the pair. *Courtesy Whitehall at the Villa, Chapel Hill, N.C.*

One of a pair of nineteenth-century French carved walnut *fauteuils à la reine*. Molded padded square back and armrests and loose cushions, each fluted round tapering leg headed by a square reserve centering a disc. *Courtesy Grogan & Company, Boston.* **$6,000–9,000** the pair.

Pair of mid-eighteenth-century Venetian gilt wood open *fauteuils*. Vasiform splats decorated with crests. *Courtesy Leslie Hindman Auctioneers, Chicago, Ill.* **$10,000–15,000.**

Italian rococo silvered *fauteuil*, c. 1780–1800. The arched foliate and ro15caille-carved light green satin upholstered back above scrolled arms on shaped supports, the shaped seat rails on molded cabriole legs. Silvering is rubbed. *Courtesy Butterfield & Butterfield, Los Angeles.* **$5,000–7,000.**

Swedish neoclassical mahogany *fauteuil du bureau*, c. 1825. With arched crest rail above a lyre-form splat, with bold pierced acanthus-carved scroll arms and drop-in seat above a plain rail on turned tapering legs headed by paterae ending in casters. Upholstered in leather. Very large and robust! *Courtesy Christie's New York.* **$5,000–7,500.**

Pair of eighteenth-century Venetian rococo painted parcel gilt and gessoed *fauteuils.* Floral-carved crest and shaped back and seat, on cabriole legs and trifid feet. Note the asymmetry of the crest and sides (the slight carving deviations) and the bold asymmetry of the apron. *Courtesy Leslie Hindman Auctioneers, Chicago, Ill.* **$12,000–18,000.**

Pair of c. 1800 Italian fruitwood side chairs with carved and gilded intertwined loops. Crest rails also parcel gilt. *Courtesy Whitehall at the Villa, Chapel Hill, N.C.* **$2,500–3,500** the pair. Increase geometrically in value for a set of 8 or more!

Pair of Charles X rosewood-inlaid *bois clair chaises,* c. 1825. Each with curved ladder back inlaid with paterae, the drop-in seat above a similarly inlaid seat rail on circular tapering legs headed by lappets and ending in toupie feet, upholstered in moss cut velvet. *Courtesy Christie's New York.* **$3,500–4,800.**

Biedermeier armchair, Vienna, c. 1820. Mahogany veneer on a walnut frame. An exceptionally sculptural chair of great elegance. 32 1/2" high x 23" wide x 23" deep. *Courtesy Rita Bucheit, Ltd., Chicago, Ill.* **$6,000–9,000.**

Biedermeier side chair, Vienna, c. 1825. Cherry veneer with ebonized accents. 36" high × 17 1/2" wide × 16 1/2" deep. *Courtesy Riga Bucheit, Ltd., Chicago, Ill.* **$2,500–3,500.** These also turn up quite often at "bargain" prices of $1,200 or less. But beware of bargains. They are often c. 1920 Biedermeier Revival!

One of a pair of Biedermeier side chairs, Austria, 1830–1850. Ash with ebony inlay. Each with shaped gadrooned crest rail centered by an oval ring, the shaped waisted back inlaid with ebony stringing and joined by an arched splat. Padded seat above a similarly inlaid seat rail on slightly tapering inlaid sabre legs. Upholstered in silk moiré. *Courtesy Christie's New York.* **$2,500–3,500.**

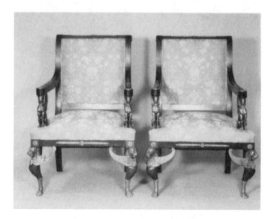

Pair of nineteenth-century French Second Empire mahogany *fauteuils*. Rectangular backs, crests set with garland-and-rosette bronze mounts, square arms with cylindrical grips. supported by female sphinx caryatids, rectangular upholstered seat with bronze-mounted apron of garland rosettes, winged lion's-head supports, above chimera legs and claw feet. Damask upholstery. 28" × 24" × 39 1/2" high (seat height is 19"). *Courtesy Frank H. Boos Gallery, Bloomfield Hills, Mich.* **$6,000–9,000** the pair.

Pair of Biedermeier neoclassical brass-mounted walnut armchairs, 1800–1825, probably Berlin. Each with overscroll-shaped crest with scroll arms, on padded seat above a plain seat rail on square tapering legs. Blue silk upholstery. *Courtesy Christie's New York.* **$6,000–9,000** the pair.

Two of a set of six Austrian Jugendstil beechwood dining chairs by Thonet, c. 1915. Caned back and seat, out-curving legs. *Courtesy Leslie Hindman Auctioneers, Chicago, Ill.* **$1,200–1,600** set of six.

Two of a set of four Austrian Jugendstil painted beechwood side chairs, designed by Otto Prutscher. Back and seat upholstered in reissued Werkstätte fabric. *Courtesy Leslie Hindman Auctioneers, Chicago, Ill.* **$1,200–1,500** the set, although specialists might well sell such a set for up to $3,500!

Austrian beechwood folding chair, c. 1910. Rectangular back and seat with bar splats on X-form curved block legs, with Hoffman-designed-fabric cushion. *Courtesy Leslie Hindman Auctioneers, Chicago, Ill.* **$800–1,200.**

Pair of bent beechwood upholstered armchairs, designed by Josef Hoffman, executed by Jacob and Josef Kohn, Austria, c. 1906. U-shaped with low back and continual slats from the crest rail to the stretcher, U-shaped seat with compressed-ball corner blocks. *Courtesy Frank H. Boos Gallery, Bloomfield Hills, Mich.* **$4,000–6,000.**

Part of a c. 1906 three-piece bent beechwood upholstered suite, designed by Marcel Kammerer, produced by Jacob and Josef Kohn, Austria. Settee (no shown) and a pair of armchairs, each U-shaped with outward scrolling arms, over a conforming seat, raised on plain rectangular legs, with conforming stretcher. Bearing metal tab inscribed "Johan Josef Mayer-Tapezierer, VII. Lindengasse 15." (Mayer did the upholstery work; tapezierer means upholsterer.) *Courtesy Frank H. Boos Gallery, Bloomfield Hills, Mich.* **$5,000–7,000** the three-piece suite.

Régence walnut settee with serpentine back and seat, c. 1730. Acanthus and shell carving on seat rail. Six whorl feet. Upholstered in a seventeenth-century verdure tapestry. Repairs. Note how only the back is purely Régence. The legs preview the fluidity of Louis XV. 42 1/2" high x 59" wide x 30" deep. *Courtesy Skinner, Inc.* **$15,000–25,000.**

Scandinavian neoclassical carved and painted settee, c. 1790. Base pulls out for a bed. *Courtesy Whitehall at the Villa, Chapel Hill, N.C.* **$4,500–6,000**.

Northern European neoclassical walnut settee, c. 1830. Bowed, reeded crest with swan-carved armrests over caned back and sides above upholstered slip seat. Sabre legs with brass sabots. 54" long. *Courtesy Leslie Hindman Auctioneers, Chicago, Ill.* **$3.600–4,800**.

Early nineteenth-century Charles X mahogany *canape,* with serpentine back, out-scrolled arms. Bracket feet. Were this in light wood such as satinwood, elm, etc., the price would be double. *Courtesy Skinner, Inc., Boston, Mass.* **$2,400–3,600**.

Dutch floral marquetry and mahogany settee, early nineteenth century. Rounded back and scroll arms, inlaid overall with chains of floral marquetry within plain or checkerboard borders, figured worn upholstery, on incurved scroll feet. 6'11" long. *Courtesy Butterfield & Butterfield, San Francisco.* **$5,000–7,000.**

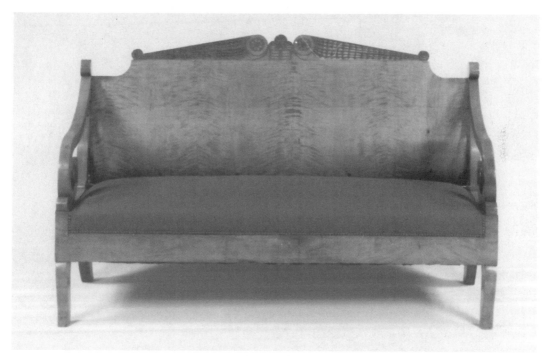

Russian neoclassical maple settee, c. 1800–1830. Rectangular arched back surmounted by a plume flanked by tapering wings ending in roundels, with bold scroll arms ending in paterae, with rectangular padded seat above a plain rail, on sabre legs. Restorations. 74" long. Very uncomfortable-looking, but visually exciting. A great hall piece. *Courtesy Christie's New York.* **$8,000–12,000.**

Turned and carved walnut early nineteenth-century country French bench. *Courtesy Whitehall at the Villa, Chapel Hill, N.C.* **$1,200–1,800**.

Late nineteenth-century Régence-style walnut bench, superbly carved and with S-scrolled stretchers. Modern tapestry upholstery. *Courtesy Whitehall at the Villa, Chapel Hill, N.C.* **$1,800–2,400**.

10

Tables

The forms of tables made on the Continent are far too numerous for a thorough discussion. There were, however, several styles that departed from the design and materials used on English tables and some of these are commonly found in the current marketplace. While English tables characteristicly featured fine wood and carving, Continental tables incorporated other elements as well. Marble tops were frequently used on Italian tables and, of course, Italian quarries supplied marble tops to France and other countries as well. Pietra dura (inlays of marble and semiprecious stones) originated in Italy during the Renaissance and by the seventeenth century was popular throughout Europe. *Scagliola,* closely related to *pietra dura,* was a process wherein powdered marble was used as tempera to paint designs into marble or composition slabs. It was a cheaper alternative to *pietra dura.* Both of these techniques made a comeback during the nineteenth century, when it was almost compulsory for travelers making the Grand Tour to pick out a *pietra dura* or *scagliola* top and have it shipped home, where it would be made into a table or incorporated in some other piece of furniture.

Italian Console Tables

Console tables, an Italian innovation consisting of a table with mirror, were products of the baroque era, an epoch in Italy that was noted for its formal furniture. The console table boasted an opulent marble top and a gilt base that was so ornately carved that it rivaled the great Italian sculpture of the day. These were imposing pieces that stood against walls of formal rooms. The console table underwent stylistic evolutions throughout the rococo, neoclassical, and Empire eras, never losing popularity after its first introduction. Console tables are popular on the American market, though seldom found as period pieces. More often they are nineteenth- or twentieth-century copies of rococo or neoclassical styles, with gilt or painted bases and marble tops.

Coiffeuse, Poudreuse, Chiffoniere

In France, the eighteenth-century *ébénistes* lavished much attention on the many small tables that catered to every need of the society at court. The varieties of small tables were almost endless. There were *coiffeuse* and *poudreuse* with lift up mirrors and compartments, used when preparing one's toilet and hair. There were small sewing or work tables called *chiffoniere,* with drawers or a cabinet mounted on four slender legs. The *guéridon,* which might be considered the French answer to the English tripod table, had a round top, sometimes with three graduated round shelves underneath. There were also games tables, such as the *bouillotte* table, dating from the Louis XVI period. It had a round, marble top with a brass gallery and four legs. *Menuisier* versions of these occasional tables were made in solid native woods.

Dining tables were introduced under Louis XVI in designs copied from the English. These were made by *menuisiers,* not the *ébénistes,* as for practical purposes the tops could not be veneer or marquetry. These tables were made of solid native woods like chestnut, oak, or fruitwoods. Besides the English forms, dining tables were sometimes made in the draw-leaf style, which dates back to the Renaissance. Draw-leaf tables have tops that extend by means of slides, unlike the English drop-leafs or gatelegs that have support legs.

Towards the end of the eighteenth century in France, another sign of English influence was the popularity of tea tables with tripod bases, sometimes incorporating Sèvres or Wedgwood plaques.

One generally expects furniture made by the *ébénistes* to have remained in better shape over the years than furniture made by the *menuisiers*—not so much because the *ébénisterie* was more soundly constructed, but because pieces made to furnish well-to-do urban homes would not suffer the same amount of wear and tear as more rustic furniture made for different surroundings. A country French table, for example, will almost always have tipped up legs (legs that have had the tips replaced due to rot). These tables sat on stone floors in provincial homes. When the floors were washed, the table legs got wet too, and the legs inevitably rotted. So you should almost always find repairs, or tipping up, on country French table legs. If you don't, the piece is probably not an antique!

Of course, on occasional tables made by *ébénistes,* you should find shrinkage in the marquetry. It is not at all uncommon to have losses to the marquetry. When judging bronze mounts for quality and signs of age, it is helpful to remember that the degree of definition indicates an early or late casting and can give some suggestion of age. An early casting from the mold will be relatively crisp, while a later casting will be somewhat muddy.

On *ébénisterie* tables with marble tops, it is not surprising to find rather sloppy construction underneath the marble (the part that is not expected to see the light of day) in contrast to the beautiful decorative work and construction of the rest of the table.

Continental, probably French, oval tole tray of deep red with black and gilt eagle-and-diamond motifs (the gilding worn away) surrounding an oval oil painting of Napoleon (victorious) and his troops on a battlefield. On a very well-made contemporary stand of coffee-table height. *Courtesy Whitehall at the Villa, Chapel Hill, N.C.* **$5,000–7,500.**

Two-tier red tole dessert tray with decoupaged central panels. Mid-nineteenth century. Now on a custom-made stand. *Courtesy Whitehall at the Villa, Chapel Hill, N.C.* **$2,500–3,500**.

Italian carved walnut and specimen marble table, c. 1860. Circular specimen marble and agate top inset in a radiating star-point pattern within a shouldered molded rim, raised on a ring-turned acanthus-carved standard on scroll-carved legs (slight worming to rim). 34"high x 28" diameter. *Courtesy Butterfield & Butterfield, Los Angeles.* **$6,000–9,000**.

Italian Rococo style gilt wood and scagliola pedestal table, c. 1880. Circular scagliola top with radiating stylized flower heads and dark-banded reserve within a leaf-tip-carved rim over a foliate-pierced apron, raised on baluster-form standard on scrolled feet. Rubbing to gilt, scratches to top. 34" high x 28" diameter. *Courtesy Butterfield & Butterfield, Los Angeles.* **$6,000–9,000**.

Charles X ormolu-mounted mahogany table, c. 1825; later green-tooled leather top above a frieze fitted with four droawers and mounted with female masks alternating with cornucopia. In-curved triangular baluster support mounted with ribbon-tied berried laurel leaves ending in lappet-carved feet on casters. 29" high × 31 1/2" diameter. *Courtesy Christie's New York.* **$10,000–15,000.**

Late nineteenth-century carved cherry wood bedside cabinet with drawer and cupboard door. Paneled sides. Short cabriole legs. *Courtesy Whitehall at the Villa, Chapel Hill, N.C.* **$1,000–1,400.**

Louis XV Revival carved walnut three-drawer table/commode, c. 1900. Very flamboyant carving. Note the over symmetry—one obvious sign that this is a revival piece. *Courtesy Whitehall at the Villa, Chapel Hill, N.C.* **$1,000–1,500.**

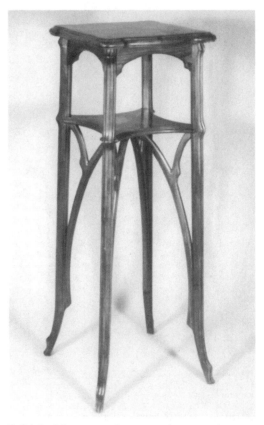

Gallé Art Nouveau mahogany and rosewood veneer marquetry inlaid side table, c. 1900; shaped square top with molded edge above a lower shelf, both inlaid in various woods with floral and butterfly supports, signed "Gallé" in marquetry. 15 3/4" square x 45" high. *Courtesy Frank H. Boos Gallery, Bloomfield Hills, Mich.* **$3,000–4,500**.

Gallé Art Nouveau marquetry inlaid fruitwood and enameled glass *coiffeuse* or dressing table, c. 1895. Shaped crest inlaid with tulips above a rectangular frame enclosing a central arched mirror flanked by arched green glass panels cut and enameled in white and pink with croci or snowdrops. Lower section with shaped top inlaid with a landscape with leafy trees by a lake, snowdrops in the foreground, spindled frieze below centered by sliding shelf inlaid with a single blossom. On two slender supports before a back panel inlaid with poppies and orchids. Shaped platform shelf raised on slightly flared legs. Crack to one glass panel. Signed "E. Gallé." 4'2" high x 23" wide. *Courtesy Butterfield & Butterfield, Los Angeles.* **$6,000–9,000**.

Marquetry top of Gallé table in previous photograph.

c. 1900 Gallé Art Nouveau marquetry occasional table of irregular outline inlaid with a bird amid stylized foliage, inscribed "Gallé," over molded out-flaring legs joined by an inlaid lower shelf. 29 1/2" high x 21" wide. *Courtesy Butterfield & Butterfield, Los Angeles.* **$3,000–5,000.**

Austrian Jugendstil bentwood dressing table by J. & J. Kohn, c 1910. Oval swing mirror over rectangular top with drawer on slightly curved legs. 51" high x 31" wide x 16" deep. *Courtesy Leslie Hindman Auctioneers, Chicago, Ill.* **$1,800–2,400.**

Late eighteenth-century Italian neoclassical carved and bicolor-gilded table with inset black and gold seventeenth-century Chinese lacquer top, frieze carved with rosettes and fitted with a drawer, on fluted tapering legs with acanthus-carved toes. 30" high x 23 1'2" wide x 18 1/2" deep. *Courtesy Grogan & Company, Boston.* **$8,000–12,000.**

Italian rococo, c. 1760, parcel-gilt and red-painted games table; shaped rectangular top with outset rounded corners, inset with red tooled-leather surface within an elevated molded edge. Scroll-carved apron centered by a crest. Foliate and scrolled cabriole legs. Burns to leather, worming to frame, losses to molding and carving. 27 1/2" high x 39 3/4" wide. *Courtesy Butterfield & Butterfield, Los Angeles.* **$8,000–12,000** restored. **$4,000–6,000** as is.

Italian neoclassical inlaid walnut drop-leaf table, c. 1770–1800. Hinged rectangular top inlaid with a central figure of a lion within a cross-banded reserve, over inlaid frieze drawers on tapering square legs ending in square caps. Cracking to veneer, small stains on top. 29" high x 33" wide (open). *Courtesy Butterfield & Butterfield, Los Angeles.* **$4,000–6,000**.

Late nineteenth-century country French oak work, writing, or dining table with a single drawer, on cabriole legs. *Courtesy Whitehall at the Villa, Chapel Hill, N.C.* **$1,800–2,400**.

Italian rococo walnut folding-top games table, c. 1725–1750. Dark marbelized top with cusped circular outset corners above a scalloped frieze fitted with end drawers, raised on square cabriole supports. Drawers rebuilt. 30 1/2" high x 30" wide. These sell for less on the East Coast. This example is top heavy. *Courtesy Butterfield & Butterfield, San Francisco.* **$4,000–6,000**.

Mid-eighteenth-century Louis XV provincial fruit-wood tric-trac table. Leather-inset lift-off rectangular top opens to reveal a later needlepoint playing surface. Shaped apron fitted with a drawer on either side. Raised on cabriole legs, which have been restored. 27 1/2" high × 36" wide. *Courtesy Whitehall at the Villa, Chapel Hill, N.C.* **$8,000–12,000**

Louis XV kingwood and tulipwood *poudreuse* (dressing table), c. 1780–1800. Divided rectangular top opening to a central mirror plate flanked by covered lift-out cases (one missing) above a central writing slide and frieze drawer flanked by false drawers, raised on cabriole legs. 28 1/2" high × 31 1/2" wide. Watch out—90% of these date from 1890–1960! *Courtesy Butterfield & Butterfield, Los Angeles.* **$4,000–6,000** if eighteenth century. **$2,500–3,600** if nineteenth to twentieth centuries.

Louis XV style c. 1920 painted wood *coiffeuse* (dressing table) with rectangular top having lift-up dressing mirror and two hinged compartments over five small drawers. Overall floral decoration on light green ground. Cabriole legs. Rough condition. 29" high × 37" wide × 20" deep. *Courtesy Leslie Hindman Auctioneers, Chicago, Ill.* **$1,800–2,400** as is. **$3,000–4,000** restored.

Mid-nineteenth-century Louis XV style parquetry *commode en console.* Serpentine-edged liver red and gray marble top above a frieze drawer raised on cabriole legs. All with rococo ormolu mounts. 32 1/2" high × 35" wide × 14 1/2" deep. *Courtesy Grogan & Company, Boston.* **$4,500–6,500.**

French gilt wood Louis XVI style marble-top console table, c. 1880. Very good carving. *Private collection.* **$2,000–2,800.**

Eighteenth-century Portuguese or Brazilian rococo jarcaranda wood side table with serpentine-molded top above a conforming molded frieze drawer and foliate-carved scalloped apron on shell-carved cabriole legs ending in scroll feet. 33" high × 35" wide × 19 1/2" deep. *Courtesy Christie's New York.* **$5,000–7,500.** (These are more common in rosewood.)

One of a pair of nineteenth-century Italian neoclassical painted and parcel gilt fruitwood demilune console tables. Each top painted with three lush floral bouqets centering an acanthus leaf-formed demirosette, with a yellow-ground ribbon-tied floral garland border, the frieze with rectangular gilt reserve centering a lyre, the square tapering legs applied with gilt rosettes, swags, and trialing bellflowers, ending in fluted toupie feet goined by shaped stretchers supporting a gilt frame. 36"high × 60" wide × 26 3/4" deep. *Courtesy Grogan & Company, Boston.* **$25,000–35,000.**

Mid-eighteenth-century Italian rococo carved gilt wood console. Serpentine outline, surmounted by a white marble top with molded edge above a central carved shell issuing folliate, raised on double C-scroll inswept supports carved with pendant flowers and ending in scrolled feet issuing beaded acanthus leaves. Note the subtle asymmetry (one of the hallmarks of the rococo style) on the lower stretcher. 37 1/2" high × 27 3/4" wide. *Courtesy Butterfield & Butterfield, San Francisco.* **$4,500–6,500.**

Mid-nineteenth-century Rococo Revival carved and gilded wood salon table with beveled shaped rectangular marble top fitting into conforming carved molding above a frieze with pierced floral, foliate, scroll-and-shell carving, raised on scrolling legs with floral, demon mask, foliate, tassel, and scale carvings terminating in C-scrolls and carved bun feet. C-scroll and X-scroll stretcher centering a bouquet of flowers. 57 1/2" long × 35" deep × 33" high. *Courtesy Frank H. Boos Gallery, Bloomfield Hills, Mich.* **$15,000–20,000.**

French Louis XV Revival parquet-top draw-leaf oak dining table, c. 1890. These tables were enormously popular at the turn of the century (1870–1920) and were made in oak, walnut, cherry, and beech. The legs and aprons may be more or less carved. Sizes vary from small (seating 4 to 6) to large (seating 8 to 12). *Courtesy Whitehall at the Villa, Chapel Hill, N.C.* Plain: small, **$1,200–1,600**; large, **$2,400–3,000**. Ornate: small, **$1,800–2,600**; large, **$4,000–5,500**.

Seventeenth-century Spanish baroque walnut library table. Rectangular top above three paneled frieze drawers, raised on square supports joined by box stretchers. Restorations. 32" high × 5'5" wide. *Courtesy Butterfield & Butterfield, Los Angeles.* **$5,000–7,000.**

c. 1820 country French walnut and cherry tapered-leg oval dining table. Tipped legs, repaired top. Courtesy *Whitehall at the Villa, Chapel Hill, N.C.* **$2,500–3,500.**

Italian baroque walnut center table, oblong top with fluted edge on later baluster-turned legs, joined by a flat stretcher and bun feet, 31" high × 91" wide × 39" deep. A very attractive and desirable size for a large hall, sofa, etc. Courtesy *Christie's New York*. **$15,000–20,000.**

Late nineteenth-century country French fruitwood banquet table with cross-banded top. Two leaves; extending ends. Tapered legs. *Courtesy Whitehall at the Villa, Chapel Hill, N.C.* **$8,000–12,000.**

11

Writing Furniture

The earliest Continental form in our listings is the *vargueño,* which originated in Renaissance Spain. It consists of a writing cabinet on a stand. The writing cabinet has a fall front that opens to reveal tiers of little drawers or compartments. The *vargueño* in our listings is a relatively plain example, but they were often heavily decorated with bone or ivory inlays in Moorish-inspired designs.

Perhaps the most characteristic French form of writing furniture is the *bureau plat,* which evolved from a Louis XIV pedestal desk. Under Louis XIV, this massive form had a flat top, two pedestals housing drawers, and eight legs supporting the pedestals. After Louis XIV, the lighter *bureau plat* remained popular through all style periods of the eighteenth and nineteenth centuries. With its expansive flat writing surface covered in leather or velvet, frieze drawers, and four legs, the form is as useful now as it was when first conceived.

The slant-front desk is a form that we associated more with England than France (although it was made in Holland and was part of the Biedermeier repertoire). In France, the slant-front desk is sometimes referred to as a *dos d'âne,* which translates literally as "back of an ass." This was a freestanding piece, un-like the English form. The fall-front secretary (*secrétaire à abattant*) was a more popular form in France and the rest of the Continent from the second half of the eighteenth century through the nineteenth century. Its simple, rectangular form was embraced during the neoclassical era and by Biedermeier cabinetmakers.

The cylinder (roll-top) desk was made from 1760 onward in France. The prototype was started by J. F. Oeben and finished by J. H. Riesener during the 1760s. It was a marvel of marquetry, movable parts, and bronze mounts. Both of the original makers were German-born, and the German talent for designing mechanical furniture is advantageously demonstrated by this innovative form. Mechanical features were much in demand on tables during the Louis XVI period, perhaps due to the influence of German-born *ébénistes.*

Another new form from the Louis XVI period was the *bonheur du jour,* a table with a back superstructure that included open or closed compartments. It was generally sized for ladies and highly decorated. Sometimes these pieces were covered entirely in Boullework, which is extremely fragile because it involves a non-wood substance laid down on wood. Pieces often pop up and are broken off.

Mid eighteenth-century Portuguese rococo walnut serpentine-fronted writing table. Rectangular top with molded edge over later drawers, raised on cabriole legs joined by an X-form stretcher, ending in ball-and-claw feet. 32" high × 46" wide. The flattened ball-and-claw foot is typically Portuguese or Brazilian. Often these are rosewood, especially the nineteenth-century examples. *Courtesy Butterfield & Butterfield, Los Angeles.* **$6,000–8,000.**

Late seventeenth-century Spanish baroque walnut *vargueño* on stand. With rectangular top above a fall front enclosing an interior fitted with numerous small drawers. Sides with wrought-iron carrying handles. Stand with arcaded splat ending in trestle feet (the stand with restorations and replacements). 55 1/2" high overall × 35 3/4" wide × 16 3/4" deep. *Courtesy Christie's New York.* **$4,500–6,000.**

Mid eighteenth-century Louis XV tulipwood, amaranth, and mahogany mechanical writing/card table, signed "Wirtz" (Henry Wirtz, who became a *maître* in 1767). Rectangular hinged top with baize-lined gaming surface, over a plain frieze with writing surface and fitted compartment, ends fitted with drawers. Raised on tapering sabre legs. 28" high × 29 1/2" long × 15" deep. *Courtesy Skinner, Inc., Bolton, Mass.* **$12,000–18,000.**

Louis XVI style gilt-bronze-mounted mahogany and parquetry *bureau plat*. Late nineteenth/early twentieth century. Rectangular top with leaf-tip cast gilt-bronze border enclosing a central oval panel of a musical trophy inlaid on a cube-parquetry ground, the frieze of slightly broken outline fitted with three drawers opposing simulated drawers and applied with plaquettes of frolicking putti all within leaf-tip cast borders, raised on inlaid square tapering supports ending in stiff leaf-cast sabots. 28 3/4" high × 45 1/4" long. *Courtesy Butterfield & Butterfield, Los Angeles.* **$8,000–12,000.**

Dutch marquetry writing desk in two parts, c. 1830. Superstructure with a central elevated cupboard flanked by shaped galleries over short drawers, the lower section with a concealed drop-front fitted writing drawer over a well flanked by small drawers. Raised on tapering ring-turned legs; inlaid overall with trailing foliage, flower heads, scrolls, and urns. Slightly losses to veneer. 47 1/2" high × 45" wide. *Courtesy Butterfield & Butterfield, Los Angeles.* **$4,000–6,000.** Add $2,000 if on square tapered legs!

Third quarter nineteenth-century Napoleon III boule (tortoise shell brass, silver or pewter) *bureau de dame* or *bonheur du jour.* Upper section with pierced gilt-metal three-quarter gallery above two doors opening to a shelf over two drawers, the lower section with a sliding green leather-lined writing surface over a frieze drawer, raised on cabriole legs mounted with gilt-metal foliate chutes and sabots. 4'3" high x 30" wide. *Courtesy Butterfield & Butterfield, San Francisco.* **$5,000–7,500.**

Napoleon III walnut and marquetry *bureau en pente,* c. 1880–1900. Galleried open shelf above a fall-front writing surface, over a frieze drawer, on tapering fluted legs joined by stretchers. 46" high x 25 1/2" wide x 16" deep. *Courtesy Skinner, Inc., Boston, Mass.* **$3,000–4,000.**

A Dutch rococo oak and marquetry slant-front bureau, mid-eighteenth-century. With rectangular cross-banded top above a fall front enclosing an interior fitted with four open compartments, four graduated short drawers centering a cupboard door flanked by two short drawers above a secret compartment. The base with four short and two long drawers, with scalloped apron on splayed feet, inlaid throughout with blossoming floral sprays, scallop shells, and flower-filled baskets. The real thing! This is what all that over-inlaid, later-inlaid, and reproduction stuff (c. 1890–1915) tries to emulate! 44" high x 47" wide x 20" deep. *Courtesy Christie's New York.* **$12,000–12,000.**

Danish provincial, c. 1760, oak slant-front desk with paneled hinged slant front opening to compartmentalized interior, over central drawer and three long drawers set on molded base and bracket feet. 42 1/2" high × 45" wide × 21 1/2" deep. *Courtesy Leslie Hindman Auctioneers, Chicago, Ill.* **$3,500–5,500.**

Austrian neoclassical inlaid fruitwood cylinder desk, c. 1800–1830. Rectangular cross-banded top above a cavetto-molded frieze and cylinder cover inlaid with a central patera, enclosing a compartment fitted with a central revolving section of angled mirrored reserves and small drawers on the reverse flanked by rounded pilasters and banks of small drawers, above a pullout felt-inset writing surface over two long drawers flanked by inlaid pilasters and sides, raised on tapering square feet. Minor cracking to veneer. 45 3/4" high × 46" wide. *Courtesy Butterfield & Butterfield, Los Angeles.* **$7,000–10,000.**

Biedermeier fruitwood and ebonized cylinder desk, c. 1830. Rectangular top over cylinder front opening to three compartments and drawers and sliding tooled-leather writing surface above two long drawers and square tapering legs. *Courtesy Leslie Hindman Auctioneers, Chicago, Ill.* **$8,000–12,000.**

A-189

Biedermeier ebony-inlaid fruitwood desk, c. 1825–1850. Rectangular top edged with stringing above a central drawer flanked by two tiers of three short drawers, on short tapering legs. Simple of form and late in the period. 31" high × 46" wide × 22 1/2" deep. *Courtesy Christie's New York.* **$6,000–9,000.**

Swedigh neoclassical gilt-metal-mounted mahogany *secrtétaire à abattant,* c. 1800–1830. Pediment top above a paneled frieze drawer fitted with a recessed mount cast with frolicking putti above a fall front enclosing an interior fitted with a central cupboard surrounded by sixteen short drawers. The base with three long drawers, the lower two with a recessed panel. 58"high × 37 1/2" wide × 21 3/4"deep. *Courtesy Christie's New York.* **$10,000–15,000.**

Third quarter nineteenth-century Napolean III inlaid and ebonized *secrtétaire à abattant*. Rectangular gray marble top above a frieze drawer over a fall front opening to a bird's-eye maple interior with suspended drawers and compartments, thre-long drawers below flanked by out-stepped gilt-metal-mounted fluted columns. Raised on short, turned feet. 4'6" high × 28"wide. *Courtesy Butterfield & Butterfield, San Francisco.* **$5,000–7,000.**

Dutch neoclassical walnut and floral marquetry inlaid *secrtétaire à abattant,* c. 1810. Case is fitted with a long drawer over fall front enclosing small drawers and pigeonholes. Lower section with two cabinet doors. All flanked by freestanding columnar stiles. Block feet. Minor losses. 60 1/2" high × 37 3/4" wide × 20" deep. *Courtesy Leslie Hindman Auctioneers, Chicago, Ill.* **$12,000–18,000.**

Late nineteenth-century Italian rococo style olive wood inlaid secretary. In two parts, the upper with elevated molded pediment over a glazed door enclosing shell-and-scroll carved shelves. Serpentine-fronted lower section with fall front opening to a fitted interior flanked by ebonized finials, three long drawers below. On flared bracket feet. Some cracking to veneer. 7'11" high × 44" wide. *Courtesy Butterfield & Butterfield, Los Angeles.* **$8,000–12,000.**

Nineteenth-century Italian rococo style olive wood secretary bookcase. In two parts, the upper section with black-painted arched outline over swelling sides and a shaped later mirrored door. Lower case with molded edge over a shaped sland front enclosing a prospect and short drawers. Out-stepped frieze and swelling sides above three long drawers; raised on shaped bracket feet. Cracks to veneer. Limited market! 6'10" high × 34" wide. *Courtesy Butterfield & Butterfield, Los Angeles.* **$7,000–10,000.**

12

Storage Pieces

Storage chests and boxes were produced throughout the Renaissance and up until recent times. They are a useful form and are among the most basic in terms of construction. We find them in provincial areas, decorated with local folk motifs. There are wonderful painted chests, for example, from Germany. Each area gave these coffers and chests its own particular form of decoration.

Renaissance Chests, Credenzas, and Buffets

In Renaissance Italy the chest was called a *cassone*—a long, low box with a flat lid (in its most basic form), meant to store linens. It often played a symbolic role in the customs of marriage, with wedding *cassoni* being ostentaciously decorated (with intarsia, painting, or carving) with the coats of arms and other symbols of the couple's families. After the sixteenth century, the form was submerged in the *cassapanca*—in essence, a cassone transformed into a settle. The *cassone* was the base and back and arms were added, turning it into a long seat or bench.

Another important piece from Renaissance Italy was the *credenza,* a sort of buffet that stood against a wall and had a closed-in plinth base. It generally had a top of dining-table height above two frieze drawers, with two cabinet doors in the base. Using the frame-and-panel construction, the design was simple, often with panels and architectural elements being the primary decoration. This was a popular form in the Renaissance and the baroque periods (German cabinetmakers also built *credenzas* in the seventeenth century), and in fact, it is one of the few forms from this period that we do see on the American market today, most often with extensive repairs and replaced parts.

The buffet of Renaissance France exhibited the same kinds of architectural motifs as the Italian *credenza.* The French buffet took the form of a chest with a stable top over a base of two frieze drawers above two cabinet doors (not drawers), usually separated by a blind panel. The buffet often had an upper section, which was smaller in proportion to the base and stepped back. We refer to this form today as a *buffet à deux corps.* These pieces had many variations of form and, indeed, of use: displaying plates and storing linens or other valuable belongings. Construction principles were much the same as for the Italian *credenza,* with frame-and-panel construction predominant.

Eighteenth- and Nineteenth-Century Commodes and Buffets

The commode (the French equivalent of the English chest of drawers) did not actually develop until the end of the Louis XIV period, around 1700, and was firmly established during the Régence period. The most interesting commodes were made by the *ébénistes* using imported woods, wonderful marquetry, and gilt-bronze handles and mounts. Tops were marble or marquetry.

The form of the commode evolved throughout the eighteenth century, as the various styles changed. The Régence commode was a large, heavy form with the carcass raised only a small distance from the ground on four short feet. There were usually three drawers of equal size, although sometimes there were two aligned drawers over two long drawers.

The Louis XV commode had a different character—a lighter, more graceful, curved carcass with a shaped apron on higher legs. It usually had two drawers, although the crosspiece between the drawers was no longer used after about 1740. The result was a form very far removed from the frame-and-panel chests of earlier times. The finest Louis XV commodes were covered in fabulous marquetry protected by elaborate bronze mounts. Other desirable commodes of this period were lacquered, a technique borrowed from the Chinese. During the seventeenth century, lacquered panels were imported and incorporated into French pieces, but by mid-century, the French were producing lacquer to suit their own rococo furniture. The Martin brothers were probably the most famous Parisian lacquerers (*vernisseurs*).

With the neoclassical style of Louis XVI, the commode lost its curvaceous form and took on a rectilinear shape. It usually had two large drawers or sometimes three aligned drawers over two long drawers. Like the Régence commode, it was raised on short legs, but these ended in *sabots*. Parquetry (geometric designs) was more common than the fanciful, floral marquetry patterns of the rococo period and bronze mounts were more restrained. A block front sometimes added interest to the rectilinear lines of the Louis XVI commode. Demilune commodes were also made during this period.

Throughout the eighteenth century, the commodes built by the *ébénistes* had carcasses made out of oak, pine, or poplar. Drawers were dovetailed (the French term, *queue d'hironde* or *queue d'aronde,* translates as swallow tail). When the top was covered in marble, the finish of the wooden carcass can be surprisingly sloppy.

The primary concern for *ébénistes* in constructing commodes with marquetry was in the handling of the veneer. Pegs were avoided since over time they tended to push through veneer. The *ébénistes* also avoided carcass wood that was cut across the grain because the glue would not adhere well. Bronze mounts were applied to protect corners and delicate marquetry.

Menuisiers made commodes out of native woods like cherry, elm, and walnut, with restrained carvings rather than marquetry. These simpler versions of the very popular work of the *ébénistes* were usually in the Régence style (with three equally large drawers, one above the other, and fairly low to the ground). The tops were wood, not the marble used by *ébénistes*. Towards the end of the eighteenth century, *menuisiers* also made Louis XVI commodes with two large drawers below a narrow frieze drawer. These provincial commodes are very popular today and are more affordable and more suitable to the average lifestyle than the *ébénistes'* formal commodes.

The *menuisiers* also made buffets in solid wood throughout the eighteenth and nineteenth centuries. Like the provincial commodes, these buffets have their own distinct appeal. There are no fancy frieze mounts on these pieces, instead they have steel hinges, hardware, and key plates in swirling designs inspired by rococo lines. Steel hardware preceded the brass parts seen on later buffets and commodes.

The commode was as popular in other parts of Europe as it was in France. Throughout the eighteenth century, it was made in Germany and Italy in forms closely related to the French prototype. German cabinetmakers began making commodes around the 1720s, when Régence styles and forms were eagerly taken up. The German commode took on its own particular pronounced bombé shape and tended to be heavier than most French commodes. The German form had short feet, sometimes of bun form. Another popular German type had a serpentine carcass and drawers. By about 1770, Louis XVI styles were being executed in Germany, giving way to the Empire style by about 1800. Biedermeier commodes or chests of drawers show the simplicity of design and clarity of wood that characterizes the Biedermeier style as a whole.

In Italy, the eighteenth-century commode was most often made in a bombe shape, sometimes quite exaggerated and top heavy. Bronze mounts were rarely as elaborate as on French commodes. Italian commodes were often lacquered, especially those made in Venice.

In France, commodes were sometimes made in pairs, and when this was the case, one would have the traditional drawers and one would have cupboard doors, the latter called a *commode à vantaux.* Corner cabinets, made to harmonize with commodes, were called *encoignures* and were usually made in pairs. They had two doors and sometimes an extra foot for stability. During the Louis XV period, matching corner shelves were made to go above the *encoignures.* The resulting pieces, called *étagères,* consisted of graduated shelves above a small cabinet with doors. As a rule, these matching pieces were separated over the intervening years and are rarely available today as sets.

Sixteenth-century Italian Renaissance walnut *cassone* with rectangular molded hinged top over conforming paneled case fitted with a pair of doors. Bracket feet. Restorations. This is a plain piece, but useful as a hall piece, server, or buffet, as well as in a bedroom. 35 1/4" high × 62 1/2" × 24 1/2" deep. *Courtesy Skinner, Inc., Boston, Mass.* **$4,000–6,000.**

Italian baroque walnut *cassone,* early eighteenth century. The hinged rectangular top with molded edge and cleated ends above a dentil and arch-carved frieze over paneled reserves centering large carved flower heads, a guilloche-carved border below, raised on later bracket feet (cracks on top, worming to carcass). 22" high × 5'1" wide. *Courtesy Butterfield & Butterfield, Los Angeles.* **$4,000–6,000.**

Italian Renaissance walnut *cassone* with hinged rectangular top above a paneled case with caryatid supports and fluted base with scalloped bracket feet. Extensive restorations make this piece undatable by Christie's standards. In a shop, however, it would probably be dated late sixteenth century, with repairs noted. 22" high × 62" wide × 20 1/2" deep. *Courtesy Christie's New York.* **$4,000–6,000.**

Italian Renaissance *cassapanca,* having an elevated back with molded edge and out-stepped ends aabove oval panels flanked by arms with mask-carved ends over a hinged seat and paneled front, raised on a molded base. With restorations, 40 1/2" high × 5'8" wide. This form is closely related to the *cassone,* with added back and arms. *Courtesy Butterfield & Butterfield, San Francisco.* **$5,000–7,000.**

Norwegian painted pine coffer, dated 1832. The domed lid with metal strap banding and foliate painting above straight sides, the front with stylized Celtic painting with two arched images, one with the initial MDA, the other with "1832" centering an elongated wrought-iron lock plate, the sides applied with bail handles. 22" high × 43 1/2" long. *Courtesy Butterfield & Butterfield, San Francisco.* **$3,000–5,000.**

Austrian baroque polychromed pine chest-on-stand, early eighteenth century. The rectangular undecorated hinged top with molded surrounds enclosing a till, above straight sides applied with wrought-iron bail handles, the front and base with painted paneled decoration. Wear to finish. This piece fits with many styles and collections, from folk art to contemporary to ultra-traditional. 36" high × 5'9" long. *Courtesy Butterfield & Butterfield, San Francisco.* **$4,000–6,000.**

Italian baroque walnut *credenza* with serpentine demi-lune-molded top above a pair of frieze drawers and pair of molded cupboard doors enclosing a shelf, the shaped sides fitted with cupboard doors, on molded plinth and bracket feet. Probably Bolognese. Typical of seventeenth-century Italian pieces, restoration is so extensive due to worm damage that the piece is undated, but *not* unsalable. 42" high × 11 1/2" wide × 23" deep. *Courtesy Christie's New York.* **$15,000–20,000.**

South German baroque burl walnut commode (c. 1750–1800). With serpentine cross-banded top above three long drawers fitted with later scrolling foliate pulls, on later bun feet. 32 1/4" high × 43 1/2" wide × 22 1/2" deep. *Courtesy Christie's New York*. **$8,000–12,000.**

A north Italian rococo walnut commode. Mid-eighteenth-century. With serpentine top centrally inlaid with a cartouche above four similar long paneled drawers, the sides similarly inlaid, on short cabriole legs. 37 1/2" high × 60" wide × 26 7/8" deep. *Courtesy Christie's New York*. **$10,000–15,000.**

Mid-eighteenth-century south German inlaid walnut commode with serpentine top over conforming case with three drawers and scrolling apron. On scrolled feet. Although this is Louis XV in feel and period, the heavier nature of Germanic pieces supresses the prices compared to a French example. 36 1/2" high × 45 1/2" wide × 23" deep. *Courtesy Skinner, Inc., Boston, Mass*. **$6,000–9,000.**

Eighteenth-century Dutch rococo walnut bombé commode with rectangular top with four long drawers cross-banded with chevron stringing on shaped bracket feet. 30" high × 32"wide × 19" deep. *Courtesy Christie's New York*. Sold at auction for **$2,970.** This chest was fully restored by the purchaser and sold for **$8,500.**

Eighteenth-century Italian baroque walut commode. Rectangular top with carved lower edge above three long drawers with shaped panels, on later bracket feet. 38 1/2" high × 55" wide × 24 1/2" deep. *Courtesy Christie's New York.* **$5,000–7,000.**

Country Dutch walnut veneered commode with serpentine top and four serpentine drawers, c. 1830. Scrolled apron. Canted and scrolled corners. 29" high × 33" wide × 21" deep. Great small size. Needs restoration. *Courtesy Leslie Hindman Auctioneers, Chicago, Ill.* **$1,800–2,400** as is. **$4,000–6,000** restored.

Mid-eighteenth-century Louix XV provincial walnut commode with serpentine-molded top over conforming case fitted with three drawers, raised on cabriole legs. Restoration. 34" high × 48 3/4" long × 27 1/4" deep. *Courtesy Skinner, Inc., Bolton, Mass.* **$18,000–24,000.**

French provincial eighteenth-century carved walnut shaped-front commode with two short over two long drawers. Conforming molded top. Paneled sides. *Courtesy Morton Goldberg Auction Galleries, New Orleans.* **$15,000–20,000.**

Early nineteenth-century Portuguese (Dona Maria) rosewood commode with rectangular top above two short and two long paneled drawers fitted with later roundel pulls, with similarly paneled sides, on scrolling bracket feet. 37 1/4" high × 45" wide × 27 1/2" deep. *Courtesy Christie's New York.* **$3,000–5,000.**

Mid to late nineteenth-century Portuguese (or possibly Brazilian) rococo style jacaranda wood commode with serpentine-molded top above two short and two long conforming paneled drawers. Each fitted with pierced foliate handles. Voluted scrolling angles and plinth on bold scroll feet. 42" feet x 43" wide x 24" deep. *Courtesy Christie's New York.* **$6,000–9,000.**

Late nineteenth-century/early twentieth-century Louis XV style bombé commode with green serpentine top over two graduated drawers (*sans traverse*), mounted with bronze chutes and sabots. Case covered with floral chintz. 32" high x 43" wide x 23" deep. *Courtesy Leslie Hindman Auctioneers, Chicago, Ill.* **$4,000–6,000.**

Eighteenth-century Louis XV japanned pine commode with bowed marble top over two drawers decorated with gilt gesso figures in a landscape on green ground, on cabriole legs with gilt-bronze chutes and sabots. Replaced marble. 37" high x 56" wide x 24" deep. *Courtesy Leslie Hindman Auctioneers, Chicago, Ill.* **$8,000–12,000.**

Nineteenth-century Louis XV style marquetry commode. Two quarter-veneered ormolu-mounted drawers (*sans traverse*) with cartouche, acanthus leaf, and floral garland marquetry inlay, the sides similarly decorated. Marble top. 32" high × 40" wide × 21 1/2" deep. *Courtesy Grogan & Company, Boston.* **$4,500–6,500.**

Eighteenth-century Italian neoclassical parquetry fruitwood commode. Top inlaid with an eight-pointed star within a circular reserve, over a single cube-work-inlaid frieze drawer and two string-inlaid deep drawers, raised on square tapering legs. 32 1/2" high × 43 1/2" wide × 24"deep. *Courtesy Grogan & Company, Boston.* **$12,000–18,000.**

Late eighteenth-century cherry buffet with two drawers over two doors. Shaped apron. Iron hinges. Shaped, paneled doors. Feet tipped. *Courtesy Whitehall at the Villa, Chapel Hill, N.C.* **$5,000–7,000.**

Louis XV walnut buffet. Fitted with two frieze drawers over two shaped arched fielded doors divided by a broad stile over a scalloped apron, all carved in low relief with stylized flowering plants. Incised paneled round stiles above short square tapered supports ending in scrolled feet. Repairs to feet and top. Carving is all of later nineteenth-century date; it is shallow and it is inset *below* the line of the surrounding wood. It is symmetrical rather than asymmetrical. 40 1/4" high x 4'4" long. *Courtesy Butterfield & Butterfield, San Francisco.* **$8,000–12,000.**

Louis XV late eighteenth-century burl elm buffet with simple carved decorations. The spectacular wood needs little embelishment, although burl is fragile and difficult to carve. *Courtesy Whitehall at the Villa, Chapel Hill, N.C.* **$8,000–12,000.**

Mid-eighteenth-century Louix XV provincial walnut buffet. Rectangular top above a pair of frieze drawers over cabinet doors, raised on cabriole legs. 45 1/2" high x 49 1/2" long x 24 1/4" deep. *Courtesy Skinner, Inc., Bolton, Mass.* **$6,000–9,000.**

Pair of Louis XV style marquetry *encoignures,* stamped "Nogaret à Lyon," third quarter nineteenth century. Each mottled pink marble top above a pair of cupboard doors inlaid with ribbon-tied floral sprigs within gilt-bronze foliate-scroll borders, raised on shaped cross-banded feet ending in cast hoof-form sabots. One marble top cracked. Minor chips and losses. 36" high × 28 1/2" wide. *Courtesy Butterfield & Butterfield, San Francisco.* **$6,000–9,000** the pair; when period, **$15,000–25,000** the pair!

Eighteenth-century Louis XV marquetry *encoignure,* stamped "J. Bircle." Marble top above a conforming cupboard door, with central oval medallion enclosing a figure in landscape with ivory bust and arms, enclosed by floral, foliate, and ribbon design, flanked by plume, facial, floral, and foliate bronze dore mounts, raised on tapering square legs. Crude inlay in the door panel, perhaps and alteration or replacement. Good provenance. 27 1/2" × 19 1/2" × 34 1/4" high. *Courtesy Frank H. Boos Gallery, Bloomfield Hills, Mich.* **$5,000–7,000.**

One of a pair of turn-of-the-century French marble-top and gilt-bronze-mounted *credenze,* signed "Paul Sormani," serpentine shape, decorated with fine floral inlay. 41" high × 45" wide × 16" deep. *Courtesy Dunning's Auction Service, Elgin, Ill.* **$8,000–12,000.**

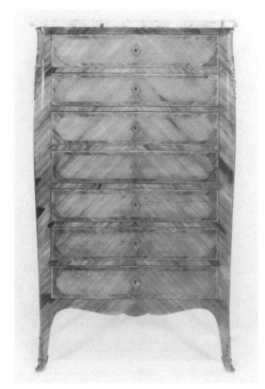

Louis XV style kingwood *semainer,* c. 1900. Shaped rectangular marble top with molded edge above seven parquetry drawers within a chevron-inlaid outline, raised on shaped feet ending in foliate sabots. 4'5 1/2" high × 32 1/2" wide. *Courtesy Butterfield & Butterfield, San Francisco.* **$3,000–5,000.**

Dutch c. 1800 Directoire cherry wood tambour-door cabinet with two drawers and black marble top. Original hardware and leg trim. *Private collection.* **$5,000–7,000.**

Nineteenth-century German neoclassical ormolu-mounted mahogany commode with rectangular top above a frieze drawer and three further recessed long drawers flanked by columnar supports on block feet. 38" high × 49" wide × 20 1/2" deep. *Courtesy Christie's New York.* **$5,000–7,000.**

North German Biedermeier birch commode, c. 1820. Rectangular top above pedimentd frieze and three long drawers flanked by Corinthian columns. These very strong architectural forms are the most highly prized of the Biedermeier pieces. 33" high × 38" wide × 20 1/2" deep. *Courtesy Christie's New York.* **$4,000–6,000.**

13

Armoires and Display Pieces

Country Armoires

Although the *ébénistes* made spectacular armoires covered in exquisite marquetry work and bronze mounts, they did not make them as frequently after 1700. The spectacular armoires are rarely found outside museums and chateaus. The more affordable armoires are the country French pieces made by *menuisiers*. Armoires were an important part of the repetoire of *menuisiers* in Paris and in the provinces. On the market today, we find armoires dating from the eighteenth century and ones made throughout the nineteenth century.

Construction of the country French armoires was conservative and rarely strayed from the time-tested method of frame-and-panel construction, in which panels slid into grooves in the frame and the frame members were secured with the mortise-and-tenon joint and pegs. Essentially, the panels floated in the grooves of the frame and, thus, were allowed to move rather than split as they shrank. The panels may have raised areas, and the frames always have the decorative molding that give these pieces such appeal. The pegs used were squarish, not perfectly round.

Country French armoires are made out of solid native woods, never veneer. The cornices were constructed of solid wood also, in contrast to English cornices which were always built up on a core of secondary wood. One of the exciting things about country French furniture was the use of panels of burl and figured woods in solid form, something rarely seen in English furniture (where burl was used only as veneer). Armoires and buffets with burl panels are relatively common, as are ones entirely constructed of burl wood. Another desirable feature for armoires and buffets is herringbone door panels.

Most country French armoires were inspired by the curvaceous Louis XV style. Even if they were made in 1830, they more than likely have curved moldings that show the influence of the rococo style. In country pieces, older styles were kept alive long after they had gone out of fashion in urban areas. Obviously, these armoires have rectilinear carcasses, not the curved form of Louis XV furniture. However, the influence of Louis XV can be seen in the curved crown moldings, the asymmetrically shaped door panels with curved moldings, hardware with swirling cutout designs, gracefully shaped aprons, and whorl feet. The *menuisiers* were a more conservative breed than the *ébénistes,* and this is clearly reflected in the anachronistic decoration of armoires.

So although an armoire may show Louis XV influences, we certainly cannot date it to 1750. In fact, armoires that we see on the American market are *rarely* that old; more often than not, they are nineteenth-century pieces. However, stylistic features can be helpful in dating a piece. We do know, at least, that a piece can be no older than the most recent stylistic element. So if an armoire has some Louis XV attributes but also some Empire motifs, we know the piece could not have been made before the Empire period. Pieces of provincial furniture often include motifs from more than one style period. The *buffet à deux corps* shown on page 212 is a good case in point, combining eighteenth- and nineteenth-century design motifs.

EXPECTED REPAIRS

Feet will often be replaced, as country furniture frequently sat on stone floors. When the floors were washed, the feet naturally got wet and rot set in. The interiors are rarely original and have been customized to suit today's uses. Crown moldings have sometimes been replaced, as these can be broken fairly easily. Look for a good fit between molding and carcass and for consistent oxidation patterns on the two pieces.

SIGNS OF AGE

The frame-and-panel construction should show signs of movement. You may be able to see this where the very edge of the panel goes into the frame. Since the entire piece was rubbed down with a finish only after completion, the part of the panel inside the frame should be unfinished. The panel should have shrunk, leaving a bit of the unfinished edge visible. On the sides of armoires, the panels may have been constructed of two or three boards held in the frame. You will often see gaps between the boards as they have moved due to shrinkage (Fig. 13-1).

It is common to see signs of worm damage, particularly if the piece is walnut. The evidence is little round holes about the size of a pin head (the exit holes of the worm). If you see tracks made by a

Fig. 13-1 Panel showing signs of age: visible unfinished edges and gaps between the boards.

worm burrowing through the wood, you are not looking at an original surface. This is a sign that the wood has been sanded down. If you see carving that shows worm tracks (not holes), again, this carving was added later after the worm had done its damage. The carving in Fig. 13-2 has exposed the worm tracks beneath the surface of the cornice. Worm-eaten wood would not have been used by a legitimate cabinetmaker.

Fig. 13-2 Later carving as indicated by worm tracks.

Solid burl elm, c. 1800, armoire with original crown molding, having unusual corner projections. Tipped feet. *Courtesy Whitehall at the Villa, Chapel Hill, N.C.* **$7,500–9,500.**

Chapeau gendarme two-door cherry wood armoire, c. 1780, with Louis XV and XVI stylistic elements. Central pilasters. Original brass hinges and escutcheons. Feet tipped. Some repairs to crown molding. This type is named for its bonnet, which is shaped like a French policeman's hat. *Courtesy Whitehall at the Villa, Chapel Hill, N.C.* **$6,500–8,500.**

"Rare" pair of eighteenth-century French provincial oak *bonnetiers,* each with single-paneled door on French feet. Originally one piece. *Courtesy Morton Goldberg Auction Galleries, New Orleans.* **$6,000–9,000.**

Late eighteenth-century Louis XV/XVI provincial oak armoire or *bibliotèque.* Molded cornice above a foliate vine-carved frieze over a pair of grilled doors centering a reserve carved with scrolling tendrils issuing foliage and flower heads, a scroll-carved apron below, raised on later scrolled feet. losses to cornice. 8' high x 4'9 1/2" wide. The grills are of a later date—this was originally an armoire. Glass and grills are often added; be aware of these potential changes. *Courtesy Butterfield & Butterfield, San Francisco.* **$8,000–12,000.**

Ash *bonnetier,* c. 1800, with a large, single-panel door, exposed brass over iron hinges, and typical ornate brass escutcheon. *Courtesy Whitehall at the Villa, Chapel Hill, N.C.* **$4,000–6,000.**

Eighteenth-century French provincial oak and walnut buffet à deux corps with arched molded cornice above a pair of cupboard doors openingn to shelves above a lower section fitted with two long drawers and a pair of cupboard doors with stained parquetry cartouches on short cabiole legs. A dymanite piece. One must, however, be drawn to ask a few questions (which cannot be answered except by a personal inspection): 1. Why is there a chevron design between the lower doors and fluting between the upper doors? 2. Why are the lower panels solid wood parquetry while the upper are plain? 3. Why are the hinges different in finial shape and in width of mounting rings from top to bottom? 4. Why are the escutcheons different top and bottom? The answers to these questions will tell you whether or not the piece was a marriage. 93" high × 56" wide × 27" deep. *Courtesy Christie's New York.* **$8,000–12,000** as a marriage.

Charles X burl elm *bonnetier,* c. 1830; simple, paneled design. Concealed pinned legs. *Courtesy Whitehall at the Villa, Chapel Hill, N.C.* **$4,000–6,000.**

French Empire *buffet à deux corps,* c. 1805–1810; columned corners, paneled central decoration, and a few Louis XV flourishes. Oak with a carved cherry central panel on top section. Brass grills added (originally had blind doors like the base). *Courtesy Whitehall at the Villa, Chapel Hill, N.C.* **$12,000–18,000.**

Note the vestiges of eighteenth-century design that endure on Empire piece shows in previous photograph.

Ash and elm country French *buffet à deux corps,* with a blind door, c. 1800–1830. Lightly carved top panel, scalloped apron. Cracks in doors are endemic to this design because the door panels were often set too tightly in the surrounds. Original hinges, replaced pulls. Three drawers. *Courtesy Whitehall at the Villa, Chapel Hill, N.C.* **$8,000–12,000.**

Late eighteenth-century French provincial buffet/ *vaisselier* with pedimented top section with four open shelves, each with plate brace. Lower half with rectangular top above two frieze drawers, over a pair of hinged cupboard doors, on square bracket feet. Original hinges. Possibly replaced escutcheons. Pulls on drawers are replaced. 79" high x 21" deep. *Courtesy Wolf's Fine Arts Auctioneers, Cleveland, Ohio.* **$8,000–12,000.**

Country French cherry hanging vaisselier, c. 1800–1820. Bottom board added (shelves originally sat on a buffet base). *Courtesy Whitehall at the Villa, Chapel Hill, N.C.* **$1,800–2,400.**

Mid nineteenth-century diminutive (about 6' high) painted (and repainted) French vaisselier. *Courtesy Whitehall at the Villa, Chapel Hill, N.C.* **$3,500–4,500.**

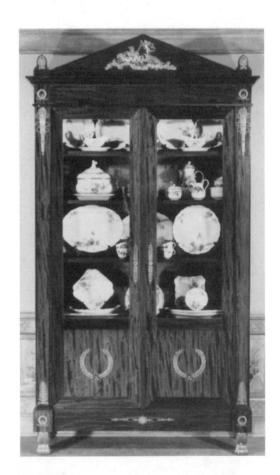

French Second Empire (c. 1850–1870), *biblioteque/ vitrine* for books or porcelains. Rich mahogany with spectacular bronze doré mounts and solid bronze doré feet. Triangular pediment. Laurel wreath, acanthus leaf, charioteer decorations, etc. *Courtesy Whitehall at the Villa, Chapel Hill, N.C.* **$15,000–25,000.**

Italian crimson-japanned and parcel-gilt corner cabinet, c. 1770. Bowed upper part enclosed by a triple panel glazed door beneath a carved shell cresting. Base enclosed by a paneled door, decorated overall with sprays of gilt foliage within broad gilt borders. On shallow bracket feet. Painting refreshed. 6'2" high × 26" wide. *Courtesy Butterfield & Butterfield, San Francisco.* **$8,000–12,000.**

Early twentieth-century French kingwood ormolu-mounted vitrine with rectangular marble top above hinged door with cartouche-shaped glazed panels with ormolu scroll borders. Sides similarly glazed, opening to mirrored interior, raised on square legs mounted with ormolu sabots. 62" high × 23" wide × 15" deep. *Courtesy Wolf's Fine Arts Auctioneers, Cleveland, Ohio.* **$6,000–9,000.**

Late nineteenth-/early twentieth-century Louis XV style lacquered vitrine cabinet. Serpentine front with one long door, with figures in a landscape decoration, opening to reveal shelves, mirrored back and silk-lined bottom shelf, the sides with drum-and-scroll decoration, overall multicolored floral and foliage design on the interior and exterior and bronze-ormolu mounts overall, raised on cabriole legs. One bronze mount impressed "PE Guerin. NY." 27" × 16" × 69" high. *Courtesy Frank H. Boos Gallery, Bloomfield Hills, Mich.* **$3,000–5,000.**

One of a pair of c. 1870 French bronze doré mounted rosewood parquetry *encoignure* (corner cabinet) with glazed upper and contoured lower doors. The bases are actually eighteenth century and the tops were added c. 1870 to create more useful display pieces. 82" high × 24" deep. *Courtesy Whitehall at the Villa, Chapel Hill, N.C.* **$15,000–25,000.**

Art Nouveau Marjorelle marquetry armoire, c. 1900: arched cornice over a mirrored door flanked by a cabinet door, open shelf and molded short drawers above a long drawer. 7'6" high × 4'3" high. *Courtesy Butterfield & Butterfield, Los Angeles.* **$4,000–6,000.** A suite with this armoire, plus a bed, nightstand, and dresser would sell for **$8,000–12,000.**

Renaissance-style carved oak cupboard, c. 1880. In two parts, the upper section with egg-and-dart and dentil-carved cornice above a deeply carved guilloche frieze; two paneled doors below flanked by scale-carved pilasters. The lower section with dentil-carved apron raised on fluted corinthian columns; paneled back above a platform shelf. Compressed ball feet. 7'6" high × 4'3" wide. Most Renaissance-style furniture was newly made from 1880 to 1930. However, some very interesting examples used period parts, especially wainsoting and paneling from churches, etc. On this example the doors and lower panels appear to be made from authentic wall paneling. *Courtesy Butterfield & Butterfield, Los Angeles.* **$4,000–6,000.**

Flemish baroque inlaid walnut cabinet-on-stand, c. 1730–1750. Stepped rectangular pediment fitted with drawers and topped with turned finials. Above a pair of cabinet doors inlaid with coats of arms and crowned rampant lions wielding swords, enclosing an interior fitted with central prospect door flanked by columns and small drawers. Out-stepped long drawer below. Stand with inlaid frieze drawer and molded edge on ball-turned baluster-form supports joined by curving X-form stretcher on compressed-ball feet. 5'4 1/2" high × 34 1/2" wide. *Courtesy Butterfield & Butterfield, Los Angeles.* **$8,000–12,000.**

Italian Renaissance style walnut two-part *credenza*, c. 1865–1885. Molded, carved cornice over two wrought-iron grill doors and two small drawers. Base with frieze drawer over two cabinet doors. Paw feet. Acanthus and figural carving. 67" high × 33 1/2" wide × 15" deep. *Courtesy Skinner, Inc., Boston, Mass.* **$4,000–6,000.**

Austrian baroque walnut inlaid *schrank*. Top with rectangular canted cornice and inlaid frieze, above two inlaid doors over a molded base. With bun feet, etched steel escutcheons, hinges, and keys. Some shrinkage. 80" high × 65" wide × 22 1/2" deep. *Courtesy Skinner, Inc., Boston, Mass.* **$6,000–8,000.**

14

Unusual Forms and Eccentric Pieces

Included here are mirrors, beds, and a few other interesting items. Mirrors were a specialty of the Venetians, who began making them in the early fourteenth century and who monopolized the mirror trade until the eighteenth century. Venice was known for its production of glass, but it also had a specially trained group of artisans to make mirrors. This group of artisans lived on the island of Murano, where their methods were carefully guarded secrets. Venetian mirrors with glass-and-mirror frames are especially coveted on today's market.

Aside from Venetian mirrors, the rococo period produced many remarkable mirrors with gessoed frames formed in extravagant undulating curves. In France during this period, mirrors were often designed as part of the overall wall paneling. Not just an afterthought or a decorative touch, the full effect of the room was dependent upon their proper placement. An often-found combination in France and Italy was the console table with pier mirror above. These formal pieces frequently boasted the most elaborate and fanciful rococo carving.

The French produced a great variety of beds, many of which we still find on the market today. The most common form was known to the French as the *lit à la Française* (French bed). It was a four-poster bed with headboard, footboard, and a canopy of a size equal to the bed. The *lit à la Polonaise* also had a canopy, but it was supported on iron uprights and was smaller than the bed itself. During the Napoleonic era, a new bed form was introduced, and it is considered highly desirable today. The *lit en gondole* or *lit bateau* has a boatlike shape, with head and footboard equally balanced and the crest rails of each curving gracefully over and outward. The headboard and footboard are joined by side rails that attach high on the ends and scoop down in the middle, so the sleeper has a feeling of being enclosed somewhat by the side rails. The side rails provide a sweep of beautiful wood which is often accented with bronze mounts. The *lit bateau* can be found scaled down for use as a daybed. Besides being distinguished by their small size, daybeds never have canopies. The *lit d'alcove,* another variety of daybed, was placed in an alcove against a wall, and thus decorated on one side only.

Continental rococo gilt wood wall mirror, eighteenth century; the crest carved with scrolling flourishes, rocaillerie, and acanthus leaves. 42 1/2" × 33 1/2". *Courtesy Grogan & Company, Boston.* **$3,000–4,500.**

Italian c. 1720 baroque gilt wood and gesso mirror. Rectangular mirror plate within a scrolling foliate-carved frame with mirrored reserves headed by an arched foliate and rocaille-carved crest fronting mirrored reserves. Losses to gilt and gesso, creacks to some reserves. 6' high × 41" wide. *Courtesy Butterfield & Butterfield.* **$12,000–18,000.**

Late nineteenth- to early twentieth century Venetian rococo-style molded and etched glass mirror. Arched crest with leaf-cast cartouche and etched mono-grammed reserve above an elongated octagonal frame and conforming beveled mirror plate, with etched foliate-and-scroll reserves flanked by ribbon-and-flower-head divides above a scroll-and-floral cast cartouche. 6'4" high × 42" wide. *Courtesy Butterfield & Butterfield, Los Angeles.* **$4,000–6,000.**

Late nineteenth-century Continental baroque-style carved walnut mirror. Rectangular mirror plate within a leaf-tip-carved inner border, contained within an elaborate foliate-scroll-carved frame. 5'11" high × 41" wide. *Courtesy Butterfield & Butterfield, Los Angeles.* **$4,000–6,000.**

Louis XVI revival ormolu-mounted mahogany bedstead, c. 1900. 6" wide. *Courtesy Morton Goldberg Auction Galleries, New Orleans.* **$1,500–2,500.**

Late eighteenth-century Louis XVI painted and parcel-gilt *trumeau* (mirror with painting above in one frame). Vertical plate within beaded and husk-carved borders beneath a ribbon-tied trophy, surmounted by a painted arched oil-on-canvas panel of a female goat herd with her flock in a mountain landscape, the broad paneled stiles carved in the upper and lower corners with ribbon-tied pendant foliate and neoclasical two-handled urns respectively, painted pale green. 6'6 1/2" high × 3'7" wide. *Courtesy Butterfield & Butterfield, San Fransisco.* **$5,000–8,000.**

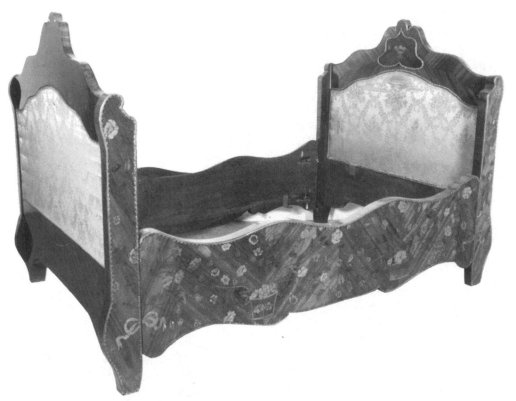

Napoleon III kingwood and marquetry *lit du jour,* c. 1880. Note the exterior of the ends is less decorated as the bed was placed in an alcove with the ends hidden. *Courtesy Morton Goldberg Auction Galleries, New Orleans.* **$2,500–3,500.**

Late eighteenth-century Louis XVI painted *lit d'alcove.* Padded head and footboard with scrolling foliate and rosette carving. Raised on fluted tapering legs, painted white, and upholstered in white silk. 77" long. *Courtesy Grogan & Company, Boston.* **$3,500–5,500.**

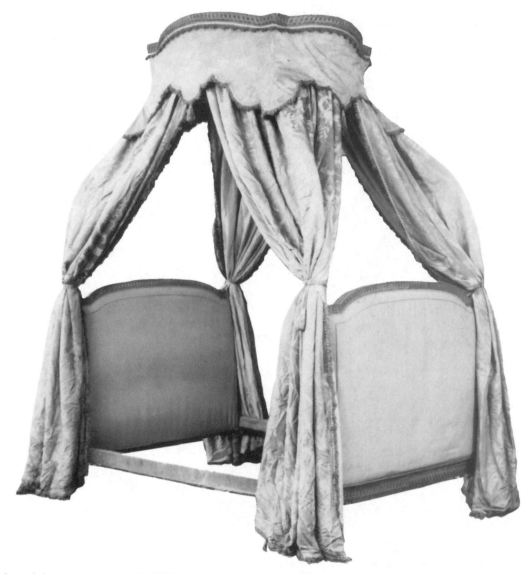

Late eighteenth-century Louis XVI *lit à la Polonaise.* Head and foot with scroll carving and celadon upholstery, raised on fluted tapering legs; with curved iron supports concealed by fringed celadon brocade draperies. 84" long × 57" wide. *Courtesy Grogan & Company, Boston.* **$7,000–10,000.**

Italian late-neoclassical walnut sleight bed with ebonized applied decoration. c. 1830. 47" high × 53" wide × 69" long. *Courtesy Skinner, Inc., Boston, Mass.* **$2,000–3,000.**

French painted four-fold screen, nineteenth century. Decorated to simulate an eighteenth-century "print room," applied with hand-colored engravings depicting views of Paris and other eighteenth-century world capitals within painted faux frames and all on green-striped faux wallpaper. 69" high × 19" wide (each panel). *Courtesy Grogan & Company, Boston.* **$5,000–8,000.**

BIBLIOGRAPHY

Bizot, Chantal. *Mobilier Directoire, Empire.* Paris: Editions Charles Massin (n.d.)

———. *Mobilier Restauration.* Paris: Editions Charles Massin (n.d.)

Burckhardt, Monica. *Mobilier Louis XVI.* Paris: Editions Charles Massin (n.d.)

Cescinsky, Herbert. *The Gentle Art of Faking Furniture.* New York: Dover Publications, 1967.

Chippendale, Thomas. *The Gentleman and Cabinet-Maker's Director* (3rd edition, 1762). New York: Dover Publications, 1966.

Edwards, Ralph and Percy Macquoid. *The Dictionary of English Furniture.* Country Life Ltd., 1924–1927 (three volumes). Revised, 1954. Reissued by Barra Books, 1983.

English Chairs. Victoria and Albert Museum Publications. London: Her Majesty's Stationery Office, 1970.

* Feild, Rachel. *Macdonald Guide to Buying Antique Furniture.* London: Macdonald & Co., 1986; Radnor, Pa.: Wallace-Homestead, 1989.

Gilbert, Christopher. *The Life and World of Thomas Chippendale.* New York: Tabard Press, 1978.

* Hayward, Charles H. *Antique or Fake? The Making of Old Furniture.* New York: Van Nostrand Reinhold Company, 1970.

Hepplewhite, George. *The Cabinet-Maker and Upholsterer's Guide* (3rd edition, 1794). New York: Dover Publications, 1969.

Honour, Hugh. *Cabinet Makers and Furniture Designers.* London and New York: Spring Books, 1969.

Jourdain, Margaret and F. Rose. *English Furniture: The Georgian Period (1750–1830).* London: B. T. Batsford, 1953.

* Macquoid, Percy. *A History of English Furniture.* Four volumes. 1904–1908. Reissued in two volumes. Woodbridge, Suffolk: Antique Collectors' Club, 1987.

Mannoni, Edith and Chantal Bizot. *Mobilier 1900–1925.* Paris: Editions Charles Massin (n.d.)

* Massin, Charles. A series of books on all periods of French furniture from the eighteenth to the twentieth centuries. Published in Paris by Editions Charles Massin.

* Mitford, Nancy. *The Sun King, Louis XIV at Versailles.* New York: Harper & Row, 1966.

* Musgrave, Clifford. *Adam and Hepplewhite and Other Neoclassical Furniture.* New York: Taplinger, 1966.

———. *Regency Furniture.* Glascow: MacLehose and Co., 1961.

Oliver, Lucile. *Reconnaitre Les Styles Regionaux.* Paris: Editions Charles Massin (n.d.)

Praz, Mario. *An Illustrated History of Furnishing.* New York: Thames and Hudson, 1964, 1982.

Sheraton, Thomas. *The Cabinet-Maker and Upholsterer's Drawing-Book.* New York: Dover Publications, (reprint) 1972.

Smith, Nancy. *Old Furniture: Understanding the Craftsman's Art.* New York: Dover Publications, 1990.

* Stone, Dominic R. *The Art of Biedermeier, Viennese Art and Design—1815–1845.* Seacaucus, NJ: Chartwell Books, Inc., 1990.

Symonds, R. W. *Furniture Making in Seventeenth and Eighteenth Century England.* London: Connoisseur, 1955.

———. *The Present State of Old English Furniture.* London: Duckworth, 1921.

Tardieu-Dumont. *Le Mobilier Regional Francais: Normandie.* Paris: Berger-Levrault, 1980.

* Verlet, Pierre. *French Furniture of the Eighteenth Century,* translated by Penelope Hunter-Stiebel. Charlottesville, Virginia: University of Virginia Press, 1991.

* Viaux, Jacqueline. *French Furniture,* translated by Hazel Paget. New York: G. P. Putnam's Sons, 1964.

---

* Denotes books particularly useful when studying furniture periods and styles.

CONTRIBUTING AUCTION HOUSES AND DEALERS

Frank H. Boos Gallery
420 Enterprise Court
Bloomfield Hills, MI 48301
(313) 332-1500

Rita Bucheit, Ltd.
449 North Wells St.
Chicago, IL 60610
(312) 527-4080

Butterfield & Butterfield
220 San Bruno Ave.
San Francisco, CA 94103
(415) 861-7500

Leighton Adair Butts
1900 Carolina Dr.
Tryon, NC 28782
(704) 856-6849

Christie's
New York, NY 10022

Dunning's Auction Service, Inc.
755 Church Rd.
Elgin, IL 60123
(708) 741-3483

Freeman/Fine Arts
1808-10 Chestnut St.
Philadelphia, PA 19103
(215) 563-9275

Morton Goldberg Auction Galleries
New Orleans, LA 70113

Grogan & Company
890 Commonwealth Ave.
Boston, MA 02215
(617) 566-4100

Leslie Hindman Auctioneers
Chicago, IL 60610

James D. Julia, Inc.
Route 201, Showhegan Rd.
Fairfield, ME 04937
(207) 453-7125

Queen's Quest, Inc.
Edenton, NC 27932

Skinner, Inc.
Auctioneers and Appraisers of Antiques
    and Fine Art
63 Park Plaza
Boston, MA 02116
(617) 350-5400

Sotheby's
1334 York Ave.
New York, NY 10021
(212) 606-7000

Weschler's
909 E. Street NW
Washington, DC 20004
(202) 628-1281

Whitehall at the Villa
David Lindquist; Elizabeth Lindquist
    Mann
1213 E. Franklin St.
Chapel Hill, NC 27514
(919) 942-3179

Wolf's Fine Arts Auctioneers
1239 West 6th St.
Cleveland, OH 44113
(216) 575-9653

INDEX

COLONIAL REVIVAL

FURNITURE

WITH PRICES

CONTENTS

ACKNOWLEDGMENTS

A book of this scope would be impossible without the help of many people. We would like especially to thank all of the auction houses and antiques dealers who generously loaned us photographs. Our thanks go to Marisa Capaldi of Frank H. Boos Gallery, Bloomfield Hills, Michigan; Rita Bucheit, Ltd. of Chicago; Pamela Tapp at Butterfield & Butterfield of Los Angeles and San Francisco; Leighton Adair Butts of Tryon, North Carolina; Mary Lou Strallindorf at Christie's of New York City; Barbara Clare of Edenton, North Carolina; Dunning's Auction Service, Inc. of Elgin, Illinois; Leslie Lynch Clinton at Freeman/Fine Arts of Philadelphia; Morton Goldberg Auction Galleries of New Orleans; Grace Yeomans at Grogan & Company of Boston; Whitney McCune at Leslie Hindman Auctioneers of Chicago; Clarence Pico at Litchfield Auction Gallery of Litchfield, Connecticut; James D. Julia, Inc. of Fairfield, Maine; Cynthia Tashjian and Ann Trodella at Skinner, Inc. of Boston; Sotheby's of New York City; Weschler's of Washington, D.C.; and Wolf's Fine Arts Auctioneers of Cleveland, Ohio.

We are grateful to the Sloan Art Library at the University of North Carolina at Chapel Hill for the use of their fine collection of materials about the decorative arts and the history of furniture.

Finally, we would like to thank the editors at Wallace-Homestead for their patience and suggestions for improving the book and this series.

Introduction and State of the Market

*C*olonial Revival in the context of this book is furniture made in America between 1870 and 1940 that copies seventeenth- and eighteenth-century American styles. These styles include Jacobean, William and Mary, Queen Anne, Chippendale, Hepplewhite, Sheraton, and American Empire. One may rightly protest that not all of these styles were Colonial. However, around the turn of the century, when so much Colonial Revival furniture was made, the label "Colonial" was frequently applied to Empire-style reproductions and, indeed, to all the other original styles as well. The term "Colonial" has been used loosely since the time it was coined and we use it just as freely here as the Colonial Revivalists did. Although Colonial-style reproductions are still being made today, we chose to end our coverage at 1940. The creativity of the Colonial Revival movement had reached its peak during the 1920s, and the 1930s saw few new developments in terms of style. In the 1930s Colonial Revival furniture became more predictable, often copying specific museum pieces. There were larger numbers of accurate reproductions, but the interesting developments in Colonial Revival furniture had faded by the beginning of World War II.

This ground-breaking book will be of interest to collectors not only for the compilation of photographs of the seemingly infinite variety of Colonial Revival pieces found on the market today by also for the prices attached to these pieces. Colonial Revival furniture is in the process of undergoing a rapid expansion in the antiques and decorative arts markets in the United States as it moves from flea markets, mall shows, and group or mall shops into respected antiques and decorative arts shops. Colonial Revival pieces are turning up in auctions, including the major houses in New York. Almost every major auction contains numerous examples of Colonial Revival furniture. In addition, the number of specialists in the field is increasing, and they are concentrating their time and effort on just a few Colonial Revival furniture makers. Furthermore, we see specialists developing. One example is Michael Ivankovich, who has made a name for himself writing about and selling the work of Wallace Nutting's shop. Another is Nadeau's Auction Gallery in Windsor, Connecticut, which has annual sales featuring the work of the Nathan Margolis Shop, the work of Abraham Fineberg, and other fine shops in the Hartford, Connecticut, area from the 1920s on. Along with this mobility, of course, has come a rapid increase in value. As these pieces have become more respectable in the collecting/decorating scheme, prices have escalated.

Two qualities must be present in a Colonial Revival piece in order for it to increase rapidly in value. First, it must copy a difficult-to-find genuine period antique. Second, to reach the highest levels of value, the piece must be faithful to the original design, and it must copy designs of the finest quality from the eighteenth and early nineteenth centuries. Perfect supporting examples are found the sections on Colonial Revival dining chairs. The reader will immediately notice striking differences in price. Those differences are clearly attributable to the rarity of authentic antiques upon which these pieces are based, as well as to the high quality of the copies. For dining tables, too, we see a considerable increase in value. Fine antique banquet tables are rarely found on the market today, and when they are found, they are excruciatingly expensive. And again, only the very finest examples of chairs or tables command the highest prices on today's market.

Since the first edition of this book the most staggering price jumps have involved sets of dining chairs. It is not at all unusual to encounter fine sets of 12 dining chairs priced from $36,000 to $75,000! These prices reflect the staggering prices for period sets and the equally staggering prices for fine new reproductions from companies such as Bakov and Kindel.

It seems clear that there is a high level of sophistication among both buyers and purveyors of Colonial Revival furniture. Collectors and dealers focus on faithfulness to style, quality of materials used, rarity of the originals, and the makers and their reputations both at the time of manufacture and over the decades. This latter point is extremely important because it documents the likely longevity of pieces. Pieces made to exacting standard of quality in solid wood; or of heavy, thick veneers are proving to have great durability. Collectors and dealers know the companies whose merchandise from this era has survived in fine condition. Such large companies as Paine Furniture Company of Boston, small companies such as Sypher & Company of New York City, or cabinet makers such as Potthast Brothers of Baltimore come readily to mind as highly collected makers of fine-quality pieces.

The expansion of the Colonial Revival market is nothing short of staggering. In twenty years we have seen a considerable expansion of interest in the market into what is clearly twentieth-century-manufactured Colonial Revival furniture. These pieces, which were until recently found only in yard sales, house sales, or mall shows, are now found in nearly every antiques and decorative arts shop in cities and towns across America.

This guide provides many keys to evaluating the pieces that are so changing the face of the antiques shops of America. We hope you enjoy using it.

PART I

History of Colonial Revival Furniture

1

Construction Techniques

Because Colonial Revival furniture attempts to copy the design of seventeenth- and eighteenth-century American furniture, the collector must understand first and foremost how to tell the difference between an original period piece and the nineteenth- or twentieth-century copy it inspired. In many cases, just a glance or a casual inspection will tell you that the style is not authentic and that the proportions do not replicate the original. The collector new to Colonial Revival furniture should also know something about the construction techniques of each period. We will not attempt an exhaustive discussion of construction techniques here since they have been covered so thoroughly in other books.[1] We do, however, want to provide you with some basic information that you will need as you become more familiar with Colonial Revival furniture.

In this brief guide to construction techniques, we will not discuss seventeenth-century construction apart from eighteenth-century methods. The fact is that most seventeenth-century American pieces are in museums and private collections. You will seldom find on the market a Jacobean or William and Mary piece that was made in America that is not a later

reproduction. When you do see seventeenth-century-style pieces, you *must* find real signs of age—shrinkage, warping of boards, patina, hand-saw marks, mortise and tenon joints, and the like—before even considering that it might be a period piece. Of course, when looking at seventeenth-century-style pieces, it is imperative to know seventeenth-century forms. William and Mary coffee tables, for example, were not made until the 1920s.

A piece of Colonial Revival furniture is often easy to spot because it does not copy an earlier style accurately. Sometimes one Colonial Revival piece will even combine elements from several different style periods. Proportions tend to be irregular on Colonial Revival pieces, sometimes because the maker was not familiar with earlier designs, but just as often the reason is that the piece was made to accommodate modern ceiling heights and room sizes. Colonial Revival desks are smaller; highboys and secretaries are shorter. Colonial Revival chairs, on the other hand, are often taller and narrower than eighteenth-century chairs. Colonial Revival Chippendale-style chairs seldom capture the feeling of the substantial weight found in the originals.

The differences in the tools used to

---

1. Particularly good is Nancy A. Smith's *Old Furniture: Understanding the Craftsman's Art* (New York: Dover Publications, 1990).

construct and refine furniture are also important to know. The main difference between the hand tools used in the seventeenth and eighteenth centuries and the machine tools used in the nineteenth and twentieth centuries is that the marks left by machine tools are perfectly regular, whereas the marks of hand tools are not. You will find the marks left by various saws on areas of furniture that were not meant to be seen—on the undersides of skirt aprons, on the backs of case pieces, or underneath seat rails, for example.

Figure 1–1 shows the marks left by an eighteenth-century bow saw. You will notice that the up-and-down marks are not perfectly parallel. These marks are typical of uneven hand sawing. Figure 1–2 shows the easily identifiable, sweeping marks created by a circular saw, which was not used in America until about 1830. Figure 1–3 shows band-saw marks, which are even and parallel. You will find this perfect regularity, a telltale sign of machine work, on late nineteenth- and twentieth-century furniture.

In figure 1–4, we turned over a c. 1890 Colonial Revival Chippendale-style chair to check for machine-made marks. Although the chair might confuse the novice because of its relatively good design, underneath the seat rail we found visible machine saw marks, a sure sign of a late nineteenth-century reproduction. Circular-saw marks are visible on the seat rail and band-saw marks are noticeable under the applied shell.

The underside of legs is another good place to look for saw marks. In figure 1–5 we examined a c. 1900 Colonial Revival

Fig. 1-1 Bow-saw marks.

Fig. 1-2 Circular-saw marks.

Fig. 1-3 Band-saw marks.

tea table for saw marks and found band-saw marks, which designate the table as a turn-of-the-century reproduction.

Figure 1–6 shows bow-saw marks on the inside of the apron on an eighteenth-century lowboy. The irregular marks are a clear sign of handwork. On the back of a drawer, we see the furrows or troughs of the hand plane that have worn and softened with time (figure 1–7).

Another aspect of furniture construction that helps us date a piece is the method of joinery, especially on case pieces. When you examine a case piece, always look at the dovetails on the drawers to see if they are handmade. Of course, small shops even in the twentieth century still make dovetails by hand. But even

these dovetails will not be as fine as an eighteenth-century handmade dovetail. Figure 1–8 shows fine handmade dovetails on an eighteenth-century secretary drawer. Note how small the dovetails are, how sharp the angles are, and that the spacing is not perfectly regular. Finally, note the dovetails on the c. 1930 sewing table in figure 1–9, which are obviously machine-made.

To determine the age of Colonial Revival chairs, here are several tips you will find helpful. If you look at the back of a good eighteenth-century chair, you will see that the outline of the splat has been "silhouetted" (figure 1–10). The edge of the design has been beveled so that it is thicker in front than in back. The purpose

Fig. 1-4 Underside of a c. 1890 Colonial Revival Chippendale-style seat rail showing circular-saw marks on the rail and band-saw marks on the underside of the scalloped shell.

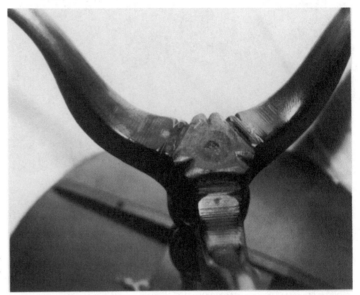

Fig. 1-5 Underside of a c. 1900 Colonial Revival tea table showing bandsaw marks on underside of legs.

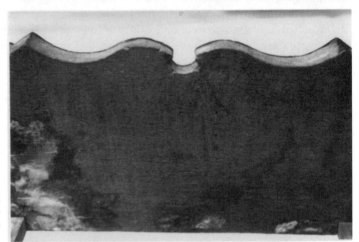

Fig. 1-6 Underside of the shaped apron on an eighteenth-century lowboy. Note the irregular marks of the bow-saw.

Fig. 1-7 Random hand-planing marks on the back of a drawer.

Fig. 1-9 Machine-made dovetails from the drawer of a c. 1930 Colonial Revival sewing table. The dovetails are small, perfectly regular, and not sharply angled.

Fig. 1-10 Back of an eighteenth-century chair showing silhouetting (or chamfering) of the splat.

of silhouetting is to maintain crisp design definition when viewed from an angle. On a chair without silhouetting, the splat will look muddy or fuzzy when viewed from an angle. Silhouetting was one extra step that the furniture maker took in making a fine eighteenth-century chair, and it was the sort of step that was omitted when making machine copies in the late nineteenth and early twentieth centuries. You

will not find silhouetting on Colonial Revival chairs (see figure 1–11).

Still looking at the back of the chair, notice how the splat is attached to the shoe. As a rule, the shoe on an eighteenth-century chair will be separate from the seat rail. Look closely at the eighteenth-century chair in figure 1–12 and you will see the separate shoe. The Colonial Revival chair in figure 1–13 has an integral

Fig. 1-11 Back of a c. 1910 Colonial Revival Chippendale-style chair showing no silhouetting of the splat.

Fig. 1-12 Back of an eighteenth-century chair showing the two-part shoe.

Fig. 1-13 Back of a c. 1890 Colonial Revival chair showing an integral (one-piece) shoe.

shoe, in which the shoe and the seat rail are in one piece. This is another step that was omitted in the process of making a chair after the eighteenth century.

Next, look at the chair to see how the stretchers were joined together. Furniture makers in the eighteenth century used the mortise-and-tenon method for joining stretchers to legs. To do this by hand required great precision, and the stretcher was lined up flush with the edge of the leg to make measuring and cutting easier. The tenon was simply inserted into the mortise, a little glue was used, sometimes a peg was added (perhaps later for more strength), and that was it. In the late nineteenth century these same joints would have been produced by machine, and the stretchers will be positioned in the center of the legs rather than flush with the edge.

Figure 1–14 shows a centered stretcher on a Colonial Revival chair. Often dowels were used on Colonial Revival pieces instead of the mortise-and-tenon joint. Figure 1–15 shows a dowel joint on a Colonial Revival chair. This type of joint is not

Fig. 1-14 Centered stretcher on a c. 1890 Colonial Revival chair.

Fig. 1-15 Use of a dowel on a c. 1915 Colonial Revival chair.

as strong as the mortise-and-tenon joint, but it is simpler to implement. A dowel joint is made simply by cutting two round holes—one in the stretcher and one in the leg—and then inserting the round dowel in each hole. You can sometimes see the dowel if the joint is a little loose. You will see light through the joint, since the dowel itself is not as thick as the pieces it joins. These joints tend to loosen more easily than do mortise-and-tenon joints. Figure 1–16 shows a double dowel joint, used for extra strength, on a Colonial Revival tea table.

Weight is a dead giveaway when trying to determine the age of a piece of furniture, especially if the piece is made of mahogany. Eighteenth-century Santo Domingo mahogany is dense and heavy. If you have ever had to move eighteenth-century furniture, you know that! In contrast, a Colonial Revival chair that may have a good Chippendale look will be much lighter in weight. Why is this? The supply of Santo Domingo, Cuban, and Honduran mahogany began to diminish after 1800 and furniture makers had to turn to other geographic locations, such as South America and the Philippines, for

Fig. 1-16 Double dowel joint on a c. 1900 Colonial Revival tea table.

stock. The wood from each of these areas has its own characteristics. Cuban mahogany is very strong, and African mahogany has a finer texture than the wood from Mexico and the Philippines. All of these woods, however, are lighter in weight than Santo Domingo mahogany.

Not only is the wood lighter in Colonial Revival furniture, but boards were not as wide as those used in the eighteenth century. Often, an eighteenth-century tilt-top table will have a top made of only one board—or no more than two. If a table top has been made from a board less than 20″ wide, that's a good sign that it is not an eighteenth-century piece. Nineteenth-century boards tend to be thinner, as, of course, does veneer. In fact, in furniture made in the 1920s through the 1940s, you will find plywood used in drawer bottom and for the backs of case pieces.

Another thing you must know about wood is that, as it ages, it shrinks across the grain. In other words, a round table top from the eighteenth century will simply not be perfectly round today. You may not be able to see the shrinkage with the naked eye, but get out your ruler and the numbers will tell the tale. You will not find this kind of shrinkage on a Colonial Revival piece from the 1920s or 1930s, or even on a piece from the 1880s or 1890s.

Carving will tell you a great deal about the age of a piece of furniture. After you have examined many eighteenth-century pieces, as well as Colonial Revival ones, you will be able to recognize that later carving is flatter, neither as deep nor as detailed (see figure 1–17). Ball-and-claw feet will display these same characteristics. Genuine eighteenth-century American feet have strength and vitality, whereas Colonial Revival examples from the early twentieth century are more stiffly schematic, lacking the energy and grace of the originals. Some carving styles, like the roundel on the Colonial Revival lowboy in figure 1–18, are borrowed from late nineteenth-century carving styles, not from the eighteenth century.

Fig. 1-17 Hand-carved drawer front from a c. 1920 Colonial Revival highboy. The carving, though by hand is flat and stiff, with very little undercutting, cruder than eighteenth-century carving.

Fig. 1-18 Applied roundel on a c. 1880-1900 Colonial Revival lowboy, a machine-made ornament often used on Renaissance Revival and Eastlake furniture. A roundel on a Chippendale-style piece is a clear sign of Colonial Revival decoration.

When looking at fluted or reeded carving, you can determine if it was machine-made by its perfect regularity. On handmade carving you will notice slight imperfections and irregularities. Again, this is something you will learn to recognize once you have spent time looking at actual examples.

In addition to design and construction materials and techniques, you will notice the difference in the kinds of nails and screws used in the eighteenth century as opposed to the late nineteenth and early twentieth century. This is a specialized area of study, but we can suggest a few rules. From about 1815 to 1890, machine-cut or square nails were used, and they have square heads. After 1890 you will find wire nails with round heads: this is what you will find on Colonial Revival furniture. The slots in the heads of early screws are off-center because they were made by hand. Machine-made screws will have perfectly centered slots.

Hardware offers easier clues to dating a piece. Rarely will you find original brasses even on eighteenth-century pieces because they do wear out, so this point is almost academic. On Colonial Revival pieces, the brasses have been stamped rather than cast. In the second half of the nineteenth century, they were stamped by hand, and in the twentieth century they are machine-stamped. You will see little wear or patina on Colonial Revival brasses.

This basic discussion of construction techniques will get you started as you examine Colonial Revival furniture. Learning to distinguish Colonial Revival furniture from original period antiques involves studying the history of American furniture design, along with plenty of hands-on experience with antiques, in order to become familiar with the true signs of age.

2

Colonial Revival Furniture
before 1900

mportant and informative articles
have been published on the Colonial
Revival movement, and we will syn-
thesize information from these sources
here as it applies to furniture. Late nineteenth-century trade catalogues, manuscripts, and contemporary accounts of
nineteenth century exhibitions and fairs
that sometimes featured antiques have all
been used as source material for this history.

One of the subjects we explored in
doing our research for this book was the
misleading term "Centennial," which is
often applied to early Colonial Revival
furniture. Antiques dealers, auctioneers,
and collectors often use the term to add
cachet to a Colonial Revival piece. "Centennial," used loosely at best, carries the
connotation of a good-quality piece from
around the time of the United States Centennial, the year 1876, that makes attractive use of eighteenth-century American
design elements. The use of this term
might lead one to think that Colonial designs were popular at the Centennial Exhibition, held in Philadelphia. This is
simply not true, however. Rodris Roth
and Kenneth Ames have shown that practically no Colonial-style furniture was on
display at the Centennial Exhibition.
What was marketed at the Centennial was
Renaissance Revival, Rococo Revival,
Eastlake, Neo-Grec (a term used in the

1870s to describe a subset of Renaissance
Revival style which incorporated Egyptian and Greek motifs in a somewhat fanciful way), and patent furniture. It would
be more accurate to call these styles "Centennial" than to apply that term to Colonial Revival furniture.

Why not abandon the label "Centennial" altogether? We suspect that dealers
and collectors like the term because it sig-
nifies the beginnings of the movement,
and of course everyone tends to think the
earlier, the better. But with Colonial Revival furniture, *earlier* is not necessarily
better. The best pieces produced throughout the Colonial Revival period tended to
be made in small shops by workers who
either had access to originals to study and
copy or who had benefited from some of
the scholarship on American antiques
published during the 1890s. A few small
shops were making fairly faithful copies
of Colonial designs in the 1880s and
1890s: for example, Meier and Hagen as
well as Sypher & Company of New York
City, and Potthast Brothers in Baltimore.
However, small shops were also making
good handmade reproductions in the
1920s and 1930s, such as Margolis of
Hartford, Connecticut, and Wallace Nutting of Framingham, Massachusetts. Soon
after the Centennial some inaccurate (read
ugly) Colonial designs were also being
sold. Paine Furniture Company of Boston,

Wanamaker's of Philadelphia, and several Grand Rapids, Michigan, companies produced more than a few hideous pieces. So, simply because a piece was made near the time of the Centennial Exhibition is no guarantee of quality. Rather than an early date, what you want to look for is (1) good design, (2) good materials, and (3) high-quality workmanship. We can find all these elements in the 1880s and also in the 1920s and 1930s.

In the middle of the nineteenth century, the popular furniture styles in America were Renaissance Revival, Rococo Revival, and Eastlake. At the same time, a small segment of the population began to take an interest in antique furniture. This interest first manifested itself in *collecting* and reclaiming family heirlooms from the attic or barn—or in coercing unsophisticated neighbors to give up an old table or two from their garage. Only as antiques became more popular did reproductions begin to appear in order to meet public demand for the tastes of the past.

Christopher Monkhouse and Thomas Michie have documented the earliest beginnings of the Colonial Revival movement, evident in the nation's first local bicentennial celebrations. Plymouth, Massachusetts, had its Bicentennial in 1820, and Providence, Rhode Island followed in 1836.[1] In the 1840s antiques were the rage in towns or cities such as Providence and to a lesser extent, Boston. Then, as ever, it was common to exaggerate the merits of the provenance of a piece. An article from a Providence newspaper from the 1840s mocked the huge quantities of furniture reportedly brought over on the Mayflower.[2] Even as early as the 1840s, reproductions were being made, but the evidence suggests that the

numbers were far smaller than those later produced in the 1880s and after. In the 1840s Daniel Wadsworth had copies made of a seventeenth-century chair to give to the Connecticut Historical Society and the Wadsworth Atheneum. The copies were made by Smith Ely of New York City, and one chair is now at Pendleton House in Providence.[3] These were early signs of the movement that would be felt strongly in the rest of the country around the time of the nation's Centennial, held in Philadelphia in 1876. Providence and Boston were ahead of their time in celebrating the past.

Turning to the past became a theme in other fine and decorative arts as well and in literature, too. Nathaniel Hawthorne used a seventeenth-century New England chair as the focus for his historical narrative about Puritan New England, *Grandfather's Chair,* published in 1841. In 1843, Henry Wadsworth Longfellow published his poem "The Old Clock on the Stairs," which featured what was called in the eighteenth century a long-case clock. Subsequently it came to be known as a grandfather clock. In 1868 the artist Edward Lamson Henry used the same title as Longfellow's poem for one of his paintings. The painting was displayed at the Centennial Exhibition and undoubtedly increased the demand for the grandfather clock, which became an essential piece of furniture in a Colonial Revival home.[4]

One kind of celebration that put antiques before the general public was the Colonial Kitchen exhibit, which was a part of fund-raising fairs for the U.S. Sanitary Commission, a precursor of the Red Cross, for the Union army. Colonial Kitchens were part of the Sanitary Fairs at

---

1. Christopher P. Monkhouse and Thomas S. Michie, *American Furniture in Pendleton House* (Providence: Museum of Art, Rhode Island School of Design, 1986, 188.

2. Ibid., 10.

3. Ibid., 188–89.

4. Ibid., 11, 13, 15.

Brooklyn, Poughkeepsie, New York City, Saint Louis, Philadelphia, and Indianapolis during the Civil War. Women organized sanitary fairs featuring Colonial kitchens furnished with antique furniture. Meals were served by costumed waitresses serving Colonial fare.[5] Most kitchens included candlesticks on the mantel, a gun over the mantel, a tall clock, often a cupboard, table, chairs, and spinning wheels. These often were antiques, and sometimes there was even a "Mayflower" relic. An advertisement for the Colonial Kitchen at the 1864 Poughkeepsie Fair described it as follows: "Completely furnished as in that olden time, and the House-keeping carried on by Ladies in Costume, such as our great-grandmothers wore. Flax and wool spinning wheels in operation. Tea in the ancient style every evening from 5 to 10 o'clock."[6]

By the 1870s "antiquing" was gaining in popularity. In the 1870s *Harper's New Monthly Magazine* published many articles about the country's early days and ran features on the Colonial towns of Cape Cod, commenting on the popular pursuit of antiques.[7] When Irving Whitall Lyon published his ground-breaking book, *The Colonial Furniture of New England,* in 1891, he explained that he began collecting furniture in 1877 around Hartford, Connecticut, and that many others were doing the same.

The Centennial Exhibition of 1876

At the time of the Centennial Exhibition in 1876, New Englanders certainly had cultivated an interest in antiques, but that interest was still focused almost exclusively on the real thing, not on new reproductions. At the Centennial Exhibition itself, the great majority of the displays showcased the industrial might and ingenuity of American manufacturers, rather than promoting nostalgia for the past. Renaissance Revival and Eastlake were popular styles at the Centennial, along with patent furniture, innovative designs combining two pieces of furniture into one, or that folded into smaller spaces, such as the fold-down Renaissance Revival bed in figure 2–1; Colonial styles were not to be found for sale by American manufacturers. There were more than 2,000 exhibits featuring products of American manufacturers, and about 130 of these were furniture manufacturers. Kenneth Ames points out that holding the Centennial Exhibition in Philadelphia naturally skewed the geographic selection of manufacturers, bringing proportionately greater numbers of exhibitors from the East Coast, especially from Philadelphia and New York. About fifty furniture exhibitors were from Philadelphia, and thirty were from New York. Only eighteen exhibitors were from the Midwest, although that region certainly contained several important furniture-making centers. Five exhibitors were from Grand Rapids, Michigan, and as we shall see later Grand Rapids made the most of its exposure at the Centennial.[8]

5. Rodris Roth, "The New England, or 'Olde Tyme,' Kitchen Exhibit at Nineteenth-Century Fairs," in Alan Axelrod, ed., *The Colonial Revival in America* (New York: W. W. Norton, 1985), 160–71.

6. Ibid., 161, 164.

7. Rodris Roth, "The Colonial Revival and Centennial Furniture," *Art Quarterly* 27, no. 1 (1964): 64, 49.

8. Kenneth L. Ames, "Grand Rapids Furniture at the Time of the Centennial," *Winterthur Portfolio* 10 (1975): 23–24.

Fig. 2-1 Patent folding bed displayed at the Centennial Exhibition of 1876 in Philadelphia. From James McCabe's *The Illustrated History of the Centennial Exhibition* (Philadelphia: National Publishing Company, 1876).

A few antiques were displayed as part of noncommercial exhibits. An exhibit in the United States Government Building, for example, displayed some of the personal effects of George Washington, along with what was called the "Washington Elm Chair." The chair obviously had not been made during George Washington's lifetime, and it was Renaissance Revival in style. Indeed, it was especially made for the Centennial! The only furniture exhibitor who had any pieces that might be called Colonial was George J. Henkel of Philadelphia. His exhibit boasted a "set of chamber furniture in the style of 1776, made from the wood of an old maple tree that grew in Independence Square, and

was over two hundred years old." Although we do not have any pictures of the Henkel furniture, contemporary accounts suggest that it was probably like the George Washington elm chair and Renaissance Revival in style.[9]

The Centennial exhibit of the Grand Rapids firm of Nelson, Matter and Company represented that era's tribute to the spirit of 1776, which was not an emulation of eighteenth-century design at all but rather an attempt to incorporate the heroic stature of the Founding Fathers in the context of the monumental—and then popular—Renaissance Revival style. The company pulled out all the stops for the exhibit and created a massive Renaissance Revival bedstead and dresser, both decorated with niches holding full-body statues of American patriots—George Washington, Thomas Jefferson, and Benjamin Franklin. Each piece was topped with a carved American eagle (fig. 2–2).[10]

So of the American exhibits at the Centennial, the furniture that tried to commemorate the nation's early days—the Washington elm chair, the Henkel furniture, the Nelson and Matter bed and dresser—did so in the Renaissance Revival style, not in Colonial styles.

The visitor at the Centennial Exhibition could find antique furniture on display at "The New England Log House and Modern Kitchen," which was set up to provide food for Centennial-goers. There visitors could see a spinning wheel, a two-hundred-year-old chest of drawers, and other pieces of seventeenth-century American furniture associated with the Pilgrims.[11] This popular exhibit was patterned after the Sanitary Fair Colonial Kitchens and featured the same kinds of artifacts.

Although American manufacturers did not display eighteenth-century de-

9. Roth, "The Colonial Revival and Centennial Furniture," 63.

10. Ames, "Grand Rapids Furniture," 31.

11. Roth, "The Colonial Revival and Centennial Furniture," 60.

Fig. 2-2 Nelson, Matter and Company display at the Centennial Exhibition of 1876 in Philadelphia. Massive Renaissance Revival-style bedstead and dresser, with niches holding full-body statues of patriots, including George Washington. *Collections of the Public Museum of Grand Rapids.*

signs at the Centennial, there were several English furniture manufacturers that featured Queen Anne–style and Jacobean-style furniture and eighteenth-century furniture.[12]

One of the few examples we have found of "Centennial" furniture from the 1870s comes from a toy catalogue from C. W. F. Dare of New York City dated 1878, which included two examples of toy chairs inspired by the Centennial.[13] Both are fairly simple ladder-back chairs with a Pilgrim Century look. (*Pilgrim Century* style refers to furniture of the first century that European settlers were in America; this seventeenth-century furni-

ture is sturdy and simple, with turned posts and spindles.) The description for one chair calls it both "Centennial style" and "style of 1776." The other chair, a "Toy chair of 1776," is a good example of what the term "Centennial" meant in the 1870s: it was not literally the copying of styles from 1776 but simply adapting an early American style, here from the Pilgrim century. Early reproductions were often at odds with historical accuracy.

Toward the end of the 1870s we do find some evidence that reproductions were being produced. In Providence, Rhode Island, fine-quality reproductions were being made by Charles Dowler, Wil-

---

12. Monkhouse and Michie, *American Furniture in Pendleton House,* 197.

13. We would like to thank Neville Thompson, Librarian-in-Charge at the Winterthur Library, for bringing this catalogue to our attention.

liam Morlock (who formed the firm Morlock and Bayer, 1877–1908), and Rudolph Breitenstein. All of these men were fine carvers who had emigrated from England and Germany to the United States, and who put their skills to use in making interior woodwork and furniture.[14] In England, the work of Thomas Chippendale (1718–79) had never lost favor, and his styles from the mid-eighteenth century were reproduced in England as early as the 1830s. Woodworkers coming from England obviously would have been familiar with eighteenth-century furniture design.[15]

Interior Decoration: A New Simplicity

In 1878 Clarence Cook published his influential book, *The House Beautiful,* in which he advocated decorating with antiques, or, for those who did not own family heirlooms or antiques, with reproductions. Although Cook acknowledged the value of family provenance, he also admitted, "But everybody can't have a grandfather, nor things that came over on the 'Mayflower,' and those of us who have not drawn these prizes in life's lottery must do the best we can under the circumstances."[16] Cook espoused one of the central tenets of the Colonial Revival movement—that one's environment had the power to shape character. Antiques and reproductions, associated with a braver and simpler time, might inspire the same qualities in modern Americans.

The House Beautiful is full of illustrations showing how to decorate by combining antique furniture and reproductions. Cook even recommends a few firms as sources of good reproduction furniture—for example, Cottier and Company of Boston. Cook writes, "The Messrs. Cottier long since found themselves obliged to give up importing furniture from England, as all the pieces that came from over seas had to be overhauled before they had been many weeks in this country. The chair shown in cut No. 22 [a Chippendale-style corner chair] is not a modern one, but the Cottiers have used it, or one like it, as a model, and have produced a design that takes the eye of every one who sees it."[17]

In the 1870s architects began designing Colonial Revival pieces for their Colonial Revival homes. George Fletcher Babb of New York was one.[18] Many of the architects of Colonial Revival homes must have had a hand in designing furniture as well. Another influential architect who also designed furniture was Arthur Little, who used English Chippendale designs as the basis for a set of dining chairs for a house in Boston's Back Bay in 1899.[19]

---

14. Monkhouse and Michie, *American Furniture in Pendleton House,* 23, 24.

15. Ibid., 22.

16. Clarence Cook, *The House Beautiful* (New York: Scribner, Armstrong and Company, 1878), 162, quoted in Elizabeth Stillinger, *The Antiquers* (New York: Alfred A. Knopf, 1980). 58.

17. Ibid., 71.

18. William B. Rhoads, *The Colonial Revival* (New York: Garland Publishing, 1977), 358.

19. Bainbridge Bunting, *House of Boston's Back Bay* (Cambridge: The Belknap Press of Harvard University, 1975), 41.

Furniture Makers in New York City

In the early 1880s Sypher & Company of New York City (a firm that dates back to the 1840s) was making fine reproductions. The chair in figure 2–3 is faithful in spirit to the Philadelphia Chippendale style. Obadiah Sypher made no apologies for making and selling reproductions, as he stated in an 1887 article: "My strict prin-ciple is to sell goods for what they are, copies if they are copies, originals when I am lucky enough to find any. But good, faithful, honest copies are of such worth in the market that they do not need being presented, and passed for what they are not."[20] This is certainly true of the chair pictured, which, barring close scrutiny, would pass as an eighteenth-century chair.

Sypher & Company published a pamphlet in 1885 entitled "The House-keeper's Quest: Where to Find Pretty Things" to advertise its interior decoration using both antique and modern styles. The pamphlet included numerous illustrations of antique china, silver, and pieces of furniture from Europe. "The Housekeeper's Quest" also comments on Sypher's reproductions, praising the "old colonial days" as a time when furniture "gave an air of refinement" to a home:

Such were the chests of drawers, the knee-hole tables, the high-backed chairs, the claw-foot tables and light stands, the eight-day clocks, which are again becoming familiar sights, since the renewal of old fashions has not only brought the genuine pieces out of their obscurity, but, the demand being much greater than could be supplied by the real thing, has led to the making of copies. The Messrs. Sypher & Co. produce copies of these old pieces which are in every way as handsome and well made as the originals, and so far as interior finish is concerned, their copies are often much better than their models.[21]

Take particular note of the last part of this statement: when assessing hundred-year-old items and two-hundred-year-old pieces, this distinction can be vital to sep-

Fig. 2-3 Sypher & Company (New York) 1880–83 Chippendale-style armchair in the Philadelphia taste. Shell-and-tassel carved crest rail, gothic splat, fluted stiles, shell-carved seat rail, acanthus-carved cabriole legs with ball-and-claw feet. Rear stump legs. Mahogany, with pine slip seat. This chair actually combines disparate Philadelphia design elements that would not have been found together on one eighteenth-century chair. 29 3/4" wide × 24" deep × 41" high. *Museum of Art, Rhode Island School of Design, Providence. Gift of Commander William Davis Miller.* **$4,000–6,000.**

---

20. "Bric-a-Brac," *The Curio* 1, no. 2 (October 1887): 192. Quoted in Monkhouse and Michie, *American Furniture in Pendleton House,* 197, 198.

21. Sypher & Company, "The Housekeeper's Quest: Where to Find Pretty Things," New York, 1885, 3–4. Courtesy of The Winterthur Library.

arating the real from the hundred-year-old copy.

In the 1880s in New York City, the firm of Meier and Hagen was making reproductions as well as doing restoration work and buying antiques. Ernst Hagen's career reflected the trends in furniture making in the late nineteenth century. Hagen had been an apprentice under Duncan Phyfe and was one of the first persons to study his life. Hagen's notes tell about the difficulties of running a small shop at a time when competition from midwestern factories was becoming more intense. After 1867, he wrote, many smaller cabinetmakers were wiped out, or they found employment doing repair work for the larger concerns. Hagen was fortunate enough to survive, and his firm established private trade with some of New York's wealthy families.[22] In 1885 Louis Tiffany ordered "10 Maple Dining Chairs," ladder-back chairs with a high-arched crest,[23] a Colonial Revival interpretation of a Pilgrim Century chair. In the 1890s Meier and Hagen continued to produce high-quality reproductions, which are still desirable today. Since Hagen had been an ardent student of Duncan Phyfe, many of his reproductions copy the designs of Phyfe.

Another cabinetmaker in New York City in the 1890s was R. J. Horner, who made Colonial Revival pieces as well as English reproductions into the twentieth century (see page 142).

Furniture Makers in Baltimore, Philadelphia and Boston

Baltimore in the 1880s was another furniture-making center where Colonial Revival reproductions were being made. Henry W. Jenkins & Sons, founded in 1799, made high-quality furniture, including some faithful reproductions. The company did not attempt to compete with mass-produced, machine-made furniture.[24] An 1898 publication described the firm:

Half a hundred expert upholsterers and furniture workmen are employed, and all of the resources, facilities, energies, and equipment of the establishment are devoted to the production of the finest grades of furniture and upholstering possible to American designers and *American skilled workmanship. The business of the house is conducted upon a retail basis, and is largely local, with all the leading families in Maryland, and all over the country. . . . Henry W. Jenkins & Sons takes charge of the entire job, making the necessary sub-contracts and assuming the responsibility from start to finish.*[25]

A drawing from about 1880 shows "a 3'6" Sofa in Silk Plush—Like in Sheraton's book," the design indeed being faithful to Sheraton's.[26] An undated drawing from the Jenkins archives shows a Hepplewhite *demi-lune* (or halfmoon) table of very good proportions and style with bell-flower inlay. These pieces were expen-

22. Elizabeth A. Ingerman, "Personal Experiences of an Old New York Cabinetmaker," *The Magazine Antiques*, November 1963, 580.

23. Elizabeth Stillinger, *The Antiquers* (New York: Alfred A. Knopf, 1980), 54.

24. John H. Hill, "Furniture Designs of Henry W. Jenkins & Sons Co." *Winterthur Portfolio* 5 (1969): 162.

25. *Baltimore 1898,* compiled by the Mercantile Advancement Company of Baltimore (Baltimore: The Company, 1898), 181. Quoted in Hill, "Furniture Designs of Henry W. Jenkins & Sons Co.," 163.

26. Hill, "Furniture Designs of Henry W. Jenkins & Sons Co.," 180.

sive, with Jenkins charging for a Hepple-white secretary-bookcase "without lid & no inlaying $115.00, without lid & with inlaying $135.00, with lid and with inlay $150.00."[27]

Also working in Baltimore in the 1880s was C. F. Meislahn & Company. Part of its output is a chair that reminds us that Colonial Revival furniture often added on to eighteenth-century designs: Figure 2–4 shows a Chippendale-style rocking chair with ball-and-claw feet and, yes, rockers! This is not a design that we take seriously today, but it demonstrates that the Colonial Revival movement certainly was not tethered to slavish copies.

Philadelphia's furniture makers were also engaged in making reproductions. According to *The Decorator and Furnisher,* August Wunsch was making reproductions in the 1880s. No doubt there were other small cabinetmakers as well. In the last quarter of the nineteenth century, Philadelphia still had many small cabinetmaking shops of one or two skilled craftsmen producing good-quality reproductions.

Beyond the small cabinetmaking firms, larger companies such as Wanamaker's of Philadelphia also sold Colonial Revival furniture in the 1880s. One of Wanamaker's catalogues from around 1887 advertised a "Dining Room in Colonial style," which although mostly heavy golden oak, did include dining chairs in a quasi-Chippendale style with rather elongated gothic-inspired splats, cabriole front legs, and paw feet, available in oak or mahogany. The same catalogue also featured a chair with a gothic-inspired splat, tufted seat, and straight legs.[28]

Paine Furniture Company was one of the largest furniture manufacturers in Boston, and it was producing Colonial Revival furniture, along with other styles, in the 1880s. One of its catalogues from the

Fig. 2-4 C.F. Meislahn & Company (Baltimore) c. 1880 mahogany Chippendale-style rocking chair—an imaginative adaptation of Chippendale. *Copyright© Smithsonian Institution. Courtesy Paul Mason.* **$1,200–1,800.**

end of that decade shows a number of "colonial desks"—slant-front desks, some with galleried tops, most with some carving on the slant front and/or drawers, and bracket feet, available in cherry, oak, or mahogany. Paine Furniture Company's 1890 catalogue, "Suggestions to Those Who Would Furnish," contains several illustrations of Colonial Revival furniture, along with advice on how to decorate the home by avoiding excessive ornament and instead striving for grace and simplicity. The catalogue shows a "Colonial Desk Chair," a Chippendale chair with straight legs, and a "Colonial Desk," a broadly carved, blocked slant-front desk with quarter-columns on bracket feet. Also illustrated is a "Colonial Sideboard," which owes more inspiration to Empire than to Chippendale, with a heavy backsplash incorporating beveled glass

27. Ibid., 181.

28. "Wanamaker's Furniture," c. 1887, 155, 189, 135. Courtesy of The Winterthur Library.

and scrolling brass. The dining chairs in the same illustration are Chippendale in style. The dining-room chair in figure 2–5 was made by Paine Furniture Company around 1890.

Paine's summer catalogue from 1897 includes Windsor chairs, accompanied by a whimsical explanation of their origin: "When George II was hunting one day in Windsor Forest he was overtaken by a storm, and took refuge in a shepherd's hut. He was surprised to find there one of the most luxurious chairs he had ever oc-

Fig. 2-5 Paine Furniture Company (Boston) c. 1890 mahogany dining chair in the Chippendale style, with gothic splat, slip seat, front cabriole legs with ball-and-claw feet, rear stump legs. Labeled. 23 1/8" wide × 19" deep × 40 1/2" high. *Collection of Dr. and Mrs. Bernard Carroll.* Side chair **$500–700.** Armchair **$800–1,200.** Set of 12 **$18,000–24,000.**

cupied, and upon inquiry it was found that the shepherd had made it himself, largely with his pocket-knife. The king purchased it, and had duplicates promptly made. This is the chair. It has been known ever since as the Windsor chair."[29] This kind of narrative, associating a prestigious historical figure with a piece of furniture, was a popular sales device for Colonial Revival furniture.

In the 1880s Goldthwait Brothers and Bancroft and Dyer in Boston made fine furniture for the upper-middle class.[30] For this top-of-the-line furniture, designers were becoming important. George Clark was a trained architect who designed his own furniture for George Clarke & Company, which also provided complete decorating advice.[31] Conant, Ball and Company produced chairs in Gardner, Massachusetts, and sold them in Boston. In general, Boston furniture manufacturers around 1880 did not try to compete with the larger midwestern factories, and they relied more on word of mouth than on advertising. Many shops were relatively small and maintained traditional woodworking techniques.[32]

An interesting furniture concept from the 1880s is the spinning-wheel rocking chair (see figure 2–6), which appears to have been made in Boston and other parts of New England. These chairs embody several aspects of the Colonial Revival movement: a romanticization of the hearth and home and the roles played there by women, a glorification of handmade items as opposed to machine-made goods, and the use of older design elements in new context—not always such a practical idea!

As Christopher Monkhouse has pointed out, the spinning wheel became

29. Courtesy of The Winterthur Library.

30. Edward S. Cooke, "The Boston Furniture Industry in 1880," *Old-Time New England* 70 (Winter 1980): 86.

31. Ibid., 89.

32. Ibid., 93.

Fig. 2-6 Spinning-wheel rocking chair, New England, c. 1880. *Courtesy Leslie Hindman Auctioneers, Chicago.* **$800–1,200.**

one of the central artifacts of the Colonial Revival movement.[33] As New England towns began to celebrate their bicentennials early in the nineteenth century, a few relics were usually brought out for display, and spinning wheels were particularly important.

Henry Wadsworth Longfellow's

poem "The Courtship of Miles Standish," published in 1858, did much to popularize the spinning wheel. In the poem, John Alden is sent to propose to Priscilla Mullins on behalf of his friend, Captain Miles Standish. The courtship takes place while Priscilla works at her spinning wheel. The spinning wheel also became the subject of several nineteenth-century paintings.[34]

William B. Savage of Boston capitalized on the popularity of old spinning wheels by remaking old, broken spinning wheels into rather odd-looking chairs, which he advertised in *The Decorator and Furnisher* in 1886–87. The advertisement alluded to Longfellow's poem, quoting: "So as she sat at her wheel one afternoon in the autumn / Alden, who opposite sat, and was watching her dexterous fingers / As if the thread she was spinning were that of his life and his fortune . . ." Not surprisingly, the chair was advertised as a good wedding present.[35]

In the 1880s we see Colonial Revival furniture being produced by some of the larger companies in the East and also some good pieces being produced by small firms in the major cities on the East Coast. The 1890s continues the trend in both directions. Some good pieces were advertised by Daniels, Badger & Company of Boston. Its 1890 catalogue, "How to Furnish Our Homes," contained mostly pieces in golden oak, but it also featured a shield-back Hepplewhite chair of good proportions, called a "reception chair," which was available in cherry and mahogany as well as oak. Also advertised were parlor desks with galleried tops, slant fronts, and ogee bracket feet, all with some carving. The catalogue also offered decorating advice, which shows a reac-

---

33. Christopher Monkhouse, "The Spinning Wheel as Artifact, Symbol, and Source of Design," in Kenneth Ames, *Victorian Furniture* (Philadelphia: Victorian Society of America, 1983), 159.

34. Ibid., 157, 159.

35. Ibid., 163.

tion against Victorian clutter. Grotesque ornament, an overabundance of curving lines, and suffocating Victorian bric-a-brac were now frowned upon. The author instead praises the virtues of the early days of New England, when interiors featured European and Chinese porcelains, and furniture with simpler lines.

In 1893 the World's Columbian Exhibition was held in Chicago to celebrate the 400th anniversary of Columbus's discovery of America. Like the Centennial Exhibition of 1876, this world's fair showcased the industrial might of many nations. Colonial Revival architecture was much in evidence, particularly in the group of state buildings, many of which incorporated Colonial design elements. The most recognizable building was a replica of Mount Vernon. Included in these state houses were displays of colonial relics—documents, furniture, and often anything having to do with George Washington.

Many of the furnishings for these houses were actual antiques. Other pieces were made especially for the exhibits. However, the makers of these reproduction pieces were rarely mentioned.[36] Although antiques and reproduction Colonial Revival furniture were included in the historic exhibits, Colonial Revival furniture was not being exhibited by furniture manufacturers; neither was it being displayed for purchase by the general public.[37] The importance of the Columbian Exhibition to the Colonial Revival movement lies in the fact that more than twenty million people visited the fair with its exhibits of Colonial architecture and interiors. Furthermore, what had previously been an eastern-seaboard movement now had a chance to spread to the heartland of the nation.[38] Certainly the fair must have influenced the "Colonial" designs that midwestern factories soon began to produce.

Furniture Makers in Chicago

According to Sharon Darling, who has written extensively about the Chicago furniture industry, during the 1890s several small cabinetmaking shops were producing good-quality reproductions. John A. Colby & Sons, one of Chicago's oldest furniture retailers, had been making Colonial Revival furniture as early as 1894, and by the turn of the century its factory employed one hundred workers. During the 1890s Colby produced custom-made interior woodwork, along with custom-made furniture, a popular combination in the late nineteenth century, as we have

seen in eastern cities. By 1900 designer William F. Halstrick was selling handmade reproductions of antique Dutch chairs, and the Storey Furniture Company offered a Windsor armchair that claimed to be "a faithful reproduction of one the Mayflower patterns."[39]

In 1899 William Kennett Cowan opened a showroom for his Empire-style furniture and copies of eighteenth-century American furniture of solid mahogany and walnut. His output included such popular items as George Washington's desk (modeled after a desk that Washing-

36. Susan Prendergast Schoelwer, "Curious Relics and Quaint Scenes: The Colonial Revival at Chicago's Great Fair," in Alan Axelrod, ed., *The Colonial Revival in America* (New York: W. W. Norton, 1985), 193.

37. Roth, "The Colonial Revival and Centennial Furniture," 75.

38. Schoelwer, "Curious Relics and Quaint Scenes," 32.

39. Sharon Darling, *Chicago Furniture: Art, Craft, and Industry, 1833–1983* (New York: W. W. Norton, 1984), 203.

ton had used in New York City) and Martha Washington's sewing table.[40]

Beginning in the 1890s, department stores such as Marshall Field & Company created their own cabinetmaking shops to make reproductions. Marshall Field & Company also bought large quantities of furniture from midwestern factories.[41]

An article in the *Furniture Worker* in 1900 notes that Chicago probably had five thousand craftsmen working as wood-carvers for furniture factories. Some probably also worked for firms making mantels and millwork or in shops that specialized in carving. Many of these craftsmen had been trained in Europe.[42]

Bench-Made Reproductions

According to Gregory R. Weidman in his *Furniture in Maryland, 1740–1940,* in the last years of the nineteenth century the furniture industry in Baltimore showed many of the same characteristics seen in other eastern cities as they absorbed the competition of mass-produced furniture from midwestern factories. Weidman credits the decline in the number of furniture manufacturers and cabinetmakers to several causes in addition to competition from midwestern factories, including larger firms squeezing out smaller firms and the trend toward eclecticism in interior design. Large department stores edged out small furniture stores by selling a wide array of household furnishings to the public. On top of that, several midwestern factories had retail stores in Baltimore, so competition was fierce. One could also buy furniture through interior decorators, who bought from a variety of sources and sometimes had furniture made to order.[43]

By 1900, as the antiques trend continued, eighteen Baltimore furniture dealers had begun selling antiques. As the market for antiques grew in Baltimore, so did the manufacture of reproductions. As noted earlier, beginning in the 1870s, fine reproductions were produced by Henry W. Jenkins & Sons. By the 1890s, a number of firms were making what was called "artistic furniture," which copied the old English masters. This furniture has come to dominate the Baltimore furniture industry in this century.[44]

The most successful of these firms was Potthast Brothers, founded in 1892 by German immigrants who had been trained in woodworking techniques in Germany. Potthast Brothers specialized in fine-quality reproductions, which were popular in Maryland and the surrounding area and continue to be sought after today (see figures 2–7 and 2–8). The firm focused on dining-room furniture, often in the Hepplewhite and Empire Revival styles, and the design sources were often local, building on the tradition of Baltimore furniture design. The furniture was mostly handmade and usually was labeled. The firm proudly called its pieces "The True Antiques of Tomorrow." The firm was in business until 1975.[45]

Also in Baltimore, C. F. Meislahn & Company, founded in 1887, advertised itself as "Sculptors, designers, and manu-

---

40. Ibid., 210.

41. Ibid., 208.

42. Ibid., 197.

43. Gregory R. Weidman, *Furniture in Maryland, 1740–1940* (Baltimore: Maryland Historical Society, 1984), 213.

44. Ibid.

45. Ibid., 214.

Fig. 2-8 Potthast Brothers (Baltimore) 1910-30 Hepplewhite Revival shield-back armchair, based on a piece in a Baltimore collection. Reeded arms and legs, spade feet. Mahogany. 23 3/4" wide x 20 1/4" deep x 36 3/4" high. *Courtesy Maryland Historical Society, Baltimore.* Single, **$500–750.** Pair, **$1,200–1,800.** Set of eight **$8,000–12,000;** Set of 12, **$18,000–24,000.**

Fig. 2-7 Potthast Brothers (Baltimore) c. 1903 Chippendale-style side chair in the Philadelphia manner, based on an original in a Baltimore collection. This chair is labeled "Potthast Bros/Antique Furniture/ Artistic Furniture Mfrs./507 N. Howard Street, Baltimore, Maryland." Mahogany, with oak corner blocks. 24" wide x 21 3/4" deep x 40 1/4" high. *Courtesy Maryland Historical Society, Baltimore.* Single, **$800–1,200.** Set of six, **$6,000–9,000.** Set of eight **$10,000–16,000.** Set of 12 with two arm chairs, **$24,000–36,000.**

facturers of plain and artistic furniture and interior work."[46] An example of Meislahn's work from about 1880 is the Chippendale-style rocking chair shown in figure 2–4. The firm was in business until 1941.

One Baltimore manufacturer that turned out reproductions and fine custom

furniture around the turn of the century was J. W. Berry & Son, a company that is still in business today (see figure 2–9). Enrico Liberti opened a shop in 1930, and built an excellent reputation during the 1930s. He made reproductions for a number of public buildings, and his shop continues to make reproductions today.[47]

Figures 2–10 and 2–11 show examples of Empire Revival pieces made in Baltimore around the turn of the century. Empire pieces at that time were often called "Colonial," although the style ante-

46. Ibid.
47. Ibid.

Fig. 2-9 Chippendale Revival desk and bookcase, c. 1910-20, made by J.W. Berry & Son of Baltimore. Based on a Massachusetts prototype found in a Baltimore collection at the turn of the century. Mahogany and white pine. 44 1/2" wide × 25 1/4" deep × 96" high. *Courtesy Maryland Historical Society, Baltimore.* **$12,000–18,000.**

dates the Colonial era. Nevertheless, Empire-style pieces were an important part of the Colonial Revival.

Other furniture centers active in the 1890s included Cincinnati, Saint Louis, Louisville, Indianapolis, Rockford, Illinois, Williamsport and Allentown, Pennsylvania, and Columbus, Ohio. Grand

Rapids, Michigan, a major furniture-making center, will be discussed in Chapter 3.

Before the nineteenth century drew to a close, books on American antiques began to appear. The first, published in 1891, was Irving Whitall Lyon's *The Colonial Furniture of New England.* Lyon's work was well researched and has stood the test of time, as opposed to other books of that vintage. Completing the research for his great work took Lyon to the homes of numerous collectors as well as to many antiques shops. In his journal of 1883 he describes a visit to a shop in Salem, Massachusetts, where he spotted new "antiques": "His Oaken chests were most all reproductions, newly carved brand new, & he so told me. The price was always about $75, & he said his customers bought these tight new pieces in preference to the old."[48]

Lyon studied furniture in England and France to try to uncover some of the roots of American furniture design. One important result of his pioneering research was that he proved that much of the seventeenth-century furniture then extant in New England had actually been made there, whereas previously most people assumed it had been imported from England.[49]

In 1895 Alvan Crocker Nye published *A Collection of Scale Drawings, Details, and Sketches of What Is Commonly Known as Colonial Furniture, Measured and Drawn from Antique Examples.* No doubt Nye's work, together with Lyon's was a great help to furniture manufacturers in their efforts to build good-quality reproductions.

By the turn of the century, the Colonial Revival movement had come of age,

---

48. I. W. Lyon, "Notes from Inventories on Old Furniture, etc.," manuscript, Winterthur No. 76 × 99.17. Quoted in Stillinger, *The Antiquers,* 73.

49. Stillinger, *The Antiquers,* 74.

Fig. 2-10 Empire Revival sofa made in Baltimore c. 1880-1910, a popular style around the turn of the century. Although this looks very much like a c. 1825 piece, the carving is flat and not as extensive as on an earlier piece, and the legs are too short. Mahogany and white pine. 93 1/2" long × 24 1/2" deep × 35 3/8" high. *Courtesy Maryland Historical Society, Baltimore.* **$1,200–1,800.**

Fig. 2-11 Empire Revival window seat made in Baltimore, c. 1880-1910. The heavy diagonal molding on the arms, the claw feet, and the flat are typical of Colonial Revival pieces rather than period Empire pieces. Mahogany, with oak. 47 1/2" wide × 19 5/8" deep × 27 7/8" high. *Courtesy Maryland Historical Society, Baltimore.* **$800–1,200.**

and reproductions were popular at all levels of society. As we have seen, good-quality reproductions were readily available from small shops, and they were becoming more plentiful from larger factories as well. In the next chapter we will discuss the production of these larger factories, focusing on the furniture industry of Grand Rapids, Michigan, which was one of the most important centers of factory production by the turn of the century.

3

Grand Rapids Furniture Makers and the Advent of Mass Production

By the turn of the century, Grand Rapids, Michigan, became one of the major producers of furniture. As in Chapter 2, there were several important centers of mass-produced furniture around the country. We chose Grand Rapids as the example to show how factory production fed the popular demand for Colonial Revival furniture. Grand Rapids was an important furniture producer even before the Colonial Revival gained momentum, so it is interesting to see how and when the furniture manufacturers responded to the popularity of Colonial styles. It is one of the ways that we can gauge the widespread popularity of the movement.

Much of the output of Grand Rapids factories was intended for the mass market and was affordable. In order to produce reasonably priced furniture and to increase profitability, factories used machines wherever possible to speed up production and cut costs. Thus, the great majority of these pieces could not be as well-made as the work of smaller cabinet-making shops where traditional woodworking techniques were still used. We will look at the sorts of machines used in large factories in Grand Rapids to under-

stand their limitations and the kind of furniture they were capable of producing.

The first Colonial styles coming out of Grand Rapids around 1890 were far from faithful copies, and many of these pieces do not succeed from an aesthetic point of view.

Factory-produced furniture from before the turn of the century is less desirable to today's buyer. However, we do see a great deal of it at flea markets and antiques malls, and we need to know how to distinguish among levels of quality. This mass-produced Colonial Revival furniture is what was available through mail order and to the average household, so it was influential in its own time if not in our own. The furniture coming out of Grand Rapids generally improved after the turn of the century and, by the 1920s, high-quality reproductions were available, along with plenty of low-end pieces for the mass market.

Grand Rapids was an ideal location for making furniture. There was the abundant supply of timber—both hardwood and softwood—and the town was located on the Grand River, which provided transportation for the raw timber as well as for the finished product. The river rapids provided water power for the sawmills and furniture factories. In addition, Grand Rapids had had railroad service since 1858 and could ship its products both to the South and the West, thus meeting the requirements of an expanding nation.

Many of the furniture companies in Grand Rapids began as millworks, making architectural pieces such as banisters, stairs, doors, and sashes. Nelson, Matter and Company began as a sawmill, then became a barrel factory, then expanded into making chairs, and by the 1870s had established itself as one of the mainstays of the Grand Rapids furniture industry. Chris Carron, Curator of History at the Public Museum of Grand Rapids, points out that many of Grand Rapids' successful furniture companies started out this way. Carron notes that Grand Rapids had already laid the foundation for mass production from its days in millworking. It was just a few short steps from processing lumber to making furniture. Companies were already established to take advantage of the water power, and they were easily able to transform water-powered mills into powering machines to mass-produce furniture.

During the 1870s Grand Rapids greatly increased its share of the nation's furniture industry. By 1880, it ranked seventh in the nation in the production of furniture.[1] In 1878 the city established its semiannual Furniture Market, through which it displayed and sold its products to retailers. This important marketing arena led not only to sales through furniture and department stores but also to contracts for large quantities of furniture to be sold through such mail-order giants as Sears Roebuck and Montgomery Ward. Of course, furniture made for the mail-order business was inexpensive, and

some companies in Grand Rapids that wished to be associated only with high-quality goods scorned the mail-order business. Grand Rapids indeed had companies that made cheap furniture, but many companies produced a great deal of good-quality furniture as well.

The three main furniture companies that were established by the 1870s and led the industry were the Berkey and Gay Company, the Phoenix Furniture Company, and Nelson, Matter and Company. In the 1870s these three companies built new factories that proved vital to their later success. The Phoenix factory covered 12,000 square feet of space, with four stories. The nearby sawmill had two veneer saws in addition to the usual saws. Wood was treated on site in dry kilns that had a capacity to hold 90,000 feet of lumber. The machines were powered by a two-hundred-horsepower steam engine fed by four boilers.[2]

The Nelson, Matter and Company factory was equally impressive, with its largest building covering 11,000 square feet. Machines for cutting, planing, and turning occupied the first floor. A Grand Rapids historian describes the layout in detail: "Two cutoff saws were used to cut the lumber into desired lengths, and four strip, or splitting, saws and a band saw aided by three planing machines cut the lumber to the proper width and thickness. Two jointers, six turning lathes, and a gauge lathe accomplished the remaining preliminary processes. The second floor had twenty machines for cutting, mortising, tenoning, grooving, moulding, boring, and scroll sawing. Cabinet work, veneering, and carving were done in the top two stories of this building."[3] The factory was laid out for maximum efficiency. Iron tracks allowed the lumber and other

---

1. Kenneth L. Ames, "Grand Rapids Furniture at the Time of the Centennial," *Winterthur Portfolio* 10 (1975): 25.

2. Frank Ward Ransom, *The City Built on Wood: A History of the Furniture Industry in Grand Rapids, Michigan, 1850–1950* (Ann Arbor: Edwards Bros., 1955), 32.

3. Ibid., 33.

heavy materials to move easily in and out of the building. The tracks were routed near a steam-powered elevator, so materials could be sent to upper floors efficiently. Such planning helped give Grand Rapids factories an advantage over the older companies in the East.[4]

In the 1870s Berkey and Gay Furniture Company built one of the largest factories in the country. Offices, showrooms, shipping facilities, storage space, and the finishing department were housed in a 16,500-square-foot, six-story building. Three other buildings housed the manufacturing processes. The company operated its own lumberyard and dry kiln. In 1889 Berkey and Gay built another six-story building, which allowed the company to double its production.[5]

One important asset of the Berkey and Gay factory in the 1870s was its two steam-powered elevators. Another is that the new factory had been designed to include space for a photography studio, as furniture manufacturers produced illustrated catalogues to help the companys' salespeople sell their products.[6]

With major factories up and running, the 1870s was the decade in which Grand Rapids established its national reputation in furniture making. In 1876 the three major Grand Rapids companies took part in the Centennial Exhibition in Philadelphia, and all received awards. The companies made good use of the opportunities for promotion and about the same time began to open showrooms in New York City to sell their furniture in the East. By the end of the decade, Grand Rapids was exporting furniture to Europe and South America.[7]

The furniture style produced in the 1870s was predominantly Renaissance Revival—massive pieces that could be ornamented to a greater or lesser degree depending upon the desired price range. It is difficult to determine which company made a particular piece of furniture from this period as many companies were producing a similar look.[8]

During the 1880s the Grand Rapids furniture industry continued to expand, fueled by westward migration. The Grand Rapids companies continued to update their equipment and added new machinery, while factories in the East lagged behind because their capital was tied up in old factories. In 1880 Berkey and Gay employeed 400 people, Phoenix employed 520, and Nelson, Matter and Company employed 380.[9]

Rather than using mass-production techniques, most Grand Rapids factories used the method of "batch" production. The companies would display several samples at exhibits such as their semiannual Furniture Markets or in their showrooms and take orders from retailers. In general, furniture was not mass-produced and then warehoused as inventory to await sales. Pieces were made in batches of twenty-five or fifty or one-hundred as orders came in.

We tend to think that Grand Rapids produced relatively inexpensive furniture and relied heavily on mechanized processes, while smaller shops in the East and elsewhere maintained the old woodworking traditions, making furniture of higher quality for people of means. While this assumption is fairly accurate, it is instructive to look more closely at how machines were actually used in the furniture industry at the end of the nineteenth cen-

4. Ames, "Grand Rapids Furniture," 30.

5. Ransom, *The City Built on Wood*, 33.

6. Ames, "Grand Rapids Furniture," 28.

7. Ibid., 30.

8. Ibid., 34.

9. Ibid., 31.

tury. Grand Rapids furniture, though made in large quantities, still required handwork, especially on high-end pieces. Machines, after all, could not duplicate handwork. Machines allowed workers to take shortcuts and produce furniture more quickly, but they could not replicate hand-carving. Mechanization had the greatest impact on the methods of furniture making that were already inexpensive.[10]

Since the early nineteenth century, furniture manufacturers used circular saws for cutting boards and machines to plane and sand the boards, make mortise-and-tenon joints, and mass-produce dowels. Workers experimented with machines to cut dovetails and pins, the most successful being the rotary, or gang, dovetailer.[11] Band saws, which could cut curved forms, were in wide use by the 1880s, as were scroll saws or fretsaws.[12] Machine-powered lathes and gauge lathes were used to turn wood. Gauge lathes could turn several pieces of wood at a time, but they did not completely replace hand turning. Gauge lathes required many different settings to do anything beyond basic turnings, so they were cost-effective only when producing thousands of identically turned pieces. On a smaller scale, it was more economical to do simple turnings by hand rather than fit machines to do the turning automatically. Powered lathes were used, but they were not always automatic.[13]

Molding machines were available, but molding was often contracted out and done at mill-work houses. Shapers and routers were used on edges or, with attachments could cut fluted legs or regular, geometrical, applied ornaments such as the sunburst and fan patterns one often finds on Colonial Revival pieces from this era. The router, or edge molder, could make roundels and other geometric patterns also found on Colonial Revival pieces.[14]

The only machine that could come close to duplicating hand carving was the spindle carver, also in use by the 1880s. This machine required a highly skilled operator, who did the work freehand. And even with the spindle carver, the work had to be completed by hand. Even at the turn of the century, the Sligh Furniture Company of Grand Rapids employed forty hand carvers in its factory producing middle- and low-end products.[15] On pieces with any value, the carving was always finished by hand. While other "carving" machines were available, they could be used only on low-end furniture since the results obviously looked machine-produced.

By the late 1880s an embossing machine was in use but it was only capable of making a relief design, a shallow impression with no undercutting, and it was not used on high-quality furniture.[16] The multiple carver, capable of cutting several identical designs simultaneously, was limited to incising; using it for anything more complex was not cost-effective.[17]

Most of the woodworking machines in use at the end of the nineteenth century had limitations, one being that the end product was obviously machine made.

10. Michael J. Ettema, "Technological Innovation and Design Economics in Furniture Manufacture," *Winterthur Portfolio 16* (1981): 198, 201.

11. Ibid., 212.

12. Ibid., 213.

13. Ibid., 215.

14. Ibid., 216–18.

15. Ibid., 202.

16. Ibid.

17. Ibid., 220.

When producing Colonial Revival furniture, these machines could not duplicate the fine work or hand carving of early American craftsmen. Machines could produce only adaptations. The marks left from machine carving on lower-end pieces is one of the easy ways to spot Colonial Revival furniture. Large companies did have their own carvers, and on better pieces the carving was sometimes done by hand, but some pieces were contracted out to specialty carving works in Grand Rapids. Even when the carving was done by hand, however, it was not as deep or crisp as eighteenth-century carving. Anyone familiar with good eighteenth-century carving can easily spot most Colonial Revival–era carving.

After 1900 the finishing process was done by machine and often the hand-rubbing was eliminated. By the 1910s furniture was being spray finished, a process that offered great potential savings to furniture manufacturers. With a spray gun, two men could finish twenty-four chairs in an hour. With the brush-and-dip method, one man could finish only four chairs in an hour.[18] Hand-rubbing between each coat of finish added to the cost, and of course the number of coats increased the cost as well. On pieces that are beautifully and carefully finished, the finishing process can easily account for half of the final cost. The method of finishing is one important aspect of quality that collectors today look for. Not surprisingly, hand-finishing will always be more highly valued than machine-finishing.

In 1895, George Gay of Berkey and Gay described a furniture industry that manufactured two classes of furniture—low-end furniture for the general public and high-end furniture that was made to order and combined old traditional methods with new machine methods.[19] At the turn of the century, Grand Rapids produced large quantities of low-end furniture, but its manufacturers also produced high-quality pieces that still required a great deal of hand work.

Not only did the Grand Rapids furniture companies make efficient use of the available technology at the end of the nineteenth century, but they also understood the art of promotion. Grand Rapids had always marketed itself aggressively, and the semiannual Furniture Market was an essential marketing tool. Beyond that, the major companies advertised in the most important national magazines. For instance, Berkey and Gay advertized in *The Saturday Evening Post*. At the turn of the century, Grand Rapids also founded several trade journals, including *The Furniture Manufacturer, The Stylist, Furniture Record,* and *Good Furniture and Decoration.*

By the 1890s Grand Rapids had begun to promote itself as a "style center." Companies hired furniture designers who had been trained in London, New York, and Chicago and began producing copies of period pieces and furniture in the Arts and Crafts style. The Phoenix Furniture Company employed the services of David W. Kendall, who was a major designer of period furniture from 1895 to 1910. In his search for authentic period designs, he traveled to England to study examples.[20] Around the turn of the century, Grand Rapids became the home of the College of Furniture Designing, headed by Arthur Kirkpatrick, who designed for Berkey and Gay. Students could take classes at the school or through correspondence courses.

In addition to the three major Grand Rapids companies at the turn of the century, several other large companies were founded in the nineteenth century in

---

18. Ransom, *The City Built on Wood,* 61.

19. Edward S. Cooke, "The Boston Furniture Industry in 1880," *Old Time New England* 70 (Winter 1980): 85.

20. Ransom, *The City Built on Wood,* 27.

Grand Rapids and remained prominent through the 1920s. All these companies produced a good line of furniture that established their reputations. Phoenix Furniture Company, founded in 1870, was sold to Robert W. Irwin in 1911, who reorganized under the name Robert W. Irwin in 1920 and operated until 1953. Irwin specialized in high-quality paint-decorated furniture that emulated French designs, Japanese lacquer, and Chinese Chippendale. Imperial Furniture Company (fig. 3–1) was founded by E. H. Foote in 1903 and was bought by another company in 1954.

The Century Furniture Company was founded in 1900 (hence the name) and incorporated in 1905. From its inception, Century produced some fairly faithful copies of Empire pieces and other Colonial styles. In the 1920s Century offered a line of reproductions copying furniture from Knoll House in England. Century was in operation until 1942.

Luce Furniture Company was also founded in 1900 and made mid-priced furniture and many Colonial Revival pieces. Colonial Furniture Company of Zeeland, Michigan, was founded in 1899 and did not move to Grand Rapids until 1947. Colonial specialized in making clocks, but in the 1930s it also made reproductions of pieces in the Henry Ford Museum. Widdicomb and Sligh were two other prominent companies. Sligh made cheap to mid-range furniture and is still in business today, making desks and clocks.

Gustav Stickley does not fit the profile of the average Grand Rapids manufacturer, but he and his small firm of Stickley Brothers, which made Arts and Crafts furniture, did participate in the Furniture market in 1900. The Arts and Crafts movement had its origins in late nineteenth-century England and was devoted to craftsmanship and simple, purposeful designs meant to be used by all. The Arts and Crafts movement rejected furniture

Fig. 3-1 Imperial Furniture Company c. 1920 Hepplewhite-style card table with shaped flip top. Mahogany, with diamond and line inlays and satinwood center panel. Labeled. 36" wide x 18" deep x 28 3/4" high. *Private collection.* **$800–1,200.**

that was too ornate to be practical, and furniture that was intended for the elite only. Stickley was the main popularizer of the movement in America, producing good quality, simple, sturdy, oak furniture that had the look of hand craftsmanship. Stickley's magazine, *The Craftsman* (1901–1916) promoted the ideals of the Arts and Crafts movement, with articles on household and decorative arts, as well as philosophy, economics and politics. Stickley had been influenced by the simplicity of early American furniture, and recalled that in 1886 he turned his attention to "reproducing by hand some of the simplest and best models of old Colonial, Windsor, and other plain chairs, and to a study of this period as a foundation for original work along the same lines."[21]

21. William B. Rhoads, *The Colonial Revival* (New York: Garland Publishing, 1977), 368.

Although we remember Stickley for his Arts and Crafts furniture, in 1914 he was also making Jacobean Revival pieces.

Stickley admired some eighteenth-century designs, but he did not approve of copying. Economic necessity alone had forced him to make reproductions. In a 1913 issue of *The Craftsman,* in which Colonial Revival furniture was discussed, he admitted that some early American designs would, in fact, harmonize with Craftsman designs. The 1915 *Craftsman* advertises Windsor chairs made by Stickley.[22]

Berkey and Gay is probably more representative of the mainstream furniture producers in Grand Rapids. It certainly was one of the most successful, and by the 1920s was employing 600 to 1000 people. Even with so large a factory, orders were still processed in batches of twenty-five or fifty or one-hundred. Berkey and Gay made some high-quality furniture but its major market was for mid-priced furniture.

Berkey and Gay's 1900 catalogue, "The Old Feeling, or the Past Revived," was based on the theme offered by Clarence Cooke in *The House Beautiful,* that one's surroundings—including furniture—influence a person's character. The Berkey and Gay catalogue is full of what it calls "antique reproductions" of earlier styles. Each illustrated piece is accompanied by an elaborate description of how the piece captures certain desired characteristics of the past. Over and over again, we are assured that environment shapes character—that furniture and interiors can strengthen moral fiber. As part of the description of the Colonial Toilet Table, a vanity with attached mirror, the writer waxes eloquent: "Who could be brought in daily association with such unassumed, impressive elegance, without being somewhat fashioned after it? As well say that the rays of a 4th of July sun could not warm your body as to say that such furniture can have no bearing on the development of refinement in character."[23]

The description of the Empire Revival sofa with scrolling arms and feet and tufted back and seat gives us an idea of why Empire Revival is associated with the Colonial era: "Here you have a glimpse of magnificent Colonial ideals. There is not a monotonous line in sight, yet the design is as simple as a child, as pure as a lily. . . . There is nothing else that can more adequately portray the pure ideas of Puritan life. . . . Can you conceive of the influence of such a piece in the home?"[24] While the writer has his historical periods confused, and a Puritan certainly never came near an Empire-style sofa, it is clear that Empire Revival represents the virtues of simplicity and purity, virtues also associated with the early American life. Writing about another Empire Revival piece—a three-drawer dresser with ogee mirror attached to rope-turned standards, with convex overhanging top drawer—he describes it as a "well-balanced pure Colonial reproduction."[25] He goes on to quote Henry Wadsworth Longfellow, often pressed into service by Colonial Revivalists: "In character, in manners, in style, in all things, / the supreme excellence is simplicity."

Capping off his praise of simplicity in furniture, the writer says: "Cheap, meaningless furniture rabble, may need a whole retinue of glued on filigree, of flimsy embellishments, but furniture of the Berkey and Gay quality needs no irrelevant decoration. . . . You can feel Puritan

---

22. Ibid., 373.

23. Berkey and Gay Furniture Company, *"The Old Feeling, or the Past Revived"* (Grand Rapids: Dickinson Bros., 1900), 5.

24. Ibid., 9, 10.

25. Ibid., 13.

chasteness running all through this class of workmanship."[26] The Puritans, often invoked, are praised for their quiet spirit and simple elegance.

Berkey and Gay's 1910 catalogue, "Character in Furniture," dispatched with the fulsome prose of the 1900 catalogue and exhibits a better understanding of historical style periods. The broad use of the term "Colonial," while not historically accurate, has now become standard. In the catalogue, "Colonial" is applied to Empire-style furniture, with its carved columns, claw feet, pineapple finials, and overall simplicity, which was highly valued. The catalogue explains that "Colonial" is in fact Empire style, an American adaptation of French styles after the War of 1812.

The catalogue is illustrated with "Colonial" characters posing amid period furniture. The styles include Louis XV and XVI, "Colonial" (what we would call Empire Revival), Sheraton, Flanders furniture (Elizabethan and Jacobean), the Flemish Renaissance, Chippendale (mainly Chinese Chippendale), and William and Mary. All are adaptations, but the writing reflects greater historical accuracy and understanding of the history of furniture design.

In the 1920s Berkey and Gay produced a limited number of an interesting table. The USS *Constitution,* which had been active in the War of 1812, was being restored in Boston Harbor. Part of the wood from the oarlock deck had to be replaced. Berkey and Gay bought the discarded wood and made it into one hundred "Old Ironsides" tables, modeled from a Wallace Nutting design, complete with carved eagles.

W. L. Kimerly's book on style, *How to Know Period Styles in Furniture,* published in 1912, helps explain how styles were perceived at the time. Kimerly sums up the common view on most nineteenth-century furniture when he described it as "furniture loaded with cheap ornament and meaningless carving. The main idea seemed to be 'how much' and not 'how good.' This was partly due to the introduction of labor-saving machinery, but more to untrained men going into the furniture business, many of them being entirely ignorant of the first principles of design."[27] Kimerly acknowledges that the term "Colonial" is broadly applied to describe furniture made well after 1776. The chapter "Early American or Colonial Furniture" shows Windsors, Louis XVI (a chair owned by George Washington), Sheraton, Empire, William and Mary, Dutch (or Queen Anne), Jacobean, Chippendale, and Duncan Phyfe. Kimerly notes that the most popular style of "modern Colonial" is derived from the Empire style.[28]

In the years immediately preceding 1900, many styles were produced in Grand Rapids, with no single one dominating the trade. The semiannual Furniture Market held in Grand Rapids may have encouraged regular shifts in styles. In the last years of the nineteenth century and the first years of the twentieth, the most popular styles in Grand Rapids included the French styles, English styles, and American Colonial styles. By 1915 Adam, Hepplewhite, and the French styles were no longer as popular. Chippendale remained popular, and William and Mary, Queen Anne, and Charles II were becoming more popular. Jacobean pieces hit their stride in the 1920s, and Colonial styles continued to gain in popularity throughout the 1920s[29]

Because so much furniture was being

26. Ibid., 14.

27. W. L. Kimerly, *How to Know Period Styles in Furniture* (Grand Rapids: Periodical Publishing Company, 1912), 131.

28. Ibid., 145.

29. Ransom, *The City Built on Wood,* 62.

produced in period styles, finishing processes became more important. Manufacturers turned to mahogany and walnut for these period pieces. Because of its superior strength, Cuban mahogany was especially preferred for legs, while African mahogany was prized for its fine texture. Honduran and Mexican mahogany were also used.[30] Walnut, more costly and scarce than mahogany, was used only for legs or as veneer on expensive high-quality pieces. Low-priced furniture was often made from white woods such as maple and birch. Gum was used as a secondary wood; when it was used as a primary wood, it was painted because it did not finish well. Cheap furniture from the 1920s was often made from gum.

Nearby, in Holland, Michigan, a major force in the furniture industry was about to be established, led by Siebe Baker. Cook and Baker started out in 1890 in Allegan, Michigan, making golden oak combination bookcases and china closets. In 1903 the name was changed to Baker and Company. Siebe Baker died in 1925 and his son, Hollis Baker, took over as president. Hollis Baker had a passion for antiques and made numerous trips to the East Coast, England, and the Continent in search of designs to reproduce.

In the 1920s Baker was eager to capitalize on the public's interest in Colonial Revival furniture. In 1922 it introduced a line of Colonial furniture and in 1923 produced a Duncan Phyfe suite, which was copied from the original at the Metropolitan Museum of Art in New York City. In 1926 Baker came out with a popular line of Pilgrim Century dining-room suites.[31] In 1927, under a new name, Baker Furniture Factories was producing complete living-room and bedroom suites. And in 1931 Baker introduced its first "Old World Collection" of Georgian mahogany furniture.[32] For the next fifteen years Baker produced many eighteenth-century reproductions in the English and French styles. In 1932 the company opened the Manor House in New York City, created to produce top-of-the-line furniture that was virtually handmade, including the dovetails and finishing work. By now, of course, it has sixty years of patination, wear and tear. The Baker Museum for Furniture Research was established in 1941 in Holland, Michigan, and it remains today a wonderful source of information for furniture lovers.

In the 1920s Grand Rapids began to lose some of its market to southern companies, who had access to cheaper labor and materials. The Depression spelled the end for many Grand Rapids companies, and by the end of the Depression Grand Rapids had relinquished its reputation as a national furniture center to High Point, North Carolina. As the public began to spend its money on new goods such as cars and radios, they seemed less willing to spend as much money on furniture. High Point now was the new center of inexpensive, mass-produced furniture.

Grand Rapids continued to be a center for furniture design and continued to make high-quality furniture, but the South now dominated in producing cheaper grades. In the 1930s Grand Rapids produced high-quality Colonial designs that included handwork, but by the 1940s its furniture industry was dominated by "contract" furniture—furniture made for offices, stadiums, theaters, schools, and other public places.

---

30. Ibid.

31. Sam Burchell, *A History of Furniture—Celebrating Baker Furniture: One Hundred Years of Fine Reproductions* (New York: Harry N. Abrams, 1991), 8.

32. Ibid., 109.

4

The Peak Years: 1900–1930

Elizabeth Stillinger has documented the growing interest in American antiques in the early twentieth century in her book *The Antiquers,* in which she describes the major museum exhibits and events that shaped the public's interest in antiques and subsequently increased the demand for Colonial Revival furniture. After the great exhibition fairs of the nineteenth century, the most influential exhibits in the early twentieth century were sponsored by museums, which now began to display American antiques. In 1909, the Hudson-Fulton Celebration at the Metropolitan Museum of Art in New York City held an exhibition of American furniture from Colonial times up to 1815. This was the most comprehensive and well-organized exhibit of American antiques to date, focusing primarily on furniture from New York and New England (the Midatlantic states and the South were not yet included). Objects were arranged by period and displayed in their proper context in rooms that traced the evolution of American furniture design. One result of these period rooms was that the public went away with concrete ideas about how to incorporate antiques—or reproductions—in their own homes.[1]

After the turn of the century, the Colonial Revival movement became widely popular in architecture and home furnishings. Architecture tended toward homogenous plans for homes that were smaller, had fewer rooms, and more open floor plans, and with an emphasis on efficiency and hygiene. This was an era that saw the rise of the interior decorator and the reliance on architects to bring the best of Colonial design elements to bear on homes designed for modern living.[2]

One can see from the furniture catalogues of this period the value placed on simplicity and the rejection of the excesses of the Victorian era. Simplicity came to stand for purity and for the simpler life of the early republic. Doing away with Victorian clutter, ornamentation and overdecoration was encouraged not only for aesthetic reasons but also as a means to promote a healthy, sanitary environment. The walls of Colonial Revivalists' houses were often painted white because white and ivory were colors associated with purity and it was also believed (incorrectly) that they were used by early Americans.

1. Elizabeth Stillinger, *The Antiquers* (New York: Alfred A. Knopf, 1980), 129–32.

2. Bridget May, "Progressivism and the Colonial Revival: The Modern Colonial House, 1900–1920," *Winterthur Portfolio* 26 (Summer/Autumn 1991): 108.

Covering wood floors only with area rugs was another way to diminish dust and dirt. The simple lines of Colonial Revival furniture fulfilled this desire for simplicity, cleanliness, and order.[3]

A writer for *House Beautiful* in 1904 testifies to the strength of the Colonial Revival movement:

Every year sees the Colonial reaching more perfect expression, not only in furniture but in hangings, draperies, and all the accesories of decoration. Even in the cheaper priced furniture exact Colonial reproductions may be had now, and the makers who are not content to depend on antiques alone for designs are producing a modern Colonial series that would have been creditable to Hepplewhite, Sheraton, or Chippendale. So we say that there will be no successor to the Colonial style. It is as near perfection in household furniture as can be created, and as such it needs no successor.[4]

A survey of furniture catalogues in the Winterthur Library from the early twentieth century confirms that Colonial Revival furniture was widely available. The designs vary greatly in historical accuracy, and the furniture itself varies in the quality of its construction. We should note, however, that furniture catalogues tend to reveal what was being made in fairly large shops rather than in the smaller shops, whose quality would be higher.

Given the popularity of Colonial styles, it is not surprising that quite a bit of the furniture available was not of the highest quality and was sold at low prices. Ekin Wallick's *Inexpensive Furnishing in Good Taste* (1915) includes a wide variety of factory-made, low-priced pieces in simplified forms, such as wing chairs, slant-front desks on straight legs, and stripped-down Sheraton-style dining-room pieces. The Sheraton style was recommended for its simple lines: "For a small apartment or country dining room there is probably no style of furniture more suitable than Sheraton. The simple gracefulness of its lines will add a certain dignity to any room. . . . Sheraton furniture calls for white woodwork and light colored walls and will lend itself admirably to any color scheme which might be chosen."[5] These inexpensive pieces were often made of gum, which was stained dark to look like mahogany. Some popular, relatively new forms in this book include pieces for men—smoking stands, book troughs, and book racks—and for women, new designs of sewing stands.

The 1910 catalogue of Brandt Cabinet Works of Hagerstown, Maryland, describes that company as makers of parlor and library tables. Brandt produced broad adaptations of Colonial designs, all of quartered oak or imitation mahogany. Most looked more like golden oak than anything from the eighteenth century.

In 1913, S. Karpen and Sons of Chicago, New York, and Boston advertised "Colonial suites," each consisting of a sofa, an easy chair, and a rocker. Most owe a debt to Empire design, with massive scrolling crest rails and arms and scrolling legs with upholstered backs and seats. These inexpensive suites were still heavily influenced by the massiveness of Victorian furniture, and most collectors today would not find them appealing.

Peck and Hills of New York, a large mail-order company, advertised Colonial Revival furniture in its 1916 catalogue, most of it in quartered oak, with some mahogany. There are dining-room suites in the Queen Anne and Sheraton styles,

---

3. Ibid., 116.

4. Quoted from Cheryl Robertson, "Women, Style, and Decoration: Inside the Colonial Revival Home," in *The Colonial Revival in Rhode Island, 1890–1940* (Providence: Providence Preservation Society, 1989), 12.

5. Ekin Wallick, *Inexpensive Furnishings in Good Taste* (New York: Hearst's International Library Company, 1915), 91.

rather broadly interpreted, Jacobean furniture, and "period" tea carts—another popular item in the first quarter of the twentieth century.

The Danersk Furniture Company of New York advertised inexpensive-looking furniture in its 1917 catalogue, the most interesting being a gateleg desk consisting of a slant-front desk on a gateleg table base.

After 1900, and even more so after 1910, we see in furniture catalogues evidence of fairly faithful reproductions being manufactured in large numbers. By then, designers had absorbed some of the lessons offered by Irving Whitall Lyon in *The Colonial Furniture of New England,* which had been published in 1891, and Alvan Crocker Nye's 1895 book of designs of early American furniture, along with the period furniture included in the Hudson-Fulton Exhibition at the Metropolitan Museum. Well-researched books on American antiques continued to appear, such as Luke Vincent Lockwood's *Colonial Furniture in America* (1901). Lockwood's book covered the seventeenth century through the early nineteenth century, with furniture arranged according to period and style.

From 1900 on, many companies offered good-quality reproductions. Shaw's Furniture Company of Boston published a catalogue in 1910 with pen-and-ink drawings of elaborately carved Jacobean and Flemish pieces and living-room and dining-room suites in many styles. The quality appears high, though it is difficult to tell from the drawings alone.

The 1914 catalogue of the Richter Furniture Company of New York City shows many faithful adaptations of eighteenth-century designs, including Chippendale chairs of various grades. There is also a model called the "Puritan," a Queen Anne–style side chair with rockers, its selling price listed as $17.50.

Rocking chairs seem to have been irresistible to Colonial Revival designers.

A persuasive tribute to the popularity of Colonial Revival furniture during the 1910s is the 1915 *Craftsman* catalogue, which one would expect to find full of Mission furniture, identified with Gustav Stickley. Surprisingly, it also offered a number of Colonial designs, including several Chinese Chippendale pieces, Jacobean-inspired pieces with caning, a Windsor chair, a mahogany tilt-top table, a Chippendale pedestal, a gateleg table, and a mahogany slant-front desk.

Few of us associate Tiffany and Company with the Colonial Revival, but the company in fact did sell Colonial Revival furniture after 1907. Tiffany Studios had absorbed the Schmidt Brothers Furniture company in 1898. After 1907 Tiffany provided furnishings that it described as "artistic furniture" and "quality reproductions."[6] Tiffany catalogues from the 1910s show high-quality, generally faithful copies of dining-room and bedroom suites in many period styles (see figs. 4–1, 4–2, and 4–3).

Fig. 4-1 Duncan Phyfe-style mahogany extension table made by Tiffany Studios of New York City in 1915. Tiffany loosely described the table as being "in the Georgian style." Made from Cuban mahogany, it is inlaid with satinwood and ebony around the frieze. It sold for $215 in 1915. 5' diameter × 28 3/4" high (leaves each 14" × 60"). *Private collection.* Round tables now command an enormous premium. **$6,000–9,000.**

6. Robert Koch, *Louis Tiffany: Rebel in Glass,* updated third edition (New York: Crown, 1982), 135, 136.

Fig. 4-2 Matching sideboard made by Tiffany Studios, 1915. With biscuit corners, serpentine front inlaid and crossbanded in satinwood and ebony. Legs are turned and reeded. Three cock-beaded drawers over one central drawer flanked by two cabinets. Shaped, beaded apron. Back with chamfered panels. Drawer interiors with quarter-molding. Shellac finish. Sold for $256 in 1915. 77" long x 23 1/2" deep x 39" high. *Private collection.* **$5,000–7,500.**

Fig. 4-3 Mahogany server to match sideboard and extension table, by Tiffany Studios, 1915. Three drawers above shelf. Sold for $113 in 1915. 46 1/4" long x 20 1/8" deep x 35" high. *Private collection.* **$1,800–2,400.**

Many small cabinet shops were making reproductions during this period. Nathan Margolis in Hartford, Connecticut, and Meier and Hagen in New York City are two of the better-known shops.

Nathan Margolis opened his cabinet-making shop in Hartford in 1893 after emigrating from Yanova, Russia. He began by restoring and selling antique furniture but soon concentrated on making reproductions. By the mid-1920s the Margolis Shop was doing a flourishing business in handmade reproductions. The shop records are now in the Winterthur Museum Library. Most of these records cover the years from 1925 to 1974, when Harold Margolis, Nathan's son, ran the business. The Margolis Shop made furniture for the upper-middle class, for whom Margolis furniture was a highly desirable alternative to the prohibitive cost of antiques. The majority of the craftsmen employed by Margolis were European immigrants, who brought with them a tradition of skilled woodworking (figs. 6–30 and 6–31).

In the manuscript collection at the Winterthur Library, we came across a billhead from 1911 from a New York City cabinetmaker, who advertised himself as "Caspar Sommerlad, Dr. Antique Furniture. Furniture made to order, repairing, upholstering and polishing. Furniture boxed and shipped." His billhead includes a drawing of a Colonial patriot holding a walking stick and wearing a tricorner hat and breeches standing next to a long-case clock, a mantel, and a Windsor chair.[7] No doubt there were many other small shops like Sommerlad's in every city.

At the turn of the century, Chicago had several makers of good-quality Colonial Revival furniture. Marshall Field & Company hired Frederick Walton who had been trained at the Art Institute of Chicago, to head its custom shop. In the 1910s Marshall Field made pieces according to the directions of decorators as well as its own in-house designs.[8]

Also in Chicago, W. K. Cowan and Company, founded in the 1890s, was showing Colonial Revival furniture in period rooms as early as 1906. By 1909 Cowan was making furniture in six hundred patterns and included Queen Anne, French Colonial, Chinese Chippendale, and Hepplewhite styles.[9]

The W. K. Cowan Company's 1915 catalogue, "Things Colonial," contains Empire Revival pieces masquerading as Colonial, in addition to a Washington writing table for $150 and a Martha Washington sewing table for $30 (for an example, see page 140). These two patriotic items became popular pieces. The Washington writing table was raised on reeded legs with a central drawer. The writing surface has shelves not on the back of the desk but on both sides and apparently was modeled after a desk used by Washington

in New York City (for a similar example, see page 142).

The David Zork Company in Chicago, founded in 1914, made and sold antiques and reproduction furniture, some of which was produced for midwestern interior designers.[10] A few years later, in 1920, the Chicago firm of Tapp, De Wilde and Wallace was established. It built a reputation for making top-quality, exact copies of existing pieces in eighteenth-century styles. It also produced designs gracefully adapted to modern living requirements, using the best woods and finished by hand. The furniture was sold in Chicago, New York, and Los Angeles.[11]

From the 1920s on, the Chicago company of Watson and Boaler imported European antiques and paneling. It also made its own reproductions, sometimes doctoring an actual antique, sometimes making the reproduction from scratch.[12]

Interest in the Colonial Revival reached a fever pitch in the 1920s with a series of important exhibits and the beginnings of the historic preservation movement, with the efforts of the Rockefellers in Williamsburg, Virginia, the du Pont family at Winterthur, near Wilmington, Delaware, and Henry Ford at Greenfield Village, in Dearborn, Michigan. In 1922 the Metropolitan Museum held an exhibition of Duncan Phyfe furniture. In the same year *The Magazine Antiques* was founded. The American Wing of The Metropolitan opened in 1924, featuring period rooms complete with paneling, furniture, and appropriate accessories on permanent display. The display was not limited to antiques from New England—now it also included the Midatlantic states and the South.

As Elizabeth Stillinger notes, exhibits

7. From the Joseph Downs Collection of Manuscripts and Ephemera, The Winterthur Library.

8. Sharon Darling, *Chicago Furniture: Art, Craft, and Industry, 1833–1983* (New York: W. W. Norton, 1984), 208.

9. Ibid., 210.

10. Ibid., 210, 211.

11. Ibid., 212.

12. Ibid.

in the American Wing, bringing together furniture with other decorative arts from the same style period for a complete experience, presented to the public a lesson in the aesthetics of the seventeenth and eighteenth centuries. Finally the public had learned to appreciate the more restrained and simple aesthetic of Colonial America without having to embellish it or "Victorianize" it. With the American Wing as one of the focal points of antiques in the country during the 1920s, New York overtook Boston as the country's leading antiques center. By 1930, *The Magazine Antiques* had moved from Boston to New York, as had the influential antiques dealer Israel Sack.[13]

Furniture manufacturers naturally made the most of the museum exhibits. In 1923, on the heels of the 1922 exhibit, Baker Furniture Company offered a line of Duncan Phyfe furniture. The Charlotte Furniture Company of Charlotte, Michigan, advertised itself as makers of "Reproductions and Adaptations of Antique Furniture." In a catalogue from the 1920s, many pieces are inspired by specific antiques from museums or important private collections. The catalogue included copies from the American Wing, the Bolles Collection in the Metropolitan Museum, the collections of Mrs. Frances Garvan and Wallace Nutting, and pieces featured in Lockwood's *Colonial Furniture in America.*

The 1920s continued to see mass-produced Colonial Revival furniture from Grand Rapids and the Midwest. One of the prospering midwestern manufacturers from the 1920s was Wilhelm Furniture of Sturgis, Michigan. Its 1924 catalogue showed spinet desks, gateleg tables, tea carts, and other popular items. One intriguing catalogue from around the 1920s is from the Hand Made Furniture Shop of Chicago, advertising a "complete line of correct tea carts and ferneries." This com-

pany, and many others, produced tea carts in all the popular styles—Chippendale, Queen Anne, William and Mary, Adam, Jacobean, Sheraton, and "Colonial." In mahogany, a tea cart was priced around $40; in oak, $35.

Paine Furniture Company of Boston continued to produce large quantities of Colonial Revival furniture. Its catalogues from about 1920 show "Colonial style" (read "Empire style") twin beds, wing chairs, "Colonial sideboards" (which look like Empire pieces), music stands and "tip tables."

The 1920s witnessed the application of Colonial styles to new forms, such as coffee tables, tea carts, telephone tables, book stands, and radio tables. One mail-order company offering these new forms was the W. A. Hathaway Company of New York City. Its 1924 catalogue, "Furniture for the Home Emphasizing the Early American Period," showed desks of many forms (spinet, kneehole, George Washington), sofas, chairs, telephone cabinets, tea carts, and more. Judging from the catalogue, "Colonial" referred to Empire style, and "Early American" pieces were spool-turned.

The catalogue for the Winthrop Furniture Company in Boston from about 1925 shows another adaptation of the popular gateleg form. Winthrop offered a "Colonial Gateleg Corner Cabinet"—an odd-looking piece of furniture, consisting of a cabinet with a broken-arch pediment and central flame finial above doors with gothic arches. Below is the gateleg table with an oval top. In the same catalogue, Winthrop offered a mahogany library table with quarter-columns, cabriole legs, and ball-and-claw feet—sort of an elongated lowboy form, and one that is popular with buyers today (see a similar example on page 126). The catalogue also shows a "Colonial Chest," said to be an exact reproduction of a Salem (Massachu-

13. Stillinger, *The Antiquers*, 196–97.

setts) chest, a tallish chest with fluted quarter-columns and fan-carved apron (see page 143 for a similar chest).

Leavens of Boston, which sold mass-produced furniture in the 1920s, took liberties with earlier styles, applying older design motifs to new forms, such as telephone sets, gateleg desks, and smoking stands.

Although many companies in the 1920s made low-priced mass-produced Colonial Revival furniture, some companies sought to distinguish themselves from the fray and made good-quality, well-designed reproductions. A catalogue from about 1920 for the Old Colony Furniture Company of Boston and New York emphasizes the high quality of its furniture. With a design department headed by an antiquarian of note, Old Colony produced furniture that, according to the catalogue, was all handmade and hand-carved, with no spindle carving. Furthermore, the finishes were hand-rubbed. The company made bedroom suites, cabinets, chairs, desks, secretaries, mirrors, sideboards, sofas, and tables, as well as other furniture.

In the 1920s, the Kensington Manufacturing Company of New York City made good pieces in the Hepplewhite, Duncan Phyfe, Sheraton, seventeenth-century English, and Italian Renaissance styles. Kensington won a gold medal for craftsmanship at the 39th Annual Exhibition of the Architectural League in 1924. The award was for excellence in design, restraint in the treatment of details, workmanship (joinery, carving), and versatility of styles and periods.

The Chicago companies that were making reproductions included Watson and Boaler, John A. Colby & Sons, and Tapp, De Wilde and Wallace. Cleveland was the home of the design firm Rorimer-Brooks, known for its fine custom furniture. In the 1920s and 1930s, to meet public demand, Rorimer-Brooks also made Colonial Revival pieces in William and Mary, Queen Anne, and Duncan Phyfe styles. Some were faithful reproductions, and some were made using old parts.[14]

Ferdinand Keller of Philadelphia advertised in "Antiques, Reproductions," a catalogue of about 1920, good-quality pieces that were largely handmade, in the styles of Duncan Phyfe, Hepplewhite, Queen Anne, and Elizabethan. Karcher and Rehm was also making Colonial Revival furniture in Philadelphia around the same time.

The 1920s also saw the rise to prominence of such large department stores as Wanamaker's, Lord & Taylor, Jordan Marsh, and Marshall Field, some of which sent their buyers to Europe in search of antiques. Wanamaker's, of New York and Philadelphia, sold excellent-quality reproductions from many different periods in suites and as individual pieces. Beginning in 1918, Wanamaker's offered the first department-store decorating service, called "Au Quatrieme," in the New York store.[15]

Wanamaker's had offered Colonial Revival pieces as early as 1887 in its mail-order catalogue, where it advertised a library chair with a mahogany frame in the "English wing pattern" for $42.50 and a three-piece parlor suite (a settee, armchair, and side chair), featuring solid mahogany frames, in a generally faithful Sheraton square-back style. Also advertised were bedroom, dining-room, and desk chairs in a Chippendale style of rather elongated proportions.

By the 1920s Wanamaker's was advertising its high-quality Colonial-style furniture with finesse. Its 1927 catalogue, "Reflections in Good Taste," featured

14. Leslie Pina, *Louis Rorimer: A Man of Style* (Kent, Ohio: Kent State University Press, 1990), 48–49.
15. Ibid., 38.

room settings with an elegant, though lived-in, look. In each photograph, something is nonchalantly draped over a chair—a bathrobe, a towel, etc. Each photograph is described in breezy terms, casually invoking historical figures. The illustration of a study is entitled "Things to think with" and includes a George Washington desk and a John Hancock chair. Another library scene is labeled "In the Jeffersonian key." "Chippendale, Moderato" describes a comfortable living room, complete with camelback sofa, kneehole desk, lowboy, and tennis racket.

Fine department stores on the West Coast, notably S. and G. Gump Company of San Francisco, sold Colonial Revival furniture and other styles. Gump's catalogue, "Furniture of Individuality," included furniture copying Jacobean, early Italian, Renaissance, Louis XV, and Louis XVI styles.

In the 1920s Wallace Nutting in Massachusetts and Nathan Margolis and Abraham Fineberg in Hartford, Connecticut, were producing good-quality furniture. High-quality bench-made reproductions were being made in New England towns and elsewhere. In most areas where there was any money at all, by the 1920s and certainly by the 1930s, local cabinetmakers in small shops were selling their furniture locally to people of means. Figure 4–4 shows an example of a fine-quality bench-made reproduction made around 1930 in a shop in North Carolina.

The 1920s were famous for conspicuous consumption, and this was demonstrated in the antiques world as well. The decade ended with two highly publicized auctions of American antiques—the Reifsnyder Sale and the Flayderman Sale, both held in New York City in 1929. These two sales brought staggering prices

Fig. 4-4 Handmade copy of an eighteenth-century lowboy, c. 1930, made in a small cabinetmaking shop in Elizabeth City, North Carolina. A copy of a local c. 1760 piece. Cabriole legs with volutes, pad feet. Shell-carved apron. Walnut. 34 1/8" wide x 24 3/8" deep x 28 3/4" high. *Private collection.* **$2,400–3,600.**

as a result of the competition between the major collectors Henry Ford, Henry Frances du Pont, and Frances Garvan. These millionaire collectors certainly impressed upon the public the value and importance of American antiques.[16]

The 1920s ended with the Girl Scouts Loan Exhibition in New York City in 1929, an important exhibit that widened its focus on American antiques from seventeenth-century New England to include New York and Pennsylvania and Queen Anne, Chippendale, and Duncan Phyfe styles. This exhibition brought together the cream of the crop of American antiques, each piece having been carefully selected to demonstrate the best design characteristics of its kind. By the end of the 1920s American antiques were without question validated for their artistic merit.[17] As the public demanded copies of the finest museum-quality American antiques, the market for reproductions became increasingly strong.

---

16. Stillinger, *The Antiquers,* 200–202.

17. Ibid., 202–3

5

The Furniture of Wallace Nutting

By Michael Ivankovich

Michael Ivankovich is widely recognized as the country's leading authority on Wallace Nutting pictures, books, and furniture. He is the author of four books on Wallace Nutting, including The Guide to Wallace Nutting Furniture, The Price Guide to Wallace Nutting Pictures *(4th edition),* The Alphabetical and Numerical Index to Wallace Nutting Pictures, *and* The Guide to Wallace Nutting–Like Photographers of the Early Twentieth Century. *He has also published five other reference guides on Wallace Nutting and has written numerous articles. He conducts periodic Wallace Nutting specialty auctions. Ivankovich can be reached at P.O. Box 2458, Doylestown, PA 18901; (215) 345-6094.*

Many people no doubt know the name Wallace Nutting from his landscape photographs, and some may be aware that he wrote nearly twenty books, but, surprisingly, relatively few people know much about Wallace Nutting's bench-made reproduction furniture.

Working in Southbury, Connecticut, from 1905 to 1912, Wallace Nutting, a retired Congregational minister, moved his already profitable picture business to Framingham, Massachusetts, where it began to flourish. He sold his pictures in department stores and gift shops, and the public soon became fascinated by his pleasant pastoral scenes of flowering trees, birches, streams, and lakes. By 1912 Nutting's picture business was grossing more than a thousand dollars a day.

As the public became more interested in the Colonial Revival movement, Nutting began to compose and photograph Colonial interior scenes in his home or in the homes of friends. He would dress his models in Colonial outfits and pose them among fine antiques and decorative items of various forms and styles.

Over a five-year period, starting in 1915, Nutting purchased, restored, and furnished five historic homes in New England. Each house was selected because of its historical charm and its particular decorative style. These houses were the Wentworth-Gardner House in Portsmouth, New Hampshire (Chippendale style); the Hazen-Garrison House in Haverhill, Massachusetts (Pilgrim, with English influence); the Culter-Bartlett House in Newburyport, Massachusetts (Chippendale, Hepplewhite, and Sheraton); the Saugus Iron Works, or Broadhearth, in Saugus, Massachusetts (Pilgrim with Gothic influence); and the Webb House in Wethersfield, Connecticut (Dutch and Chippendale).

As a result of his research into such a wide variety of styles during these five years, Nutting became recognized as an expert of early American antiques. The lack of scholarship on early American antiques led Nutting to write and publish three books of his own. His first book, *Windsor Chairs* (see figure 5–1), published in 1917, became the definitive work on Windsor chairs. In 1921 Nutting published a book on Pilgrim-style furniture, *Furniture of the Pilgrim Century* (see figure 5–2), and in 1928 he published *The Furniture Treasury,* which is still in print and is still considered to be the most complete pictorial reference book on early American antiques.

Nutting knew that he was only one of many collectors of antiques. As early as 1915, with the Colonial Revival movement well under way, the finest examples of early American antiques were frequently unavailable even to those who

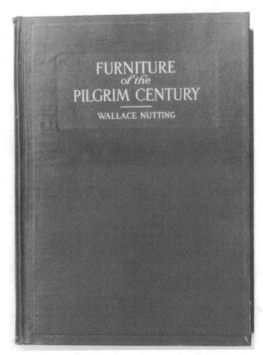

Fig. 5-2 Wallace Nutting's *Furniture of the Pilgrim Century,* published in 1921, covered not only Windsors but also other types of chairs, American chests, desks, tables, mirrors, clocks, utensils, and hardware. More than five hundred pages long, with more than a thousand photographs of items dating from 1620 to 1720. This was the period from which the early Nutting reproductions were taken. *Courtesy Michael Ivankovich, Diamond Press.*

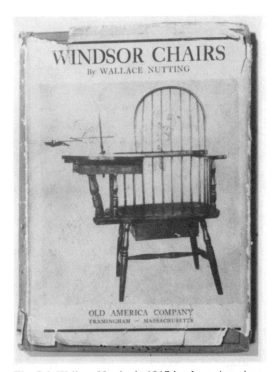

Fig. 5-1 Wallace Nutting's 1917 book on American Windsors, the first serious study of the Windsor form, discusses chairs from 1725 to 1825 and pictures nearly one hundred Windsors, many of which Nutting owned himself. *Courtesy Michael Ivankovich, Diamond Press.*

could afford them. Thus Nutting decided, in 1917, to start his own furniture reproduction business.

In 1918 Nutting published his first reproduction furniture catalogue, this one on Windsor Chairs (see figure 5–3). Nutting had become an expert on Windsor chairs, so, logically, this was the first style he began reproducing. His sales catalogue contained more than one hundred different Windsor styles that were available from his shop. Nutting continued producing Windsor chairs through the 1930s, so Windsors account for a large percentage of his production and are the most common, available form of Wallace Nutting furniture. When Nutting decided to create the "perfect" Windsor chair, he could use as a

Fig. 5-3 Wallace Nutting's 1918 catalogue of Windsor chairs from his workshop, his first furniture sales catalogue. *Courtesy Michael Ivankovich, Diamond Press.*

Fig. 5-4 Wallace Nutting c. 1921 no. 420 bow-back Windsor armchair with a block brand. Fairly common. Very good condition. 41" high. *Courtesy Michael Ivankovich, Diamond Press.* **$1,800–2,400.**

model one of the 150 Windsors in his own collection.

Nutting made his Windsors entirely by hand, even though he could have made them by machine for one-twentieth of the cost of hand production. With so much handwork involved, a craftsman was capable of completing only three or four chair seats a day. Each seat was shaped from a single piece of country pine 2" thick. All legs and stretchers were finished on a hand lathe because machine lathes could not make cuts deep enough for the look Nutting wanted to achieve. All chair legs were raked 4" within 18" in order to provide the greatest strength and stability. Bow backs and combs were bent with wet steam and shaped by hand. Arm rails ending in knuckles were carved by hand.

Nutting used three different woods in making his Windsors: rock maple for the legs, country pine for the seats, and hickory for the spindles, bows, bent arm rails, and combs. The finishing process was an important part of Windsor construction. Each part of the chair was finished at least five times by hand with a special shellac. The chairs were rubbed by hand between each coat.

After mastering the Windsor form, Nutting designed furniture in the Pilgrim Century style. He made court cupboards, paneled and sunflower chests, oak chests, tables of many designs, including butterfly, gateleg, refectory, trestle, folding gate, and tavern tables, framed desks, ladderback chairs, joined and rush stools, and pilgrim and Carver chairs. He ventured into other styles only when forced to do so by economic pressures. As he wrote in the *Wallace Nutting General Catalogue, Supreme Edition* in 1930, "a stop is made just short of the cabriole leg." In the mid-1920s Nutting began to sell other furniture styles in order to maintain his business's profitability: Chippendale, Hepplewhite, Queen Anne, Sheraton, Duncan Phyfe,

Fig. 5-5 Wallace Nutting c. 1921 no. 329 swivel Windsor side chair with a block brand. Unusual, but not rare. Normal wear. 18" wide × 16 3/4" deep × 40" high. *Courtesy Michael Ivankovich, Diamond Press.* **$500–750.**

Fig. 5-6 Wallace Nutting c. 1921 no. 415 comb-black Windsor chair with New England turnings and block brand. Unusual, but not rare. Very good condition. 45" tall. *Private collection.* **$1,800–2,400.**

Federal—he copied them all. His advertisements in *The Magazine Antiques* helped him reach an affluent market.

At his peak, Nutting employed about twenty-five craftsmen. By 1927–28, however, sales had begun to lag. Nutting was aware of the demand for eighteenth-century designs, so he began to copy Queen Anne, Chippendale, Hepplewhite, and Sheraton styles. In his autobiography he wrote: "My first attempt at mahogany was to copy the most beautiful and elaborate piece of American furniture—a secretary in Providence which had been bought from Goddard. I took six of my craftsmen to study it by the hour and to make all measurements and sketches. . . . I knew if I had made that piece as well as the old,

that I could make anything." In the late 1920s he produced Savery (of Philadelphia) style highboys and lowboys, Queen Anne, Chippendale, and Hepplewhite style armchairs and side chairs, carved walnut sideboards, a Goddard chest-on-chest, Welsh dressers, and a carved corner cupboard. In all, Nutting offered eighty different types of chairs, thirty beds, sixty tables, twenty chests and chests of drawers, twenty cupboards, and twenty desks and secretaries.

Nutting took an analytical approach to the furniture reproduction process. First, he would locate the finest examples of authentic American antiques. After studying each piece with his master craftsmen, they would draw detailed

Fig. 5-7 Pair of Wallace Nutting c. 1921 no. 33 Windsor comb-back side chairs, block branded. Unusual, but not rare. Normal wear. 44" tall. **$1,800–2,400** the pair. *Center:* Wallace Nutting c. 1921 no. 660 tavern table, block brand. Unusual, but not rare. Normal wear. 36" wide x 24" deep x 27" high. **$1,200–1,800.** Pair of Wallace Nutting c. 1921 no. 22 cross-bow candlestands, one with block brand, one unmarked. Unusual, but not rare. Normal wear. 14" diameter x 25" high. *Courtesy Northeast Auctions, Hampton, New Hampshire.* **$500–750** each.

sketches to determine what made each piece unique.

Rarely did he find an antique he felt was perfect. To him, most pieces needed some improvement—and extra inch added to the legs, a crisper turning, a narrower drawer. He then incorporated these improvements in his final drawings and sketches.

After deciding which pieces to reproduce, Nutting drew precise patterns. His craftsmen used the patterns, whether of paper or wood, to ensure uniformity in size for each individual component. The final step before production was to assemble a model of the piece of furniture. Every craftsman was required to duplicate the master prototype exactly. Once a piece reached the production stage, Nutting as-

signed it a three-digit Furniture Design Number for his sales catalogues. For example, the 300s represented side chairs, the 400s were armchairs, the 900s were cabinet pieces, etc.

Nutting's furniture reproductions represented one of the finest styles of any twentieth-century furniture maker. What sets his furniture apart was his production method. He insisted that his craftsmen follow the old, traditional methods. All turnings and carvings were executed by hand, and all assembly was done with foxtail wedges and hot glue. Each step contributed to a finer, more accurate piece of furniture. Nutting, however, never cut corners and produced each piece regardless of expense.

Maintaining such a high level of qual-

Fig. 5-8 Pair of Wallace Nutting c. 1921 no. 408 bow-back Windsor armchairs with block brands. Unusual, but not rare. Normal wear. 41" tall. *Courtesy Northeast Auctions, Hampton, New Hampshire.* **$2,800–3,600** the pair.

ity had its consequences. Nutting's furniture was expensive, and the Depression signaled the decline of his business. Nutting had always relied on his picture business to carry the furniture business. Now the picture business was hard hit as well. By 1930 Nutting was making a commercial line of furniture for businesses—check-writing desks for banks, typewriter desks, executive desks, stenographer's chairs, a spinning-wheel hatrack, and even an oak radiator cover. By the late 1930s, he had only three or four employees.

Wallace Nutting died in 1941, and his remaining furniture and antique collection was sold at Parke-Bernet in New York.

Markings

Wallace Nutting marked most of his furniture using one of five distinct markings:

1. Paper labels were Nutting's earliest form of identification; he used three different labels between 1917 and 1922.

2. Script-branded signature: In 1922, Nutting sold his business, along with the right to continue using the Wallace Nutting name. The new owners did not maintain Nutting's high standards, and in 1924 Nutting repurchased the business. Although script-branded furniture is collect-

Fig. 5-9 Set of eight Wallace Nutting c. 1921 no. 408 bow-back Windsor armchairs, block branded. A set of eight is rare; this is an assembled set. Normal wear. 41" high. *Courtesy Northeast Auctions, Hampton, New Hampshire.* **$12,000–18,000.**

ible in its own right, it is not as desirable as paper-label and block-branded furniture.

3. Block-branded signature: From 1924 to his death in 1941, Nutting marked his furniture with a distinctive block brand. This marking indicates furniture that was made *after* Nutting repurchased his business.

4. Punched, or incised, marking: This much smaller, block-type marking was usually used on small items such as treenware. This marking can be found on significantly larger pieces as well, such as chairs, tables, and corner cupboards.

5. Punched number: Some pieces of Nutting furniture retain their three-digit punched number, although the paper label may be missing.

Wallace Nutting Fakes

At present, fake Wallace Nutting furniture presents minimal problems. Pieces of inferior furniture marked with a fake, stenciled "Wallace Nutting" are rare.

Fig. 5-10 Set of six Wallace Nutting c. 1921 no. 301 bow-back, brace-back side chairs, block branded. Individual chairs are fairly common; sets are unusual, but not rare. Normal wear, 39" tall. *Courtesy Northeast Auctions, Hampton, New Hampshire.* **$4,500–6,500.**

The best defense against fake Wallace Nutting furniture is to learn the difference between ordinary and superior examples. Nutting represents the finest of twentieth-century reproductions available, and, although anyone can fake a paper label or a branded signature, no one can profitably reproduce a piece of fine Nutting furniture, add seventy-five years of age and patina, and make it look as good as the original.

The Future of Wallace Nutting Furniture

Wallace Nutting furniture can be found in shops and shows all over the country, but especially in New England, where it was originally made. Over the past several years, major regional auction houses have included significant amounts of Nutting furniture. In 1989 Skinner's of Bolton, Massachusetts, had a sale devoted entirely to Nutting and a few other makers of fine reproductions.

A highly successful March 1992 auction at Northeast Auctions in New Hamp-

Fig. 5-11 Set of six Wallace Nutting c. 1921 no. 393 Pilgrim side chairs, block branded. Individual chairs are fairly common; sets are unusual, but not rare. Normal wear, except for damaged rush on several seats (easily restored). 43" tall. *Courtesy Northeast Auctions, Hampton, New Hampshire.* **$2,400–3,000.**

shire contained over twenty lots of Wallace Nutting furniture. Several lots consisted of sets of chairs and commanded substantial prices.

A January 1993 Americana sale at Sotheby's in New York City contained four lots of exceptional Wallace Nutting furniture, three of which sold for well over estimate. A Chippendale-style shell-carved secretary in the Newport manner sold for almost $15,000; a Federal-style desk with bookcase sold for $3450; a Chippendale-style bonnet-top highboy with shell carving sold for over $7000; and a Chippendale-style lowboy sold for $3162. All of these were formal pieces, made in styles that Nutting turned to in the late 1920s, after his Pilgrim Century pieces. His high style pieces will probably continue to command the highest prices. With such major auction houses selling Nutting furniture, we can assume that the market for Wallace Nutting furniture is in a strong position to improve into the twenty-first century.

Fig. 5-12 Set of eight Wallace Nutting c. 1921 New England ladder-back chairs (two no. 490 armchairs, six no. 390 side chairs), block branded. Individual chairs are fairly common; sets are unusual, but are not rare. Normal wear, except for damaged rush on several seats (easily restored). 50" tall. *Courtesy Northeast Auctions, Hampton, New Hampshire.* **$3,000–4,800** the set, as is.

Fig. 5-13 Two armchairs from a set of eight Wallace Nutting c. 1928 ribbon-back Chippendale chairs (*two* no. 459-B armchairs, *six* no. 359-B side chairs), block branded. Individual chairs are rare; sets are extremely rare. Normal wear. 40" tall. *Courtesy C. G. Sloan and Company. North Bethesda, Maryland.* **$6,000–9,000.** Set of 12 **$18,000–24,000.**

Fig. 5-14 Set of four Wallace Nutting, c. 1928 Queen Anne-style mahogany side chairs (similar to no. 399), branded signature. Extremely rare. 42 1/2" high. *Courtesy Skinner, Inc., Bolton, Mass.* Single, **$1,000–1,5000.** Eight for **$10,000–15,000.** Twelve for **$18,000–24,000.**

Fig. 5-15 Wallace Nutting c. 1928 upholstered wing chair with large ball-and-claw feet, carved legs, and block and turned stretcher base. *Courtesy Nadeau's Auction Gallery, Windsor, Conn.* **$3,000–4,500.**

Fig. 5-17 Wallace Nutting c. 1921 no. 17 Windsor candlestand, block brand. Fairly common. Excellent condition. 14" diameter × 25" high. *Courtesy Michael Ivankovich, Diamond Press.* **$450–650.**

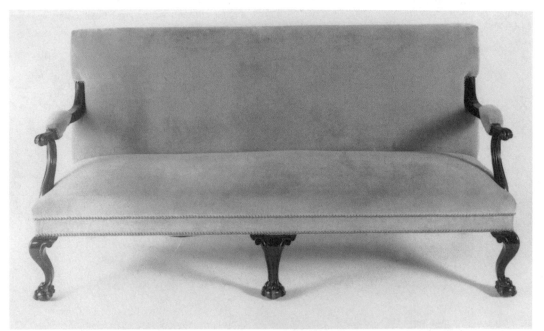

Fig. 5-16 Wallace Nutting c. 1928 no. 525 Chippendale-style mahogany sofa, no visible signature. Extremely rare. 75" long × 37". *Courtesy Skinner, Inc., Bolton, Mass.* **$3,000–5,000.**

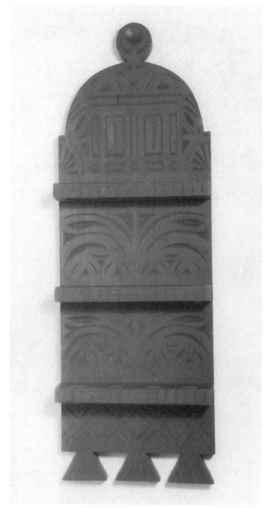

Fig. 5-19 Wallace Nutting c. 1928 large Chippendale-style giltwood and mahogany-veneer looking glass, branded signature. Rare. 53" high. *Courtesy Skinner, Inc., Bolton, Mass.* **$2,500–3,500.**

Fig. 5-18 Wallace Nutting c. 1920s no. 903 spoon rack, unmarked. Extremely rare. Normal wear (this piece is in its original red paint, which is quite unusual). 24 3/4" high. *Courtesy Michael Ivankovich, Diamond Press.* **$800–1,200.**

Fig. 5-20 Wallace Nutting c. 1928 no. 693B Chippendale-style carved mahogany piecrust tip-top tea table, branded signature. Rare. 27 1/2" high × 33" diameter. *Courtesy Skinner, Inc., Bolton, Mass.* **$3,000–4,500.**

Fig. 5-21 Wallace Nutting c. 1921 no. 615 trestle table, block brand. Unusual, but not rare. Very good condition. 50" long × 30" high. *Courtesy Michael Ivankovich, Diamond Press.* **$800–1,200.**

Fig. 5-22 Wallace Nutting c. 1921 no. 613 ball-turned tavern table with paper label. Rare. Very good condition. 36" x 25 1/2". *Courtesy Michael Ivankovich, Diamond Press.* **$1,200–1,800.**

Fig. 5-23 Wallace Nutting c. 1928 block-front chest with four graduated drawers, bracket feet. Top is molded and shaped. Drawer openings are lipped. Rare. A 1940 advertisement in *The Magazine Antiques* described it as "one of the simplest examples of the Goddard style. Heavy Cuban mahogany in three-inch thickness used for the drawers." *Courtesy James D. Julia, Inc., Fairfield, Maine.* **$3,000–5,000.**

Fig. 5-24 Wallace Nutting c. 1928 no. 979 Chippendale-style mahogany bureau in the Goddard manner, branded signature. Extremely rare. 39 1/2" wide x 18 1/2" deep x 34 3/4" high. *Courtesy Skinner, Inc., Bolton, Mass.* **$5,000–8,000.**

Fig. 5-25 Wallace Nutting c. 1928 no. 729 Chippendale-style maple slant-front desk, branded signature. Rare. 36" wide × 19" deep × 39" high. *Courtesy Skinner, Inc., Bolton, Mass.* **$3,000–4,500.**

Fig. 5-26 Wallace Nutting c. 1928 no. 729 Chippendale-style mahogany blind-door secretary, branded signature. Extremely rare. 42" wide × 23" deep × 103" high. *Courtesy Skinner, Inc., Bolton, Mass.* **$18,000–24,000.**

Fig. 5-27 Wallace Nutting c. 1928 no. 989 Chippendale-style mahogany highboy, unsigned. Extremely rare. 39 1/2" wide × 20" deep × 85 1/2" high. *Courtesy Skinner, Inc., Bolton, Mass.* **$8,000–12,000.**

Fig. 5-29 Wallace Nutting c. 1928 no. 846B Federal-style maple tester bed, branded signature, with net and dust ruffle. Rare. 54" wide × 76 1/2" long × 68" high. *Courtesy Skinner, Inc., Bolton, Mass.* **$2,000–3,000.**

Fig. 5-28 Wallace Nutting c. 1928 no. 832B Federal-style carved mahogany tester bed, branded signature, with net and dust ruffle. Rare. 54" wide × 74" long × 82" high. *Courtesy Skinner, Inc., Bolton, Mass.* **$3,000–4,500.**

6

The 1930s: Diverted by the Depression

The Depression brought an abrupt end to the public's eager acquisition of all things Colonial. The interest may have continued to exist, but the means to buy did not. The decline of Wallace Nutting's furniture business can be taken as an example of the toll exacted by the Depression. Colonial styles remained popular, but the general public simply could not afford to buy as it had in the 1920s. Not surprisingly, many furniture companies failed completely.

By the end of the Depression, several changes were evident in the furniture industry as a whole. The South, with its cheap labor and plentiful raw materials, had emerged as a powerful new furniture producer, overtaking Grand Rapids as a maker of low-grade residential furniture. Furniture manufacturers in the Midwest, New York, and other areas responded to the Depression by marketing smaller pieces, when the public could not afford to buy large case pieces. Popular items included magazine racks, radio cabinets, and telephone stands—all made in a variety of period styles. The production of these novelty items helped places like Chicago and New York maintain their furniture production throughout the 1930s.

Finally, several companies capitalized on the partnership between museums and the Colonial Revival movement that had begun in the 1920s. These companies were granted the rights to reproduce items from museum collections. This trend has lasted through the decades and, in recent years, several museums have strengthened their furniture reproduction programs, providing the public with a good source of reproductions.

During the 1930s Grand Rapids was losing its grip on the market for low-end furniture. Grand Rapids continued to produce high-quality expensive furniture, but it was not able to compete with the low-priced furniture being produced in the South in increasing quantities in the 1920s and 30s.

The Southern furniture industry had been in existence from the 1880s, soon after the Civil War and Reconstruction, making inexpensive furniture for Southerners recovering from the economic deprivations of war. Furniture factories in North Carolina, Georgia, Virginia, and Tennessee were locally owned, and produced furniture largely for the local population. It was not marketed widely. However, the South had abundant lumber and cheap labor: fine potential for a successful furniture industry.

During the last quarter of the nineteenth century, as many of the large furniture manufacturers moved from the Northeast to the Midwest, some of the Northeastern firms began to explore opportunities in the South, and began to in-

Fig. 6-1 The display room of the Continental Furniture Company of High Point, North Carolina, in 1936. Continental prospered throughout the 1920s and 1930s. Displayed are Chippendale-style secretary-bookcases, kneehole desks, a block-front slant-lid desk, Windsor chairs, and ladder-back chairs. *Courtesy Kate Cloninger, International Home Furnishings Center, High Point, N.C.*

vest in already existing factories there. By 1890 North Carolina had six furniture factories; by 1900 this number had increased to forty-four, with twelve of those plants located in High Point, indicating an early strength that would solidify in the twentieth century.[1]

High Point copied the same proven marketing strategies used in Grand Rapids. Furniture manufacturers came together in High Point to pool their strengths and compete more effectively against Grand Rapids, rather than compete against one another. In 1913 High Point had its first semiannual Southern Furniture Exposition, patterned after the Furniture Market in Grand Rapids. The first Exposition consisted mainly of cheap and medium-grade bedroom furniture, including pieces in Colonial styles. Not only

did furniture manufacturers participate in the Exposition, but suppliers of materials attended as well. Lewis Thompson and Company, a Philadelphia firm then the largest handler of mahogany in the world, owning 640,000 acres of timberland in Mexico, was on hand to display its mahogany and Circassian walnut veneers.[2]

World War I disrupted the progress of the Southern Furniture Exposition, but only temporarily. By the mid-1920s, High Point's exposition was attracting national attention and it led to the growth of the furniture industry not only in North Carolina, but also in Tennessee, Georgia, and Virginia (figures 6–1 and 6–2 illustrate the work of two High Point area companies). By 1926 North Carolina had 133 factories, while Tennessee, Georgia, and Virginia combined had 100 factories. During

1. David N. Thomas, "A History of Southern Furniture," *Furniture South* 46, no. 10, sec. 2 (October 1967): 14, 25.
2. Ibid., 37, 46, 47.

Fig. 6-2 Chippendale-style c. 1930 mahogany kneehole desk with shell-carved apron, fluted quarter-columns, cabriole legs, pad feet. Labeled "Thomasville Chair Co. Character Furniture Since 1904." From the High Point North Carolina area. 49" long × 19 1/2" deep × 30" high. *Courtesy Willow Park Mall, Durham, N.C.* **$900–1,200.**

the 1920s, the North Carolina furniture industry produced more bedroom and dining room furniture than any other part of the country. By 1929 producers from most of the important furniture-making centers attended the semiannual Exposition.[3]

The Depression slowed the progress of the Southern furniture industry for a few years, but as the nation began to recover from the Depression, it was clear that High Point had surpassed Grand Rapids in the production of cheap and medium-range furniture for the general public. By 1937 North Carolina and Virginia were producing 38 percent of the country's bedroom furniture and 37 percent of its dining room furniture. In 1937 North Carolina ranked second after New York in overall furniture production.[4]

Most of the Southern companies began the same way the Grand Rapids companies began: dealing with the raw product, making wood products, and then making furniture using mass production. There were, however, smaller cabinet shops also producing higher-quality furniture. One such firm that grew into a successful company throughout the first half of the twentieth century was Biggs Furniture Company of Richmond, Virginia. Biggs is an example of the firms producing high-quality bench-made reproductions in the 1930s.

Like many businesses specializing in reproductions, Biggs began with a cabinetmaker who knew antiques, who repaired them, and soon got into the profitable business of making reproductions. In 1890 Joseph Franklin Biggs, an En-

3. Ibid., p. 55, 59, 66.

4. Ibid., p. 72.

glishman, opened up his shop in Richmond. Apparently, he came to Virginia looking for antiques to sell. When he realized that his customers would sometimes be forced to wait a year before he could locate the antiques they wanted, he began to make reproductions. Biggs copied originals for his customers and he gradually built up the business to employ many craftsmen to produce handmade reproductions. Biggs also continued to carry antiques until the 1930s. Eventually, Biggs had shops in Atlanta, Washington, Baltimore, Pittsburgh, and New Orleans. In the 1930s Biggs had a flourishing mail-order business, with catalogues advertising "Fine Colonial Reproductions" (see figure 6–3). Biggs pieces were popular throughout the South, and Biggs reproductions show up for sale all around the country today. Though acquired by several larger firms, Biggs continued to do business in Richmond until 1989.

Also in Richmond, and for a while next door to Biggs, was H. C. Valentine

Fig. 6-3 Biggs Furniture Company catalogue from the early 1940s, Richmond, Virginia.

and Company, which produced bench-made furniture of the same quality, using similar designs (see figures 6–4 and 6–5). Valentine's catalogue from around 1930 contains a series of individual pamphlets on each American style period, even "Colonial," which they admit to be Empire style (they continue to use the term "Colonial" because the public seemed to insist on it). Each pamphlet provides a brief history of the style, and illustrates several pieces made by Valentine in that particular style. Valentine apparently started out as an antiques dealer and appraiser who employed craftsmen to build reproductions. Valentine's catalogue claims that no modern methods were used in the shop. Finishes were hand-applied and hand-rubbed, with at least seven coats of finish. During the 1930s Valentine sold antiques as well as reproductions. Although Biggs continued to expand its business throughout the 1930s, Valentine must have suffered during the Depression, as the business did not survive the 1930s.

One large Virginia firm that prospered during the first half of the twentieth century was Bassett Furniture Industries. Bassett was founded in 1902, by J. D. Bassett, who began by selling oak lumber to companies in Grand Rapids and Jamestown, New York. Then Bassett began to produce bedroom suites in golden oak. Prices were cheap—one bed actually sold for $1.50. As the firm prospered and hired furniture designers, it began to produce some Colonial designs, like those shown in figure 6–6. During the 1930s, eighteenth-century styles in mahogany were popular sellers.

Southern furniture companies also forged relationships with regional museums to make reproductions from their collections. Virginia Craftsmen, Inc. of Harrisonburg was granted exclusive rights to reproduce antiques from Monticello, home of Thomas Jefferson. Pieces shown in the catalogue included Jefferson's music rack, a card table, and a sewing table.

Fig. 6-4 The showrooms of H.C. Valentine Company, Richmond, Virginia, showing its period and reproductions. From the H.C. Valentine Company catalogue, c. 1930.

Fig. 6-5 The showrooms from the H.C. Valentine Company, Richmond, Virginia, showing a variety of Chippendale, Empire, and other period reproductions for the dining room. From the H.C. Valentine Company catalogue, c. 1930.

Fig. 6-6 Bassett Furniture Industries Jacobean-style dining-room suite from the 1920s. Mahogany and walnut. Gate-leg table with molded top and Jacobean-type turnings. Chairs with cutout carrying handles, strong turnings. Buffet and server complete the set. *Courtesy Bassett Furniture Industries, Bassett, Virginia.*

In the late 1940s, Biggs took over the furniture reproduction program at Monticello.

Other museums around the country also began sponsoring reproductions in the 1930s. In 1936, Kittinger began reproducing selected pieces for Colonial Williamsburg. This relationship continued until 1989, when Kittinger went out of business. Baker Furniture Company makes the Colonial Williamsburg reproductions today. In Zeeland, Michigan, the Colonial Manufacturing Company began making reproductions for the Henry Ford Museum in Dearborn, including several tall case clocks (Colonial's specialty), corner chairs, a tambour desk, highboys, and several Duncan Phyfe-style pieces. Colonial continued making reproductions for the Henry Ford Museum into the 1960s.

Individual craftsmen working in small cabinetmaking shops also continued to make high-quality, largely handmade reproductions, often based on a local antique. In Baltimore, Potthast Brothers continued making high-quality reproductions, as did J. W. Berry and Son. Enrico Liberti opened up his Baltimore shop in the 1930s. The Liberti Shop built an excellent reputation during the 1930s and was employed to make reproductions for a number of public buildings. Liberti still makes reproductions today.

In Hartford, Connecticut, the Margolis Shop continued to make Colonial reproductions of the highest quality. Between 1926 and 1950, the shop produced approximately 7,400 pieces of furniture. Margolis furniture is a very strong seller today. Figures 6–30 and 6–31 show work from the Margolis Shop.

Margolis also fostered the talents of other cabinetmakers, like Charles Post, who went on to form his own shop and to do fine work. Abraham Fineberg set up his shop in Hartford in 1932, having come from Lithuania in 1929. He and his son, Israel, produced high-quality custom-

(Text continued on page 79)

Fig. 6-9 Biggs c. 1925-40 Queen-Anne-style mahogany tea table. Rectangular top with raised thumb-molded edge, above a plain frieze, above an ogee serpentine apron. C-scrolled bordered knees, cabriolet legs with pad feet, with two candle slides on either side. 30" wide × 18 1/2" deep × 26 1/2" high. *Courtesy Frank H. Boos Gallery, Bloomfield Hills, Mich.* **$1,000–1,500.**

Fig. 6-7 Biggs c. 1940 dish-top candlestand, which sold for $15.50 around 1940. Very light weight. Three-board top. 15 1/2" diameter × 25" high. *Private collection.* **$175–275.**

Fig. 6-8 Biggs c. 1930 Hepplewhite-style *demi-lune* card table with five legs, flip top, line inlays on frieze and on square, tapered legs. 36" diameter × 30" high. *Private collection.* **$500–750.**

Fig. 6-10 One of a set of eight Biggs c. 1915 side dining chairs in Hepplewhite Revival style, with line inlays on chair back, seat rail, and legs. Chair back of dowel construction; legs are mortise-and-tenon joined. 18 1/2" wide × 17 1/2" deep × 38" high. *Private collection.* **$2,800–3,800** the set.

Fig. 6-11 Biggs Hepplewhite-style c. 1915 round mahogany dining table with three leaves, line inlays. En suite with the dining chairs. 60" diameter × 29 1/4" high. *Private collection.* **$3,600–4,800.**

Fig. 6-12 Biggs Hepplewhite-style c. 1915 mahogany sideboard with slightly bowed front. Line inlays on front and on the six square, tapered legs. En suite with table and chairs. 72" long × 28" diameter × 40 1/4" high. *Private collection.* **$1,800–2,400.**

Fig. 6-15 Biggs c. 1930 four-drawer Hepplewhite-style mahogany chest of drawers with French splay feet, oval brasses. Stringing around drawers. Top not molded–a lack of detail typical of Colonial Revival pieces. Top made of three boards, plywood back and drawer bottoms. 39 1/4" wide x 20 1/2" deep x 38" high. *Private collection.* **$800–1,200.**

Fig. 6-13 One of a set of eight Biggs c. 1910 solid mahogany Chippendale-style dining chairs (two arms chairs, six side chairs). Mortise-and-tenon construction, rear legs chamfered. Integral shoe, no molding on backsplat, stiles, or crest rail. Heavy in weight. Sides 20" wide x 16 1/2" deep x 38 1/2" high. *Private collection.* **$3,600–4,800.**

Fig. 6-14 Biggs c. 1930–40 "Colonial" ottoman as described in the Biggs catalogue. 20" long x 16" wide. *Private collection.* **$125–225.**

Fig. 6-16 Biggs c. 1937 writing desk. The 1937 catalogue describes it as follows: "Late Sheraton mahogany writing table, with reeded legs. Reproduced from a period about 1760. 44" long x 25" deep x 40" high overall, with two large drawers, three small drawers, two cupboards, and the letter boxes. $127.50." The description is not quite accurate. This is actually a reproduction of a c. 1800 style. The Biggs model has nailed drawers. *Private collection.* **$1,200–1,800.**

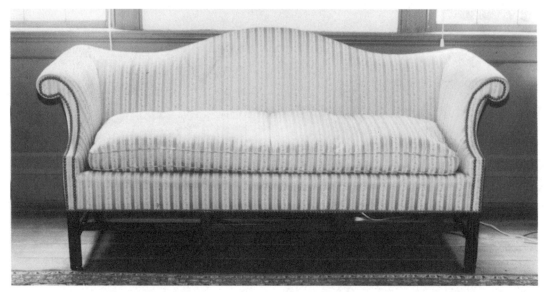

Fig. 6-17 Biggs c. 1938 Chippendale-style camelback sofa with single loose down cushion, on straights, molded legs. 80" long × 32" deep × 36" high. *Private collection.* **$1,000–1,500.**

Fig. 6-18 Biggs c. 1938 Queen Anne-style wing chair with cabriole legs and pad feet. Back flares out nicely. 27 1/2" wide × 21 1/2" deep × 44" high. *Private collection.* **$500–750.**

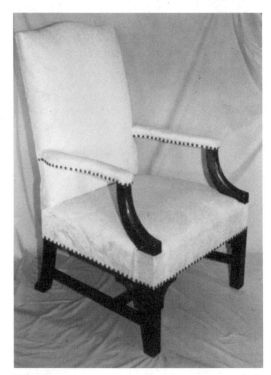

Fig. 6-19 Biggs c. 1938 Martha Washington-style mahogany chair. Very heavy and sturdy. 27" wide × 26 1/2" deep × 24 1/2" high. *Private collection.* **$600–900.**

Fig. 6-20 Biggs c. 1930 Queen Anne-style wing chair. 34" wide × 25" deep × 40" high. *Private collection.* **$250–350.**

Fig. 6-21 Biggs c. 1937 card table. From the 1937 catalogue: "Duncan Phyfe card table—has the typical reeded pedestal and reeded legs with brass claw feet. An impressive occasional table for use in Living Room, Dining Room, or Hall. Open, 36" square, closed 18" × 36". Height 30". Made of selected, solid mahogany with Biggs' dull antique finish. $75." *Private collection.* **$375–575.**

Fig. 6-22 Biggs c. 1937 armchair. From the 1937 catalogue: "Duncan Phyfe armchair of unusually graceful lines, has carved cross slat in back and is shaped to the back for comfort. Seat is filled with finest quality hair. This chair is justly popular because of its comfort and its appropriateness as an occasional chair, desk chair, or at the dining or bridge table. $35. *Private collection.* **$350–475.**

made reproductions that were often inspired by Lockwood's or Nutting's books. Fineberg adapted an original piece to suit the client's needs, which usually meant that the pieces were scaled down to accommodate lower ceiling heights. Fineberg generally did not mark his pieces. Post and Fineberg reproductions are eagerly sought today.

In Framingham, Massachusetts, Wallace Nutting continued making his high-quality reproductions during the 1930s. However, his business never fully recovered from the Depression; his business declined all through the 1930s, ending with his death in 1941.

There were many small shops around the country making reproductions of an-

Fig. 6-23 Biggs c. 1940 mahogany lowboy/desk of simple form. One long over two short cock-beaded drawers. Square, tapered legs. *Courtesy Whitehall at the Vila Antiques and Fine Art, Chapel Hill, N.C.* **$500–750.**

Fig. 6-24 Biggs c. 1920 Queen Anne-style settee with shell-carved knees, pad feet. 45 1/2" long × 24" deep × 39" high. *Private collection.* **$2,400–3,600.**

tiques, often local pieces. These cabinetmakers did not market their reproductions beyond their locality. Instead, they made pieces to meet specific demands of local clients, who may have wanted a copy of a local antique. We all know of estate settlements in which one family member gets the fine eighteenth-century table, and the other family member gets an exact copy of the antique. These pieces were produced by local cabinetmakers all around the country, and still are today.

The Depression in general had a detrimental effect on the Colonial Revival movement. Most people could no longer afford to indulge their interest. However, if one did have money during the Depression, it was a great time to buy antiques, since people who normally would have cherished family heirlooms were forced to sell fine antiques. We know of one case in which a museum buying the family antique commissioned an exact copy for the owners! This must have happened often when museums, dealers, or private collectors purchased family pieces. No doubt, this type of transaction led to many fine local reproductions. It also led, no doubt, to those dubious and astounding stories dealers often encounter—of reproductions thought by owners to be real.

The furniture industry of the 1930s

Fig. 6-25 Biggs c. 1937 Sheraton-style four-poster bed. Headboard with acanthus-carved broken arch with rosette terminals and urn finial. Posts are reeded, with acanthus carving. 81 1/2" long x 58" wide x 92" high. *Private collection.* **$2,000–3,000.**

Fig. 6-26 Valentine tilt-top tea table of mahogany, with chamfered underside, two-board top. Richmond, Virginia, c. 1925. 20" diameter x 30" high. Finish ruined. *Private collection.* **$145–195.**

Fig. 6-27 Valentine c. 1930 Queen Anne Revival wing chair with schematized, shell-carved knees, pad feet. Virginia walnut or mahogany. 48" high. H. C. Valentine Company catalogue, c. 1930. **$800–1,200.**

was hampered in the early years by the Depression, and at the beginning of the next decade by the entry of the United States into World War II. Naturally, with the gathering clouds of war and the lend-lease boom, large furniture factories turned their energies toward the war effort. Smaller cabinetmakers all around the country often disappeared into the armed forces. The entire furniture industry restructured to manufacture goods needed for the war. The Colonial Revival movement in furniture suffered as a result.

The Colonial Revival had been the focus of great national interest and was directed toward greater historical accuracy by the influential museum exhibits and the flamboyant collectors of the 1920s. By the end of the 1920s, all of the trends in Colonial Revival furniture were established: reproductions were available for all pocketbooks, including mass-produced pieces that took great liberties with

Fig. 6-30 Three of a set of twelve mahogany Chippendale-style chairs (ten side chairs and two arm chairs) with interlaced gothic splats, scrolled arms, and molded seat frames and front legs. Branded "Margolis 1929." From the Nathan Margolis Shop, Hartford, CT. *Courtesy Nadeau's Auction Gallery, Windsor, Conn.* **$12,000–18,000.**

Fig. 6-28 Valentine c. 1930 "Colonial" or Empire Revival dressing table and stool. Dresser has acanthus-carved standards and legs, three-over-two cock-beaded drawers. Mahogany and mahogany veneer. 48" wide × 24" deep × 71" high. Stool is solid mahogany with acanthus-carved legs. 24" wide × 15" deep × 20" high. H. C. Valentine Company catalogue, c. 1930. Dresser. **$600–900.** Stool. **$175–275.**

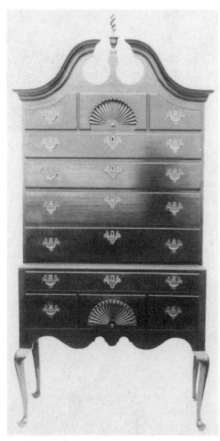

Fig. 6-29 Valentine c. 1930 Chippendale-style block-front, slant-lid desk with four graduated drawers, shell-carved apron, ball-and-claw feet, fitted interior. Solid mahogany. 42" wide × 22" deep × 42" high. H. C. Valentine Company catalogue, c. 1930. **$800–1,200.**

Fig. 6-31 Queen Anne-style c. 1937–41 mahogany highboy, with broken-arch pediment, two fan carvings, cyma carved skirt, cabriole legs with pad feet. Branded: "Handmade by the Nathan Margolis Shop Hartford, Conn." *Courtesy Nadeau's Auction Gallery, Windsor, Conn.* **$3,000–4,500.**

Hepplewhite-style c. 1930 secretary. Top with brass finials, central brass eagle finial. Two faux-paned doors, above central door with eagle and shield inlay. Tambour sides and fitted interior. Below are two drawers with line inlay on square, tapered legs with brass cuffs. Rabetted drawers. 36 1/4" wide x 18" deep x 81" high. *Courtesy Whitehall at the Villa Antiques and Fine Art, Chapel Hill, N.C.* **$3,000–4,500.**

William and Mary Revival c. 1915 small candlestand with shaped, molded top of beautiful burl veneer. Trumpet-turned legs, X-stretchers, ball feet, shaped apron (with band-saw marks). 19 1/2" x 19 1/2" x 24 1/2" high. *Courtesy Reynolda House, Museum of American Art, Winston-Salem, N.C.* **$250–350.**

William and Mary-style c. 1920 needlepoint bench with six whorl-carved feet, two curving, molded X-stretchers with central finials, trumpet-turned legs. Excellent style and fine upholstery. 44 1/4" long x 18 1/2" deep x 18 1/4" high. *Courtesy Reynolda House, Museum of American Art, Winston-Salem, N.C.* **$900–1,500.**

Jacobean-style c. 1920 open armchair with dramatically scrolling arms, stretcher base, block turnings. Handmade needlework back and seat, along with strong turnings, enhance this type of chair. 25 1/4" wide x 21 1/2" deep x 44" high. *Courtesy Reynolda House, Museum of American Art, Winston-Salem, N.C.* **$2,400–3,000.**

Opposite page: Very good quality c. 1890-1910 Chippendale-style armchair in the Philadelphia manner. Pierced, molded gothic splat. Molded and carved crest rail, shell-carved apron, acanthus-carved knees, ball-and-claw feet. Rear stump legs. Needlepoint seats. 22 3/8" wide x 19" deep x 41" high. *Private collection.* Set of eight (six side chairs, two arm chairs), **$8,000–12,000.** At right: Side chair from the same set. 20 1/2" wide x 17 3/8" deep x 41" high. *Private collection.* Single, **$700–1,000.**

A creative c. 1920 adaptation combining tea table with wash basin or wig stand into one piece. Transitional Chippendale/Sheraton style. Mahogany. Top with floral inlay in a cartouche, edged in cross-banding. Shell-carved knees, pad feet. Rabetted drawers. 30" diameter x 30" high. *Courtesy Reynolda House, Museum of American Art, Winston-Salem, N.C.* **$450–750.**

Elizabethan Revival c. 1920 open armchair with acanthus-carved scrolling arms. Shell-, scroll-, and flower-carved seat rail and stretcher. Carving is flat and schematic. New machine tapestry. Found in oak or walnut. 26" wide x 24" deep x 48 1/4" high. *Private collection.* **$1,800–2,400.**

Sheraton-style c. 1890-1910 sofa with turned, reeded legs and carved, straight crest rail. Doweled construction. *Courtesy Whitehall at the Villa Antiques and Fine Art, Chapel Hill, N.C.* **$2,400–3,600.**

William and Mary-style c. 1910 walnut high-back hall chair with elaborate pierced and carved back and front stretcher. Cabriole legs with hoof feet. Lovely old English needlepoint seat adds to the value of this chair. 20" wide x 17 1/2" deep x 47" high. *Courtesy Reynolda House, Museum of American Art, Winston-Salem, N.C.* **$500–750.**

Set of six c. 1880-1900 side chairs with bellflower and rosette carving done by hand. Molded and shaped crest rail. *Courtesy Whitehall at the Villa Antiques and Fine Art, Chapel Hill, N.C.* **$4,500–6,500.**

Chippendale-style c. 1920 highboy with two fan-carved drawers (hand-carved, but shallow). Broken-arch pediment, three flame finials. Handmade dovetails on drawers. Drawer openings cock-beaded. Acorn drop finials, shaped apron. Cabriole legs with volutes, pad feet. 40 3/8" wide x 20 1/2" deep x 81 1/8" high. *Courtesy Whitehall at the Villa Antiques and Fine Art, Chapel Hill, N.C.* **$5,000–7,500.**

style and attempted only to suggest a nostalgic past. The major museum exhibits of the 1920s validated early American furniture and design as a field worthy of collecting and scholarship. These exhibits also led to more accurate, higher-quality reproductions. After the Great Depression, the Colonial Revival movement was no longer the center of national attention, as the country was diverted by the war and by rebuilding for peacetime. The new modernism caught on during this era and became central to large factory production, as did the use of new materials arising from wartime production. Colonial styles continued to be produced and a few museums began to formalize their reproductions, providing the public with a source of good-quality reproductions. Certainly by the end of the 1930s the Colonial Revival movement had successfully established Colonial styles as a mainstay of the furniture industry that prevails even today.

PART II

Furniture Forms
and Prices

7

Chairs and Sofas

William and Mary or "Flemish"-style c. 1910-20 oak side chair with applied half-spindles on the stiles, spindle arcades showing influence of Spanish design, carved top and lower rails, block-turned front legs, spool-turned front stretcher. Needlepoint seat. Mortise-and-tenon joints, a sign of high-quality workmanship. Probably made in New York City. 19" wide × 17 1/4" deep × 40" high. *Private collection.* **$275–425.**

One of a pair of c. 1910 tall, dramatic Jacobean-style open armchairs with strong sweeping arms hand-carved with acanthus leaves curling under at knuckles. Barley-twist stretchers. Arched and shaped backs. Beautiful old needlework. The somewhat exaggerated arms and the poorly proportioned bun feet are our of character and lower the value of this chair. 27 1/4" wide × 19 1/4" deep x 53" high. *Courtesy Reynolda House, Museum of American Art, Winston-Salem, N.C.* **$1,500–2,000,** single. **$3,000–4,000,** the pair.

Cromwellian-style c. 1920 oak open armchair with barley-twist legs and stretchers, scrolled arms with acanthus carving. Needlepoint seat and back. 24 1/2" wide x 26" deep x 38 1/2" high. *Courtesy Chameleon Antiques, Newport News, Virginia.* **$400–600.**

William and Mary-style c. 1920 cane-back side chair with double-scroll front legs and scrolling un-der-bracing. Block-turned rear legs and stretchers. Worn needlepoint seat. 20 1/2" wide x 19" deep x 49 1/2" high. *Courtesy Chameleon Antiques, Newport News, Virginia.* **$600–900,** single. **$1,500–2,200,** the pair.

Open armchair, c. 1910, with out-curving arms ending in spiral turns. Front legs ending in hoof feet. Upholstered back and seat in old needlepoint. Knees with rosette terminals, acanthus and bellflower carving, beaded rim above hoof feet. Strong legs, weak arms, low back. 24 1/2" wide x 17" deep x 36" high. *Courtesy Reynolda House, Museum of American Art, Winston-Salem, N.C.* **$1,000–1,500,** (high price due to needlework).

Jacobean-style c. 1910 straight-back open armchair with curving arms ending in spiral terminals. Legs and stretchers are block-turned. This typical adaptation does not retain the vigor of the original chair. 25" wide × 21 1/2" deep × 44" high. *Courtesy Reynolda House, Museum of American Art, Winston-Salem, N.C.* **$100–175.**

William and Mary-style c. 1920 factory-made hall chair with caned back and seat, carved crest rail, turned stretchers. Refinished. 22" wide × 18" deep × 54" high. *Collection of Naomi and Norman Ludwig.* **$800–1,200.**

Pair of c. 1930 William and Mary/Spanish-style walnut medallion-carved side chairs with stretcher bases. Stiles and backs are carved. 35" high. *Private collection.* **$300–500.**

Jacobean-style c. 1920 open armchair with barley-twist stretchers, supports, and arms. Arms end in wonderful hand-carved recumbent lions. 25 1/2" wide x 20 1/2" deep x 37 1/2" high. *Courtesy Reynolda House, Museum of American Art, Winston-Salem, N.C.* **$1,800–2,400.**

Queen Anne transitional-style lolling chair, c. 1910, with shepherd's-crook arms and ball-and-claw feet. Knees with C-scroll carving. Upholstered back and seat. Philadephia. *Private collection.* **$800–1,200.**

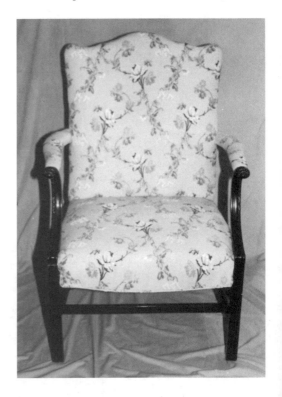

Sheraton-style c. 1900 open armchair. *Courtesy Reynolda House, Museum of American Art, Winston-Salem, N.C.* **$400–600.**

Sheraton-style c. 1900 mahogany open armchair or lolling chair with wheat carving. Reeded and turned front legs, on rollers, reeded arms. 21" deep x 47" high. *Private collection.* **$800–1,200.**

Stretcher-based lolling chair, c. 1910, with shaped apron, cabriole legs. Pad feet in front, straight legs in rear. Curving arms with scroll terminals. Upholstered back and seat. *Private collection.* **$300–500.**

Fireside pull-up chair, c. 1920, in the Chippendale style. Mahogany legs, 25" wide x 23" deep x 35" high. *Courtesy Chameleon Antiques, Newport New,s Virginia.* **$275–375.**

Rocking chair, c. 1890–1900, showing the influence of Chippendale with its pierced splat. A far cry from eighteenth-century Chippendale, we would call this a Colonial Revival adaptation of Chippendale. Found in oak, mahogany, mahoganized cherry or birch. *Private collection.* **$175–275.**

Sheraton-style racket-back child-size rocking chair with needlepoint seat. Splat groken. The rocking chair was especially popular as an adaptive Colonial Revival form. *Private collection.* As is, very little. Perfect **$300–475.**

Adapted Sheraton Revival-style armchair, c. 1905–20, with line inlay on crest rail and arms. Doweled construction, mahogany, 22" wide x 19" deep x 30 1/4" high. *Private collection.* **$175–325.**

Child's Windsor-style rocking chair with turned arm supports and legs, c. 1920. Labeled "J. B. Van Sciver Co. Camden, N.J." *Private collection.* **$125–225.**

American walnut slat-back Empire Revival-style rocker, c. 1900. 21 1/2" wide x 19" deep x 37 1/8" high. *Private collection.* **$150–250.**

Open armchair, c. 1895–1905, with mother-of-pearl inlay and applied acanthus carving on crest rail, pierced splat. Spindles and legs show a Sheraton influence. Mahogany or mahoganized native woods. 24 1/2" wide x 17 3/4" deep x 35 1/2" high. *Private collection.* **$275–475.**

Pastiche window seat/armchair with caned seat, applied carvings on crest rail and arms, odd little splat, shaped apron, and front stretchers. Factory made, c. 1910. *Private collection.* **$175–275.**

Sheraton Revival side chair, c. 1900, with reeded stiles, line inlay and pattera on crest rail, stringing on tapered front legs. Doweled construction, mahogany. 19" wide x 15 3/4" deep x 36" high. *Private collection.* Single, **$175–275.** Set of six (two plus four), **$1,800–2,700.** Set of eight (two plus six) **$3,600–4,800.**

Hepplewhite Revival-style mahogany fan-back side chair of doweled construction. 22" wide x 19" deep x 30 1/4" high. *Private collection.* Single, **$100–175.** Set of six (two armchairs, four side chairs), **$1,500–2,400.** Set of eight (two armchairs, six side chairs), **$3,000–4,000.**

Underside of one of the dining chairs *(opposite page, bottom)* showing the label for Moser Furniture Company.

Open armchair, c. 1900, in a Duncan Phyfe design after the English Regency. The flatness of the sides of the legs is indicative of factory work and depresses the value of this otherwise fine Colonial Revival chair. *Private collection.* **$350–550.**

One of a set of four c. 1920 Empire-style dining chairs made by Moser Furniture Company of Lynchburg, Virginia. The company was founded in 1915 and sold bench-made reproductions using hand-dovetailing, mortising, hand carving, and good-quality woods. Each chair is labeled. Note the urn-shaped splat. In the late nineteenth century, these chairs would have been called "Grecian" in style. 18" wide x 17" deep x 33" deep. *Private collection.* **$500–750** set of four.

Sheraton-style c. 1900 lyre-back side chair with acanthus-leaf and other carving on back, turned and reeded front legs. Doweled construction. Back legs of glued-up stock. 19 1/4" wide x 18" deep x 32 1/4" high. *Private collection.* **$150–225.**

One of a set of eight (two armchairs, six side chairs) dining chairs, c. 1905, combining Queen Anne with other sylistic elements. Crinoline stretchers. 19 1/2" wide x 17 1/2" deep x 39 1/2" high (sides). *Private collection.* **$2,400–3,600** the set of eight.

Sheraton-style c. 1900 lyre-back side chair with upholstered back and seat, turned and reeded front legs. Doweled construction. Back legs of glued-up stock. 20" wide x 18 1/4" deep x 33 1/2" high. *Private collection.* **$375–550** for a pair.

One of a set of six (two armchairs, four side chairs) Chippendale-style c. 1900 solid mahogany ladder-back dining chairs with straight legs and well-carved interlaced back supports. Arms very poorly shaped. Rear legs of glued-up stock. 20" wide x 18 3/4" deep x 39" high (sides). *Private collection.* **$1,200–1,800** the set. **$3,600–4,800** for 12.

One of a set of eight (two armchairs, six side chairs) Sheraton-style dining chairs made by Tiffany Studios, 1915. Cuban mahogany. Molded back and arms, reeded and turned front legs. 19 1/2" wide x 18" deep x 38" high (sides). *Private collection.* In 1915, Tiffany sold the side chairs for $20 and the armchairs for $25. Today they are valued at **$175–275** (side) and **$450–650** (arm). Furniture is the one area where the name Tiffany is decidedly not magic.

Elaborately carved Chippendale-style c. 1890 mahogany corner chair. Hand-carved, with swags, flowers, and scrolling foliage. Pierced backsplats similarly carved. Backsplats are silhouetted, an unusual touch on chairs of this date and a sign of quality workmanship. Arms are leaf-carved, as are stiles and three legs. Front leg is cabriole, with ball-and-claw foot. The elaborate carving is a good example of an exuberant Victorian interpretation of a typically more restrained Chippendale design. 17 3/4" x 17 3/4" x 23 3/4" high. *Private collection.* **$1,200–1,800.**

Solid mahogany c. 1900 bench-made corner chair in the Chippendale style with front cabriole leg ending in ball-and-claw foot. Other legs are chamfered. Turned uprights, molded arms, pierced splats. *Private collection.* **$800–1,200.**

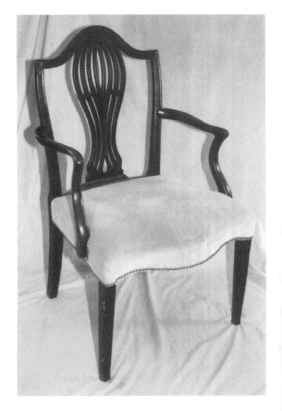

Single c. 1925 Hepplewhite-style mahogany armchair with molded back and front legs, shaped arms. Good form and quality mahogany. *Courtesy Reynolda House, Museum of American Art, Winston-Salem, N.C.* **$400–600**, (single). **$1,000–1,500** the pair.

Chippendale-style c. 1900 mahogany ladder-back or ribbon-back armchair with needlepoint seat. Light weight, small size. Curving seat rail is a nice touch. Stiles are molded; otherwise, arms and legs are devoid of any carving. This example is somewhat battered. *Private collection.* **$450–650.**

Chippendale-style chairs in the gothic taste were manufactured in many versions around the turn of the century. Collectors should be discriminating and look only for the best. This chair is a basic mahogany c. 1910 Chippendale-style side chair with a pierced gothic splat and cabriole legs ending in well-articulated ball-and-claw feet. It is otherwise devoid of carving. *Private collection.* **$350–550,** side chair. **$800–1,200,** arm-chair. Set of eight, **$8,000–12,000.**

Nicely proportioned Chippendale-style side chair with pierced and molded gothic splat, shell carving on seat rail, acanthus carving on knees, ball-and-claw front feet. Needs to be refinished. Baltimore, c. 1915. *Private collection.* **$600–900.**

An interesting, rather outlandish pair of c. 1880–1920 Chippendale-style mahogany chairs (six side chairs and two armchairs). Carved crest rails with ears, backsplats with scrolling entwined snakes, fleur-de-lys (an odd combination). The arms have snake ends curving inward. Gadrooned seat rails, acanthus knees, well-articulated ball-and-claw feet. What these chairs lack in unity of design, they make up for in visual interest. *Courtesy Richard Beecher.* **$8,000–12,000** the set of eight.

Chippendale-style mahogany carved side chair, Philadelphia, 1880–1910. Old refinish. Good gothic and rococo carving, well-articulated claws on the feet. Highly carved stiles and crest rail. This chair has wonderful carving. 38" high, seat height 17 1/2" high. *Courtesy Skinner, Inc., Bolton, Mass.* **$1,000–1,500,** side chair, **$1,500–2,400,** armchair. **$18,000–24,000** for eight. **$24,000–36,000** for 12.

Chippendale-style c. 1920 side chair with shell-carved crest rail, pierced backsplat. Rear legs chamfered, shaped apron, front cabriole legs with ball-and-claw feet, large size. Mahogany. Rather stiff back. 22" wide x 17 1/4" deep x 41 3/4" high. *Private collection.* Single, **$400–600.** Set of six (two plus four), **$2,800–3,800.** Set of eight (two plus six), **$6,000–9,000.**

Chippendale-style c. 1890–1910 armchair of mahogany in the Philadelphia manner. Acanthus carving on the knees and applied shell on the straight seat rail. The arms are shaped, with knuckle terminals. The arms are slightly contoured rather than flatly horizontal. *Private collection.* **$500–700,** side chair. **$800–1,200** armchair. Set of eight, **$12,000–18,000.**

A similar Chippendale-style c. 1890–1910 mahogany armchair in the Philadelphia manner with gothic splat. Porportions are squatter. The arms have no contouring on the horizontal axis, legs are thicker and stockier, squarish. Applied shell on straight seat rail. Acanthus carved knees, ball-and-claw feet. Carving on legs and feet is flat and schematic. The shaping of the legs is not complete; the legs are not fully rounded. This is part of a set of eight (two plus six) dining chairs. *Private collection.* **$8,000–12,000.**

This side chair is similar, but the proportions are better. The shape and curve of the legs are closer to the grace of the eighteenth-century original. The shaped seat rail adds grace. The mahogany is of a better quality and a heavier weight than the last set. However, one should not mistake this for an eighteenth-century chair. Some clues indicate that this is Colonial Revival (the applied shell on the seat rail is not a rococo shell. It is long and pendulous—a late nineteenth-century intrpretation of rococo.) We had a chance to turn this chair upside down and found circular-saw marks under the seat rail and band-saw marks on the underside of the shell, tools not used in eighteenth-century America! **$800–1,200.**

Armchair from the same set as the preceding side chair. The set consists of two arms and six sides. **$800–1,200,** side chair. **$1,000–1,500,** armchair. **$8,000–12,000** the set. Very serious money in sets of eight or 12. **$12,000–18,000** for eight. **$22,000–28,000** for 12.

Chippendale Revival-style c. 1920 armchair with shell-carved knees and pad feet. Not true to period forms. 29 1/2" wide x 20" deep x 39" high. *Courtesy Reynolda House, Museum of American Art, Winston-Salem, N.C.* **$300–450.**

One of a set of six c. 1880 transitional Chippendale side chairs with pierced splats and and "bird" backs, rush seats, block-turned front legs, Spanish feet, bulbous-turned front stretchers. 18 1/4" wide x 15" deep x 39 1/2" high (sides). From a small shop. *Private collection.* Set of six, **$1,800–2,400.**

Queen Anne-style c. 1930 armchair with pad feet and shell-carved knees. Walnut legs. True to early forms, except back is too short and arms are too thick. 34 1/2" wide x 25 1/4" deep x 38 1/4" high. *Private collection.* **$400–600.**

Queen Anne-style c. 1900 mahogany wing chair with heavy, rather straight back legs. 28 1/2" wide x 22" deep x 43" high. *Private collection.* **$400–600.**

Chippendale-style c. 1915 wing chair with straight, molded legs and stretcher base. 32" wide x 20" deep x 41" high. *Private collection.* **$800–1,200.**

Chippendale-style c. 1900 wing chair with short cabriole legs and ball-and-claw feet. 28" wide x 22" deep x 43 1/2" high. *Private collection.* **$800–1,200.**

Pair of c. 1920 Chippendale-style mahogany open armchairs, each with upholstered back, seat, and arm rests. Acanthus-carved handrests and arms. Carved, scrolled apron on cabriole legs. Acanthus-carved knees and feet. *Courtesy Leslie Hindman Auctioneers, Chicago.* **$5,000–8,000** the pair.

Chippendale-style c. 1930 carved mahogany wing chair with arched back and rolled arms. Cabriole legs with acanthus- and cabochon-carved knees and whorl feet. Fat arms, poor crest rail, good legs. *Courtesy Leslie Hindman Auctioneers, Chicago.* **$1,800–2,400.**

Empire Revival c. 1890 loveseat and armchair. Backs, seats, and rear backs upholstered. Winged paw feet, scrolled arms, carved crest rail. Cherry, now with black lacquer. Doweled construction. 53 3/4" long x 23" deep x 37" high. *Collection of Naomi and Norman Ludwig.* **$1,800–2,400** the set.

Empire Revival armchair matching the loveseat.

Modified wing chair in the Chippendale-style, c. 1920. Machine carving, doweled construction. 28 1/2" wide x 24 1/2" deep x 34" high. *Private collection.* **$500–750.**

Empire Revival c. 1890 armchair and settee of mahogany and mahogany veneer. Armchair with lion's paw feet (missing applied decoration), scrolling acanthus carving on arms and crest rail. 39" wide x 20 1/2" deep x 32 1/4" high. Settee with back crest sides of carved cornucopia and flowers, with winged lion's paw feet. 79" long x 28" deep x 34" high. *Courtesy New Orleans Auction Galleries, New Orleans.* Chair, **$350–475.** Settee, **$750–1,200.**

Jacobean Revival c. 1920 sofa with triple-curved back, turned legs and stretchers. Found in mahogany, oak, and maple. 76" long x 21 1/2" deep x 39" high. *Courtesy Reynolda House, Museum of American Art, Winston-Salem, N.C.* **$800–1,500.**

Sofa en suite with the armchair *below.* 72" long x 21" deep x 38 3/4" high. *Private collection.* **$800–1,200.**

Empire Revival c. 1890 armchair of mahogany veneer. Scrolled crest rails, cartouche backs, gadrooned seat rails, paw feet. These massive pieces were popular in the 1890s, when factories produced three-piece suites for the living room. These two pieces at one time may have had a matching rocker. Suites were often in a heavy, Empire style, but this one, interestingly enough, combines Empire with Queen Anne, Chippendale, and Adam features—an indication of the early Colonial Revival misunderstanding of historic design periods. This is as wild as it gets, folks! Chair is 40 1/2" wide x 21" deep x 38 1/2" high. *Private collection.* **$350–475.**

Sheraton Revival c. 1900 factory-made settee with cabriole legs, applied ribbon and floral decoration. 42 1/2" long x 20" deep x 29" high. *Private collection.* **$350–550.**

William and Mary-style c. 1920 sofa with turned legs and stretchers. A rather odd adaption, but in leather, and very comfortable. *Courtesy Reynolda House, Museum of American Art, Winston-Salem, N.C.* **$800–1,200.**

Chippendale-style c. 1900 camelback sofa of good proportions. Ball-and-claw feet, boldly carved, with shell knees. Down cushion, fine fabric. 82" long x 23" deep x 32 1/2" high. *Private collection.* **$800–1,200.**

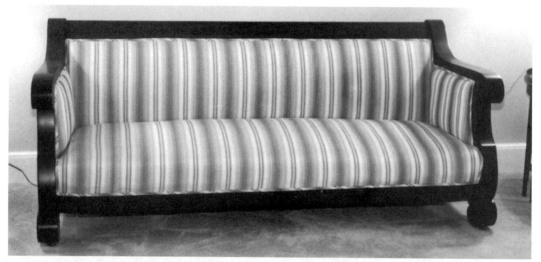

Empire Revival c. 1910 sofa with scrolled arms and feet of solid mahogany. During the Colonial Revival period, this sofa would have been called "Colonial" or "Empire Colonial". 77 1/2" long x 28" deep x 32" high. *Private collection.* **$450–750.**

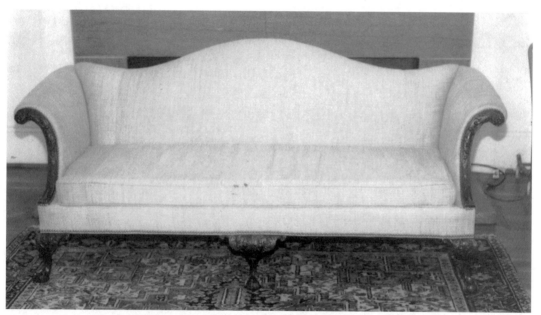

Camelback sofa, c. 1880-1900, with carved mahogany arm supports and cabriole legs with ball-and-claw feet. Richly carved mahogany arms and legs. Very good quality. *Private collection.* **$3,000–4,500.**

Federal-style c. 1920 serpentine mahogany sofa, with burl panels on the seat rail and inlaid legs. 84" long x 23" deep x 32" high. *Private collection.* **$1,800–2,400.**

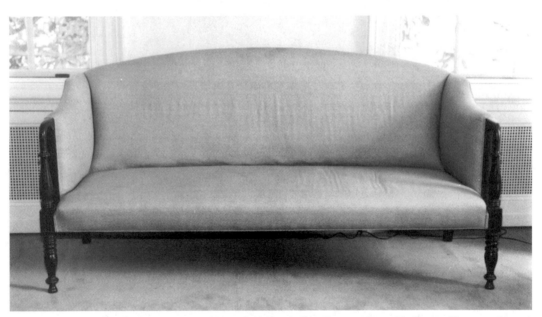

Sheraton-style c. 1915 sofa. Legs are not well turned and are bulky. *Courtesy Reynolda House, Museum of American Art, Winston-Salem, N.C.* **$800–1,200.**

Federal-style c. 1920 mahogany and figured maple veneer sofa, made in Portsmouth, New Hampshire. Reeded and turned arms and front legs. 79" long x 36" high. *Courtesy Skinner, Inc., Bolton, Mass.* **$1,800–2,400.**

Chippendale-style c. 1900 solid mahogany camelback sofa with straight, molded legs, molded base trim and returns, and stretcher base. Down cushion. 84" long x 21" deep x 36 1/2" high. *Private collection.* **$1,200–1,800.**

William and Mary-style c. 1920 kidney-shaped fireside seat with three caned panels, black lacquer. 54" long x 12 3/4" deep x 12" high. *Collection of Naomi and Norman Ludwig.* **$400–600.**

Chippendale-style c. 1920 footstool with strongly turned handles, ball-and-claw feet, shaped apron, needlepoint covering. 20" long x 9" deep x 7 3/4" high. *Courtesy Reynolda House, Museum of American Art, Winston-Salem, N.C.* **$75–125.**

8

Tables, Lowboys, and Stands

Factory-made trestle-based table, c. 1930, with molded top and turned legs. Labeled "French Trade mark, Minneapolis." 24" wide x 14 1/8" deep x 22 1/2" high. *Private ollection.* **$125–165.**

Tea cart or tea wagon, c. 1920. From 1890 to World War II in mahogany, strained soft woods, and mahoganized cherry or birch, and in all style periods. *Private collection.* **$300–450.**

Spider-leg gateleg table, c. 1920, possibly by Hungate, Schmeig, and Kotzian of New York City. 25 3/4" long x 12" deep x 27" high. *Private collection.* **$350–550.**

Rococo-style c. 1915 boldly carved ashtray stand with triangular base, button feet, acanthus carving, cabochons. Usually in oak or walnut. 27 3/4" high. *Courtesy Reynolda House, Museum of American Art, Winston-Salem, N.C.* **$150–225.**

Well-turned ashtray stand, c. 1915. Tripod base with beading and acanthus carving, spiral turning. Paw feet. Usually found in oak or walnut, sometimes in mahogany. 28 1/4" high. *Courtesy Reynolda House, Museum of American Art, Winston-Salem, N.C.* **$125–175.**

Late nineteenth-century Sheraton Revival mahogany nest of four tables with molded tops and "bamboo"-turned legs. *Private collection.* **$900–1,200.** These tables can be found in more ornate styles with fine veneers and inlays at **$2,400–3,600.**

Small sofa or side table, c. 1915, with trestle base and turned stretchers and legs. Top is a shaped oval with raised, molded edge with book-matched veneers. This is an adaption of an earlier style to modern use. 21 1/2" long x 16" wide x 23" high. *Courtesy Reynolda House, Museum of American Art, Winston-Salem, N.C.* **$145–225.**

Jacobean-style c. 1920 oak tavern table or joint stool with turned legs and molded stretchers and frieze. Pegged, but top also secured with screws. 18" long x 8 1/2" wide x 18" high. *Private collection.* **$300–450.**

Jacobean- or Flemish-style c. 1915 triangular table with veneered top and double C-scroll legs, molded and shaped stretchers, bun feet. Frieze with pierced scroll and floral carving, carved with a band saw. 19" sides, 23" high. *Courtesy Reynolda House, Museum of American Art, Winston-Salem, N.C.* **$175–225.**

Small c. 1920 side table. Lifting lid has elaborate and delicate marquetry and burl panels. Thin legs end in pad feet. Burl veneer and line inlays all around frieze. A weak adaptive form. 16 1/4" long x 11" deep x 26 1/4" high. *Courtesy Reynolda House, Museum of American Art, Winston-Salem, N.C.* **$125–175.**

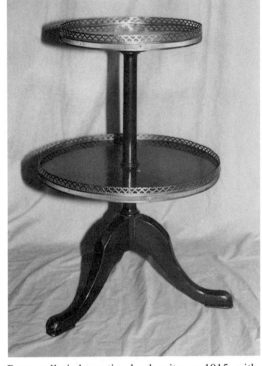

Brass-galleried two-tier dumbwaiter, c. 1915, with striking exotic wood veneers, edged in contrasting wood. Tripod base with slipper feet. 16" diameter x 25 1/2" high. *Courtesy Reynolda House, Museum of American Art, Winston-Salem, N.C.* **$145–225.**

Kidney-shaped side table, c. 1915, with burl veneer top, brass gallery, and one hung drawer. Brass-galleried middle shelf. Trestle base. 37 3/4" long x 18 1/2" deep x 30" high. *Courtesy Reynolda House, Museum of American Art, Winston-Salem, N.C.* **$300–450.**

William and Mary Revival c. 1915 walnut center table with round top with panels of burl and geometric inlay. Trumpet-turned legs and curving stretchers. Shaped, lipped apron. A scaled-down adaptation. 36" diameter x 28 1/2" high. *Courtesy Reynolda House, Museum of American Art, Winston-Salem, N.C.* **$500–750.**

Transitional William and Mary/Queen Anne-style c. 1915 six-sided table with centered underbracing. Legs turned and eight-sided, ending in whorl feet. Top with six inset burl panels. 29 1/2" x 29 1/2" x 24" high. Found in oak or mahogany. *Courtesy Reynolda House, Museum of American Art, Winston-Salem, N.C.* **$450–650.**

Elizabethan-style c. 1915 oak console table with shaped top, apron with pierced scroll carving. Laminated legs with bulbous turnings. Molded stretcher base. Conspicuous square pegs on the front of the piece, but a closer look reveals dowels. 38" long x 18 1/2" deep x 29 1/2" high. *Courtesy Reynolda House, Museum of American Art, Winston-Salem, N.C.* **$500–750.**

Jacobean-style c. 1930 flip-top, gateleg games table (the entire top flips up) of curly walnut and tulip poplar. Turned legs, ball feet. Octagonal top is molded. 30 3/8" x 30 3/8" x 28" high. *Private collection.* **$175–275.**

Hepplewhite-style c. 1930 Pembroke table with leather inset top. One real and one false drawer. Tapered legs end in brass casters. Mahogany cross-banded in satinwood. 29 7/8" long x 18" wide x 27 1/2" high. *Private collection.* **$400–600.**

Two-drawer stand of mahogany, maple, and cherry, c. 1900. Cock-beaded drawers with handmade dovetails. Square, tapered legs. 20 3/4" wide x 18 3/4" deep x 28 3/4" high. *Courtesy Whitehall at the Villa Antiques and Fine Art, Chapel Hill, N.C.* **$500–750.**

Tilt-top table, c. 1880, with scalloped, molded top, bird cage, flattened ball-and-claw feet. 31" diameter x 28 1/2" high. *Courtesy Reynolda House, Museum of American Art, Winston-Salem, N.C.* **$800–1,200.**

Federal-style c. 1930 tiger maple candlestand with three spider legs, rather crude turnings on shaft. 16" x 16" x 29 1/2" high. *Courtesy Whitehall at the Villa Antiques and Fine Art, Chapel Hill, N.C.* **$250–400.**

Factory-made round mahogany dish-top table, c. 1900, with turned baluster pedesal with acanthus-leaf carving, tripod base with drop finial, ending in laminated lion's paw feet. Refinished. Legs are schematized and two-dimensional rather than fully rounded. *Private collection.* **$300–450.**

Acanthus carving on pedestal. Note how shallow and schematized the machine carving is; hand-carving is much deeper and crisper.

Stylized paw foot of the tea table. Again, note the shallow machine carving, only touched up by hand. Carving done completely by hand would have more depth and detail.

Underside of the dish-top table. The top is stamped with a model number (manufacturer unknown). Note the bottom of the lion's paw feet, with laminated wood added for necessary width. Top made of five boards.

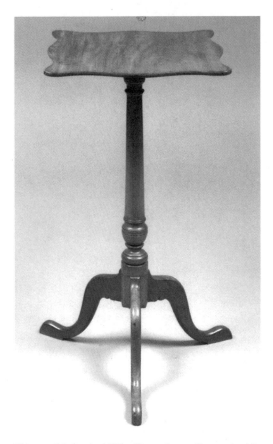

Late nineteenth-century mahogany Hepplewhite-style five-leg *demi-lune* card table with line inlay. Tapered legs end in cuffed feet. Refinished. Probably from Maryland. 36" diameter x 30" high. *Private collection.* **$800–1,200.**

Chippendale-style 1920–40 maple candlestand with serpentine square top over turned pedestal support and three down-curving legs, slipper feet. 16" x 16" x 27 1/2" high. *Courtesy Leslie Hindman Auctioneers, Chicago.* **$300–450.**

Hepplewhite-style c. 1900 mahogany *demi-lune* card table with various line inlays. Five tapered legs and cuffed feet. 35 1/2" diameter x 30 3/8" high. *Private collection.* **$800–1,200.**

Hepplewhite-style c. 1890 serpentine front flip-top games or tea table of mahogany with elaborate inlays. Apron with curly maple panels inset with marquetry. From Virginia area, bench-made (see detail below). 35 3/4" long x 17 3/4" deep x 31" high. *Private collection.* **$1,200–1,800.**

Hepplewhite-style c. 1930 five-leg *demi-lune* table with line inlays. Tapered legs with cuffed feet. Bench-made in a small cabinet shop in Raleigh, North Carolina. 36" diameter x 29" high. *Private collection.* **$800–1,400.**

Detail of the marquetry on the frieze of the tea table. The floral style is typical of 1890s work.

Chippendale-style c. 1910 square tea table with intricate shell-and-leaf carvings applied to the blocked center and ends on the skirt and gadrooned skirting fitting over the legs and around the corners, with no break. Laminated legs with carved knees and ball-and-claw feet. This table is a copy of an original New York table featured in Luke Vincent Lockwood's *Colonial Furniture in America*, published in 1901. It is highly likely that this table would have been manufactured after that date. The original table does not have gadrooning on the top edge, or shell carving on the sides. This copy is a good example of the way Colonial Revival pieces lack the retraint of eighteenth-century designs. The decoration on Colonial Revival pieces is often overdone. 37 3/4" wide x 23 3/4" deep x 29" high. Poplar, pine and mohogany with mahogany veneers on top and skirt. *Courtesy Chesapeake Antique Center, Queenstown, Maryland.* **$2,800–4,500.**

Sheraton-style c. 1920 mahogany flip-top games table. The fifth leg draws our with a drawer for holding card and chips. Shaped top with reeded edge, reeded and turned legs. Marked: "Elite Tables, Elite Furniture Company, Jamestown, NY." Elite Furniture Company, founded in 1909, specialized in living-room tables and other occasional pieces. 35 7/8" wide x 17" deep x 28" high. *Private collection.* **$450–750.**

Chippendale-style c. 1920 carved mahogany lowboy in the Philadelphia manner. Molded-edge rectangular top above one long over three short thumb-molded drawers, flanked by fluted, canted lamb's-tongue corners. Cabriole legs with foliate-carved knees end in ball-and-claw feet. While this piece captures more of the spirit of eighteenth-century design than many, note the crude, shallow carving on the knees and the ungraceful apron. 34" long x 30 1/2" high. *Courtesy Butterfield & Butterfield, San Francisco, Calif.* **$2,400–3,500.**

Magnificent Chippendale-style hand-carved lowboy after a Philadelphia prototype illustrated in Wallace Nutting's Furniture Treasury, 1928. Fully carved ends and front-carved quarter-columns. Crosshatching on leg and skirt is an unusual characteristic found on few Philadelphia lowboys or highboys. This piece copies the highest form of the Philadelphia Chippendale style. Handmade and beautifully carved. This piece probably was made after the publication of Wallace Nutting's book; it is possible that the maker had access to the original, as the copy is so well executed. Mahogany with chestnut and pine secondary wood. 33 1/8" wide x 20 1/2" deep x 30" high. *Courtesy Chesapeake Antique Center, Queenstown, Maryland.* **$4,000–6,000.**

Queen Anne-style c. 1930 tiger maple desk or lowboy with molded top and three-over-two drawers. Fluted quarter-columns, shaped apron, cabriole legs. Similar models sold at Wanamaker's (Philadelphia) in 1927 for $110. 41 3/4" long x 19" deep x 29" high. *Collection of Naomi and Norman Ludwig.* **$500–750.**

Queen Anne-style c. 1920 library table with shaped and shell-carved apron, laminated legs. Refinished. 46" wide x 29" deep x 30" high. *Collection of Diana L. Altman.* **$400–600.**

Chippendale-style c. 1910 mahogany partner's desk with two-over-two drawers on two sides, gadrooned top, shaped and carved apron, cabriole legs with acanthus carving and ball-and-claw feet. Made with a combination of machine and hand work. Dovetails on drawers are handmade, but the carving is flat and lacks depth, typical of machine-made Colonial Revival carving. Top constructed of four boards, probably roughed out by machine and finished by hand. Cast brasses. 53 1/4" long x 29 3/4" deep x 30 1/2" high. *Private collection.* **$1,800–2,400.**

Chippendale-style c. 1910 mahogany writing desk with gadrooning around top, cabriole legs with acanthus-carved knees and ball-and-claw feet, corners with inset spiral-turned columns, ankles with exaggerated curves. This is a good example of a Colonial Revival piece using earlier design motifs but changing the proportions. Underside bears the label of Karcher and Rehm Company of Philadelphia. *Private collection.* **$1,200–1,800.**

Chippendale-style c. 1900 lowboy with molded top, cock-beaded drawers with handmade dovetails. Shaped apron on sides and front with applied rosette-type roundel—a typical Colonial Revival attempt to add some carving while saving the expense of hand-work. Cabriole legs, ball-and-claw feet. 29 3/4" wide x 19 1/2" deep x 30 1/2" high. *Courtesy Whitehall at the Villa Antiques and Fine Art, Chapel Hill, N.C.* **$900–1,600.**

Handmade dish-top tea table, c. 1930, an exact copy of an original eighteenth-century table. Shows hand-tool marks. Cabriole legs with acanthus and bell-flower carving. Vigorous ball-and-claw feet. Mahogany. 30 3/8" wide x 19 1/8" deep x 26 3/8" high. *Private collection.* **$1,800–2,400.**

Chippendale Revival c. 1900 mahogany dressing table with rectangular top with gadroon border above a single drawer, over leaf corner brackets with applied brass rosettes, flanked by rope-carved quarter-columns with brass capitals, supported on cabriole legs with shell-carved knees, ending in ball-and-claw feet. The legs and shell carving are sinewy and elongated. Flattened Victorian-type carving on frieze, topped off with rosettes, which have an Eastlake feeling. 34" wide x 18" deep x 32" high. *Courtesy Osona Auction Gallery, Nantucket, Mass.* **$1,800–2,400.**

Chippendale-style c. 1920 mahogany lowboy with molded top over two-over-three drawers. Central drawer with fan carving. Shaped apron, cabriole legs ending in ball-and-claw feet. 36" wide x 20" deep x 29" high. *Private collection.* **$450–650.**

Queen Anne-style c. 1880 maple lowboy with molded top above long drawer over a central shell-carved drawer flanked by two drawers, on cabriole legs ending in pad feet. Handmade and handcarved. Top made of two boards. The stamped brasses look tinny. Pegged. Finish not original and in need of repair. Good proportions. 30 1/2" wide x 21" deep x 31 1/2" high. *Courtesy Leslie Hindman Auctioneers, Chicago.* **$1,200–1,800.**

Queen Anne-style c. 1920 tea table with burl top and candle slides (oak), one cock-beaded drawer. Legs are solid walnut, pad feet, shell-carved knees. 33 1/4" wide x 19 1/2" deep x 30" high. *Private collection.* **$1,800–2,400.**

Queen Anne-style c. 1920 factory-made tea table with applied shells on front and back apron. Pad feet, cabriole legs. 27 3/4" long x 18" deep x 25 1/4" high. *Private collection.* **$600–900.**

Empire Revival-style flip-top table with one drawer, scroll feet, mahogany veneers. Purchased in Baltimore, 1915, when this piece would have been considered "Colonial" or "Empire Colonial." Empire Revival was popular with Baltimore furniture makers around the turn of the century. *Private collection.* **$275–375.**

Empire Revival-style c. 1910 library table with laminated scroll legs and feet. Mahogany veneers. One drawer. 49 3/4" long x 29 1/2" deep x 28 3/8" high. *Private collection.* **$300–475.**

William and Mary or Tudor-style c. 1900 oak buffet with bun feet, molded top, front with geometric panels of burl in fields of oak, with applied half-spindles. Dovetailed drawers with drop pulls. Three drawers over three cabinets. 71 1/2" wide x 24" deep x 35 1/4" high. *Courtesy Reynolda House, Museum of American Art, Winston-Salem, N.C.* **$1,800–2,400.**

Renaissance-style c. 1900 buffet with molded top over frieze with dentil carving. Three drawers with burl panels divided by acanthus scrolls. Drawers of oak, dovetailed. Front with four stop-fluted columns and three doors with burl panels. Gadrooned lower edge. Paw feet. 64" long x 23 1/4" deep x 39" high. *Courtesy Reynolda House, Museum of American Art, Winston-Salem, N.C.* **$3,200–4,200.**

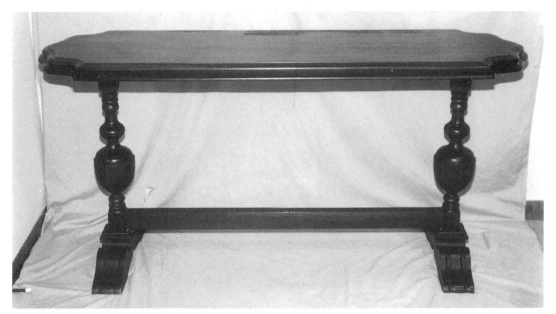

Jacobean-style c. 1920 factory-made refectory table with molded and shaped top, center stretcher base, turned supports with simple machine-carved fluting. Various woods. 61" long x 19 1/2" deep x 28" high. *Private collection.* **$300–475.**

William and Mary-style c. 1930 library table with molded top, three drawers, turned and fluted legs. Walnut and walnut veneers. 72" long x 28" deep x 30 1/2" high. *Private collection.* **$800–1,200.**

Hepplewhite-style c. 1940 walnut drop-leaf dining table with six square, tapered legs. Made by E.A. Clore and Sons, Madison, Virginia. 42 1/8" long x 20 1/2" deep x 29 7/8" high (leaves 20 1/8"). *Private collection.* **$450–650.**

Regency-style c. 1925 inlaid mahogany sofa table, manufactured by Kittinger. The rectangular cross-banded top is flanked by two rounded drop leaves, over a frieze with two drawers and a trestle base joined by an upper stretcher on down-swept legs ending in brass casters. 32" wide x 24" deep x 29" high. *Courtesy Leslie Hindman Auctioneers, Chicago.* **$3,000–4,500.** Kittinger signed furniture is skyrocketing.

Federal-style c. 1925 dining table with rectangular top and turned double-pedestal base, four down-curving legs ending in casters. With three leaves. A popular form copied throughout the twentieth century. 65" long and leaves x 41 3/4" wide x 30" high. *Courtesy Leslie Hindman Auctioneers, Chicago.* **8,000–12,000.**

Hepplewhite-style c. 1940 walnut single-drawer server, raised on tapered legs, en suite with the dining table (p. 133, top right) and chairs. Drawers with nailed construction. Made by E.A. Clore and Sons, Madison, Virginia. En suite with above table. 42 1/2" long x 20 1/4" deep x 29 7/8" high. *Private collection.* **$275–375.**

Hepplewhite-style c. 1940 simple walnut sideboard with low backsplash, four graduated drawers flanked by two cabinets, on six turned legs. Labeled E. A. Clore and Sons, Madison, Virginia. 60 1/8" long x 20 1/8" deep x 39 1/4" high. *Private collection.* **$800–1,200.**

Hepplewhite-style c. 1900 mahogany sideboard, the overall frame inlaid with rosewood, ebony, and satinwood bands. 74" long x 30" deep x 41" high. *Courtesy Neal Auction Company, New Orleans.* **$4,000–6,000.**

Hepplewhite-style c. 1900 round mahogany dining table with four leaves, satinwood line inlays on legs and frieze. On casters. From the Fredericksburg, Virginia, area. 54" diameter x 30 1/2" high. *Private collection.* **$4,500–6,500.**

Hepplewhite-style c. 1900-1915 mahogany sideboard with bellflower inlays and pattarae on cabinets. Plywood drawer bottoms and back, machine-made dovetails. 59 1/2" long x 21 3/4" deep x 39" high. *Private collection.* **$800–1,200.**

Hepplewhite-style c. 1900 sideboard, accurately styled. Mahogany with line inlay and flame veneers. *Courtesy Skinner, Inc., Bolton, Mass.* **$4,500–6,500.**

Jacobean Revival c. 1910 solid walnut stretcher-based serving table with drop leaves and gate legs. *Private collection.* **$500–750.**

Hepplewhite-style c. 1900 bench-made mahogany bow-front server with gallery back featuring pattera inlay. Line inlay on frieze and legs. Underside of bow front has blocks of wood glued to make the curve. From the Fredericksburg, Virginia, area. 52" long x 21 1/2" deep x 28 1/8" high. *Private collection.* **$800–1,200.**

Federal-style c. 1940 factory-made mahogany buffet with six drawers and two cabinets. Applied moldings, applied carving on canted corners, with fluting. Machine dovetails, 58 3/8" long x 18 3/4" deep x 34 1/2" high. *Private collection.* **$450–650.**

Jacobean Revival c. 1920–30 solid walnut server or hall table with two full drawers flanked by two small drawers, raised on turned, stretchered legs. Applied half-spindles on front. 54" long x 15 3/4" deep x 37 3/4" high. *Private collection.* **$400–600.**

9

Case Pieces, Beds, Clocks, and Oddities

Empire Revival c. 1910 mahogany pedestal sewing table with two drawers and drop leaves. Base with acanthus carving and paw feet. Drawers with nailed construction. A popular Colonial Revival piece. (Remember that around the turn of the century what we would normally refer to as Empire style was then called "Colonial" or "Empire Colonial.") 17 3/8" wide x 18" deep x 29 3/4" high. *Private collection.* **$300–450.**

Hepplewhite-style c. 1930 mahogany-veneered round end table with line inlay around top, sides, and drawers. Modified cabriole legs. Sides and top veneered. 20" diameter x 27 1/2" high. *Private collection.* **$225–325.**

Martha Washington-style c. 1920 walnut sewing cabinet with lift-up top on central section fronted by three graduated drawers. Rounded, scalloped side sections have molded lift-up lids, scalloped bases. Cabriole legs with pad feet. This was a popular piece in the 1910s and 1920s. This particular example has several nice, unusual touches, especially the scalloping and cabriole legs. 27" long x 13" deep x 28" high. *Collection of Diana L. Altman.* **$450–650.**

William and Mary-style c. 1915 sewing cabinet of Circassian walnut, by Tiffany Studios, New York City. Lift top, trumpet-turned legs, curving X-stretchers. 22" long x 11" deep x 28" high. *Private collection.* **$300–450.**

Oak music cabinet, c. 1920, with door opening to reveal shelves for music or records. A popular, mass-produced item. *Courtesy Boulevard Bed and Breakfast, Wilmington, Del.* **$275–475.**

Dressing table, c. 1920, with two glove boxes, applied beading and carving. Square back legs, turned front legs. Dentilated trim on frieze. Machine-made dovetails on drawers. Applied carved scrolling on backsplash. 32" wide x 20" deep x 28 7/8" high. *Private collection.* **$150–250.**

Hepplewhite Revival c. 1920 mahogany Edison Victrola with tapered legs and brass cuffs. 18 3/4" wide x 19 1/2" deep x 44 3/4" high. *Private collection.* **$600–900.**

Factory-made lady's small desk, c. 1890, with fitted interior. Slant front has applied scrolls, typical of early c. 1890 Colonial Revival decoration. One central drawer with applied carving. Cabriole legs. Once had a backsplash. This type of desk was produced by large companies such as Paine's of Boston and by midwestern factories. Usually found in oak or mahogany. 41 1/2" wide x 16" deep x 28" high. *Collection of Diana L. Altman.* **$300–450.**

Small spinet desk of light mahogany, c. 1930, on turned legs, with writing slide and fitted interior. 32 1/8" wide x 18 1/2" deep x 32" high. *Private collection.* **$300–450.**

Carved mahogany vanity c. 1890, with beveled glass mirror with scrolling carving flanked by scrolling stiles. Two glove drawers, shaped top, bow front with cock-beaded drawers, shaped and carved apron, cabriole legs with carved knees. Signed "R.J. Horner, N.Y." *Courtesy Southampton Antiques, Southampton, Mass.* **$800–1,200.**

Chippendale-style c. 1920 slant-front desk with oxbow front, during the Colonial Revival period often called a Governor Winthrop desk. Lupers extend automatically when slant-front is pulled down. Prospect door with pressed, carved fan. Ball-and-claw feet. *Private collection.* This kind of desk found in mahogany or stained soft wood. In mahogany. **$800–1,200.** In soft wood, **$450–675.**

George Washington writing table, c. 1920, modeled after one used by Washington in New York City. False drawers in back, working drawers in front, cockbeaded drawers, eight reeded legs, applied roundels. *Private collection.* **$1,800–2,400.**

Chippendale-style c. 1920 bench-made solid mahogany slant-front desk with two-over-two drawers. Fine fitted interior with three shells, blocked drawers. Ball-and-claw feet. Top of carcass with exposed dovetails. From the New York area. 37" wide x 17" deep x 40" high. *Private collection.* **$800–1,200.**

Hepplewhite-style c. 1910 bench-made solid walnut chest of drawers. Carcass front and drawers with stringing, bracket feet. Walnut lightly figured. Drawers with handmade dovetails. 42" wide x 44" high. *Private collection.* **$600–800.**

Walnut veneered, adapted Chippendale-style cabinet, c. 1920, with molded top, ogee bracket feet. Doors with hook-matched veneers and cross-banding. 36 1/4" wide x 17 1/2" deep x 41 1/2" high. *Private collection.* **$500–750.**

Queen Anne-style c. 1930 mahogany chest of drawers with four graduated drawers. Molded top, inset reeded quarter-columns, shell-carved apron, cabriole legs, and pad feet. Drawers with machine-made dovetails. In the Colonial Revival era this would have been called a "Salem chest." 37 1/4" wide x 20 3/8" deep x 38 1/4" high. *Private collection.* **$400–600.**

Chippendale-style c. 1920 inlaid bow-front chest of drawers. Double stringing around drawer fronts. Molded, slightly bowed top, with conforming, graduated drawers. Awkward ball-and-claw feet. This piece is typical Colonial Revival in that it combines motifs from different design periods, in this case Federal-era stringing with Chippendale-style feet. *Courtesy Morton Goldberg Auction Galleries, New Orleans.* **$800–1,200.**

Chippendale-style inlaid mahogany highboy with three urn finial (finials missing) and broken-arch scrolled pediment with floral carving, over shell-carved center drawer flanked by two small drawers over four graduated drawers. Lower portion with one long drawer over one shell-carved drawer flanked by two small drawers over carved apron and cabriole legs with carved knees and pad feet. Drawers with cross-banding and line inlays. This example shows the flat carving often found on Colonial Revival pieces (even good ones like this), which is an easy tip-off for late nineteenth-century work. Flattened and more attenuated than good eighteenth-century carving (note especially the lines of the apron). 35" wide x 19" deep x 79" high. *Courtesy Leslie Hindman Auctioneers, Chicago.* **$2,400–3,600.**

Factory-made c. 1920 Chippendale-style mahogany highboy of ordinary form, with little carving. Five graduated drawers in the top section over two graduated drawers in the lower part. Broken-arch pediment with turned finial and applied acanthus carving below. Shaped apron. Resting on cabriole legs with ball-and-claw feet. *Courtesy Motley's Auctions, Inc., Richmond, Virginia.* **$800–1,200.**

Chippendale-style c. 1880-1900 highly carved mahogany glazed-front bookcase. Pierced, scrolling, broken-arch pediment with rosette terminals. Blind-fret carving on door fronts. Legs and apron with shell carving, paw feet. 48" wide x 15" deep x 19 1/2" high. *Courtesy New Orleans Auction Galleries, New Orleans.* **$3,000–5,000.**

Chippendale-style c. 1900 mahogany chest-on-chest, a beautiful bench-made repoduction of a classic piece. Broken-arch bonnet top with three flame finials. Top section headed by shell-carved central drawer flanked by two short drawers over four long drawers. Lower section with two short drawers over three long drawers. Top and bottom with reeded, quarter-column case. Resting on ball-and-claw feet. Bat-wing brasses. 41" wide x 18 1/4" deep x 87" high. *Courtesy Anthony J. Nard & Company, Milan, Penna.* **$6,000–8,000.** A good investment, especially considering that an eighteenth-century American piece of the same stylistic quality would cost over $100,000!

Chippendale-style mahogany chest-on-chest, in the manner of Newport, Rhode Island, another fine example of late nineteenth-century work. Scrolling broken-arch pediment with rosette terminals, three flame finials. Upper section with three aligned shell-carved drawers over four block-front graduated drawers with molded drawer openings. Lower section with four block-front graduated drawers, also with molded drawer openings. Conforming molded base, resting on ball-and-claw feet. Bat-wing brasses. 37" wide x 21 1/2" deep x 6' 8 1/2" high. *Courtesy William Doyle Galleries, New York City.* **$12,000–18,000.** A comparable eighteenth-century American piece would cost over $1 million.

B-147

Chippendale-style c. 1880-1900 mahogany secretary bookcase. Broken-arch pediment of scaled-down proportions, with rosette terminals and acanthus carving, urn finial. Thirteenth-pane glazed doors above slant-front lower section. Interior with serpentine drawers and compartments, shell-carved door flanked by columns with flame finials. Four long graduated drawers. Resting on squat ball-and-claw feet. 42 1/2" wide x 21" deep x 92 1/2" high. *Courtesy New Orleans Auction Galleries, New Orleans.* **$1,500–2,400.**

Chippendale-style c. 1900 mahogany secretary bookcase with broken-arch pediment mounted with three urn and flame finials and shell and acanthus carving; over a pair of mullion-glazed doors above fall-front writing surface, over block-front case with carved shells comprised of four drawers, on ball-and-claw feet. Inset, reeded quarter-columns. 43" wide x 22" deep x 94" high. *Courtesy Leslie Hindman Auctioneers, Chicago.* **$4,000–6,000.**

Hepplewhite-style c. 1880-1900 secretary with two eight-pane doors enclosing shelves and fitted interior. Fold-out writing surface over four graduated cock-beaded drawers. Apron and cornice with inlay. French splay feet. *Courtesy Richard Beecher.* **$1,800–2,400.**

Seth Thomas c. 1920 mantel clock with molded top, gilded columns, rose-painted face, molded base. Features an image of Mount Vernon, much loved in Colonial Revival era. 10 3/4" wide x 5" deep x 14 1/4" high. *Private collection.* **$125–175.**

Carved oak tall-case clock, c. 1880-1900, probably by Walter H. Durfee and Company, Providence, Rhode Island. Broken-arch pediment (finials missing) over arched case flanked by rope-turned columns on all three parts of case. Shell carving above pendulum (missing). Paw feet. Moon phase. 8" high. *Courtesy Skinner, Inc., Bolton, Mass.* **$3,000–5,000.**

Left: Tiffany and Company mahogany tall-case clock with gold and silver face beneath curved bonnet top supported by reeded columns. Original finish and presentation plaque. 24 1/2" wide x 16 1/4" deep x 86" high. **$6,000–8,000.** *Right:* Tiffany and company tall-case clock, c. 1910. Iodized mahogany, with lion's paw feet, broken-arch pediment. 24 1/2" wide x 15" deep x 97" high. **$5,000–7,000.** *Courtesy New Orleans Auction Galleries, New Orleans.*

Similar to the clock at *right* on page 149, this is another c. 1880-1900 carved mahogany tall-case clock, by Walter H. Durfee and Company, Providence, Rhode Island, with carved, scrolled bonnet, three pairs of twisted columns with brass capitals and moon dial. 98 1/2" high. *Courtesy Rafael Osona, Nantucket, Mass.* **$5,000–7,000.**

Mahogany tall-case chiming clock, c. 1900, by Walter H. Durfee and Company, Providence, Rhode Island. Swan-neck pediment with three urn and flame finials, on a glazed case flanked by columns with capitals, shell carving above pendulum, gadrooning and acanthus carving. Paw feet. Arched dial with painted moon phase, silvered chapter and subsidary rings, chiming on eight tubes with Westminster and "Eight Bells" chimes. 96" high. *Courtesy Northeast Auctions, Hampton, New Hampshire.* **$8,000–12,000.**

Roxbury-style c. 1920 mahogany tall-case clock with Westminster chimes. Made by Bigelow and Kennard Company, Boston. 7' 6" high. *Courtesy Southampton Antiques, Southampton, Mass.* **$8,000–12,000.**

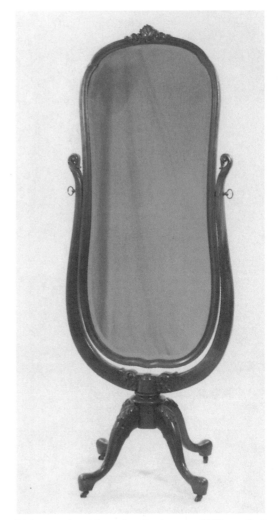

Mahogany hourglass cheval mirror, c. 1900, applied leaf carvings. *Courtesy of Southampton Antiques, Southampton, Mass.* **$1,200–1,800.**

Tall-case clock of simple form with molded, arched bonnet, c. 1913. Face flanked by columns. Silent or hour strike. Revolvng landscape and seascape and two moons above clock face. Pendulum flanked by columns. Lion's paw feet. By H. Mahler's Sons, Raleigh, North Carolina. 24 1/4" wide x 14 1/4" deep x 90 1/4" high. *Private collection.* **$4,000–6,000.**

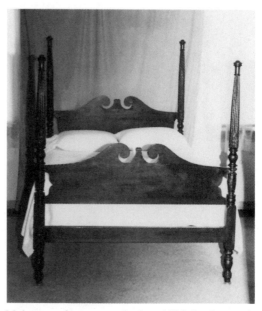

Mahogany four-poster bed, c. 1920, broken-arch headboard and footboard. Posts are reeded and carved with acanthus leaves and swags. 54" wide x 80" long. *Private collection.* **$225–425.**

Federal-style maple four-poster single bed, c. 1930–1940. High, turned posts with urn finials. *Courtesy of Neal Auction Company, New Orleans.* **$1,000–1,800,** pair.

POSTSCRIPT

We end this book with World War II because national attention had by then been diverted from the Colonial Revival movement—first by the Great Depression and, later, by the war. With returning soldiers interested in some of the styles they had seen abroad, the furniture industry had new postwar tastes to accommodate. The Colonial Revival began to settle into the familiar, ubiquitous style that we take for granted today. In 1993 we Americans seem to be just as interested in our past as ever, and we find Colonial designs all around us in the designs of our homes and furnishings. Colonial designs constitute a solid, dependable segment of the current furniture market, and it seems likely that they always will.

Probably the most important development in Colonial reproductions in the decades since World War II has been the increase in museum-sponsored reproduction programs that began in the 1930s. Reproductions from museum collections are generally more accurately styled than pieces commonly available in the Colonial Revival era, although museums also sponsor reproductions that adapt the original form to modern needs. The highest level of accuracy is found in the hallmarked pieces offered by several museums. These reproductions duplicate the primary and secondary wood of the original, along with many of the construction techniques. While there are certainly small custom shops making reproductions with even higher levels of hand work, museum-licensed reproductions are more readily available and more widely marketed.

In 1936 Colonial Williamsburg licensed a line of English and American reproductions to be made by Kittinger of Buffalo, New York. Kittinger made high-quality reproductions, with a good deal of hand work and finishing. In 1991 Colonial Williamsburg contracted with Baker Furniture Company to continue and expand the line of reproductions that Kittinger had begun. There are now around thirty-three pieces from Colonial Williamsburg's collections being reproduced by Baker, with the highest level the hallmarked pieces. Most of the pieces are American in origin, with several from Virginia.

One example from the current Baker/Williamsburg catalogue shows a c. 1753 Philadelphia Chippendale-style high chest (or highboy) with cartouche-carved finial, scrolling pediment, flame finials, two shell- and acanthus-carved drawers, carved knees, cabriole legs, and ball-and-claw feet. It represents the highest caliber of eighteenth-century American design. According to the catalogue, the piece is made up of nearly four hundred parts, with two hundred ninety-eight hand-cut dovetails and hand carving. The catalogue also describes some of the construction techniques used in hallmarked pieces: hand-cut dovetails, mortise and tenon construction, floating panel construction, and stacked core surfaces. Other hallmarked pieces from this catalogue include a c. 1790 Norfolk, Virginia, serpentine chest with a floating panel back, a top made from a single board, inlaid chamfered corners and splay feet. There is a c. 1770 Philadelphia Rococo armchair and side chair, both with carved crest rail, fluted stiles, shell-carved apron, acanthus knees, ball-and-claw feet, and through mortise and tenon construction. Also included in the catalogue are a Philadelphia armchair with Marlborough legs; a c. 1750 Massachusetts tea table; a c. 1800 New England easy chair; a c. 1790 Virginia Pembroke table; and many other pieces. All are branded with the marks of Colonial Williamsburg and Baker. There are a number of lacquer finishes available to match the exact color of the original pieces. The finishes are largely done by hand.

The Henry Ford Museum in Dearborn arranged with Colonial Furniture Company of Zeeland, Michigan, to reproduce a number of pieces from the collection in the 1930s. This relationship continued until fairly recently. The Henry Ford Museum has been active in keeping up its reproduction program, with new efforts launched in the early 1960s, in 1975, and again in 1991. The American Life Collection debuted in 1991, featuring clocks made by Sligh Furniture Company of Holland, Michigan. Sligh currently makes four tallcase clocks for the Henry Ford Museum, based on originals by Jacob Eby, Joseph Doll, Thomas Harland, and Simon Willard. Sligh also makes a William Gilbert mantel clock and a Benjamin Morrill wall clock as part of the American Life Collection. The tallcase clocks apparently are scaled down for modern ceiling heights. Sligh promotional material describes the Doll tallcase clock as being hand finished with a hand-painted face, moving moon dial, and an eight-day, weight-driven triple-chime pendulum movement.

Century Furniture Company of Hickory, North Carolina, also contracted with the Henry Ford Museum in 1991 to produce pieces for the American Life Collec-

tion, including furniture for the bedroom and dining room, occasional and upholstered pieces made from cherry, mahogany, and pine. Promotional literature from Century details a Queen Anne-style highboy with cabriole legs, pinwheel carvings, and flame finials. Century also reproduces several rustic pieces and a few Federal era pieces.

In 1982 Winterthur Museum began a reproduction program with Kindel Furniture Company, copying some of the finest pieces in its collection, including the famous Goddard-Townsend secretary/bookcase from Newport, Rhode Island. Of the several made around 1760, one recently sold at auction for 12 million dollars! This obviously represents the height of eighteenth-century American design. The Kindel reproduction from the Winterthur Museum Collection is a hallmarked piece, copying the primary and secondary woods of the original, as well as many aspects of the original construction. Kindel also produces dining room furniture patterned after eighteenth and nineteenth-century American pieces at Winterthur. However, these pieces are not exact reproductions, but make accommodations to current customers' needs.

Kindel began making reproductions for the National Trust for Historic Preservation in 1984, based on originals from the various properties owned by the organization. In general, these tend to be more vernacular in style than the pieces reproduced for Winterthur.

The Society for the Preservation of New England Antiquities has had a reproduction program since 1983 in conjunction with Southwood Reproductions, Henkel-Harris Furniture Company, Frederick Duckloe and Bros., and Eldred Wheeler. These reproductions are all based on New England originals, from the many properties owned by the SPNEA. SPNEA materials from the 1980s show a Portsmouth, New Hampshire, Chippendale corner chair; a Maine blockfront chest of drawers; a Newport card table; a

c. 1735–1750 Massachusetts chest on frame; a Portsmouth Queen Anne dropleaf table by Henkle-Harris; a Boston comb-back Windsor chair by Duckloe and Bros.; a Boston easy chair with shell-carved knees and ball-and-claw feet; a Chippendale lolling chair; and a Federal sofa by Southwood Reproductions. Currently the firm of Eldred Wheeler makes a New Hampshire six-drawer chest on frame from the 1770s, and an eighteenth century oval-top tavern table from Portsmouth, New Hampshire.

Public interest in and support of these museums and their reproduction programs continues. With several new programs begun in the 1980 and 1990s, museums will probably provide a source of good quality Colonial reproductions for the foreseeable future. It will be interesting to see how these reproductions fare in the secondary market, particularly as we enter the twenty-first century, and twentieth-century reproductions become "antiques" in their own right. We suspect that museum-sponsored reproductions and the work of the smaller cabinetshops will be among the most sought-after reproductions, which is exactly what is happening with signed Kittinger furniture.

BIBLIOGRAPHY

American Manufactured Furniture. West Chester, PA: Schiffer Publishing Ltd., 1988.

Ames, Kenneth L. "Grand Rapids Furniture at the Time of the Centennial." *Winterthur Portfolio* 10 (1975): 23–50.

Axelrod, Alan, ed. *The Colonial Revival in America.* New York: W. W. Norton, 1985.

Bainbridge, Bunting. *Houses of Boston's Back Bay.* Cambridge: The Belknap Press of Harvard University, 1975.

Bassett Furniture Industries. *A History of Bassett Furniture Industries, Inc.* Bassett, Virginia, c. 1985.

Betsky, Celia. "Inside the Past: The Interior and the Colonial Revival in American Art and Literature, 1860–1914." In Alan Axelrod, ed., *The Colonial Revival in America,* 241–77.

Burchell, Sam. *A History of Furniture— Celebrating Baker Furniture: One Hundred Years of Fine Reproductions.* New York: Harry N. Abrams, 1991.

Cook, Clarence. *The House Beautiful.* New York: Scribner, Armstrong and Company, 1878.

Cooke, Edward S. "The Boston Furniture Industry in 1880." *Old-Time New England* 70 (Winter 1980): 82–96.

Darling, Sharon. *Chicago Furniture: Art, Craft, and Industry, 1833–1983.* New York: W. W. Norton, 1984.

Dietz, Ulysses G. *Century of Revivals: Nineteenth-Century American Furniture from the Collection of the Newark Museum.* Newark NJ: Newark Museum of Art, 1983.

Ettema, Michael J. "Technological Innovation and Design Economics in Furniture Manufacture." *Winterthur Portfolio* 16 (Summer/Autumn 1981): 187–223.

Fennimore, Donald L. "Fine Points of Furniture, American Empire: Late, Later, Latest." In Kenneth L. Ames, *Victorian Furniture.* Philadelphia: The Victorian Society of America, 1983.

Hill, John H. "Furniture Designs of Henry W. Jenkins & Sons Co." *Winterthur Portfolio* (1969): 154–87.

The Housekeeper's Quest: Where to Find Pretty Things. New York: Sypher & Company, 1885.

Ingerman, Elizabeth. "Personal Experiences of an Old New York Cabinetmaker." *The Magazine Antiques* 84 (November 1963): 576–80.

Ivankovich, Michael. *The Guide to Wallace Nutting Furniture.* Doylestown, PA: Diamond Press, 1990.

Kimerly, W. L. *How to Know Period Styles in Furniture.* Grand Rapids, MI: Periodical Publishing Company, 1912.

Koch, Robert. *Louis C. Tiffany: Rebel in Glass.* Updated third edition. New York: Crown, 1982.

Lockwood, Luke Vincent. *Colonial Furniture in America.* New York: Scribner's, 1901.

Lyon, Irving Whitall. *Colonial Furniture of New England*. Boston and New York: Houghton Mifflin Company, 1891.

May, Bridget A. "Progressivism and the Colonial Revival: The Modern Colonial House, 1900–1920." *Winterthur Portfolio* 26 (Summer/Autumn 1991): 107–22.

McCabe, James D. *The Illustrated History of the Centennial Exhibition*. Philadelphia: National Publishing Company, 1876.

Monkhouse, Christopher P. "The Spinning Wheel as Artifact, Symbol, and Source of Design." In Kenneth Ames, ed., *Victorian Furniture*, Philadelphia: Victorian Society of America, 1983, 155–72.

Monkhouse, Christopher P., and Thomas S. Michie. *American Furniture in Pendleton House*. Providence: Museum of Art, Rhode Island School of Design, 1986.

Nutting, Wallace. *Wallace Nutting General Catalog, Supreme Edition*. 1930.

———. Wallace Nutting Windsors: Correct Windsor Furniture. Framingham, Mass: 1918.

———. *Wallace Nutting's Biography*. Framingham, Mass.: Old America Co., 1936.

Nye, Alvan Crocker. *A Collection of Scale-drawings, Details, and Sketches of what is commonly known as Colonial Furniture, Measured and drawn from antique examples by Alvan Crocker Nye*. New York: William Helburn, 1895.

Otto, Celia Jackson. *American Furniture of the Nineteenth Century*. New York: Viking Press, 1965.

Paine Furniture Company. "Suggestions to Those Who Would Furnish." Boston: 1888.

Pina, Leslie. *Louis Rorimer: A Man of Style*. Kent, Ohio: Kent State University Press, 1990.

Ransom, Frank Edward. *The City Built on Wood: A History of the Furniture Industry in Grand Rapids, Michigan, 1850–1950*. Ann Arbor, MI: Edwards Bros., 1955.

Rhoads, William B. *The Colonial Revival*. New York: Garland Publishing, 1977.

Roth, Rodris, "The Colonial Revival and Centennial Furniture." *Art Quarterly* 27, no. 1 (1964): 57–81.

———. "The New England, or 'Olde Tyme,' Kitchen Exhibit at Nineteenth-Century Fairs." In Alan Axelrod, ed., *The Colonial Revival in America*, 159–83.

Schoelwer, Susan Prendergast. "Curious Relics and Quaint Scenes: The Colonial Revival at Chicago's Great Fair." In Alan Axelrod, ed., *The Colonial Revival in America*, 185–216.

Seale, William. *The Tasteful Interlude: American Interiors Through the Camera's Eye, 1860–1917*. New York: Praeger Publishers, 1975.

Smith, Nancy A. *Old Furniture: Understanding the Craftsman's Art*. New York: Dover Publications, 1990.

Smith, Ray C. *Interior Design in Twentieth-Century America: A History*. New York: Harper and Row, 1987.

Stillinger, Elizabeth. *The Antiquers*. New York: Alfred A. Knopf, 1980.

Sypher & Company. "The Housekeeper's Quest: Where to Find Pretty Things." New York, 1885.

Thomas, David N. "A History of Southern Furniture." *Furniture South* 46, no. 10, sec. 2 (October 1967): 13–109.

Vollmer, William. *A Book of Distinctive Interiors*. New York: McBride, Nast, 1910.

Wallick, Ekin. *Inexpensive Furnishings in Good Taste*. New York: Hearst's International Library Company, 1915.

Weidman, Gregory R. *Furniture in Maryland, 1740–1940*. Baltimore: Maryland Historical Society, 1984.

LIST OF CONTRIBUTORS

Antique Shops, Auction Houses, and Producers

Baker Furniture Company
1661 Monroe Ave. NW
Grand Rapids, Michigan 49505

Bassett Furniture Industries, Inc.
P.O. Box 626
Bassett, Virginia 24055

Frank H. Boos Gallery
420 Enterprise Court
Bloomfield Hills, Michigan 48301
(313) 332-1500

Butterfield & Butterfield
220 San Bruno Ave.
San Francisco, CA 94103
(415) 861-7500

Century Furniture Company
P.O. Box 608
Hickory, NC 28603

Chameleon Antiques
10413 Warwick Blvd.
Newport News, Virginia 23601
(804) 596-9324

Chesapeake Antique Center, Inc.
Route 301
Queenstown, Maryland 21658
(410) 827-6640

William Doyle Galleries
175 East 87th Street
New York, New York 10128
(212) 427-2730

Dunning's Auction Service, Inc.
755 Church Road
Elgin, Illinois 60123
(708) 741-3483

Eldred Wheeler
60 Sharp Street
Hingham, Massachusetts 02043

Flomaton Antique Auction
207 Palafox Street
Flomaton, Alabama 36441
(205) 296-3710

Freeman\Fine Arts
1808-10 Chestnut Street
Philadelphia, Pennsylvania 19103
(215) 563-9275

Morton Goldberg Auction Galleries
New Orleans, Louisiana

Grogan & Company
890 Commonwealth Ave.
Boston, Massachusetts 02215
(617) 566-4100

Henkle-Harris Furniture Company
Winchester, Virginia

Leslie Hindman Auctioneers
Chicago, IL

Michael Ivankovich
P.O. Box 2458
Doylestown, Pennsylvania 18901
(215) 345-6094

James D. Julia, Inc.
Route 201, Showhegan Road
Fairfield, Maine 04937
(207) 453-7125

Kindel Furniture Company
P.O. Box 2047
Grand Rapids, Michigan 49501

Merriwood Antiques
3318 West Cary Street
Richmond, Virginia 23221
(804) 288-9308

Motley's Auctions, Inc.
2334 Willis Road
Richmond, Virginia 23237
(804) 743-8891

Nadeau's Auction Gallery
184 Windor Avenue
Windsor, Connecticut 06095

Nansemond Antique Shop
3537 Pruden Boulevard
Suffolk, Virginia 23434
(804) 539-6269

Anthony J. Nard & Company
U.S. Route 220
Milan, Pennsylvania 18831
(717) 888-7723

Neal Auction Company
4038 Magazine Street
New Orleans, Louisiana 70115
(504) 899-5329

New Hampshire Antique Co-Op
Route 101A, Box 732
Milford, New Hampshire 03055

New Orleans Auction Galleries, Inc.
801 Magazine Street
New Orleans, Louisiana 70130
(504) 566-1849

Northeast Auctions
P.O. Box 363
Hampton, New Hampshire 03842
(603) 926-9800

Rafael Osona
P.O. Box 2607
Nantucket, Massachusetts 02584
(508) 228-3942

Skinner, Inc.
Auctioneers and Appraisers of Antiques
   and Fine Art
357 Main Street
Bolton, Massachusetts 01740
(508) 779-6241

Sligh Furniture Company
201 W. Washington Avenue
Zeeland, Michigan 49464

C. G. Sloan & Company
4920 Wyaconda Road
North Bethesda, Maryland 20852
(401) 468-4911

Southampton Antiques
172 College Highway (Route 10)
Southampton, Massachusetts 01073
(413) 527-1022

Kimball M. Sterling, Inc.
125 West Market Street
Johnson City, Tennessee 37601
(615) 928-1471

Whitehall at the Villa
David Lindquist; Elizabeth Lindquist
   Mann
1213 East Franklin Street
Chapel Hill, NC 27514
(919) 942-3179

Wolf's Fine Arts Auctioneers
1239 West 6th Street
Cleveland, Ohio 44113
(216) 575-9653

Museums and Libraries

Baker Furniture Company
1661 Monroe Ave. Northwest
Grand Rapids, Michigan 49505

The Bennington Museum
West Main Street
Bennington, Vermont

The Colonial Williamsburg Foundation
P.O. Box 1776
Williamsburg, Virginia 23187

The Furniture Library
1009 North Main Street
High Point, North Carolina 27262

Grand Rapids Public Library
60 Library Plaza, Northeast
Grand Rapids, Michigan 49503

Henry Ford Museum
P.O. Box 1970
Dearborn, Michigan 48120

Edison Institute
20900 Oakwood Blvd.
Dearborn, Michigan 48121

International Home Furnishings Center
210 East Commerce Street
High Point, North Carolina 27260

Museum of Art
Rhode Island School of Design
Providence, Rhode Island 02903

Newark Museum
419 Washington Street
Newark, New Jersey 07101

Public Museum of Grand Rapids
54 Jefferson Southeast
Grand Rapids, Michigan 49503

Reynolda House
Museum of American Art
P.O. Box 11765
Winston-Salem, NC 27116

Smithsonian Institution
Washington, DC 20560

Society for the Preservation of New
    England Antiquities
141 Cambridge Street
Boston, Massachusetts 02114

The Winterthur Library
The Henry Frances du Pont Winterthur
    Museum
Winterthur, Delaware 19735

Index

VICTORIAN

FURNITURE

WITH PRICES

CONTENTS

Introduction

As you look through this book, you will be astounded by the great variety of styles that can all be called *Victorian*. The Victorian market truly offers something for everyone, with a huge range of prices and styles to suit almost every taste. This era takes its name from Queen Victoria, the English monarch who reigned from 1837 to 1901. Our book covers Victorian furniture in America from about 1830 to 1900, a period of immense energy and optimism during which furniture in exuberant designs was produced.

Each chapter in the book is devoted to a type of Victorian furniture: Gothic Revival, cottage, Rococo Revival, Renaissance Revival, patent, Eastlake, and golden oak. While these all constitute distinct styles, there are some underlying characteristics that apply overall. There was a love of rich effect, manifested in pieces of massive size and in the use of high-relief carving, flame veneers, burl panels, line-incised decoration, gilt or ebonized accents, marquetry, porcelain plaques, marble, tufted upholstery and rich fabrics. Even towards the end of the century, when reform was attempted in the name of Eastlake and the English Aesthetic Movement, American mass-produced versions still could not resist ornamentation. Victorians are famous for their "horror vacuii": no surface could be left without decoration. This holds true for furniture throughout the entire period— even on many pieces dating from the reform-influenced 1870s and 1880s.

Picturesque Eclecticism

A good way to understand what seemed beautiful to the Victorians is found in the idea of picturesque eclecticism.[1] We can better understand Victorian aesthetics by realizing that it was fundamentally Romantic, very different from 18th-century classicism and also from 20th-century modernism, two sensibilities that currently appeal to us. Ideas about the picturesque were germinated by the 18th-century author Edmund Burke, who wrote *A Philosophical Enquiry into the Origin of Our Ideas of the Sublime and Beautiful* (1757). Burke explored the emotions associated with the sublime and beautiful, and he found that astonishment and terror heightened the experience of beautiful things. These qualities were celebrated in Romantic art, and the earliest phase of Victorian furniture, the Gothic

---

1. A concept originating with Carroll L. V. Meeks in his work The Railroad Station (New Haven: Yale University Press, 1956).

Revival, is rooted in these notions about the picturesque.

For the Victorians, the picturesque translated into aesthetic pleasure found in visual surprises, which took the form of unexpected silhouettes or shapes, variety in texture and decorative treatment, and sharp contrasts. Victorian furniture often displays a virtual cacophony of unusual shapes and motifs with little overall unity. We might be tempted to look at these creations and think the designers had aimed for unity and failed. They had not. The kind of tension created by jarring elements is exactly what appealed to the Victorian sensibility. They wanted every inch to be interesting—by virtue of its shape, texture or decoration—rather than have the piece as a whole embody the classical ideals of good proportion and unity of design.

In contrast to the Victorian aesthetic, 18th-century classicism valued an overall unity, which was achieved through fine proportional relationships between parts to the whole, often accomplished through repetition of a single small decorative motif. The Victorians could never limit themselves to repetition of a single decorative element. They insisted on variety and contrast. The whole idea that parts should make up a coherent, unified whole—and the classical means to achieve it—was rejected by Victorian furniture makers.

Victorian aesthetics also rejected the principle that designs should be primarily functional. With our 20th-century viewpoint, most of us look at Victorian furniture and find it impractical. For Victorians, form did not follow function. The Victorian love of the picturesque meant that visual qualities were paramount, with concerns about function lagging far behind. In Victorian furniture, dramatic forms were valued for their visual impact, even though they might be structurally weak. Victorian high-backed chairs, seating furniture with scrolling and curved backs and tables with central pedestal supports make interesting visual statements, but at a sacrifice to structural integrity.

A significant function of Victorian furniture was to convey the status and importance of the owner. This was achieved through rich effect and also through sheer bulk. Furniture of great size and weight created a grand and formal look and reflected on the owner's station in life. The honorific function of Victorian furniture comes across clearly in the massive sideboards, ten-foot hall stands, eight-foot bedsteads and dressers, and all sorts of weighty pieces.

What about the other half of "picturesque eclecticism"? The idea of eclecticism is seen in the many varied styles used as inspiration for Victorian furniture. Furniture designers studied the masters' works and the old historical styles, but not for the sake of copying them. The idea was to create a new synthesis from those styles. The Victorians were far less interested in reproduction than in originality. Over the course of the 19th century, designers borrowed freely from the Middle Ages, the Renaissance, the Baroque, the Rococo style of 18th-century France, Japanese decorative arts, and even exotic Moorish designs. They did not feel constrained by notions of academic correctness (some might say good taste), but mined earlier styles purely to suit their whimsy. In this great age of empire building, styles were appropriated worldwide. So although we can divide the era into several distinct periods, there are many pieces that display features of more than one style.

It has been said that Victorian furniture represents the first truly American style in furniture. While it is true that Victorian furniture did not copy historical styles, the inspiration was certainly European in design, coming from imported furniture and European style books, and—this is important—often brought into American culture by recent European immigrants, especially those who fled

France and Germany after the revolutions of the 1840s. The influence of French- and German-born immigrant cabinetmakers, carvers and designers cannot be underestimated in American Victorian furniture. They were major players in the 19th-century American furniture industry.

Technological Innovation

The originality and variety prized in furniture and the decorative arts correspond to the love of progress that epitomized Victorian culture. This was a time of tremendous technological innovation, and each new mechanical invention was greeted with pride. Technology and the capability of machines were allowed to drive design to a great extent—so much so that reform was attempted during the last quarter century in response to the shoddy design on display at the great mid-century international exhibitions. But we should note that although the reformers were very much in earnest, their reforms were embraced by only a few, and otherwise their ideas were watered down almost beyond recognition by the time they reached the broad population. Most people still loved every bit of Victorian ornamentation, despite the reformers. Socialites in Manhattan might be impressed by the clean, spare lines of true Eastlake furniture, but settlers on the prairie wanted all the ornament that new factories could produce.

Quality Levels and Pricing

How does the market set a value on Victorian furniture? Several factors come into play—including quality of design, workmanship, a known maker, condition, rarity, provenance, and usefulness for today's lifestyle. The work of several fine cabinetmaking firms is known for good design and workmanship, and thus highly valued. For example, makers like Belter and Herter Brothers are currently expensive. However, poor condition, even for these makers, will lower the price. A piece by an unknown maker in poor condition should be shunned or bought only at bargain prices. An especially rare form can command a higher price. Knowing who owned the piece—perhaps one of the great robber barons or railroad magnates of the 19th century—can add to the value. The one aspect that can be particularly problematic with Victorian furniture is how useful a piece will be for today's lifestyle.

The real problem in the marketplace for Victorian furniture is not poor design or craftsmanship but size. Many pieces are simply not practical in today's homes. Towering hallstands and massive beds just don't fit into most houses. Consequently, the market is not as strong for such things.

Serious scholarship on Victorian furniture is still relatively new and is just beginning to piece together a picture of the 19th-century furniture trade. The old stereotype of cheap, mass-produced Victorian furniture made of shoddy materials is being reexamined as furniture historians begin to document many of the smaller cabinetmaking firms that produced extraordinary pieces. There was, of course, a great deal of factory-produced furniture, made to suit a range of pocketbooks. However, in recent years, the market has been exciting for the work of the fine cabinetmaking firms of John Henry

Belter, Herter Brothers, J. and J. W. Meeks, Alexander Roux, Kimbel and Cabus, and others. Not surprisingly, just as there is a clear difference in quality between the production of smaller firms and mechanized factories, there is a huge difference in prices. Those pieces by known makers have been showing up in prestigious auctions with increasing regularity since the early 1980s.

In the last 20 years important books have been published and exhibitions mounted on Victorian styles and makers. Books and corresponding museum exhibitions of Gothic Revival, John Henry Belter, Herter Brothers, Eastlake, and the Aesthetic Movement have provided us with information on fine makers and interesting design movements. This kind of scholarship almost always enhances the value of the subject being studied. The trend is certainly towards more scholarship on 19th-century furniture and more interest in building serious collections. As 18th-century American furniture becomes increasingly scarce and prohibitively expensive, we are seeing more serious collectors of American Victorian furniture.

Museum collecting has also changed radically in the last ten years or so. Regional museums cannot compete for 18th-century goods. The finest examples are often already in museums. To build exciting, affordable collections, museums have turned to 19th-century pieces for which a $50,000 expenditure buys quality and rarity that would perhaps cost $500,000 to over $1,000,000 for a comparable 18th-century item. Also, museums of the South, Midwest and West have realized that local history is more strongly grounded in the 19th century than the 18th-another very good reason to collect 19th-century pieces.

Victorian furniture has become so important in some areas of the market that an "upper tier" of dealers has emerged— just as existed for years in the period American, English and French markets. These dealers often ask two or three times that a piece would bring at auction or from a generalist. They try to deal only in the most exemplary, labeled or attributed pieces in the finest original state. In dealing and collecting at a rarefied level, subtle distinctions—and the prestige of the dealer—become highly important to value.

A number of these high-end pieces are featured in this book. We have benefited from the help of several dealers in fine Victorian furniture. Picture captions will sometimes include the notation "dealer estimate." This refers to price ranges provided by such a specialized dealer, and we defer to their expertise at this level of the market. Buying from a specialist means that you do not have to scour the countryside seeking the perfect piece; they will do the work for you and will bring you the highest quality. They will, of course, charge accordingly. The prices of a specialist tell us the value of a piece at its highest level, but that does not rule out the possibility that you might find a similar piece at a lower level of the market. It is worth remembering that since Victorian furniture is still not universally appreciated, one can (with luck) buy a fine piece by a known maker for less money at auction or through a general dealer. Collectors of Victorian furniture can still "hit the jackpot" at estate sales, auctions, and general antiques shops, partly because some dealers still don't realize that there is a difference between factory Victorian and fine Victorian. As we say in the antiques business, knowledge pays.

Aside from this rather glamorous segment of the Victorian market, there is factory-made Victorian furniture at every antiques mall and small antiques shop in America. This kind of furniture is plentiful, so you have the opportunity to pick and choose carefully. With so much available, you must insist on good condition, solid construction, and pleasing design. There is no need to buy a piece in poor condition since you will undoubtedly find another in good shape. With this in mind, all of the prices in our book refer to pieces in good condition. The price ranges reflect retail prices that one can expect to pay for similar pieces in antiques shops across the country.

We have had a wonderful time creating this book. Almost every aspect of the Victorian era is fascinating, especially the decorative arts. Social customs, expanding technologies, the story of 19th-century immigrants-all shaped the evolution of furniture in Victorian America in interesting ways. We hope our book adds to your understanding and appreciation of this fascinating period of American furniture, and we hope it adds to your confidence in collecting Victorian furniture.

1

Gothic Revival
1830–1850

The Gothic Revival had its roots in 18th-century English Romanticism, with its love of the picturesque and the unusual. English designers of this persuasion felt that houses should be designed in harmony with their natural surroundings, and the results would be more picturesque if those surroundings were wild and scenic. Houses, like the landscape, should exhibit plenty of variety, contrast, a sense of movement, and even surprise. It was felt that Gothic architecture, one of the glories of England's past, best captured the picturesque aesthetic. Probably the best-known example of Gothic Revival architecture from the mid-18th century was Horace Walpole's Strawberry Hill, while in furniture, the designs of Thomas Chippendale featured many Gothic motifs. But aside from a few motifs in American Chippendale furniture, the Gothic Revival did not come to America until the 1820s and '30s, where it was first seen in church architecture. By the 1830s it was more widespread as an architectural style, with furniture also designed to complement it.

Architectural Antecedents and Furniture Makers

How were Gothic designs transmitted from England to America? The Englishman Robert Smith published *The Cabinet Maker and Upholsterer's Guide* in 1826 and it was filled with designs that could be produced for the middle class. The furniture included Gothic motifs such as arches, clustered columns, trefoils and quatrefoils, crockets and finials. Robert Conner, also English, borrowed from some of these designs, and published them in New York in 1842 in his book *The Cabinet Maker's Assistant*.[1]

Alexander Jackson Davis is probably the best-known American architect who designed Gothic Revival houses, the most famous being Glen Ellen in Baltimore (built in 1832) and Lyndhurst in Tarrytown, New York (built for New York mayor William Paulding in 1838). Davis's 1838 publication, Rural Residences, encouraged rural Gothic architecture—

---

1. Robert C. Smith, "Gothic and Elizabethan Revival Furniture, 1800-1850," *The Magazine Antiques* 75 (March 1959): 275.

houses that were meant to fit into the landscape and echo its picturesque qualities. These houses included features like gables, carved vergeboards, turrets, pinnacles, battlements, and tinted windows.[2] Bringing all these features together resulted in a varied outline—an interesting silhouette that was indeed unpredictable. The Hudson River Valley probably had the densest population of Gothic Revival homes. During the 1830s the American authors James Fenimore Cooper and Washington Irving built and added Gothic touches to their homes in New York State. Cooper turned his Otsego Hall into a Gothic mansion, and Irving created his Sunnyside on the Hudson River.

Davis designed furniture to go with his Gothic Revival houses, and the furniture was executed by New York cabinetmakers, such as Alexander Roux and the firm of Burns & Trainque. The best Gothic Revival furniture was often designed by architects, and much of this furniture is now in museums, or if not, is eagerly sought by specialized collectors. The motifs used on furniture were somewhat different from those found on architecture, although the furniture—like the architecture—is distinguished by the use of arches, clustered columns, trefoils and quatrefoils, crockets and finials.

Andrew Jackson Downing, a landscape gardener who worked with Davis and who helped popularize the movement, noted the furniture style in his 1850 publication *The Architecture of Country Houses*, which included designs for elaborate Gothic villas and modest cottages. Downing praised the work of Burns & Trainque and the firm of Alexander Roux, saying "The most correct Gothic furniture

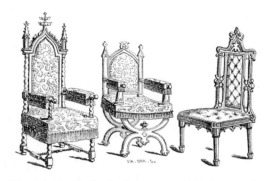

Fig. 1-1 Gothic Revival chairs, c. 1850, from A. J. Downing's *The Architecture of Country Houses* (1850). Downing writes, "Drawing-room and library chairs in the Gothic style are generally expensive and elaborate, being covered with rich stuffs, and highly carved." He also hints at a weakness of the style. The chair on the left, he says, "is too elaborate and ecclesiastical in character for most private houses. … We much prefer, when richness is requisite, to get it, in Gothic furniture, by covering rather plain and simple designs with rich stuffs rather than by the exhibition of elaborate Gothic carving, the effect of which is usually rather severe and angular, when applied to furniture."

that we have seen in this county is by Burns and Tranque (sic), Broadway, New York. Some excellent specimens may also be seen at Roux."[3]

The firm of J. and J. W. Meeks of New York City produced much fine Gothic furniture in the 1830s and '40s. The Meeks firm took a different approach to the Gothic Revival than architect-designers did. Meek's furniture was generally based on late Empire forms which showed off richly figured veneers and was highlighted by Gothic accents. This combination was especially successful on large case pieces such as secretary/bookcases. An indication of the company's prestige

2. Katherine S. Howe and David B. Warren, *The Gothic Revival Style in America*, 1830-1870 (Houston: Museum of Fine Arts, 1976), 1.

3. Andrew Jackson Downing, *The Architecture of Country Houses* (New York: D. Appleton, 1850; reprint, New York: Dover Publications, 1969), 440.

is the fact that the White House ordered Gothic chairs from them between 1845 and 1849. These chairs, which were of simple design with four Gothic arches and three trefoils incorporated into the backs, were later used during Lincoln's administration in the Cabinet Room.[4] Meeks's furniture was very well made and still finds a good market today.

John Jelliff of Newark, New Jersey, was best known for his Renaissance Revival furniture, but he did make Gothic Revival furniture as well, mainly in rosewood and walnut

Form and Function

Gothic Revival pieces from the first half of the 19th century did not revive Gothic furniture forms but simply displayed Gothic motifs—crockets and finials, arches, tracery, trefoils and quatrefoils, and rose windows—on contemporary furniture forms. Aside from pieces designed by architects like Davis, cabinetmakers like the Meeks firm added Gothic details to late Empire designs, creating pieces that were subtly Gothic. This is the kind of furniture we are likely to find outside of museums.

In general, during this period, Gothic Revival furniture was considered most suitable for the library, halls, and sometimes for the dining room. Gothic furniture for halls included hall chairs with hinged seats, the lids lifting up for storage of small items like gloves. Hall chairs often with unupholstered wooden seats, were primarily ceremonial and decorative and not intended for lengthy sitting.

As interesting as this furniture is, even writers from the period felt that heavily Gothicized furniture was really not suited for most homes. A. J. Downing, for instance, found it too angular and not domestic in feeling. He wrote, "We much prefer, when richness is requisite, to get it, in Gothic furniture, by covering rather plain and simple designs with rich stuffs, rather than by the exhibition of elaborate Gothic carving, the effect of which is usually rather severe and angular, when applied to furniture."[5] Downing much pre-

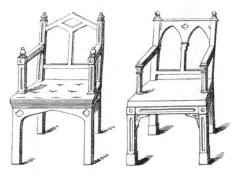

Fig. 1-2 Two Gothic Revival chairs, c. 1850, from Downing's *The Architecture of Country Houses* (1850). He promotes these because they are relatively simple and can be made fairly easily. He recommends them for the hall or living room.

Fig. 1-3 Gothic Revival bed, c. 1850, from Downing's book. Very popular with certain collectors today, this "sanctified" bed was a rarity even in the period.

4. John N. Pearce and Lorraine W. Pearce, "More on the Meeks Cabinetmakers," *The Magazine Antiques* 90 (July 1966): 70-73.

5. Downing, 447-48.

ferred plainer Gothic furniture that could be made by local carpenters or cabinet-makers. Simply by adding a few Gothic details to sturdy rectilinear forms, one could make furniture that was functional and stylish—and not the special preserve of the wealthy.

Gothic Revival furniture was found not only in homes but also in many of the Gothic Revival churches that proliferated in 19th-century America. In fact, churches have continued to demand it throughout the 20th century. Apart from choir stalls, altars, and church pews, one often finds on the market today Gothic thrones or bishops' chairs, which originally would have been in a church.

One final note about Gothic Revival furniture from the 1830s and '40s: it is not to be confused with "Modern Gothic" furniture of the 1870s and '80s. The later Modern Gothic can be distinguished by the inclusion of shallow, incised carving of geometric forms and stylized floral designs, along with Gothic motifs. It is related to the designs of Charles Eastlake and Bruce Talbert, but more on that in Chapter 6.

Gothic Revival oak hall chair, c. 1850, not designed for comfort but for ornament. Wooden seat lifts for storage of small items like gloves. Gothic pierced back. Spool-turned legs. 18" wide × 17 1/2" deep × 43 1/2" high. *Private collection*. **$400–600.**

Gothic hybrid carved walnut armchair, c. 1860, with spired crest surmounted with finials and pierced with quatrefoil above upholstered oval back, joined with open armrest continuing to a shaped seat frame raised on ring-turned legs. The spool turnings are typical of a mid-century look. This may have been made for a church. *Courtesy Neal Auction Company, New Orleans, Nicholay & Morgan photographers.* **$1,200–1,800.**

Pair of walnut Gothic Revival side chairs, c. 1850, each back rising to a pointed arch enclosing Gothic tracery. With turned stiles and legs. *Courtesy Neal Auction Company, New Orleans, Nicholay & Morgan photographers.* **$800–1,200** the pair.

Good Gothic Revival oak armchair, c. 1850, probably made in New York. With well-turned double-spiral legs and stiles. Back with "rose window," Gothic arches, quatrefoil, crest with crockets and fleur-de-lys finial. On rollers. Tufted seat. Original condition, old finish. *Courtesy Neal Auction Company. New Orleans, Nicholay & Morgan photographers.* **$2,400–3,600.**

Pair of rosewood Gothic Revival side chairs, c. 1855, attributed to Thomas Brooks, Brooklyn, N.Y. Relatively simple design with cutout quatrefoils and trefoils, fleur-de-lys finials. On rollers. 46 1/4" high × 19" wide × 18" deep. *Courtesy Neal Auction Company, New Orleans, Nicholay & Morgan photographers.* **$800–1,200** the pair.

Gothic-Empire mahogany cabinet, c. 1840. Molded frieze over one cupboard door, flanked by curved sides and scrolling stiles. Scroll feet. Typically extravagant use of flame mahogany in this Restauration-Gothic hybrid. 30 1/2" wide × 17 3/4" deep × 39" high. *Courtesy Frank H. Boos Auction Gallery, Bloomfield Hills, Mich.* **$1,000–1,500.**

Gothic Revival dresser, c. 1840, based on a late Empire/Restauration design featuring flame mahogany veneers, with a few Gothic touches. Two over three drawers. Two glove boxes with cabinets above with glazed, pointed-arch doors and fleur-de-lys finials. Mirror also with fleur-de-lys finial. *Courtesy Flomaton Antique Auction, Flomaton, Ala.* **$1,800–2,400.**

Gothic Revival wardrobe, c. 1850, featured in Downing's book. He believed this type of simple but attractive furniture could be available to the general public, and he championed many of these straightforward designs.

Gothic Revival rosewood library table, c. 1840-50. Inset marble top above a shaped apron with reticulated border, resting on bracketed cusp-carved supports containing pierced Gothic panels, joined with an arched stretcher. 29 1/2" high × 49" wide × 25" deep. *Courtesy Neal Auction Company, New Orleans, Nicholay & Morgan photographers.* **$8,000–12,000.**

Gothic Revival carved oak library table, c. 1850, with variegated inset marble top with outset corners. Conforming apron decorated with quatrefoils and foliated medallions. Raised on an arched trestle-form base, architecturally buttressed by a span of Romanesque arches. 343/4" high × 83" wide × 35" deep. *Courtesy Neal Auction Company, New Orleans, Nicholay & Morgan photographers.* **$10,000–15,000.**

Gothic Revival carved rosewood library table, c. 1845, by J. and J. W. Meeks (labeled). Marble top with rounded corners and molded edge above pierce-carved quatrefoil frieze, raised on scrolled legs joined by a scrolled stretcher, mounted at the intersections with turned finials, ending in scrolled feet on rectangular pads, casters. 41" long x 301/4" high. *Courtesy Butterfield & Butterfield, Los Angeles.* **$12,000–18,000.**

A highly important rosewood Gothic Revival center table attributed to A. J. Davis, c. 1840. Pie-veneered top, frieze with wave molding, beading, and Gothic arches alternating with drop finials. Very distinctive base with six columns joined by Gothic arches and trefoils, resting on pie-veneered base with three feet terminating in Gothic trefoils. This piece has it all— excellent provenance, association with the founder of the Gothic Revival movement in America, very good condition-all the drop finials (acorns) are original (this may sound insignificant, but it is crucial to the integrity of a fine piece). These factors have a strong impact on value. *Courtesy loan Bogart, Rockville Centre, N.Y.* Dealer estimate: **$30,000–50,000** plus (depending on condition).

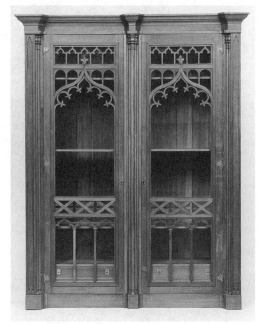

Gothic Revival mahogany double-door armoire, c. 1840. Projecting molded cornice with rounded corners, above a pair of generously proportioned doors displaying inset Gothic-arch panels, opening to a well-fitted interior with graduated drawers and pull-out slides. On conforming base with short vasiform-turned feet. Original untouched finish, as found. *Courtesy Neal Auction Company, New Orleans, Nicholay & Morgan photographers.* **$4,500–6,500.**

Walnut Gothic Revival double-door bookcase, c. 1860. Cornice with chamfered crenelated blocks above an applied Gothic fretwork frieze. Glazed doors with Gothic tracery carving and the sides with applied fretwork. Plinth base. 71" high × 52" wide × 12" deep. *Courtesy Neal Auction Company, New Orleans, Nicholay & Morgan photographers.* **$3,600–4,800.**

Gothic Revival carved walnut bookcase, c. 1840, with molded, projecting cornice above cluster columns. Two doors with Gothic tracery. Inside are shelves and a pair of drawers below. Plinth base. 95" high × 72" wide × 21" deep. *Courtesy Neal Auction Company, New Orleans, Nicholay & Morgan photographers.* **$4,500–6,500.**

A magnificent Gothic Revival bookcase, c. 1840, of mahogany and mahogany veneers. Breakfront form, with four drawers in base. Doors with Gothic arches and quatrefoil mullions. Pediment with band of acorn and leaf carving. Made by Richard Byrne of White Plains, New York, who is known to have executed designs by A. J. Davis for the Gothic mansion *Lyndhurst*. This piece has been in the *Lyndhurst* area since it was made and has a closely documented provenance, including families of note and even the name of the railroad station where the piece was originally delivered. The documented maker, wonderful form and excellent provenance enrich the value of the piece. *Courtesy of Joan Bogart, Rockville Centre, N.Y.* Dealer estimate: **$40,000–50,000.**

Gothic Revival carved mahogany bedstead, c. 1840. Flamboyant headboard in a highly stylized Gothic manner, yet held within a traditional set of columns and connecting boards such as were used from 1825-1865. *Courtesy New Orleans Auction Gallery, New Orleans.* **$4,000–6,000.**

Empire secretary with Gothic Revival touches by the Meeks firm, c. 1845. Typical of Empire furniture is the flame mahogany veneer and ogee cornice. The Gothic touches are seen in the arched mullions and arched interior door executed in crossbanding. *Courtesy Morton Goldberg Auction Galleries, New Orleans.* **$8,000–12,000** signed, **$4,000–6,000** unsigned.

Imposing Gothic Revival carved mahogany full-tester bed, c. 1850. Deeply molded tester with ap-plied cornice beading and richly carved acanthus leaves, with lacy arcaded gallery. Spiral-turned post stopped by carved capitals and resting on Gothicized blocks carved in full relief with figures in Renaissance dress holding symbolic objects, each standing within a Gothic arch on plinth base. Pierce-carved crested headboard panelled with blind fretwork and extensive Gothic tracery, which is also found on the rails and footboard. A commissioned tour de force by a master cabinetmaker. From a Gothic mansion in New Orleans. *Courtesy Neal Auction Gallery, New Orleans, Nicholay & Morgan photographers.* **$25,000–35,000.**

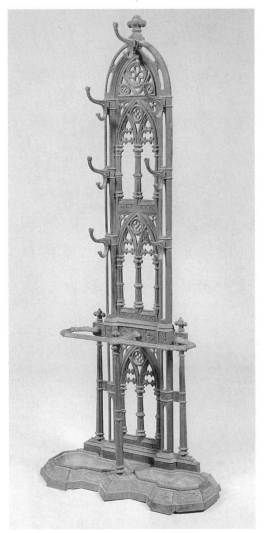

Gothic Revival mahogany hall tree, c. 1845-60, with mirror, knobs for hats/coats/umbrellas, cast iron drip pan with shell motif, pierce-carved back featuring fleur-de-lys-type shapes. 7' high. *Private collection.* **$2,400–3,600.**

Gothic Revival cast iron umbrella stand and rack, c. 1850, with repeated Gothic arches and cluster columns, quatrefoils, and fleur-de-lys finials. The Gothic Revival style was very popular with the cast iron manufacturers. 30" wide × 12" × 70 1/2" high. *Courtesy New Orleans Auction Gallery, New Orleans.* **$2,800–3,800.**

2

Cottage Furniture
1840–1890

It might be said that cottage furniture was the poor man's answer to Gothic furniture. Coming on the heels of the Gothic Revival period, cottage furniture also was rooted in a past style, being an economical interpretation of Elizabethan designs. It was inexpensive furniture, but it also could be quite charming. It was meant for simple cottages, bedrooms or other private areas of the house, or servants' quarters.

A. J. Downing reserved special praise for cottage furniture in his 1850 book *The Architecture of Country Houses*. A champion of unpretentious furniture and an influential taste maker, he even made several suggestions for creating one's own pretty furniture out of barrels, whose curves could be made into chair backs or settee backs, with ruffled skirts added to make a charming chair. Downing's suggestions remind us of the state of the furniture trade in America at mid-century. Not everyone had access to "store-bought" furniture. In rural areas or newly settled areas, or for frugality, many still depended on the skills of a family member for at least some of their furniture. If a family had only a few dollars to spend, "store bought" cottage furniture was the least expensive around.

Design Elements

Downing mentioned Edward Hennessey of Boston as being one of the best makers of cottage furniture: "This furniture is remarkable for its combination of lightness and strength, and its essentially cottage-like character. It is very highly finished, and is usually painted drab, white, grey, a delicate lilac, or a fine blue—the surface polished and hard, like enamel."[1]

Less-expensive suites were made of pine or some other soft wood and were painted as Downing described. Especially early in the period, more expensive pieces were made of mahogany or other hardwoods. These might be more elaborately decorated and have marble surfaces.

As can be seen from the Hennessey suite in Fig. 2-1, one of the chief characteristics of cottage furniture is spool or bobbin turning. This kind of decoration,

---

1. Andrew Jackson Downing, The Architecture of Country Houses (New York: D. Appleton, 1850; reprint New York: Dover Publications, 1969), 415.

Fig. 2-1 Cottage bedroom suite in an Elizabethan style, c. 1850, from A. J. Downing's *The Architecture of Country Houses*. This set, made by the Hennessey firm of Boston, was available "in dark wood, or tastefully painted, the ground of drab, enriched with well-executed vignettes in the panels, and marble tops to the principle articles, at from $70 to $100 the set, including 4 chairs." Today, a full set: **$1,800–2,400.** Chest: **$450–650.** Washstand: **$350–475.** Bed: **$275–475.** Bedside cabinet: **$400–600.** Chair: **$125–225.**

which could be inexpensively produced with the multiple-bladed lathe, had associations with the past and was seen as a variation of the barley-twist or spiral turnings on Elizabethan furniture. Elizabethan furniture, Downing felt, had a picturesque beauty, with its twisted legs, fringes, and quaint carving. As charming as Elizabethan furniture was, cottage furniture was even more so because it was available to everyone.

The picturesque *charm of this kind of furniture being conceded, to what, then, is it owing? We think, to the domestic feeling which pervades it.... It has a homey strength and sober richness....It is undeniable that, to the present age, the charm of this antique furniture is in its romance-in its long association with times, events, and names that have a historical interest, and that move our feelings deeply by means of such powerful associations... It is so much richer and more domestic than strictly Gothic furniture, that it will always be preferred to the latter by most persons."*2

Cottage furniture was especially popular for bedrooms, and the spool-turned bed got a boost from a brush with celebrity. The association with the beloved Swedish singer surely increased the popularity of the spool-turned "Jenny Lind" bed during the second half of the 19th century.

Factory Production

Cottage furniture in the spool or Elizabethan style was a snap to manufacture using the earliest steam-driven machines. Circular saws and lathes were among the first woodworking tools to be harnessed to steam power. The steam-driven lathe could make the spool or bobbin turnings with ease, and the circular saw greatly sped up the cutting of boards. These two processes were about all that was needed to make a Jenny Lind-type bed.

There were many large factories in Chicago, Baltimore, Grand Rapids and other cities that made cottage furniture and shipped it all over the country by boat and railroad.

Cottage furniture was the least-expensive mass-produced furniture available until the golden oak period, when the mail-order giants made affordable, sturdy, oak pieces in fanciful styles to the delight of households throughout America. Until then, cottage furniture was a given, maintaining its overall simplicity and affordability, while subtly adapting a silhouette and painting style to reflect the latest fashion.

2. Ibid, 451 (italics his).

Cottage bedroom suite, c. 1850, featured in A. J. Downing's *The Architecture of Country Houses*. He gives the original price for this set, which was made by Edward Hennessey, as $36—one of his least-expensive sets! Today, a full set: **$1,000–1,500.** Washstand: **$275–475.** Chair: **$100–150.** Bed: **$300–475.** Dressing table: **$300–475.**

Seven-piece New England painted cottage bedroom set in the Eastlake style, c. 1870. With floral and bird designs centering landscapes accented by pinstripes on light gray-green background. *Courtesy Skinner, Inc., Boston, Mass.* Bed: **$800–1,200.** Dresser: **$1,200–1,800.** Washstand: **$600–800.** Table: **$300–450.** Chair: **$100–175.** As a set: **$3,600–4,800.**

Child's chair, c. 1860, with spool-turned legs, stiles and spindles. Crest rail and base of back with faint remains of stenciled decoration. Caned seat. Very similar in style to the Hennessey sets—typical, charming cottage furniture. *Private collection*. **$125–150.**

Cottage bedroom Suite, C. 1850, from A. J. Downing's book *The Architecture of Country Houses*. This set (with four chairs) "without marble tops, but highly finished 'china white, peach blossom, or blue ground, single gilt lines, Ornamented,' is $68. The same, with marble top to several of the articles, $80. The wardrobe shown is $18 more." Today, a full set: **$5,000–6,000.** Washstand: **$600–900.** Dresser: **$1,000–1,500.** Bedside cabinet: **$500–750.** Sleigh bed: **$1,000–1,500.** Towel rack: **$100–150.** Chair: **$175–275.** Table: **$175–350.** Wardrobe: **$1,800–2,500.**

Faux rosewood (maple) "Grecian" rocker, c. 1860. A caned rocker like this most likely would have been kept in the bedroom. 41" high. *Private collection*. **$275–375.**

Child's caned "Grecian" rocker, c. 1860, rocker with scrolling arms, shaped seat and crest rail. *Private collection.* **$175–275.**

Boston rocker, c. 1830-60. Crest rail with stenciled landscape. The Boston rocker, probably the earliest rocking chair form-dating from around 1825—was popular throughout the century. The rocking chair originated in America, unlike many of the other popular Victorian furniture forms. 40" high. *Courtesy Butte's Antiques, Oxford, N.C.* **$400–600.**

Walnut table, c. 1860, with shaped molded top with drop finials, turned legs, trestle base with shaped shelf stretcher. 33" long × 18 1/2" wide × 29 1/2" high. *Private collection.* **$225–325.**

Table, c. 1860, with shaped top, drop finials, turned legs, trestle base, shelf stretcher. Soft wood with ebonized finish. 15" wide × 26" long × 28 1/2" high. *Private collection* **$175–275.**

Walnut Elizabethan Revival cottage table, c. 1860, with spool-turned legs on trestle base. 19" long x 15" wide x 26" high. *Private collection.* **$90–150.**

Elizabethan Revival parlor table, c. 1860, with marble turtle-shaped top. Apron with flame mahogany veneer, beading and drop finials. Shelf also accented with beading. Legs and stretchers spool turned. Sides with fret-carved scrolling decoration. Fancy cottage furniture. 29 1/2" long x 17 1/2" deep x 29" high. *Private collection.* **$800–1,200.**

Cottage pine chest, c. 1860, with original painted and gilt stenciled decoration. Original white marble top of bowed form with conforming top drawer over three drawers. Restoration overtones in the feet and decoration. Original wood pulls. *Private collection.* **$1,200–1,600.**

Black-painted pine cottage washstand, c. 1870, with stenciled decoration of graceful swirls and fruit. Scalloped, molded backsplash, molded top. One drawer over cabinet. Scalloped apron. Drawer with "button and scallop" dovetails (produced by the Knapp dovetailing machine, invented 1868). 24" high. *Courtesy The Antique Mail, Hillsborough, N.C.* **$600–800.**

Spool-turned tiger maple and maple crib, c. 1870, with turned spindles and legs, casters, 42 1/4" long × 24" wide × 34" high. *Courtesy Frank H. Boos Auction Gallery, Bloomfield Hills, Mich.* **$1,200–1,800.**

Cottage bedroom suite in the Renaissance Revival style, c. 1865. Bed with panelled headboard, finials, Renaissance-type cartouche, painted outlines and painted floral decorations. Matching dresser with candle stands, marble surfaces, original drop pulls on lower drawers. Matching washstand with marble backsplash, brackets and top, with one drawer over cabinets. With original drop pulls. *Private collection.* The set, **$4,000–6,000.**

3

Rococo Revival
1840–1865

If cottage furniture was homey and domestic, rococo furniture met another need: it was elegant and feminine and had the status associated with all things French. If cottage furniture was for the private parts of the house, rococo was for the most public parts. In 1850 a parlor furnished with Rococo Revival furniture told visitors that the homeowners were "au courant" with the latest fashions. The Rococo Revival reached its peak of popularity in the years immediately preceding the Civil War. Inspired by 18th-century French designs, the Rococo Revival was marked by curving forms—including C-scrolls, S-scrolls, and cabriole legs—and high-relief sculptural carving of fruit, vegetables and flowers. The curving forms could be as simple as the ubiquitous balloon-back lady's chair or as complex as the parlor sofa with triple arching back or the S-shaped *tête-à-tête*. Serpentine drawer fronts and sofa seat rails completed the theme. The best pieces used rosewood, though mahogany was also used, especially on earlier pieces, and walnut was widely used on less-expensive furniture. The better pieces had truly remarkable masses of carving, extravagant curves and rich upholstery.

With obvious design links to 18th-century French furniture, the style was called by an array of names in America—Antique French, Modern French, Louis XV and Louis XIV. None of these names are precisely accurate, but certainly the style does recall the sensuous curves of Louis XV Rococo furniture, a testament to the fact that at mid-century, France still dominated the decorative arts and had a rich cultural heritage that was envied by the young American nation. Even in America, French designers provided many of the best designs. In the aftermath of the revolutions of 1848, cabinet makers and woodworkers emigrated in great numbers from France and Germany to the United States. Their presence contributed significantly to the character of American Victorian furniture.

Design Elements

Elegant rococo furniture suited the Victorian mindset in several ways. Just as 18th-century France had developed a number of new furniture forms—each with a specialized use—Rococo Revival furniture also presented several new forms, commonly given French names in deference to their heritage. The *tête-à-tête*,

C-27

the *chaise légère* (reception chair), the gentleman's and lady's chairs (or *fauteuils*) from the standard parlor suite—each had a specific purpose and fit the Victorian need for hierarchy and order. One piece was for intimate conversation, one a formal piece for the hall, one for the man of the house, and one—smaller and more delicate—for the lady. Refinement, proof of man's progress, was expressed in terms of particular pieces of furniture for particular uses. It was also expressed in self control (mastery over complicated social rituals), control over natural resources and mastery over machines. There was attention to detail, from how one conducted oneself in social situations to how furniture was made. In furniture, refinement meant highly finished and polished surfaces, rich fabrics used in tufted upholstery, high-relief carving with realistic portrayals of the natural world and bountiful decoration. The French background of the Rococo Revival style greatly enhanced this sense of civilized refinement.[1]

Even though the curving lines owe an obvious debt to 18th-century French furniture, there are important differences. Eighteenth-century French furniture was lighter in weight and color, with chairs often painted in pastel colors. It had a delicate feeling, which was well suited to leisured court society. Flowers and foliage were used as decorative touches, but the effect was stylized and suggestive rather than strictly literal. In the 18th century, a simple flower or bit of foliage would suffice. The sensibility of 19th-century Rococo Revival pieces placed a premium on very realistic and detailed high relief naturalistic carving. Nature was reproduced abundantly in great heavy masses of carving, including fruit, grapes and vines, foliage and even animals (see in particular the work of Belter, and some of the re-markable sideboards illustrated in this chapter). Also, the Rococo style used *asymmetry* to create a whimsy, a constant visual delight and a lightness which is deeply contrasted with the balance and symmetry so important to the Victorian mind as it reinterpreted the 18th century into a modern sensibility. Symmetry speaks of control, perfection, strength—the dominant social goals of the 19th century.[2] Nineteenth-century Victorian furniture featured dark wood, such as walnut, mahogany or rosewood, with white marble for flat surfaces, expressing the Victorian love of contrast. This furniture obviously has a heavier, truly massive feeling. It is aggressive and ostentatious in its display of American wealth and bounty. It is vigorous and exuberant, whereas the French 18th-century Rococo is more delicate and graceful. So the Rococo Revival movement was much more than a backward-looking revival; it had a vitality and energy of its own that expressed the confidence of America at midcentury.

Although the Rococo Revival style had its finest flowering in America, this revival began in Europe and then made its way to America through immigrant cabinetmakers, style books and other means. Rococo Revival styles were popular in England and France by the 1820s, perhaps in reaction to the rather severe Empire style. On the Continent, the beginning of the reign of Charles X (1824) marks the beginning of the style. It also caught on in Germany, where the young John Henry Belter would have been exposed to it before he emigrated to America.

American cabinetmakers sold several types of Rococo Revival furniture. Some they imported from France, others they copied from the imports or based on French style books. We know something about the experience of one prominent

---

1. Katherine Grier, *Culture and Comfort: A Social History of Design from 1830-1900.* (Amherst: University of Massachusetts Press, 1988), 140-141.

2. For further discussion of 18th-century rococo, see Lindquist and Warren, *English and Continental Furniture with Prices* (Radnor, Pa.: Wallace-Homestead, 1994), 30-31.

cabinetmaking firm in Philadelphia, George Henkels, who advertised almost exact copies of furniture also found in the leading French furniture publications. It is quite possible that other cabinetmakers also produced copies of designs published in France. Sources of design included imported French furniture and French periodicals focusing on furnishings. Henkels lifted Rococo Revival designs straight out of French furniture publications from the 1840s and '50s. Apparently, Henkels also imported the latest French furniture for sale in his showrooms. In fact, it is difficult to know which of Henkels's pieces he produced himself and which were imported from France.[3]

Another means of spreading the popularity of Rococo Revival designs to the general public was the popular women's magazine *Godey's Magazine and Lady's Book,* published in Philadelphia. During the 1850s new French furniture forms and the rococo style in general were frequently discussed and clearly viewed as a desirable, stylish look.

The international exhibitions beginning in 1851 were another important way to transmit design ideas from Europe to America. They also served as an important venue for various countries to compete with each other—national rivalries ran high, fueled by a resentment against the long-standing dominance of French design. The London Crystal Palace Exhibition of 1851 and the Crystal Palace Exhibition in 1853 and 1854 in New York City displayed the latest in technology and design innovation for all the world to see. Rococo Revival was one of the major styles on display. Among the American firms documented as showing Rococo Revival pieces at the New York exhibition were Alexander Roux, A. Eliaers of Boston, Jules Dessoir, and John Henry Belter.

The popularity of the style was no doubt increased by its inclusion in the 1850 book *The Architecture of Country Houses* by influential tastemaker Andrew Jackson Downing. Downing had this recommendation for Rococo furniture:

Modern French furniture, and especially that in the style of Louis Quatorze, stands much higher in general estimation in this country than any other. Its union of lightness, elegance, and grace renders it especially the favorite of the ladies....The style of Louis XIV is characterized by greater delicacy of foliage ornamentation and greater intricacy of detail. We may add to this, that besides elegance of most French drawing-room furniture, its superior workmanship, and the luxurious ease of its admirably constructed seats, strongly commend it to popular favor.[4]

Parlor Furniture

Destined to grace the parlor, rococo furniture was often produced in parlor suites that fit a standard formula: sofa, gentleman's chair, smaller lady's chair and four side chairs, which were arranged in an ordered, symmetrical manner (Figs. 3-1 to 3-3). These suites usually matched exactly, or if not, were closely related in decorative motifs and certainly all upholstered with the same fabric. At midcentury, elegance and formality were expressed not only in voluptuous carving and curves, but also in a sense of order expressed in the matching suite—a notion that became somewhat hackneyed by the end of the century. These suites were grouped around the ubiquitous center table, which generally did not match the seating furniture but

---

3. Kenneth L. Ames, "Designed in France: Notes on the Transmission of French Styles to America," *Winterthur Portfolio* 12 (1977): 104-110.

4. Andrew Jackson Downing, *The Architecture of Country Houses* (New York: D. Appleton, 1850; reprint, New York: Dover Publications, 1969), 432.

Fig. 3-1 Rosewood Rococo Revival seven-piece parlor suite, c. 1850–60, consisting of triple-back settee, two armchairs and four side chairs, each medallion back with fruit and nut rocaille crest carved in full relief, having out-carved arms and serpentine skirts. On cabriole legs. Settee is 41" high x 63 1/2" long x 24" deep. *Courtesy Neal Auction Company, New Orleans, Nicholay & Morgan photographers.* **$8,000–12,000** the set.

Fig. 3-3 Lady's and gentleman's chairs from the set.

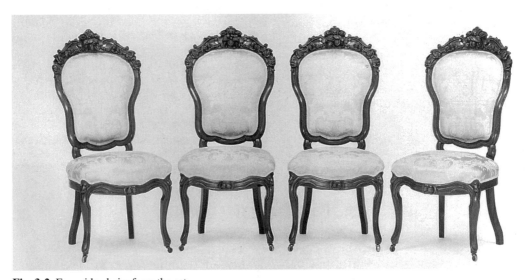

Fig. 3-2 Four side chairs from the set.

was suited in character. One reason for the prominence of the center table was that before the days of electricity the family would gather together after dark around the lamp on the center table—the main source of light by which to read or sew. Perhaps this was another way of maintaining family bonds that were so important in Victorian society.

Victorians considered the parlor part of the woman's domain, best furnished with feminine furniture Rococo Revival was perfect. High-backed chairs made by Belter and others were stylish. The Victorians loved the dramatic form, even though it weakened the structure. In fact, this might be taken as a general rule for Victorian furniture: visual qualities took precedence over solid construction. Since formality was a prime consideration for parlor suites, most did not include rockers since they were usually considered too informal. A Victorian writer cautioned against their use in 1840: "Swaying backwards and forwards in a parlour rocking chair is a most ungraceful recreation, particularly for a lady … and very annoying to spectators, who may happen to be a little nervous."[5]

Upholstery was naturally an important part of the parlor suite, being a means to make all the pieces match as well as a way to make a suite more lavish and expensive. The complex curving forms of rococo furniture seemed to demand rich upholstery. The best Rococo Revival parlor suites had elaborate tufted upholstery, which required a great deal of hand work. The fine fabric and the amount of workmanship added to the final cost of the furniture. As the 19th century progressed, machines were saving more and more money on furniture production, but the money saved could easily be spent on lavish upholstery. So in many cases, although machines took over the carving and joining of the furniture, almost as much total handwork went into a piece in the form of upholstery—an area where it was easy to indulge in "conspicuous consumption." The choice of upholstery could make a statement about the cost of the piece as well as the taste and economic status of its owner.

By this time, coil spring upholstery was no longer thought of as an aid for the infirmed or aged, as it had first been conceived. The level of comfort created by coil springs was now felt to be fitting for the parlor. Even though these pieces do not approach the comfort of 20th-century overstuffed furniture, they were a real improvement over stuffed seats supported by webbing alone.

When we think about this formal and decorative furniture, it is helpful to consider the customs of the people using it. Women at this time suffered the constraints of corsets to shape their figures and voluminous skirts under which were worn stiff "cages" or hoops. Chairs for ladies were specifically designed with no arms or with modified arms to allow room for these full skirts. Depending on the type of corset worn, women could only perch on chairs; true relaxation was not an option in the formal parlor setting.

Men fared better; uncorsetted, they could at least lean back comfortably. The gentlemen's chairs also had arms and larger proportions. So if you entered a Victorian parlor furnished with a suite, you would know exactly where to sit based on your gender.

Cabinetmaking Firms

Since parlor life in Victorian America was so indebted to French culture, it is not surprising to learn that many of the leading designers of the most fashionable style were recent French immigrants. Most of the cabinetmakers from this era were French or German immigrants as well, who brought with them fine cabinetmaking skills and a familiarity with the latest European fashions. Much of the Rococo Revival furniture that can be attributed to a particular maker was produced by one of a number of firms that were based in New York City and had shops along a fashionable stretch of Broadway during the 1850s and '60s. Charles Bauduoine, John Henry Belter, Burns & Trainque, Alexander Roux, Julius Dessoir, Rochefort and Skarren, Pottier and Stymus, Ringuet Le Prince and Leon Marcotte

---

5. Eliza Leslie, *The Handbook: or a Manual of Domestic Economy* (Philadelphia: Carey and Hart, 1840), 198. Cited in Grier, *Culture and Comfort*, 109

were among this elite group. They employed highly skilled artisans—most of whom were recent immigrants—to do the crucial work by hand. This class of furniture was not mass-produced but made to order or made for limited stock. It is important to remember that even in New York City in the 1850s and '60s, steam-powered woodworking machinery was far from common. This was still an era that depended on hand craftsmanship on the best quality furniture.[6]

Aside from the prestigious firms, there was also a lower level of furniture manufacturers who were involved in wholesale manufacturing. They made furniture, primarily in suites, to be sold to dealers. There were many of these firms in what was known as "Little Germany" in New York City.[7] In 1853, 85% of the furniture made in New York was shipped out to the West and South, especially to New Orleans.

Obviously, most of the furniture on the market today comes from these wholesale manufacturers. When compared to furniture made by the finer firms, we can see that wholesale furniture used less expensive woods, and its decoration was less developed or less finished. Fine carving, then and now, must be done by hand; this kind of expense could not be justified on wholesale furniture.

John Henry Belter

John Henry Belter was born in 1804 in Germany, came to the United States in 1840 and worked in New York City from 1844 to 1863. He was among the wave of European immigrants who helped shape the look of American Victorian Furniture, and his work represents the height of the Rococo Revival style in all its exuberance. Although the 19th century is often branded as a time when technology triumphed at the expense of design, Belter's furniture represents a happy marriage of the two. His techniques for using laminated wood were perfect for the extravagantly curving surfaces so characteristic of Rococo Revival furniture. Belter used the same principles involved in making plywood to create some of the most stunning furniture of the 19th century.

Laminated wood is made of very thin sheets of wood that are glued together, usually with the grain of the wood at right angles, thus increasing strength. Laminated wood is actually stronger than solid wood of the same thickness, and it can be steamed and bent more easily than solid wood—it has both strength and flexibility. In the case of rosewood, which has a beautiful grain but is quite brittle in solid form, using it in laminated form has definite advantages. Belter was able to use surprisingly thin pieces of laminated rosewood and not only curve them but also pierce them extensively with his patented saws.

Belter generally used rosewood for the outer layer of veneer—the part that would be seen. His famous laminated process resulted in a final product (Belter called it "pressed work furniture") that was actually stronger than if it had been created out of solid rosewood. Although rosewood is what we associate with Belter's most characteristic pieces, he also used mahogany and even oak as primary woods. The use of mahogany may indicate work of an earlier date (the 1840s), when mahogany was still widely used and before the Rococo Revival style had peaked. In his 1858 patent he explained his use of veneers:

In short, the veneers ... which, when the work is in place, are exhibited to the observer on the front side, and the veneers ... which are shown

---

6. Katherine S. Howe et al. *Heifer Brothers: Furniture and Interiors for a Gilded Age* (New York: Harry N. Abrams, 1994), 57-59.

7. Ibid., 60-61.

on the back side, should be rosewood, or the like highly-prized wood, while all the rest may be oak, hickory, black walnut, or other chea wood.[8]

Belter used molds or cauls to shape the laminated wood as the glue dried, thus forming his famous sinuous shapes. Of course, he did not invent the process of laminating, nor of bending solid wood. He did, however, patent four devices and techniques that he used in conjunction with lamination to create his unique designs. The documentation for these patents has provided valuable information about Belter.

His first patent, in 1847, was for a special saw to pierce-carve chair backs. He titled it "Machinery for Sawing Arabesque Chairs." In 1856 he got another patent for his remarkable laminated bedstead, which could be constructed in two sections rather than the traditional four. A bedstead in two sections has a headboard that flows in one piece into side rails that extend one-half the normal length. The second piece consists of a footboard that also flows into its own partial side rails. The side rails are then joined together to form the bed (see color illustration).

In 1858 Belter received a patent for laminated chair backs made with cauls or molds. Chairs made by this process had backs that curved on two planes (cut not from a cylinder, but from a spherical mold). The efficiency of this operation was increased by the fact that Belter could cut eight chair backs out of one barrel shaped mold.[9]

His final patent, granted in 1860, concerned the design of bureaus whose drawers were all cut from the same cylinder, thus assuring the absolute uniformity necessary for Belter's boldly curving surfaces. He also devised a system to lock all the drawers at one time.[10]

Collectors seek technical standards that will hold true for authenticating all Belter pieces. We have few of these rules, but furniture historians have been able to establish some facts about Belter's laminations. A high-power magnifier and very good ruler help to study his laminations which tended to be thinner and more numerous than his competitors'. In seating furniture, Belter's veneer varied from seven to nine layers, each with a thickness ranging between 0.05" and 0.07" (the average being 0.062").[11] Laminations used to make tables were also about 0.06", while those for beds were thicker, adding needed strength.[12]

Although we associate Belter's name with the lamination process, his output was not limited to this type of furniture. He is known to have made some pieces out of solid wood and also to have made others which combined laminated and solid wood. Some of his early chairs, for example, have applied solid crests which had been carved in high relief. On chairs, some side rails are solid and some veneer.[13]

It is sometimes said that one can identify a Belter chair because there will be no visible seam on the chair back. However, this is not necessarily true. If there is a visible seam, it will be vertical, and in some cases, veneers are lined up symmetrically along the seam to highlight strongly figured rosewood veneer.[14]

---

8. Marvin D. Schwartz et al, *The Furniture of John Henry Belter and the Rococo Revival* (New York: E. P. Dutton, 1981), 20.

9. Ibid., 28.

10. Ibid., 29.

11. Ibid., 16.

12. Ibid., 34.

13. Ibid., 15.

14. Ibid., 13.

Although some Belter seating furniture has plain, molded legs, most exhibit floral carving on the seat rail and legs, and as is generally true of Belter carving, it is more elaborate and realistic when compared to the stylized rendering of other makers. Rear legs generally had a noncircular (rectangular like) cross section.[15]

Belter's tables were not made to match the chairs they accompanied. Generally, parlor furniture of this period included seating furniture and tables that were related but not strictly matched. Belter's parlor furniture generally had pierce-carved chairs that went with pierce-carved tables, and solid-carved tables that went with solid-carved chairs. As with other Belter pieces, there do not appear to be any simple, hard-and-fast rules that allow foolproof identification of his tables. Pierce-carved aprons were usually laminated, and solid wood was sometimes added on. He also made tables out of solid wood, laminated wood, or a combination of laminated and solid; in any case, his stretchers were always solid wood. Cauls were used to shape table aprons, just as they were used for chair backs.[16]

These general guidelines aside, recognizing Belter furniture is really a matter of being familiar with a large body of Rococo Revival furniture and then comparing known Belter examples. In most generic Rococo Revival furniture, C-scrolls and S-scrolls are prevalent and provide the framework for the other decorative motifs. Belter occasionally used such scrolls, but even more characteristic of his work, particularly in seating furniture, is the use of naturalistic motifs like branches or vines, either rendered realistically or in a more sinuous version (as in some of his slipper chairs). These naturalistic elements provide the framework

for the rest of his carving, which includes acorns, grapes and other fruit. Stylistically, Belter's carving, with its striking sense of realism, stands out above the work of other shops. It is lifelike and not naive or stylized as in the case of lesser makers. Belter tables, like the chairs, do not incorporate as many C-scrolls and S-scrolls as are common with other makers of the period. Instead, the decoration is quite distinctive, with flowers, grape clusters, vines, leaves and branches that connect all of these elements.[17]

As with other 19th-century cabinet makers, we are able to learn some details of his business life through city directories of the time. A telling detail in Belter's case is that his listing in New York directories changed around 1853, from the designation "cabinetmaker" to "manufacturer," indicating a shift in Belter's business from custom-made furniture to furniture produced on a larger scale and warehoused for future sale. His factory at 3rd Avenue and 76th Street opened in 1854.[18] Interestingly, although the scale of his business changed, he used many of the same patterns before and after he expanded his operations. The development of the various patterns remains something of a mystery. We do not know which came first, but once in use, they were made throughout his career and not set aside in favor of a new pattern.[19]

Naming Belter patterns is problematic since none of his actual pattern books or catalogs are available today. The only pattern for which a name was actually given by Belter comes from a bill of sale for a set of furniture with cornucopias and elaborate carving. In the 1855 bill made out to the Jordan family, the name "Arabasket" is used. Through common usage, names have become associated with several pat-

15. Ibid., 35-36, 10.
16. Ibid., 10, 20, 21.
17. Ibid., 10, 20.
18. Ibid., 28.
19. Ibid., 35 and 37.

terns of seating furniture. Tuthill King was named after a Chicago family. Rosalie—the most common Belter chair pattern—was named for a set bought for Rosalie Plantation in Natchez, Mississippi, around 1860. It is one of the simpler patterns, unpierced and with a crest of flowers and fruit, a molded frame and a filler of parallel lines with dots in between (see related pattern in Fig. 3-4). Henry Clay, named for a set at Ashland—Clay's home—is unpierced and has a solid, upholstered back framed by broad sweeping scrolls and surmounted by flowers.

Most of Belter's known work consists of parlor furniture. There are several possible reasons for this. By about 1850 the Renaissance Revival style was beginning to be popular in dining rooms; Belter may have used good business instincts and created a niche for his work in the parlors of America. In general, Rococo Revival furniture was considered best suited for the parlor, which was feminine, territory in the Victorian home. Belter dining room furniture is rare indeed.[20]

Also rare, and truly remarkable, are the beds made by Belter. Because of the

Fig. 3-4 Rococo Revival rosewood side chair and armchair by John Henry Belter, New York City, c. 1845–65, in the pattern known as "Rosalie with Grapes"—one of Belter's most common patterns. Each with laminated backs with large interconnected scrolling pieces topped by heavily carved crest with roses, grapes, foliage. Molded seat rails with scroll and rose carving. Cabriole legs, whorl feet with acanthus. On casters. *Private collection.* Side chair: **$2,400–3,600.** Armchair: **$8,000–12,000.**

20. Ibid., 35.

strength needed in a bed frame, Belter used 16 to 24 layers of veneer (more layers than he used for chairs and tables). The beds were supported on four or six feet, the two additional ones being in the center of each side rail. To a modern eye, the beds are perhaps his most appealing form because the decoration does not dominate, as is often the case with other Victorian furniture. Relying less on the elaborate pierced carving that characterizes his tables and seating furniture, the beds display gracefully curving expanses of figured veneer with a proportionally smaller amount of carving. The designs appear seamless and wonderfully organic. The curving form is clearly the most essential part of these remarkable designs which are not overburdened with carving. This said, collectors today tend to pay top dollar for beds with the most carving, particularly pierced carving. On the more spectacular forms, the beds are actually constructed in two connecting parts, rather than the usual arrangement of four separate parts—headboard, footboard and side rails. These two-part bedsteads are rarely found.

In recent years, Belter beds have made headlines in auction news. For example, a very fine Belter bed sold at Pettigrew Auction Company of Colorado Springs, Colorado, in July 1990 for $101,750. The market for Belter furniture peaked at exciting levels like these. The 1990s saw a decrease in prices—a Belter bed comparable to the one mentioned above sold in June 1993 at Pettigrew for a much lower $55,000.

In light of modern resale values, it is interesting to think about prices during Belter's time. Belter's work was expensive when it was made, just as it is today. Bills show that a Belter parlor suite was priced at $1,200, costly but comparable to prices for other top-quality New York City mak-

ers.[21] Before the war newly wealthy industrialists sought out Belter's luxurious furniture to enhance their status. Belter distributed his furniture to other retailers, and we know that there were buyers in Chicago, New York City, the Northeast, and some in the South.

Although we know that Belter furniture was used at the Rosalie Plantation, it is probably a mistake to think that the Deep South antebellum mansions were largely furnished with his pieces. This seems to be a widespread misconception, probably originating with the 1939 movies *Gone With The Wind*, *Jezebel* and *Song of the South*, whose sets were full of Belter-type furniture. In fact, the furniture for these movies was all brought in from other parts of the country (mainly the Northeast). Furthermore, the South was generally a little more conservative than other parts of the country, and Southerners might not have chosen something as flashy as Belter's furniture. If one wanted that kind of furniture, there were several excellent makers in nearby New Orleans. It is difficult to say which geographic areas originally favored Belter, but there is evidence that Southerners have been strong buyers of Belter only since the 1930s.[22]

Belter died in 1863 of tuberculosis, but his partners (the Springmeyer brothers—one of whom was his brother-in-law) carried on the business until 1867, when it finally failed. Many have speculated about the reasons for the failure: the business may have been doomed without Belter or perhaps his exuberant style was out of step with the nation's somber mood after the tragedy of the Civil War. Certainly, he was known exclusively for Rococo Revival furniture, and the style was on the wane after the war. In addition, the financial depression right after the war surely had adverse affects on the business.

---

21. Ibid., 2.
22. Ibid., 3.

J. and J. W. Meeks

There are a number of other well-known furniture makers from this period, many of whom were based in New York City. The work of J. and J. W. Meeks is often compared to Belter's because Meeks too used laminations and pierce-carving. The Meeks firm was active in New York City from 1797 to 1868; however, they did not limit sales to that city. They sold much of their furniture in showrooms around the country (particularly in New Orleans). During their existence, they made furniture in all the popular styles, including Rococo Revival. Some of their rococo furniture rivals that of John Henry Belter.

Perhaps their best-known pattern is "Hawkins," so named because of the set given by Meeks to his daughter on her marriage to a Mr. Hawkins in 1859 (See Figs. 3-5, 3-6 and 3-7). Chairs of this type exhibit a construction similar to Belter's, with molded, laminated rosewood used for the chair backs.[23]

Most of the Meeks furniture that is labeled is in the Empire style. Almost none of their Rococo Revival work is marked, but we presume it to be theirs because it is strongly attributed.[24] The rococo furni-

Fig. 3-5 Laminated rosewood sofa, c. 1850, attributed to J. & J. W. Meeks. "Hawkins" pattern, after the set made by the firm for a Meeks daughter's marriage to Dexter Hawkins. Pierce-carved back with scrolling grape vines framed by heavier molded scrolls. Central crest with floral carving. Shaped and molded apron with central carving. Molded cabriole legs on casters. 63" long. *Courtesy Witherell Americana Auctions, Elk Grove, Calif.* **$8,000–12,000.**

---

23. John N. Pearce et al, "The Meeks Family of Cabinetmakers," The Magazine Antiques 85 (April 1964): 414-20.
24. Schwarz et al, 5.

Fig. 3-7 Laminated rosewood side chair, c. 1850, attributed to J. & J. W. Meeks in the "Hawkins" pattern. Courtesy Witherell Americana Auctions, Elk Grove, Calif. **$3,000–4,000.**

Fig. 3-6 Laminated rosewood armchair, c. 1850, attributed to J. & J. W. Meeks. This also in the "Hawkins" pattern. Courtesy Witherell Americana Auctions, Elk Grove, Calif. **$6,000–8,000.**

ture that is generally associated with them has thicker lamination than those used by Belter, although Meeks's Rococo Revival work was laminated and solid, just as Belter's was.

Alexander Roux

Alexander Roux worked in New York City from 1837 to 1881 and had a reputation as one of the finest cabinetmakers of the period (see Fig. 3-8). Roux apparently trained in Paris before coming to America, making the most of his French heritage at a time when it was highly valued. Like other cabinetmakers of French descent, he also imported French furniture.

He maintained close ties with his brother, a maker of fine furniture in Paris who sometimes sent pieces to America. Andrew Jackson Downing had high praise for Roux in his book *Architecture of Country Houses:*

In New York, the rarest and most elaborate designs, especially for drawing-room and library use, are to be found at the warehouse of Roux, in Broadway....At the warehouse of Mr. A. Roux, Broadway, may be found a large collection of furniture for the drawing-room, library, etc.-the most tasteful designs of Louis Quatorze, Renaissance, Gothic, etc. to be found in the country.... The chairs and sofas are particularly elegant[25] (see Fig. 3-9).

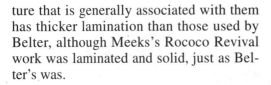

25. Downing, 432.

Fig. 3-8 Rococo Revival étagère, c. 1850, of faux-bois rosewood, attributed to Alexander Roux. Topped off by a cartouche with carved maiden's head surmounted by scrolling foliage. Central mirror flanked by exuberantly scrolling mirrored panels (compare this treatment, which is Rococo in its graceful curves, to the less graceful cutouts of the Renaissance étagères). Resting on a serpentine molded marble base on conforming scrolling base. A handsome piece. *Courtesy New Orleans Auction Company, New Orleans.* **$8,000–12,000.**

was on the cutting edge of fashion, Roux apparently left laminated furniture to Belter and Meeks.

A Roux advertisement from 1859 suggests the scope of his thriving business:

We have now on hand a large and splendid assortment of Plain and Artistic Furniture, such as Rosewood, Buhl, Ebony, and Gilt, and Marqueterie of foreign and domestic woods, and are now prepared to execute all orders for the furnishing of Houses, such as Wood Mantel-Pieces, Wainscoating, Mirror-Frames, Cornices, and Cabinet-Work in general, in the best manner and at the lowest rates.[27]

By 1855 he employed 120 people. The business peaked in the 1870s and he retired in 1881, but a son carried on until 1898.

Thomas Brooks

Thomas Brooks was another New York cabinetmaker working in Brooklyn. From the 1850s to 1870s, he made furniture in the Gothic, Rococo Revival and Renaissance Revival styles. His rococo pieces are quite distinctive, often with characteristic applied spiral or ropelike borders at the corners (see Fig. 3-10).

At the Crystal Palace Exhibition of New York in 1853, Roux's firm demonstrated its awareness of the latest fashions, exhibiting work in two styles. The company displayed a rosewood rococo armchair and sofa that won critical acclaim. Also displayed were some Renaissance Revival pieces with elaborate carving. The New York Exhibition in 1853 marked the first appearance of the Renaissance Revival style in America, so Roux was a trend-setter.[26] Although he

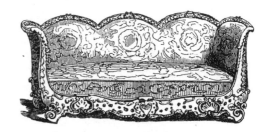

Fig. 3-9 Sofa, c. 1850, by Alexander Roux featured in A. J. Downing's *The Architecture of Country Houses.* With gracefully curving arms, well-shaped crest rail and apron, and complete with shell carving.

---

26. Diane D. Hauserman, "Alexander Roux and His 'Plain and Artistic Furniture,'" *The Magazine Antiques* 93, no. 2 (February 1968): 213.

27. Ibid., 212.

Fig. 3-10 Rococo Revival rosewood lady's secretary, c. 1860, with satinwood interior, labeled Thomas Brooks, Brooklyn, New York. Mirrored gallery with crest over two mirrored cabinet doors over slant front enclosing writing area. Applied turned pieces. Shaped apron with shell and scroll carving. Cabriole legs. *Courtesy loan Bogart, Rockville Centre, N.Y.* Dealer estimate: **$4,000–6,000.**

Charles Baudouine

Also of French descent and with a shop on Broadway in New York City was Charles Baudouine. During the 1850s he employed about 70 people and produced rococo furniture in a rather restrained manner that has more the feeling of 18th-century French furniture than most 19th-century Rococo Revival furniture (see Figs. 3-11, 3-12 and 3-13). Baudouine went to France often and imported furniture. It is difficult to know which pieces he made and which he imported, except through secondary wood analysis.[29]

Fig. 3-11 A rare pair of c. 1850 Rococo Revival carved rosewood multiform tables, attributed to Charles Baudouine, New York City. These are designed to be joined together for use as a parlor table, or kept separate as a pair of console or games tables. Each with original baize-lined interior, the apron fitted with a drawer, the carved cabriole "trick" legs extending to receive the fold-over top. Graceful, good proportions. Good condition. 46" wide × 17" deep × 30" high. An identical pair is illustrated in *19th Century American Furniture* by the Metropolitan Museum of Art. *Courtesy Neal Auction Company, New Orleans, Nicolay & Morgan photographers.* **$8,000–12,000.**

Julius Dessoir

Julius Dessoir also worked in New York City from the 1840s through the 1860s producing pieces in the Rococo Revival style. He exhibited at the New York Crystal Palace Exhibition of 1853. His shop was located with other fine cabinetmakers along the fashionable section of Broadway.[28]

28. Howe et al, *Herter Brothers*, 64.

29. Eileen and Richard Dubrow, *American Furniture of the 19th Century, 1840-1880* (Atglen, Pennsylvania: Schiffer Publishing, Ltd., 1983), 23.

Fig. 3-12 A single open Baudouine table.

Fig. 3-13 A single folded Baudouine table.

Bembe and Kimbel

In the 1850s the firm of Bembe and Kimbel worked in New York City and also had a shop in Mayenne, France. Kimbel went on to a later partnership with Joseph Cabus with whom he became renowned for Eastlake-inspired furniture.[30]

Leon Marcotte and Ringuet Le Prince

An interesting off-shoot of the Rococo Revival style can be seen in the work of Leon Marcotte and his father-in-law, Ringuet Le Prince, who worked in New York City in the 1860s. They produced furniture that was labeled Louis XVI at the time. It was, in fact, very true to Louis XVI furniture, except in the treatment of color. Marcotte's furniture was ebonized with gilt decoration, whereas in 18th-century France, the furniture would have been decorated and painted a light color—white, gray or pale blue, for example.

The proportions were quite faithful to 18th-century Louis XVI furniture. It was more restrained than most Rococo Revival furniture, with more chaste decorative touches. Although enormously popular in Europe, the Louis XVI Revival style never reached a broad audience in America, where it was not widely produced. It was largely limited to custom-made pieces manufactured in New York City for an elite clientele. Leon Marcotte sold furniture to the likes of John Taylor Johnston, who was the first president of The Metropolitan Museum of Art.[31] Like other revival styles, its arrival in America was due to events in France, where Empress Eugenie, wife of Napoleon III, redecorated in the Louis XVI style. The style was subsequently displayed at the Paris Exposition in 1855 and 1862 London Exhibition.[32]

The firm of Le Prince and Marcotte exemplifies the strong influence of French immigrants on American Victorian furniture. Le Prince had already established his reputation as a leading Paris decorator before he came to New York City in 1849, so his career spanned the old world and the new. After he retired in 1861, the firm continued very successfully under the name Marcotte and Company, both manufacturing and importing, again blurring the boundaries of American Victorian furniture. It can be difficult to determine

---

30. Ibid., 38.

31. Howe, Heiler Brothers, 69.

32. Oscar P. Fitzgerald, *Three Centuries of American Furniture* (Englewood Cliffs, N.J.: Prentice-Hall, 1982), 229.

what is American-made and what is French-made.[33]

Philadelphia Makers

Philadelphia was another center for rococo furniture. We have already mentioned George Henkels, who had a thriving business from the 1850s through the 1870s, both as a manufacturer and importer. Other Philadelphia makers include William Allen and his son Joseph, who in the 1830s sold furniture and fine woods. During the 1850s they were known for their fine rococo furniture and custom cabinetwork.[34]

New Orleans Makers

New Orleans, with its large French population, was another important center of rococo furniture. Francois Seignouret worked there from 1811 to 1852, although Prudence Mallard is probably a better-known maker from that area (see Fig. 3-14). Son of a Scottish father and French mother, Mallard worked between 1832 and 1875 and his pieces primarily reflect the Rococo and Renaissance Revivals. He produced and imported furniture from London and Paris. An advertisement from 1857 describes his firm as follows:

Cabinet Maker, Upholsterer, and Dealer in fancy articles. Has always on hand a large

Fig. 3-14 An elegant c. 1850 mahogany Rococo Revival console table, attributed to Prudence Mallard, New Orleans. Serpentine molded top of mahogany (probably marble originally). Conforming frieze is pierce-carved with scrolls and shells. Legs are made up of double C-scrolls with acanthus carving, ending in whorl feet. Molded and shaped stretchers centered by foliate carving. Very graceful overall and close in spirit to the 18th-century French Rococo style, except this piece exhibits no asymmetry, the hallmark of the 18th-century Rococo. 60" long × 19 1/2" deep × 32" high. *Private collection.* **$4,500–6,500** as is; **$12,000–18,000** with original marble.

---

33. Dubrow, 40.
34. Ibid., 13.

stock of highly finished furniture.
Imported and manufactured especially for the
  Southern climate, composed of:
    rich parlor sets, rosewood and mahogany
    bedroom sets, rosewood and mahogany
    library sets, rosewood, mahogany, and

oak—old and modern
dining room sets, rosewood, mahogany,
and oak—old and modern
hall, rosewood, mahogany, and oak—old
and modern.[35]

Factory Production

All of the makers discussed up to this point made small quantities of fine furniture for the custom trade. There were also many factories making Rococo Revival furniture. However, little of the factory output has been studied, and the great majority of it is unlabeled, making it difficult to link particular factories with particular pieces. Suffice it to say, the newly growing furniture manufacturers of the era in the major cities of the Eastern Seaboard and the Midwest strove to meet the demand for Rococo Revival pieces. These pieces would not have as much carving or carving of the same quality as that produced by the cabinetmakers for the luxury trade. Factory production captured the curving shapes of the Rococo style and used finger molding and floral carving as embellishments.

Mitchell and Rammelsberg of Cincinnati is one of the few large manufacturing firms that we actually know much about. Founded in 1847, the firm went on to become one of the largest and most successful furniture manufacturers in the Midwest. Cincinnati was one of the Midwestern cities (along with others like Grand Rapids) that had a burgeoning furniture industry and by 1850 had nine steam-powered furniture factories. In that same year, the steam-powered Mitchell and Rammelsberg factory employed 150 workers. For Mitchell and Rammelsberg, the South was an important source of revenue until the Civil War. Then the West proved to be a more lucrative source of income.[36]

Mitchell and Rammelsberg, and other companies like it, soon became a real threat to Eastern manufacturers. One disgruntled author penned this complaint against the competition in 1861:

An immense trade has sprung up in the last few years in a cheap and showy class of furniture, of mongrel design and superficial construction. The location of many dealers in the different cities and towns South and West has increased the demand for this class of good to so great an extent that a number of large steam factories are engaged in this trade exclusively. They make furiture of a showy style, with but little labor on it, and most of that done with the scroll saw and turning-lathe. The dealers both south and west, find this work very profitable, as the showy appearance gives an erroneous idea of value, and purchasers pay more profitable prices for it than they do for good but less pretentious goods. This furniture is easily detected by examination, as it consists mostly of broad, flat surfaces, cut with scrollsaws into all imaginable and unimaginable shapes, and then by a moulding machine the edges are taken off uniformly; this gives it a showy finish. The principle articles thus produced are étagères, or whatnots, fancy tables, hat-racks, bookshelves, music stands, bedsteads, cribs and fancy reception chairs. There is not much of this class of goods that will exist as long as the manufacturer, but will no doubt outlive his reputation as a cabinet-

---

35. Ibid., 40.

36. Donald C. Peirce, "Mitchell and Rammelsberg: Cincinnati Furniture Manufacturers, 1847-1881," Winterthur Portfolio 13 (1979): 217.

maker. This is not to depreciate the value of the goods of any person, but is truthful matter, properly belonging to a work of this kind.[37]

To be fair, we should hear from the other side, provided by a newspaper article in a Cincinnati paper in 1873. The article claimed that Mitchell and Rammelsberg produced "most of the best furniture in the West and South, and not a little in the East." Steam-powered production was defended because "the taste it creates and fosters, the difference in comfort it causes and the almost illimitable employment into which it branches off in every direction is a matter of which any city might boast.... By it, and it alone, the cheapness is the only means of bringing it into thousands of homes to add to their attractions, and thereby ... to lend its powerful aid in preserving unharmed the mainstay of our national strength, the homelife of our people."[38]

It is the furniture from factories like Mitchell and Rammelsberg that we most often see on the market today. This was the furniture available for those of more modest means. The pieces that we encounter in homes and shops today—with curvaceous lines, simple finger molding, and grapes or a carved flower or two—were made for the middle class. Black walnut was a popular wood; occasionally mahogany was used. The factory pieces were almost totally mass-produced, but not quite. The finger molding was done by hand, as were the carving details. The construction involved dowels and glue for joining parts together—a relatively weak method of joinery. As a result, seating furniture dating from this era often needs to be taken completely apart and reglued.

Later Revivals

Rococo Revival furniture lost popularity during the Civil War, when the Renaissance Revival style became more fashionable. For those in the know, it was becoming passe to have an entire parlor suite of Rococo furniture. However, the occasional rococo chair or table continued to turn up in the more eclectic Victorian parlors of the 1870s and '80s. This revival style had its own revival in the 1920s and again in the 1950s, and these later examples do turn up in antiques malls and estate sales. The best way to distinguish them from 19th-century pieces is to remember that the originals will have more signs of age, better-quality carving, and more generous proportions. Later copies will tend to be taller and thinner and not as graceful as the gorgeous pieces that graced Victorian homes.

37. Ibid., 217.
38. Ibid., 219.

One of four walnut side chairs from the same suite as in previous photo. Balloon-shaped back, carved crest rail and horizontal splat, finger-molded and floral-carved apron and legs. Tufted seat. 36" high. *Private collection.* **$1,800–2,400** the set.

Gentleman's chair from a walnut Rococo Revival parlor suite original to an 1859 home. Balloon-shaped back, finger-molded and carved crest rail, finger-molded arms, cabriole legs and shaped apron. Tufted seat and back. On porcelain casters, 47" high. *Private collection.* **$650–775.**

Walnut sofa with triple-arching crest rail carved with scrolling acanthus, grapes, fruit and foliage. Appropriately tufted upholstery. 44" high × 75" long (From the same set as in previous photo.) *Private collection.* **$2,400–3,600.** A note on suites: While we have typically believed that suites of exactly matching pieces were frequently acquired by Victorians, this house and its furnishings help us to expand our understanding of the period. Two suites—a minor of walnut for the lady's parlor, and a major for the gentleman's parlor—clearly show that some pieces were identical, others similar in style. All of these pieces were original to these rooms in this house, which was built in 1859. We, as dealers and collectors, need to understand this concept as we add to our collections and those of museums and other interpretive settings. Victorians apparently went to the furniture store and created a harmonious suite, with matching upholstery, but not always exactly matching pieces.

Lady's walnut parlor rocker with floral and foliate-carved crest rail, "elbows," plain apron, and appropriately tufted upholstery. 38 1/2" high. (Not an exact match but from the same suite as in previous photo.) *Private collection.* **$450–650.**

In this same parlor, and original to the 1859 house, is this center table. As is true of this table, the center table generally was not an exact "match" with the parlor seating furniture. This one is walnut, with turtle-shaped marble top. Apron with applied foliate carving. Cabriole legs with rose and scrolling foliate carving. Legs joined by scrolling stretchers centering turned finial. On porcelain casters. 36" long × 26" wide × 30 1/2" high. *Private collection.* **$3,600–4,500.**

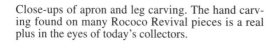

Close-ups of apron and leg carving. The hand carving found on many Rococo Revival pieces is a real plus in the eyes of today's collectors.

From the same 1859 house, another Rococo Revival parlor suite original to the house (this one for the gentleman's parlor and in rosewood). This suite retains its original upholstery—once a rich red satin, faded with time to a dark brown. The rosewood sofa with triple-arching back topped by finger-molded crest rail and scrolling cabochon crest. Shaped, finger-molded apron and cabriole legs. On white porcelain casters. Tufted upholstery. This suite is really transitional Rococo-Renaissance, the triple-arching form and overall curves being Rococo and the treatment of the crest being more Renaissance. The transitional nature of the suite is fitting to the 1859 date of the house, just about the time when the Renaissance style was overtaking the Rococo in popularity. Sofa is 86" long x 41 1/2" high. *Private collection.* **$2,400–3,600.**

Also from the suite, a rosewood gentleman's parlor chair. Again, the shape and finger molding are Rococo in style while the crest is more Renaissance in feeling. *Private collection.* **$900–1,250.**

Also from the suite, one of four upholstered rosewood side chairs. *Private collection.* **$2,400–3,600, set of four.**

Completing the suite is the lady's rosewood parlor rocker, with the same crest treatment. In both parlors in this home the owners chose to substitute the lady's rocker for the lady's chair more commonly found in parlor suites. *Private collection.* **$600–900.**

Rococo Revival walnut parlor suite, c. 1850 (actually a partial double-parlor suite) with two triple-back sofas, two gentlemen's chairs, four wall or side chairs. Tufted upholstery. Pierced and carved crest rails, carved aprons. Front legs on casters. *Courtesy Morton Goldberg Auction Gallery, New Orleans.* **$12,000–18,000.**

Rosewood six-piece Rococo Revival partial double-parlor set, c. 1850–60. With a pair of triple-medallion-back settees (one shown), pair of armchairs, pair of side chairs—all exuberantly carved with high-relief floral and fruited crests and dangling fruit clusters between medallions. Curvate molded frames with out-curved armrests, seats of generous proportions, aprons centered with fruit clusters. Cabriole legs, on casters. Settees are 67" wide x 24" deep x 44 1/2" high. *Courtesy Neal Auction Company, New Orleans, Nicholay & Morgan photographers.* **$12,000–18,000.**

Armchairs and side chairs from the set.

J. and J. W. Meeks "Stanton Hall" pattern laminated rosewood partial parlor suite, consisting of sofa, gentleman's chair, two side chairs and a hall or reception chair. Tufted backs, except for hall chair, which characteristically has an elaborately carved wooden back, meant for looks, not comfort. Pierce-carved crest rails with scrolling acanthus and grape vines within a gadrooned border, centering floral and fruit carving. On casters. *Courtesy Morton Goldberg Auction Gallery, New Orleans.* **$24,000–36,000.**

Transitional c. 1860 Rococo-Renaissance-style walnut gentleman's armchair. With a Renaissance-type crest, though the overall form is Rococo. Well-carved crest and seat rail. 43" high. *Courtesy the Howard Collection.* **$600–900.**

Rosewood Rococo Revival lady's chair, c. 1850, with tufted back and crest with C-scroll carving. Shaped apron, cabriole legs, whorl feet, on casters. Lady's chairs usually had low arms like these or more truncated "elbows" to allow for voluminous skirts. *Courtesy Crabtree & Company Antiques, Cameron, N.C.* **$800–1,200.**

Walnut Rococo Renaissance Revival gentleman's and lady's upholstered chairs, c. 1860. Each with balloon-shaped tufted backs and crest rail with vine and grape carving. Finger-molded frame, arms and apron. On casters. *Courtesy Woodbine Antiques, Oxford, N.C.* **$1,200–1,800** the pair.

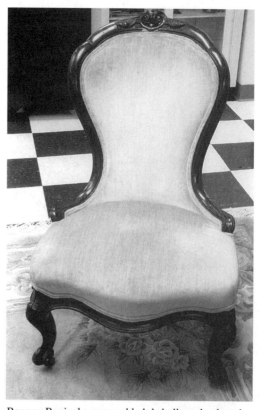

Boldly carved walnut Rococo Revival gentleman's chair, c. 1850, with strong C-scrolls, floral and shell carving surmounting and surrounding tufted back. Molded and floral-carved apron. Cabriole front legs. On casters. A strong chair—the product of a fine cabinetmaking shop. 43" high. *Courtesy the Howard Collection.* **$1,800–2,400.**

Rococo Revival rosewood lady's balloon-back parlor chair, c. 1850. Back crest with floral carving. Molded serpentine apron, cabriole legs, whorl feet, on casters. *Courtesy The Antiques Emporium, Raleigh, N.C.* **$375–475.**

Walnut Rococo Revival side chair, c. 1860–80. Caned rounded seat, balloon back with incised foilage, pierced scallops and turned spindles. Turned front legs and stretcher. Factory made. 17" deep × 17" wide × 33" high. *Private collection.* **$115–175.**

Balloon-back Rococo Revival walnut upholstered lady's chair, c. 1850–60, with finger molding, scrolling "elbow" arms, cabriole front legs on casters. 22" wide × 39" high. *Private collection.* **$400–600.**

Walnut Rococo Revival lady's rocker, c. 1860–80. Caned back and seat, scrolling "elbows," turned front legs and stretcher. This probably would have been part of a bedroom suite since the caning and informal nature of the rocker (unless upholstered) were considered more suited to the bedroom. 34" high. *Private collection.* **$275–375.**

Walnut hall chair, c. 1860, with elaborately pierce-carved back with scrolling foliage, flanked by turned stiles topped by finials. Serpentine seat front and apron. Lift lid. Turned front feet. 44" high. *Private collection.* **$400–600.**

Transitional Empire-Rococo sofa, c. 1845–55, of walnut-stained poplar with mahogany flame veneers on crest rail and apron. Triple-section serpentine back. Scrolled apron. Leaf-carved feet, uprights, and crest trims. Old refinished surfaces. 74" long. *Private collection.* **$600–900.**

Walnut transitional Rococo slipper chair, c. 1860, with elaborately pierce-carved keyhole-shaped back-splat flanked by turned stiles and topped by scrolling, foliate-carved crest rail. Rounded seat, with turned legs on rollers. 43" high. *Courtesy the Howard Collection.* **$450–650.**

Rococo Revival walnut triple-arching sofa, c. 1850. Crest rail with grape and foliate carving. Central portion of tufted back set off in heart-shaped frame. Scrolling, out-flaring arms, shaped and carved apron, cabriole legs, on casters. *Courtesy Flomaton Antique Auction, Flomoton, Ala.* **$1,800–2,400.**

Rococo Revival pierce-carved and laminated rosewood sofa by J. and J.W. Meeks, New York City, c. 1860. With pierced foliate scroll- and grape-carved back above shaped, carved seat rails, raised on cabriole legs. 65 1/2" long. *Sold by Butterfield & Butterfield, Los Angeles.* Part of a five-piece suite that sold for **$7,150,** with an estimate of $8,000–12,000.

Rococo Revival rosewood méridienne, c. 1850, attributed to John Henry Belter. Semi-uphol-stered seat back framed by large C-scrolls, shell, grape, foliate and floral carving. Shaped and carved apron, carved cabriole legs, on casters. One of a pair, and a rare, desirable form. *Courtesy Witherell Americana Auctions, Elk Grove, California.* Dealer estimate: **$20,000–30,000.**

Rococo Revival laminated rosewood armchair by John Henry Belter, c. 1855. "Arabasket" pattern. Upholstered back surrounded by broadly scrolling pieces that provide the framework for floral, fruit and grape carving. Rose-carved knees, carved apron, cabriole legs with acanthus carving, on casters. *Courtesy Witherell Americana Auctions, Elk Grove, California.* Dealer estimate: **$12,000–15,000.**

A fine c. 1850-65 Rococo Revival laminated rosewood sofa by John Henry Belter, very similar to two others in major museum collections. Three front legs support the undulated, heavily carved seat rail. Arm supports are open. Triple-arching crest rail with masses of floral, fruit and urn carving. *Courtesy Pettigrew Auction Gallery, Colorado Springs.* Sold to a dealer for **$60,500** in 1993. Similar sofas brought $38,385 in England in 1981 and $77,000 from Pettigrew in 1987. Both examples are now in museums.

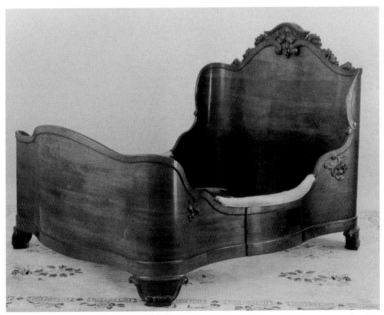

Laminated rosewood John Henry Belter patent bedstead, branded in several places "J.H. Belter/Patent/August 19, 1856/NY." This is a relatively simple example of Belter's beds, without a pierce-carved crest. Minimal decoration of carved fruit and foilage on the headboard and side rails. The visual impact relies on the beautiful sweeps of curving rosewood veneer. *Courtesy Pettigrew Auction Gallery, Colorado Springs.* Sold for **$17,600** in 1993, though it might have reached into the $25,000–35,000 range.

Laminated rosewood John Henry Belter patent bureau, c. 1860. Branded in several places "J.H. Belter/Patent/New York." With graduated serpentine drawers with scrolling handles, flanked by columns, and the curves continuing into side of the case. Conforming top with molded scrolling standards supporting arched mirror, surmounted by crest with cupids, scrolls and central cabochon. This is the only known example of a Belter patent bureau with figural crest carving, thus increasing its potential value. *Courtesy Pettigrew Auction Gallery, Colorado Springs.* Sold for **$33,000** in 1993, but it might have reached into the $40,000–60,000 range.

Walnut Renaissance Revival sideboard, c. 1860. D-shaped base with two convex doors flanking central door—all with burl panels and Renaissance medallion carving. Three drawers. Marble surface. Top has two long shelves with turned supports. Arching pediment with game and fruit carving flanked by stylized columns. *Courtesy Pettigrew Auction Gallery, Colorado Springs.* **$8,000–12,000**.

Walnut Eastlake cylinder desk, c. 1880. Base with two drawers beside cabinet below one long drawer and cylinder top, all with burl panels. With fitted interior. Two drawers above, with typical Eastlake gallery. Panelled sides and back. 35 1/2" wide x 24" deep x 59 3/4" high. *Private collection.* **$2,500–3,500.**

Walnut armchair attributed to John Jelliff & Company, c. 1870. Although many cabinetmakers produced furniture with figures on the arms, John Jelliff's usually possessed a higher level of sophistication. Bust carvings on the arm supports. Tufted back surmounted by complex crest featuring portrait medallion, burl panels, roundels, drop finials. Trumpet-turned front legs, on casters. *Courtesy Witherall Americana Auctions, Elk Grove, California.* Dealer estimates: **$2,000–3,000.**

Renaissance Revival maple and rosewood tall chest of drawers, by Herter Brothers, New York City, c. 1870. Cove-molded top incised with scrolling vines over frieze inlaid with repeating palmettes and zigzag border. Five drawers with geometric rosewood escutcheons flanked by rosewood and maple fluted columnar stiles. On stylized bracket feet. 51 1/2" high x 37" wide. *Courtesy Butterfield & Butterfield, Los Angeles.* Sold for **$20,900** in 1991, with an estimate of $8,000–12,000.

Renaissance Revival figured maple and rosewood bedstead, by Herter Brothers, New York City, c. 1870. Architectural headboard with incised and inlaid decoration. Arched, enclosed rosewood-bordered panels. Footboard with similar decoration. This use of highly contrasting woods is an exciting treatment of the Renaissance Revival style, found in the work of the best shops. 8'4" high x 7'5" long x 66" wide. *Courtesy of Butterfield & Butterfield, Los Angeles.* Sold for **$12,100** in 1991, with an estimate of $12,000–18,000.

Pair of Modern Gothic walnut and oak parlor chairs, attributed to Daniel Pabst, design attributed to Frank Furness. Probably for a San Francisco residence, c. 1877. *Courtesy of Butterfield & Butterfield, Los Angeles.* Sold in 1991 for **$1,870,** with an estimate of $3,000–5,000.

Modern Gothic carved walnut and oak settee, attributed to Daniel Pabst, design attributed to Frank Furness, Philadelphia. Probably for a San Francisco residence, c. 1877, 7' long. *Courtesy Butterfield & Butterfield, Los Angeles.* Auction estimate in 1991: **$4,000–6,000** (no sale).

Walnut Rococo Revival triple-back sofa, c. 1850, with finger molding and leaf carving on crest rail, gracefully scrolled apron. Molded cabriole legs, on casters. *Courtesy Woodbine Antiques, Oxford, N.C.* **$1,200–1,800.**

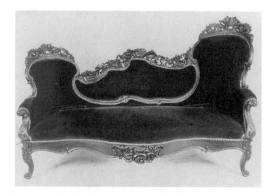

Rococo Revival rosewood asymmetrical sofa, c. 1850—an unusual form that captures the exuberance of this style. Central portion framed in scrolls and topped with elaborate carving. One side of back higher than the other, both topped with scrolls and shell carving. Scrolled arms and apron with asymmetrical carving. Carved cabriole legs. This more accurately mimics true 18th-century Rococo asymmetry than does the typical 19th-century interpretation which uses balance and symmetry throughout. *Courtesy Flomaton Antique Auction, Flomaton, Ala.* **$3,600–4,800.**

Close-up of carving: Another hallmark of Belter furniture is the depth of the carving and the realism achieved by his master carvers. Belter went far beyond most of his contemporaries in the quality of his carving. Also note the layers of lamination visible on the scrolling element below the carving.

Rosewood sofa in John Henry Belter's "Rosalie with Grapes" pattern, c. 1845–65, with triple-arching tufted back. 72 1/2" long × 40" high (14" seat height). *Courtesy the Howard Collection.* **$12,000–18,000.**

Close-up of sofa: Notice how thin the back is. This degree of thinness is possible only with the use oflaminations, rather than solid wood. This characteristic of Belter furniture would be virtually impossible to copy today—thus one doesn't have to worry about Belter fakes (only confusion over what patterns are known to have been made by Belter versus the many attributed to him).

Pierce-carved rosewood Belter armchair. New York, c. 1855. *Courtesy Joan Bogart, Rockville Centre, N.Y.* **$7,500–10,000.**

Rococo Revival rosewood slipper chair by John Henry Belter, c. 1845–65. Design of the back framed by large C-scrolls enclosing grape, leaf and floral carving. Cabriole legs. **$5,000–7,500.** With a c. 1850 rosewood center table with oval marble top. Apron with carving. Cabriole legs with carved knees and acanthus-whorl feet, on casters. Legs joined by stretchers of interconnected scrolls, centering urn finial. *Courtesy Joan Bogart, Rockville Centre, N.Y.* **$3,000–5,000.**

Pair of c. 1850–60 Belter recamiers, each with shaped and carved aprons, scrolling legs. Partial backs are tufted and surmounted by heavy scrolls enclosing foliate and grape carving, topped off by foliate-carved crest. These are in wonderful condition and in an unusual pattern, with intricate and delicate pierced carving—thus the dealer estimate of **$25,000–35,000.** *Courtesy Joan Bogart, Rockville Centre, N.Y.*

Pair of c. 1850 highly carved rosewood console tables, each with serpentine white marble top on C-scroll supports joined by arched and molded stretchers centering a rocaille-carved shell. Aprons with pierce-carved scrolling designs. These are rare and of wonderful quality. *Courtesy Neal Auction Company, New Orleans, Nicholay & Morgan photographers.* **$12,000–18,000.**

Rococo Revival walnut table, c. 1850–60, with marble turtle-shaped top with S-curved, molded legs joined by stretchers topped in center by an urn finial and drop finial. Simple applied foliate carving below table top. On casters. Original finish. *Courtesy Southampton Antiques, Southampton, Mass.* **$800– 1,200.**

Rococo Revival center table, c. 1850, with turtle-shaped marble top. Molded and shaped apron with applied dropped scrolls. Molded cabriole-type legs (square-sectioned) interrupted by a shelf on which rests a carved dog—the carving is not finely detailed, but rather sketchy. The table legs bump and flare out, creating a line admired during the era. On casters. 33" long x 20" wide x 28" high. *Courtesy Butte's Antiques, Oxford, N.C.* **$1,200–1,800.**

Rococo Revival laminated rosewood center table, c. 1850, attributed to the J. and J. W. Meeks firm, New York City. Nearly identical to a table at the Munson-Williams Proctor Institute, Utica, N.Y. Oval marble top over scrolling pierce-carved apron. Four beautifully carved cabriole legs are joined by pierce-carved stretchers that pick up motifs in the apron and center a gadrooned urn finial. Whorl feet, on casters. *Courtesy Witherell Americana Auctions, Elk Grove, Calif.* Dealer estimate: **$10,000–15,000.**

Rococo Revival marble-topped console table, c. 1850, with serpentine-shaped top and apron resting on acanthus-carved cabriole legs, shaped stretchers with turned central finial fitted with brass casters. A fairly rare and very desirable form, so long as it was not made from a games table with a replaced top! *Private collection.* **$2,500–3,500** real; **$1,000–1,500** created.

Rococo Revival walnut étagère or whatnot, c. 1850–60, with molded and shaped graduated shelves, fret-carved supports and decorations. Original finish. *Southampton Antiques, Southampton, Mass.* **$800–1,200.**

Rococo Revival walnut étagère, c. 1850–60, with shaped, molded white marble top and conforming lower shelf Scrolling bracket supports. Elaborately fret-carved pediment featuring urn overflowing with cascading scrolling foliage. Refinished. This is another one of those transitional pieces—Rococo in the scrolling vines of the crest, more Renaissance in feeling in the less-graceful side supports. *Courtesy Southampton Antiques, Southampton, Mass.* **$4,500–6,500.**

Rococo Revival rosewood center table, c. 1850–60, with original white marble, elaborately scrolled and pierced apron with mask carving and drop finials. Solid, not laminated. Scrolling, molded X-stretchers with central scrolling carving. Scrolling, acanthus-carved legs. You probably get the idea by now that C-scrolls are the dominant decorative motif of the Rococo Revival style! A handsome, formal table. Courtesy *Joan Bogart, Rockville Centre, N.Y.* **$15,000–25,000.**

Rococo-Renaissance Revival transitional carved rosewood étagère, c. 1850–60, signed by H. Iden, New York. The crest with highly carved grapevine, centered by a mockingbird (detailed and very realistic carving, indicative of the best Victorian work). Mirrored back with three shelves on shaped marble top, on cabriole legs. Apron with another mockingbird eating grapes. This piece has many transitional elements—the volutes, the turned uprights, the lion's head on the side and the repeated use of finials being more Renaissance in style. *Courtesy Neal Auction Company, New Orleans, Nicholay & Morgan photographers.* **$10,000–15,000.**

Detail of crest—spirited carving!

Rococo Revival carved rosewood cylinder desk/bookcase, c. 1855, attributed to Thomas Brooks. Mirrored upper doors. Cylinder front opens to reveal fitted maple interior with Gothic detailing. Drawer with ovolo molding and scrolling carving. Shaped, molded apron with foliate carving. Cabriole legs with heavy foliate carving on the knees. Whorl feet. Stiles with applied spiral turning. 36 1/2" wide × 23 1/2" deep × 61" high. *Courtesy New Orleans Auction Company, New Orleans.* **$8,000–12,000.**

Rococo Revival rosewood secrétaire à abattant (fall-front desk), c. 1850, with fitted interior. Base with foliate-carved cabriole legs and scrolling apron with portrait carving—also found on drawer pulls and crest. Upper section with canted corners and medallion-shaped molding and elaborate foliate carving. Pediment with scrolling foliate carving and portrait below fleur-de-lis. Profoundly influenced by Continental design. *Courtesy Flomaton Antique Auction, Flomaton, Ala.* **$4,000–6,000.**

Rococo Revival rosewood chest of drawers, c. 1850, lined in maple. Serpentine molded white marble top over four serpentine drawers with applied molding and scrolling, plumed escutcheons. No pulls—uses key to open in the European style. Canted corners with applied acanthus carving. Plinth base. Panelled sides and back. Probably made in New York City. 42" wide x 22 3/4" deep x 35 1/2" high. *Private collection*. **$2,500–3,500.**

Massive c. 1850 Rococo Revival rosewood cylinder desk with applied asymmetrical rococo carving, cabinets flanking panelled kneehole below three over three panelled drawers. Rolltop and stiles with acanthus carving. Upper section with two cabinets identical to lower ones flanking arched cabinet with applied rococo decoration. Scrolling crest centering cabochon and flanked by urn finials. *Courtesy Pettigrew Auction Gallery, Colorado Springs.* **$10,000–15,000.**

Rococo Revival walnut dresser with marble top, c. 1860. Base with four ovolo-molded drawers with wooden foliate handles. Top drawer overhangs. Mirror with beautifully scrolling standards with grapevine entwined, and scalloped upper edges and graceful crest. 44 1/2" wide x 20" deep x 81" high. *Private collection*. **$1,200–1,800.**

Walnut, flame and crotch walnut veneered Rococo Revival oversized bed, c. 1850. The headboard supported by octagonal standards topped by finials. The headboard itself is a tour de force of graceful rococo carving, complete with scrolling foliage and central cluster of fruit carving, with dangling grape bunches; over three arched panels with flame veneer. Wraparound footboard also with applied fruitful scrolling carving. Beautiful as these beds are, they tend to be so massive they do not suit every house. *Private collection*. **$3,000–5,000.**

Rococo Revival rosewood cylinder-front secretary, c. 1865. Molded cornice topped by urn finials. Two glazed doors enclose tiger maple interior. Cylinder front encloses inlaid interior with racheted writing surface. Below are two panelled cabinet doors with applied fruit carving. Chamfered sides with applied scrolling acanthus and spiral turnings. Panelled sides. Over 9' high with finials. *Courtesy Whitehall at the Villa, Chapel Hill, N.C.* **$12,000–18,000.**

Rosewood Rococo Revival wardrobe or armoire, c. 1850–60, with mirrored door. Scrolled apron, pediment and top of mirror. Fret-carved pediment. Made by Charles Baudouine, New York City. Refinished. *Courtesy Southampton Antiques, Southampton, Mass.* **$8,000–12,000.** Without a known maker, such a wardrobe would bring only **$4,000–6,000.**

A fine Rococo Revival rosewood armoire, signed by J. & J. W. Meeks, with a Vessey Street address (their place of business 1836–1855). Pediment with cabochon, shell, floral and foliate carving. Mirrored door framed by scrolls. Canted corners with scrolling acanthus and floral carving. Drawer above shaped apron. In pristine original condition (always an important factor in deciding value). This is an unusual custom-fitted piece—inside is fitted with a butler's desk with drawer and shelves. *Courtesy Joan Bogart, Rockville Centre, N.Y.* **$15,000–20,000.**

4

Renaissance Revival
1860-1880

The Renaissance style overtook the rococo in popularity around the time of the Civil War, with Renaissance remaining immensely popular through the 1870s. The new Renaissance style was inspired in part by Italianate architecture, with its interesting silhouette and arches. It had much in common with the Rococo Revival, including massive proportions, emphasis on formality and richness, and origins in France. But where the Rococo Revival was curvaceous and celebrated the bounty of nature, the Renaissance Revival was based on architectural designs, which gave it a more abstract, monumental, masculine feeling. The Renaissance Revival style was not as graceful as it was massive. Its appeal lay not in balanced curves or naturalistic motifs but in its interesting and imaginative juxtapositions of architectural elements. Arches, ovolo moldings, pediments, plinth bases, cabochons, Renaissance strapwork and scrolls were all arranged in almost endless combinations. Perhaps the exuberance of the Rococo Revival furniture seemed inappropriate for a nation torn by war. Perhaps the more abstract architectural quality and massive scale gave Renaissance Revival furniture a monumental, heroic quality that appealed to the nation at such a difficult time.

Historical Perspective

The Rococo Revival style had an underlying foundation based on C-scrolls and S-scrolls and the graceful curves inspired by 18th-century France-the same sort of unifying theme is not as evident in Renaissance Revival furniture. On the best Rococo Revival pieces the curves provide a graceful underlying structure for the furniture. The same can't really be said of Renaissance Revival, where so many elements compete with each other. The result is an energetic rather than a harmonious feeling. The same aspects that satisfied the huge Victorian appetite for ornament sometimes frustrate the 20th-century aesthetic, which prefers an organic whole. On the other hand, the more abstract, geometric qualities of Renaissance Revival tend to suit those who find the Rococo Revival too frilly by far.

The Renaissance Revival brings together a sometimes confusing melange of styles. The movement originated in mid-19th-century France—and was often referred to as "French Renaissance." The Renaissance Revival style is not at all a copy of furniture of the Renaissance period. True to the Victorian spirit, it is an eclectic borrowing and adapting of architectural motifs not only from the European Renaissance but also from the baroque and even classical periods. All of these varied elements are mixed together to suit the particular Victorian taste for richness, massive scale, variety, contrast, and visual surprises. Call it what you will, the Victorians clearly loved it.

It may help to think of the movement in two phases. The first phase was a transition from the Rococo Revival, drawing on animal and human figures, flattened arches, and ovolo molding, with walnut as the most prominent wood. Typical of this early phase is the corner cabinet, shown in Fig. 4-1, with simple applied arched and ovolo molding, carved wood fruit handles and paneled doors and sides. A common chair might have finger molding, as on rococo chairs, and a cabochon crest. As with the rococo style, one finds lots of naturalistic carving featuring fruit and sometimes animals. Fruit-carved handles are ubiquitous on these pieces. For the most part, these are conservative pieces with rela-

Fig. 4-1 Renaissance Revival carved walnut curved-front marble top corner cabinet, c. 1860. Pie-shaped white marble top over a drawer and pair of cabinet doors with arched molding and carved fruit motifs. 51" wide x 36" deep x 39" high. *Courtesy Neal Auction Company, New Orleans, Nicolay & Morgan photographers.* **$1,500–2,500.**

tively simple decoration. This style continued to be produced alongside the later phase and was sold to a more conservative segment of the market.

Néo-Grec

The later phase of the style is more assertive, moving away from naturalistic carving and becoming more abstract. The style and the name, Néo-Grec, are French in origin. Like the other Victorian styles, this one made its first appearance at the great international exhibitions. The Néo-Grec style was first displayed by the French at the 1862 London Exhibition and again at the Paris Exposition of 1867. In America the style was sometimes called Modern Greek, New Greek, New Grecian or, by the French label, Néo-Grec. Today this later phase is often simply called "Renaissance Revival," which is not incorrect. However, to be more specific, we will call it Néo-Grec.

In general, the naturalistic carving found in the earlier phase is replaced by architectural motifs and motifs borrowed from Greece, Rome and sometimes Egypt. While some naturalistic ornament is used, it is more stylized. The overall appearance is more geometrical, two-dimensional, flatter-in short, more abstract. The Néo-Grec style is highly architectural, with classical entablatures, complex pediments, medallions, columns, plinth bases, roundels, finials, drops, cabochons, palmettes and urns as hallmarks (see Fig. 4-2). Extra contrast is sometimes achieved through the use of dark and light woods.

The chief characteristics of Néo-Grec furniture are abrupt contrast and aggres-

Fig. 4-2 Richly ornamented cabinet, c. 1876, with marquetry panels and Néo-Grec detail—probably the most lavish form of furniture to appear in Victorian America. By Kimbel and Cabus, New York Citv. The firm's 1876 design book, now in the Cooper Hewitt Museum, gives us an historic and important overview of their work; this cabinet is #4 in the book, and it originally sold for $200. [Art and Antiques, ed. *Nineteenth Century Furniture: Innovation and Reform* (New York: Billboard Publications, 1982), 62.] Its purpose was purely aesthetic—to display an important piece of sculpture. Rosewood and ebonized wood, with extensive marquetry, porcelain plaques and gilt-incised decoration. *Courtesy Witherell Americana Auctions. Elk Grove, Calif.* **$15,000–25,000.**

sive, mannered design. This design treatment comes across in terms of motifs that are overdone, elongated or exaggerated-treated in a manner that brings attention to the individual motif and creates the effect of competing parts rather than an organic whole. The overall result is often bizarre composition featuring jagged outlines.[1]

The triple-back or tripartite sofas typical of both the general Renaissance Revival style and especially the Néo-Grec style provide a good example of the aesthetic. Obviously strongly divided, the parts create tension in the overall design, which is not allowed to resolve as it would in furniture of a more classical mode. When we admire this furniture, it becomes clear what the Victorians loved-novelty, strong contrasts and visual excitement. Subtlety or simplicity was not for them![2]

By the 1870s, factories were also producing this visually exciting style. In the factory setting, machine processes dictated a flatter style; high-relief carving, which had to be done by hand, was omitted on all but the most expensive pieces. Factory pieces got their Néo-Grec flare from panels of burl walnut contrasted with incised lines (sometimes with gilt), and applied roundels, turned drop finials, palmettes and complex pediments.[3] For the less expensive items, this was a popular look for small pieces like wall pockets (see Fig. 4-3), hanging cabinets, display easels, small tables, urn stands, and sewing stands. The sharp contrasts, spiky turnings, and protruding elements all create an agitated effect. It was an exciting look that seems rather eccentric to the 20th-century eye.

1. Kenneth L. Ames, "What is the Néo-Grec?," Nineteenth Century 2, no. 2 (Summer 1976): 14.

2. Kenneth L. Ames, "Grand Rapids Furniture at the Time of the Centennial," Winterthur Portfolio 10 (1975): 47-49.

3. Ames, "What is the Néo-Grec?" 18.

Fig. 4-3 Néo-Grec walnut wall pocket, c. 1870–80, with medallion of cherubs playing musical instruments. One of its uses would have been to hold sheet music. The "pocket" is secured by a chain held by a lion's head. With gilt-incised decoration, ebonized accents, applied roundels, broken pediment with stylized palmette and scrolls or plumes. 30" high x 18" wide. *Private collection.* **$500–750.**

Egyptian Revival

An interesting but limited subset of the Renaissance style was the Egyptian Revival. The fad for Egyptian things came to America by way of Napoleon's discoveries in Egypt in the late 18th century. A massive tome was published with the findings, including an exhaustive catalog of Egyptian decorative motifs. During the Napoleonic era, French furniture did not escape the Egyptian influence. From the 1860s through the 1880s the craze made its way to America, but only in the work of a few custom cabinetmaking shops in New York like Pottier and Stymus, Alexander Roux, and Leon Marcotte. The number of pieces is fairly small, but they are unmistakable, bearing motifs such as anthemion, palmettes, Egyptian animals, scarabs, the eastern star, spirals, zigzags, and bold colors.[4] These motifs are also incorporated onto Eastlake-type forms, as seen in some of the photographs in Chapter 6.

Mechanization

All of this decorative extravagance was made possible by increasing mechanization at the burgeoning factories of the period. By the 1870s the large Midwestern factories in places like Grand Rapids were able to mass-produce almost all of the decorative elements found on Renaissance Revival pieces—roundels; turned ornaments like finials, drops, urns or turned legs; paneling; molding; incised

---

4. Art and Antiques, ed., Nineteenth Century Furniture: Innovation, Revival and Reform (New York: Billboard Publications, 1982), 44-46.

decoration. Only high-relief carving still had to be done by hand. in short, the factories were perfectly suited to produce this furniture which satisfied the taste for grandeur and richness without being out of reach economically. Factories were well suited to manufacturing a range of grades-adding more ornament and using more expensive materials for the higher lines. Steam-powered woodworking machines played a significant role in producing the average factory suite of Renaissance Revival furniture; only the most expensive pieces would be accented with high-relief carving done by hand. The Rococo Revival, with its extraordinary naturalistic carving, generally required more handwork.

The comparative ease of producing Renaissance Revival styles may have led to its greater popularity. George W. Gay, partner in Berkey and Gay, one of Grand Rapids's largest furniture manufacturers, made this comment on the Renaissance Revival style: "Manufacturers looked for a fashion in which they could use their facilities to the best advantage, and at the same time retain the attractiveness of their earlier work. This they found in the Renaissance, which for a number of years superseded all other styles in the best class of furniture."[5] In fact, this kind of furniture owes its existence to mechanized factories; its widespread popularity would never have been possible in an age of cabinetmakers working by hand. In this way, the Renaissance Revival style epitomizes the Victorian age with its combined love of richness and worship of technological progress.

After the war, furniture production expanded dramatically, especially in the new Midwestern factories. Between 1860 and 1870 the furniture industry as a whole more than doubled in size, with much of thee growth occurring in the new factories in the Midwest—Cincinnati and Cleveland, Ohio; Indianapolis, Indiana; and, especially, Grand Rapids, Michigan.[6] These new furniture centers gained the advantage over more established factories on the Eastern Seaboard because, from the start, they were designed and built to incorporate the latest new machinery. This situation made furniture available to a broader range of the population, and it drove smaller operations out of business.

The number of factories producing Renaissance Revival furniture must have been legion. However, at the present time, not much is known about which factories made which pieces. Most of their production cannot be distinguished today due to lack of documentation. Also, factories all over the country tended to use the same woodworking machines, which contributed to a similarity in design. We do know that the large steam-powered factories in Grand Rapids, Michigan, were very active during the 1870s mass-producing Renaissance pieces and shipping them all over the country. Berkey and Gay, Phoenix Furniture Company and Nelson, Matter and Company all had large new factories by the early 1870s and were poised to supply the country with their goods. They had new buildings designed for optimum use with the latest equipment.[7]

These three Grand Rapids companies took full advantage of the Centennial Exhibition in 1876, where they displayed eye-catching suites in the Renaissance style. All three won awards. Nelson, Matter and Company displayed a massive beadstead and dresser in the Renaissance style with almost life-sized statues of the founding fathers. For all three companies,

5. Ames, "Grand Rapids Furniture," 34.

6. Mary Jean Smith Madigan, "The Influence of Charles Locke Eastlake on American Furniture Manufacture, 1870-90," Winterthur Portfolio 10 (1975):5.

7. Ames, "Grand Rapids Furniture," 28-31.

these were clearly exhibition pieces showing their finest materials, designs and execution—the kinds of pieces that made reputations. Of course, each produced great quantities of low-end goods as well, many of which we find on the market today. After the Centennial, several Grand Rapids firms expanded their markets with new showrooms in New York City. They further increased their market share with an important innovation—the semiannual furniture market, attended by buyers from all around the country.

By 1880 these factories had grown tremendously. Berkey and Gay employed 400 people, with product valued at $525,000; Phoenix had 520 workers and goods worth $514,000; Nelson, Matter employed 380 and valued its production at $315,000.[8] Each company had its own staff of designers to create designs to suit popular taste. A large part of the trade consisted of suites for the bedroom and parlor.[9]

Grand Rapids was, of course, not the only manufacturing center. Another important site was Cincinnati, Ohio, home of Mitchell and Rammelsberg, which was one of the largest manufacturers off the East Coast. They shipped their Renaissance Revival furniture to the South and other parts of the country. Their styles were sometimes more flamboyant while those from Eastern manufacturers were more conservative.

These large factories provided competition that threatened the livelihood of many a small cabinetmaker. Smaller firms might not be able to match the low prices of factories, but they could claim better quality. Even during the Victorian era, the attitudes towards mechanization were mixed, and smaller firms could get an edge by appealing to these misgivings. Some companies' advertisements claimed the advantages of both—the latest, most progressive machines and also a staff of skilled artisans. Others emphasized that all the work was done by hand, an attempt to distance themselves from what they would have called the shoddy work of the large new factories. Smaller firms had to appeal to a different market to stay in business at all, offering pieces that were made with time-tested construction and more handwork. appropriate for a segment of the monied population. Of course, it can be difficult to interpret advertising—we expect exaggeration—but it is clear that the advertisers were in touch with the public's mixed feelings about advancing technology.

Many smaller firms drew attention to the fact that they were not steam-run, and emphasized that much of the work was still done by hand. An older firm in Baltimore described itself thus, "...the mammoth stock of goods elegant in design, style, and finish presents one of the most complete and perfect displays of *handmade* Furniture in the city...everything in the line of first-class Fine Cabinet Furniture for parlor, chamber and office use is always to be found in stock."[10]

Furniture historians are just beginning to explore the role of mechanization in the 19th-century furniture trade. It is difficult to say with certainty when specific machines would have been used and in what settings. The process of mechanization was constantly evolving and differed depending on the size of the shop.

The furniture industry had several levels. There were large factories which used powered machinery as much as possible for the bulk of their furniture, and perhaps used hand work on a limited basis for production of high-end pieces. There were also small cabinetmaking shops, perhaps making limited use of

8. Ibid., 32.
9. 9. Ibid., 30-32.
10. Gregory R. Weidman, *Furniture in Maryland, 1740-1940* (Baltimore: Maryland Historical Society, 1984): 207.

steam-powered machinery but also keeping alive the tradition of hand work. These small firms had several options open to them. They could buy machines—steam-powered, horse-powered or foot-powered—that they could use regularly and could afford. They could also contract out to firms specializing in one aspect of the trade. For example, mill houses were equipped with circular saws and planing machines to cut boards, and they often had other machines as well—lathes, fret saws, shapers and molders to provide shaped pieces, turned pieces, roundels, etc. The third level of mechanization was exemplified by the fine cabinetmaking firms in major cities which employed many workers. They produced custom-designed furniture using quality construction methods and also used steam-powered machinery when it was cost-effective but not when it compromised the quality of the decoration.

Fine cabinetmaking firms like Herter Brothers used high-quality woods and paneled construction, and employed artisans who were skilled in carving and gilding. Obviously, there were some steps that simply had to be completed by hand. Of course, this was furniture for the luxury trade, made for wealthy clients like railroad magnates and industrialists, and today this furniture is among the most collectible of the Victorian era. Clearly, the quick dismissal of Victorian furniture on the grounds that it was all mass produced using shoddy construction techniques is neither fair nor accurate.

Period reporting of exhibits at the Centennial adds to our understanding of how new woodworking technologies were used. As a showcase for the nation's industrial strength, the Centennial had prominent displays of the latest devices. The exhibit of J. A. Fay & Company's woodworking machinery was featured in an 1876 issue of *Scientific American*, which pictured and described the various machines (see Fig. 4-4). There were machines for planing, tongue and groove (for

Fig. 4-4 The exhibit of A. J. Fay & Company's woodworking machinery at the Centennial. From *Scientific American*, November 1876.

flooring), machines for molding the edges of panels, incising, making tenons, band saws (which could cut curving outlines), rip saws and fret or scroll saws that did not run off the edge of the stock and thus could cut inside the outlines.

A few years later, an 1880 issue of *Scientific American* (see Fig. 4-5) again featured woodworking machines, this time in use at the factory of M. & H. Schrinkeisen in New York City where about 200 parlor suites in any one design could be produced at one time. There were machines for planing, turning, sanding, a jointer that smoothed the joints between boards, band saws and fret or scroll saws, a variety molder to do all sorts of moldings. But we should notice that not all of the work could be accomplished with machines. A spindle carver is pictured, and the magazine's description is

Fig. 4-5 Woodworking machinery featured in an October 1880 issue of *Scientific American*.

instructive. The wood was hand held against the cutting knives.

In this way the machine may be adjusted to do almost any kind of carving desired, but it is found more economical in practice to do a large proportion of the carving by hand, rather than fit up the knives and patterns for the machine for all the new and elaborate designs in carving which are always being introduced...The carving by hand, of which a view is given in one Of our illustrations, forms a very important part of the work done or the establishment, at which thirty to forty hands are kept regularly employed.[11]

This comment on the spindle carver illustrates several important points about emerging technologies. Some machines

(including multiple carvers or direct-copying carvers) were so complex and expensive that they were only economical in a large mass-production setting. A machine that undertook a particularly complex task could necessitate frequent changes of settings, changes of cutting tools, etc. The complexity made this type of machine practical only for a large factory making thousands of copies. These factories would also require skilled workers who knew how to operate and fix these machines. The cost of upkeep—new cutting knives, new parts-had to be considered. The cost of steam or coal or electric power had to be taken into consideration when calculating the true cost of this kind of production.[12]

Of all the carving machines, the spindle carver pictured in *Scientific American* came closest to replicating hand carving. But even it was not capable of the depth, undercutting and complexity of high-relief, three-dimensional hand carving. This kind of carving simply could not be done by machines. New technologies could not always replicate work done by hand, and when the difference between machine work and hand work was obvious to the eye, hand work would take precedence on high-quality furniture.

As we keep in mind the range of quality and degrees of mechanization in late 19th-century furniture, it is undeniable that a great deal of it was mass produced and inexpensive. The large factories in the Midwest and in major Eastern cities aimed to produce affordable furniture for an expanding population. Many factories produced goods with an eye to shipping by boat or railroad across the country or abroad. In this case, pieces were designed especially for crating and easy assembly upon arrival. Goods to be shipped were sometimes left unfinished, as the finish could be damaged by the extreme cond-

11. *Scientific American* (October 6, 1880): 229.

12. 12. Michael J. Ettema, "Technological Innovation and Design Economics in Furniture Manufacture," Winterthur Portfolio 16, nos. 2/3 (Summer/Autumn 1981): 198.

tions of long storage. Pieces could easily be finished or painted by the retailer who ordered the goods or even by the final purchaser. This kind of furniture was absolutely vital to new settlers on the Western frontier and other remote areas of the country.

Room Settings and Furniture Forms

The Hall

In Victorian America, one did not simply place furniture according to personal whim. Furniture was felt to have an important symbolic purpose, and the Renaissance Revival style was used to make a grand, imposing effect in formal areas of the home.

One often found Renaissance Revival-style furniture in halls, the area of the home where first impressions were vital. In an era when visiting was an important activity played out in subtle social rituals, the hall was a formal area that first conveyed the status of the household. In affluent households, the most prominent piece of furniture was usually the hallstand, a Victorian invention that was a mark of status and served social customs (see Fig. 4-6). It was a huge piece of furniture-often six to ten feet tall. Its bulk alone gave it importance and formality. It usually consisted of a mirror, often framed in undulating curves and studded with hooks or knobs for hats and coats. Below the mirror might be a stand with a marble top and drawer. It would be flanked by holders for walking sticks and umbrellas, with drip pans below. Elaborate hallstands had cast-metal drip pans, the best might even have marble, while cheaper models made do with tin.

The hallstand provided a formal space for visitors to leave their personal cards with subtle clues as to their feelings towards you, their status and yours. Calling cards were part of an intricate social ritual for paying respects by visiting in person or by leaving one's card. Social calling was an important and time-consuming duty of the well-to-do wife. However, the goal could also be achieved by leaving a card and not having a face-to-face visit. The person being visited could be "not at home" (upstairs, out of sight and not wanting to be bothered), and one could simply leave a card and still do

Fig. 4-6 Walnut Renaissance Revival hallstand, c. 1860, with sturdy hooks, applied veneer panels and roundels, pediment top crowned with high-relief-carved crest. Arched mirror. Base with marble-topped table with freize drawer, strongly turned legs, cast iron drip pans. Approximately 9' high. *Private collection.* **$2,400–3,600.**

one's duty without breaking a single rule of etiquette. We might consider this arrangement highly artificial, but at least it allowed social ties to be maintained without social exhaustion. Orderly social connections were a mainstay of Victorian society, and the hallstand was a prop for this vital activity. As such, it needed to take a commanding presence through the use of luxurious materials like mirrors and burl veneers, and boasting, extravagant decoration.

The Dining Room

The dining room afforded another formal setting for much Renaissance Revival furniture. For the middle class, who now bought vast quantities of furniture, a room set apart just for dining was a relatively new concept. During most of the 18th century there had been no separate room for dining, except in the grand homes of the wealthy. A drop-leaf table in the living room sufficed for a dining table. By the mid-19th century, prosperous middle class homes had a separate dining room, generally outfitted in the Renaissance Revival style. Pedestal tables had replaced the drop-leaf table for the most part. By about 1850, extension pedestal tables became fashionable, and this massive form remained the most prevalent dining table throughout the second half of the century.

The Victorians considered the dining room to be masculine. This was, of course, a carryover from the 18th century, when women retired to the drawing room (or with-drawing room) after dinner, and the men drank, smoked and conversed at the dining table. Many 18th-century and early 19th-century sideboards of the superior quality indicative of wealthy owners have a small side compartment that, surprisingly enough, contained the urinals for the men to use once the ladies departed and drinking became more robust. Screens were also kept in dining rooms for more substantial events.

In Victorian America this sort of behavior would never have been allowed. The dining room provided an opportunity to display the family's wealth—and display it they did. The massive Renaissance Revival sideboards, with their extravagant carving, were outward signs of the family's wealth and status (see Fig. 4-7). They were not particularly functional, with little storage space considering their bulk. Such a sideboard was primarily a display

Fig. 4-7 Massive oak Renaissance Revival sideboard, c. 1865. A tour de force of high-relief carving and just one step down from the fantastic sideboards on display at the international exhibitions. With intricately shaped base featuring three curved doors, each with lavish carvings of game, fish, vegetables and fruit. Pilasters between the doors also boast food carvings, including heads of cows. Oak serving surface (not marble). Top with two shelves and back with bosses framed by diamonds below carving of birds and fruit in a domed pediment. Surmounted by a gadrooned urn holding masses of fruit and vegetables. The sides are bordered by mythical beasts with web feet and griffin heads. 84" wide x 9'4" high. *Courtesy Butte's Antiques, Oxford, N.C.* **$25,000–40,000.** If walnut or rosewood, **$50,000–75,000.**

piece that made a strong symbolic and aesthetic statement. As with much high-style Victorian furniture, its visual qualities were more important than its functional ones.

At the exhibitions that shaped design evolution in the second half of the century, sideboards played an important role, representing the best and very height of carving and magnificence a country could produce. At the Crystal Palace Exhibition in London in 1851, France made an aggressive statement about its dominance in the decorative arts when it displayed an important, massive Renaissance Revival sideboard absolutely covered with high-relief naturalistic carving of foodstuffs and hunting motifs. At the 1853 New York International Exhibition, similar sideboards were on display. Steeped in motifs of the hunt, these sideboards help us understand the Victorian concept of the dining room as a masculine place. The connection between food, hunting, and death was not only made but also celebrated on these massive sideboards. Of course, these exhibition pieces were impossible to reproduce for ordinary homes. However, affluent households soon possessed similar models that copied the spirit, if not every detail, of the exhibition pieces.

The basic form was as follows: a base of four units, each with a door (the center doors being flat, the side doors convex)—all with carving and often with burl panels and molding framing the carving. Above the doors were four conforming drawers, similarly decorated with panelling and molding. The base was topped by a flat marble surface, which was divided into three sections (center and two sides) by the graduated shelves resting on it. There was often a mirrored backing for the shelves. The very top of the piece boasted a magnificent crest, usually highlighting the bounties of the hunt.[13]

In affluent Victorian homes, sideboards provided a dramatic backdrop for the important family rituals, the aim of which were to solidify bonds of community. Dining was far more than simple sustenance-it was a complex activity for the Victorians, full of significance. Above all, dining was meant to show how far man had advanced from the beast. These highly refined behaviors expressed the Victorian notion of "progress," dominance over nature and even suppression of man's own animal or bestial tendencies. For the well-to-do, seated in their opulently furnished dining rooms, the very act of eating involved using an extraordinary number of different utensils, each with a particular purpose. By the end of the century, the Victorian innovation of matching silverware meant sets of as many as 131 different pieces![14]

It is fascinating to note that even in such a setting, the violence of nature was a prominent theme and in fact, was depicted not only on sideboards but also in other 19th-century arts—for example, in the paintings of Eugene Delacroix and the bronze sculptures of Antoine Louis Barye. Romantic images glorified man's domination over nature-in savage displays of power and strength, in which man was always victorious. It seems appropriate that the same era produced Charles Darwin's *On the Origin of Species* (1859).[15]

Being such forceful pieces, these sideboards have often aroused strong feelings, not all of them positive. Reform writers in the 1870s singled them out for particular scorn. One writer described them thus: "Monsters besmeared with stain and varnish, grin at you from every point, and you cannot even open a drawer on a cupboard

---

13. Kenneth L. Ames, *Death in the Dining Room and Other Tales of Victorian Culture* (Philadelphia: Temple University Press, 1992), 67.

14. Kathryn Grover, editor, *Dining in America, 1850-1900* (Amherst: University of Massachusetts Press, 1987), 181.

15. Ames, *Death in the Dining Room*, 68.

without having your feelings outraged by coming into contact with the legs or wings of a dead bird or some other ghastly trophy of man's love of slaughter, which frequently take the place of an ordinary handle.[16]

The Parlor

In contrast to the dining room, the parlor was relatively untouched by violence and controversy. The basic forms of furniture continued unchanged from the Rococo Revival era, with only the adoption of Renaissance Revival shapes and motifs. The seven-piece parlor suite remained a middle-class convention. The sofa, gentleman's and lady's chairs and several wall or side chairs were still grouped in an orderly fashion around a marble-topped center table. Finer parlor suites often feature portrait carving or bronze medallions with busts. Whereas rococo chairs have round or oval backs, those on Renaissance Revival chairs are rectangular but flare out at the top. This is a nice effect that adds to the energetic angularity of Renaissance Revival designs.

The étagère also remained popular in the parlor as a focal point for displaying porcelains and other *objets d'art* (see Fig. 4-8). The Renaissance Revival étagères often have irregularly cutout backs with molded edges (some holding mirrors). These rather eccentric shapes create an overall unpredictable, undulating silhouette—a marked departure from the graceful, scrolling outlines of the Rococo Revival style. These irregular shapes are not a revival of any historical style—they are purely the product of a lively Victorian imagination, aided by steam-powered fret saws that could cut out almost any curve.

Renaissance Revival parlor tables and side tables eschew the obvious, functional

form of a square top with a log at each corner. This form held little interest for the Victorians, who seemed to prefer the sometimes awkward (and structurally weaker) form of a top supported by four legs clustered in the center and curving in unexpected, highly unusual ways (see Fig. 4-9). One might look at these tables and discover an underlying rule: the more

Fig. 4-8 Renaissance Revival faux-bois rosewood 6tagere, probably New York, c. 1860. Cartouche centered by clusters of nuts and leaves flanked by lavish foliate and S-scroll embellishments. Central mirror flanked by six shelves backed by interestingly shaped mirrored and cutout areas. Central marble top over drawer over shaped-apron base. The piece with the undulating, exciting silhouette favored by the Victorians. 90" high x 49" wide x 22" deep. *Courtesy New Orleans Auction Company.* **$6,000–9,000.**

---

16. Rhoda and Agnes Garrett, *Suggestions for House Decoration in Painting, Woodwork, and Furniture* (Philadelphia: Porter & Coates, 1877), 49. Cited in Martha Crabill McClaugherty, "Household Art: Creating the Artistic Home, 1868-1893," *Winterthur Portfolio* 18, no. 1 (Spring 1983): 18.

Fig. 4-9 Renaissance, Revival walnut and gilt-incised decorated fern stand, c. 1860. Molded circular top framing inset variegated rust marble raised on central column flanked by three fluted columns extending to splayed fluted legs. With applied roundels and finials. 20" wide × 18" deep × 30 1/2" high. *Neal Auction Company, New Orleans, Nicolay & Morgan photographers.* **$800–1,200.**

The Bedroom

Marble and massive furniture were also found in the bedroom, where beds and dressers were commonly over eight feet high. Suites in the early phase of the Renaissance style have applied fruit carving and arched headboards and footboards with ovolo molding. These are monumental pieces and the more architecturally styled beds, which often evoke church facades, have great dignity and a commanding presence.

Most of the beds from this period had a high headboard joined by straight side rails to a similarly decorated lower footboard. Slats supported the mattress. Canopy beds were uncommon. The more expensive the bed, the finer the wood and the more decoration, including hand carving, The companion dressers were equally impressive, with similar decoration—including veneer panels and applied carving. The form was usually three drawers below a marble surface flanked by glove boxes and supporting a tall mirror. Finer dressers with larger mirrors, were called cheval dressers or dressing cases. Because this type of dresser usually had less drawer space, a suite might also include a wardrobe for extra storage. Suites might also contain a gentleman's dresser (a tall chest with no mirror), a marble-topped washstand and night tables, as well as a shaving stand and bootjack for the gentleman. These pieces did not always match, strictly speaking, but they did make use of related motifs and materials. They were not clones but cousins.

Production of bedsteads lent itself easily to mechanization. Except for high-relief applied carving on crests, practically everything else could be done by steam-powered machines. The carving, of course, might be contracted out to a carving firm or done by carvers in-house. The construction techniques on case pieces for bedroom suites was more complicated and joinery was not entirely done by machines.

bizarre, the better. Obviously, visual surprises, complexity and richness were hallmarks of the Victorian aesthetic. Decorative effect often won out over sound principles of construction.

Atop any interesting base rested a slab of elegant marble. It offered contrast to the dark wood base, and it added richness and formality to the piece. Although it was far from practical-it was heavy, expensive, and breakable-everyone insisted on it. It, too, was an important part of the Victorian aesthetic which valued the use of contrasting materials and the effect of luxury. Marble was used extensively-on most tables (except for forms like flip-top games tables), for dressers and hallstands. Only on the cheapest grades was wood substituted for marble.

Cabinetmaking Firms

Kimbel and Cabus

Although the vast majority of Renaissance Revival furniture that we see today was made by the large factories and is rarely labeled, there were also a number of well-known highly respected firms working in the style. Kimbel and Cabus made some of the finest Néo-Grec furniture, particularly the monumental cabinets with porcelain plaques and marquetry panels, which were used as a base for sculpture (see Fig. 4-2 on page 71). Their work is characterized by the use of expensive materials like porcelain plaques (usually from France), ormolu mounts, gold-leaf accents, marquetry and exotic woods like ebony. Kimbel and Cabus operated in New York City from 1863 to 1882. Anthony Kimbel, a designer, had previously worked with Anthony Bembe and had a factory and clients in France as well as in America. Kimbel had also worked with Charles Baudouine, another maker of very fine French-style furniture. Joseph Cabus, a cabinetmaker, had worked with Alexander Roux. Obviously, Kimbel and Cabus brought to their partnership experience with some of the finest furniture makers of the period.[17]

Fig. 4-10 Renaissance Revival tripartite sofa by John Jelliff, Newark, c. 1865. Walnut, reupholstered. With busts and carved portrait medallions. Strongly turned legs, drops on apron, drop finials on sofa back. Imposing carved crest rail. Courtesy Southampton Antiques, Southampton, Mass. **$6,000–8,000.**

---

17. Art and Antiques. ed., 60-63.

John Jelliff

Another firm that produced distinctive Renaissance Revival work was John Jelliff & Company of Newark, New Jersey. At age 14, Jelliff had been apprenticed to a carver for a brief period, and his earliest training must have influenced him greatly as his designs feature strong carvings of heads and busts (see Fig. 4-10). The shop he set up in Newark, in 1843 is known to have produced pieces in several revival styles—Gothic, Elizabethan, Rococo and Renaissance. He was forced to retire in 1860 due to illness, but he continued to advise the firm. The company maintained the Jelliff name until 1890, when it was changed to Henry W. Miller, Successor to John Jelliff & Company. Jelliff died in 1893, and the business disbanded in 1901 after Miller's death.[18]

An 1874 survey of manufacturers tells us that the Jelliff factory had 40,000 square feet of floor space, employed 45 men and did an annual business of $100,000. The firm produced fine custom work, with half of the sales outside of Newark, in such places as New York City, elsewhere in New Jersey, Washington, Richmond, and further south. The firm produced furniture-from the medium grades to the finest, most expensive quality-for the parlor, dining room, library and bedroom, and for commercial offices. Jelliff is best known for his Renaissance Revival parlor sets which displayed strongly carved classical busts on the crests and arm terminals. True to his early training, his chief decoration was carving. He almost never used inlay and rarely paint, although his incised lines were often touched with gold.[19]

Alexander Roux

Alexander Roux worked in the French styles, both manufacturing and importing pieces. Roux worked in New York City from 1837 to 1881, with his firm continuing under a son until 1898. He maintained close contact with his brother, who was a maker of fine furniture in Paris.[20]

His exhibit at the 1853 Crystal Palace Exhibition in New York City proved to be on the cutting edge of fashion. In response to the fabulous Renaissance sideboards made by the French, he exhibited an ornate black walnut sideboard with game, fish and other foodstuffs. He also made other Renaissance pieces in the 1850s, along with pieces that have an Elizabethan look, characterized by vigorously spiral-turned legs and pierce-carved panels.

Thomas Brooks

Cabinetmaker Thomas Brooks (1811-1887) was also involved with the 1853 New York Exhibition. His execution of a design by Gustave Herter for a richly carved rosewood Renaissance étagère won a bronze medal.[21] Brooks worked in Brooklyn, New York, between 1850 and 1870, making fine pieces styled according to Gothic, Rococo and Renaissance Revivals.

George Hunzinger

George Hunzinger's furniture can certainly be called Renaissance in style, but because his designs were so distinctive and incorporate his own patented innovations, his work is discussed in Chapter 5.

---

18. J. Stewart Johnson, "John Jelliff, Cabinetmaker," *The Magazine Antiques*, 206 (August 1972): 256.

19. Ibid., 256-260.

20. Katherine S. Howe et al. *Herter Brothers: Furniture and Interiors for a Gilded Aged* (New York: Harry N. Abrams, 1994), 66.

21. Howe et al, *Herter Brothers*, 67.

Herter Brothers

Herter Brothers of New York City is better known for furniture in the Eastlake or Aesthetic movement style (see Chapter 6), but the company produced other styles as well. Gustave and Christian Herter were German immigrants whose furniture and decorating firm became the most prestigious of the 1870s. They were in touch with design trends in Europe and England and created their own luxurious interpretations. Their Renaissance Revival pieces, custom made for well-to-do clients around the country in the 1860s and early '70s, featured robust hand carving. Their carefully made furniture used paneled construction and fine woods and almost always demonstrates an eye for good design. Several of the Herter Brothers' Renaissance Revival pieces illustrated in this book use contrasting wood colors, a fairly unusual touch for the style as a whole (see Fig. 4-11). This use of extra contrast reflects the Néo-Grec style, with which Christian Herter would have been familiar since he had spent time in Paris.

Fig. 4-11 Renaissance Revival figured maple and rosewood library or salon table, c. 1870. Top with rounded corners and felt writing surface above frieze with one long drawer and false drawer on other side. Incurved legs with inverted trumpet and out-flared stylized bracket feet joined by interlaced stretcher with rosettes. Made for a California residence by Herter Brothers. 46" long x 28" high. Courtesy Butterfield & Butterfield, Los Angeles. **$10,000–15,000.**

Factory Production

The makers mentioned here represent the most collectible segment of Renaissance Revival furniture. Their pieces are sought by collectors and found in the best antiques shops in America. Much more common are the vast quantities of factory-made Renaissance furniture, which can be found in every small shop, antiques mall, and flea market in the country. Factory-produced Renaissance Revival suites found a ready market with the general public even when the reform ideas of Charles Eastlake were being introduced during the 1870s. These factory-made suites for the bedroom, parlor, and dining room continued to be popular well into the 1880s.

A fine Renaissance Revival walnut and ebonized portfolio stand, c. 1865, inlaid with musical trophies. Bronze medallion-mounted crest above fluted canted supports. 40" high × 23" wide. *Courtesy Neal Auction Co., New Orleans, Nicolay & Morgan photographers.* **$4,000–6,000.**

Renaissance Revival walnut firescreen, c. 1870, with ferns pressed between glass panes. Crest with "ears," acanthus scrolls, pedimented medallion. Stiles flanked by turned, reeded standards. Resting on an urn-shaped shaft flanked by four turned and reeded uprights ending in four outward-arcing feet. All with incised lines. 50 1/2" high × 23" wide. *Private collection.* **$800–1,200.**

Transitional Rococo-Renaissance mahogany Lincoln rocker, c. 1860. The Lincoln rocker has the same curving form as the Grecian rocker, but with upholstered seat, back and arm pads. It gets its name from the rocker in which President Lincoln was sitting when assassinated. This one with scrolling acanthus arm terminals and rose-carved crest. Note the elaborate scroll flipping up from the roll of the arm-sometimes these are called "whale's tails" when found on formal or country rockers of this vintage. Several Cottage furniture examples with partial "tails" can be seen in Chapter 2. 40" high x 19" wide x 20" deep. *Private collection.* **$475–675.**

Renaissance Revival carved rosewood ottoman, c. 1860, in the manner of J. and J. W. Meeks, New York City. With molded and canted square frame upholstered in tufted wine silk damask, raised on highly carved scalloped and gadrooned baluster-form legs joined by curved stretchers to a central roundel. 23" wide x 19 1/2" high. *Courtesy Neal Auction Company, New Orleans, Nicolay & Morgan photographers.* **$800–1,200.**

Left: Faux-ebonized rosewood folding carpet chair, labeled on stretcher "E. W. Vaill/Patentee and Manufacturer/Worcester, Mass./Patented April, 1873." This company was one of the largest chair manufacturing firms of that time. Bears original flower and fern tapestry. 17" wide × 20" deep × 31 1/2" high. **$250-450**. Right: Renaissance Revival walnut canterbury, c. 1875, with gilt, black and green decoration. Shaped top contains four compartments and has one central drawer to a scalloped apron which rests on trumpet feet. 23" wide × 14 1/2" deep × 21 1/2" high. *Courtesy New Orleans Auction Company, New Orleans.* **$1,500–2,400.**

Walnut Renaissance Revival side chair, c. 1860, with beaded and molded chair hack surmounted by crest featuring dolphins and cabochon set in scrolling plumes. Seat rail with cabochon and scrolls. Turned front legs, on rollers. 40 1/2" high. *Private collection.* **$350–475.**

One of a pair of walnut Renaissance Revival hall chairs, c. 1860, with pediment topped by shield and scrolling acanthus. Back with burl panel, applied roundels. Legs with applied roundels and palmettes, and ending in hoof feet. 41" high. Hall chairs and other furniture for the hall (intended not for comfort but for making formal statements) are often highly architectural, showing the true origins of the Renaissance Revival style. *Private collection.* **$900–1,500** the pair.

Renaissance Revival walnut hall chair, c. 1860, with architectural back with broken pediment over paneled back with tassel accents. Hinged seat lifts for storage of gloves, etc. (an option on hall chairs). Legs strongly turned. Apron with boss and strapwork-type applied carving. 19" wide x 17 1/2" deep x 44" high. *Courtesy Frederick Craddock III Antiques, Lynchburg, Va.* **$450–650.**

Walnut transitional Rococo-Renaissance balloon-back chair, c. 1860. With typical finger molding of the Rococo style, and burl panel and crest of the Renaissance style. *Courtesy Eileen Zambarda, 64 East Antiques, Asheboro, N.C.* **$400–600.**

Detail of chair at top right on page 89. Construction note: Chairs from this era were put together with dowels—resulting in a comparatively weak joint.

Walnut Renaissance Revival lady's parlor chair, c. 1870. with burl panels, applied roundels, incised line decoration. Bracket arms. Reeded, trumpet-turned legs (lacking casters). Factory made. *Courtesy Depot Antiques, Hillsborough, N.C.* **$300–450.**

Walnut Renaissance Revival gentleman's parlor chair, c. 1870–80, with ebonized accents, burl panels, incised line decoration, trumpet-turned front legs. Factory made. *Courtesy Carolina Antique Wall, Raleigh, N.C.* **$350–550.**

Walnut Renaissance Revival lady's parlor chair, c. 1870, with tufted upholstered back. Stiles and crest with applied burl panels and stylized acanthus carving. Bracket arms or "elbows" with incised line decoration. Round upholstered seat above trumpet-turned legs. Factory made. *Courtesy Depot Antiques, Hillsborough, N.C.* **$250–350.**

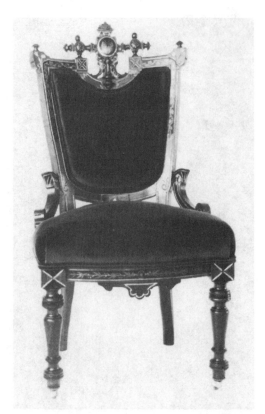

Renaissance Revival lady's chair, c. 1870, possibly by George Hunzinger, New York (the crest with its roundels and emphatic joints is reminiscent of his work). A combination of marquetry, ebony, gold incising, and burl walnut make for a finely ornamented chair. *Courtesy 19th Century America, Lafayette, La.* **$2,500–3,500.**

Renaissance Revival armchair frame, Pottier and Stymus, New York City, c. 1860. Crest rail flanked by two bronze griffin-head mounts, continuing to incised decorated stiles joined by arm rests terminating in bronze cherub heads, resting on shaped seat frame, centered with a Bacchus mask bronze mount on parcel gilt legs, terminating in hoofed feet. 28" wide x 24" deep x 42" high. *Courtesy Neal Auction Company, New Orleans. Nicolay & Morgan photographers.* **$6,000–9,000.**

Renaissance Revival tripartite sofa, c. 1865, attributed to Pottier and Stymus, New York City. Rosewood, with gilt-metal mounts, "reeded" apron, cherubs above hoof feet and tufted back. Courtesy Joan Bogart, Rockville Centre, N.Y. In restored condition. Dealer estimate: **$6,000–9,000.** (The same sofa sold for $1,000 in 1980 at auction, which gives on an idea of the recent market for quality Victorian furniture.)

A fine c. 1865–75 walnut Renaissance Revival side chair with fine carving (from a parlor suite). Closely related to a set at the Newark Museum. *Courtesy Witherell Americana Auctions, Elk Grove, Calif.* **$1,200–1,800.**

Pair of Renaissance Revival lady's chairs (related to a chair at the Houston Museum of Fine Arts and closely related to the sofa in the next photograph). Elaborately carved-note the snarling animal-head arm rests, as well as the Néo-Grec motif of the palmette on the crest and seat rail. Trumpet-turned and carved front legs. On casters. *Courtesy Witherell Americana Auctions, Elk Grove, Calif.* **$4,000–6,000.**

Walnut Renaissance Revival sofa, c. 1865, with griffin-carved crest rail flanked by acanthus-carved stiles, triple-section back and seat covered in velvet with mask-head arm supports, leaf-carved apron, cylindrical tapering legs. 78" long. *Courtesy Freeman/Fine Arts, Philadelphia.* **$3,000–5,000.**

Renaissance Revival rosewood sofa, c. 1870, from a parlor suite with triple-back sofa, two armchairs and two side chairs. Mounted with French porcelain plaques. Incised decorations, trumpet-turned legs, roundels, palmettes, drop pendants on arms, seat rails with dropped decoration. Imposing crest rails. Probably New York City. *Courtesy Morton Goldberg Auction Galleries, New Orleans.* Sofa: **$2,400–3,600.**

Chairs from the parlor suite in previous illustration. Pair of lady's & gentleman's chairs: **$2,400–3,600** the pair. Pair of side chairs: **$1,000–1,500** the pair.

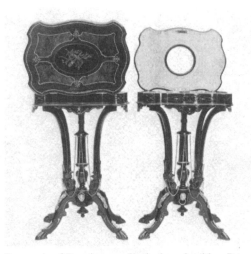

Rare pair of Renaissance Revival work tables. Rosewood, marquetry and burl hinged tops. Open to fitted bird's-eye maple interiors. Base rests on ebonized gold-incised legs with attached ormolu. *Courtesy Witherell Americana Auctions, Elk Grove, Calif.* **$4,000–6,000.**

Renaissance Revival smoking stand, c. 1870, of ebonized soft wood, with turned shaft and three attached out-flared legs with applied finials, roundels, and gilt highlights. Lion and ring with chains—a popular motif on small leggy pieces. *Courtesy the Howard Collection.* **$500–800.**

Renaissance Revival walnut oval stand, c. 1865–75, with marquetry top. Top with drop finials, which are echoed in the supports by numerous applied roundels. With lots of incised line decoration. Refinished. *Courtesy Southampton Antiques, Southampton, Mass.* **$2,500–3,500.**

Renaissance Revival ebonized and marquetry side table, c. 1875, probably by Berkey and Gay (one of Grand Rapids's largest firms). Lozenge-shaped marquetry top above conforming apron, raised on ebonized and gilt-incised turned legs joined with stretchers and surmounted by an urn finial. 27 1/2" wide × 18" deep × 28 1/2" high. *Courtesy Neal Auction Company, New Orleans, Nicolay & Morgan photographers.* **$1,800–2,400.**

Top of Berkey and Gay table, showing the marquetry work.

Renaissance Revival walnut library or parlor table, c. 1860–70, with lozenge-shaped top over base. Frieze drawer. Ball and trumpet turned legs on casters, joined by shaped and molded side stretchers and center turned stretcher. Center of top probably replaced, but not necessarily, since this is a low-end (example. 42" long × 25" deep × 29" high. *Courtesy Butte's Antiques, Oxford, N.C.* **$450–650.**

Walnut parlor table with heavy Néo-Grec detail, c. 1875, burl application and inset marble. *Courtesy Witherell Americana Auctions, Elk Grove, Calif.* **$2,000–3,000.**

Renaissance Revival figured maple and rosewood sewing table, c. 1870. Top with molded edge over single drawer. Raised on fluted columnar supports joined by shaped stretcher, on stylized bracket feet (casters replaced). Missing sewing basket and one pull. Made for a California home by Herter Brothers, New York City. Herter Brothers, though best known for their Eastlake/Aesthetic pieces, also produced custom-made top-of-the-line work in the Renaissance Revival style. The use of contrasting woods is a hallmark of their interpretations. 34 1/2" long × 30" high. *Courtesy Butterfield & Butterfield, Los Angeles.* **$800–1,200,** as is. **$2,000–3,000** perfect.

Renaissance Revival incised maple sewing table, c. 1870. Rectangular baize-inset top with reeded edge above a frieze drawer and sides applied with figured maple panels and reeded triglyphs above rounded, sliding basket. On reeded trestle supports joined by turned and reeded stretcher. Commissioned for a California residence and executed by Herter Brothers, New York City. 37 1/2" long × 29" high. *Courtesy Butterfield & Butterfield, Los Angeles.* **$6,000–9,000.**

Néo-Grec parlor table, c. 1870, with elongated rectangular marquetry top above a conforming ebonized and gilt-incised apron. Centered with medallion and raised on a pair of tapered columns and pair of griffins all joined to a shaped shelf surmounted by an urn. 43 1/2" wide × 22 1/2" deep × 31" high. *Courtesy Neal Auction Company, New Orleans, Nicolay & Morgan photographers.* **$6,000–9,000.**

Renaissance Revival walnut desk, c. 1870, with eight square-sectioned legs with Renaissance-type motifs, including pseudo-paneling, acanthus and column capitals. Heavy molded stretchers. Frieze with paneling and Renaissance decoration. 58" long × 31" deep × 29" high. *Private collection.* **$1,800–2,400.**

Renaissance Revival parcel-gilt and carved rosewood center table, c. 1870. Shaped rectangular top inset with a leather reserve over gilt-incised leaf-carved frieze fitted with two drawers, carved griffin supports on palmette-carved stretcher. On massive paw feet. Possibly by Herter Brothers. 4'7" long × 30 1/2" high. *Courtesy Butterfield & Butterfield, Los Angeles.* **$8,000–12,000.**

An unusual rosewood ivory-inlaid table, New York, c. 1865. Square top and frieze with extensive marquetry depicting birds and flowers. Supported by central turned and inlaid shaft with four strongly curving legs decorated with scrolls and rosettes. Top lifts up. *Courtesy Joan Bogart, Rockville Centre, N.Y.* **$8,000–12,000.**

Simple c. 1865 factory-made Renaissance Revival side table with slightly shaped marble top and conforming frieze. Centered undulating legs flank turned pedestal. *Private collection.* **$275–375.**

Construction note: On this table it is easy to see the most common method of joinery from the era: dowels.

Renaissance Revival walnut parlor table, c. 1860–70, with oval top and molded frieze. Supported by flat, molded legs of undulating form joined by central urn and flaring outward at base. Factory made. 27" long x 29 1/2" high. *Courtesy The Antiques Emporium, Raleigh, N.C.* **$300–450.** Wood tops are usually replacements for marble.

Walnut Renaissance Revival center table, c. 1860-70, with oval marble top. Frieze with shallow-carved motifs. Central support with turned shaft surrounded by four molded legs of undulating silhouette and applied carving. On casters. *Courtesy Rudy's Antiques. Virginia Beach, Va.* **$800–1,200.**

The same idea as in two previous tables taken further, with more decorative understructure. Made by Kingman and Murphy, New York, 1868-72. With three such closely related tables, one wonders whether they were produced by the same factory or by different factories which each purchased turned and shaped pieces from a specialized firm. Actually factories all over the country used the same machines, and this led to a certain similarity in decorative motifs. But again, the same motifs can be put together to achieve different looks. The interface between mechanization and designers permitted no small measure of variety. *Courtesy Witherell Americana Auctions, Elk Grove, Calif.* **$3,000–4,500.**

A table very similar to previous example, though with a plain frieze and more pleasing proportions. *Courtesy Southampton Antiques, Southampton, Mass.* **$900–1,500.**

Renaissance Revival parlor table, c. 1865, with oval top of inset rouge marble. Frieze with crossbanding and dropped decoration. unusual base of four centered supports with buttress-like outer elements surrounding turned pedestal and resting on four legs which arc down and end in roundels and molded round coasters. All with crossbanded accents and gilt highlights. 41" long × 28" high. *Private collection.* **$2,000–3,000.**

Walnut Renaissance Revival parlor table, c. 1865, with round white marble top. Molded apron with ovals (the effect is of gems set in jewelry) and drop finials. Four centered turned legs mounted on molded double C-scrolls, on casters, and surrounding a pierced urn. 25" diameter × 30" high. *Courtesy the Howard Collection.* **$1,200–1,800.**

Renaissance Revival walnut three-drawer bachelor's chest, c. 1860, with ovolo molding, wood foliate handles, wood top. piece is divided by band of molding below top drawer. Paneled sides. *Courtesy Woodbine Antiques, Oxford, N.C.* **$450–650.**

Renaissance Revival walnut and bird's-eye maple tall chest of drawers, c. 1870, with seven graduated paneled drawers with brass and ebonized drop pulls with molded shaped top and chambered paneled sides. 45" wide × 21" deep × 70" high. *Courtesy Neal Auction Co., New Orleans, Nicolay & Morgan photographers.* **$3,600–4,800.**

Renaissance Revival walnut side-lock tall chest, c. 1860. Six drawers with molding and wooden foliate handles. Chamfered, molded corners, one with a locking mechanism. Paneled sides. Molded top. 44" wide × 21" deep × 57" high. *Private collection.* **$1,800–2,400.**

Renaissance Revival seven-drawer side-lock tall chest, c. 1860, with burl drawer fronts, ovolo molding, wood foliate and ring handles, chambered corners, plinth base. Paneled sides. Dovetails are handmade and drawer bottoms hand planed, indicating origin in a small cabinetmaking shop. Philadelphia area. 42" wide × 22" deep × 5' high. *Courtesy Rudy's Antiques, Virginia Beach, Va.* **$2,400–3,600.**

Renaissance Revival walnut sideboard, c. 1860, with burl paneling, decorative molding, roundels, marble top. Two drawers. Side has paneled door that opens to storage area for table leaves. Handmade dovetails, machine planing. 60" long x 21 1/2" deep x 33" high. *Courtesy Rudy's Antiques, Virginia Beach, Va.* **$2,500–3,500.**

Renaissance Revival walnut sideboard, c. 1860, with plinth base, paneled doors and drawers. Architectural-facade-like upper section with applied carved trophy of fish and scroll and cartouche crest. A modest version of the great sideboards seen at international exhibitions in the 1850s and '60s which were heavily carved with food motifs and trophies of the hunt. Marble top, original finish. *Courtesy Southampton Antiques, Southhampton, Mass.* **$3,500–4,500.**

Close-up of carving on crest of sideboard.

Walnut Renaissance Revival massive sideboard, c. 1865, with base of two cabinet doors separated by a panel, all with burl panels and carved fowl and fruit. Three drawers above. Chamfered corners. Rouge marble top with mirrored back and shelf supported by cutout brackets. Domed crest topped by shield, palmette and scrolling foliage. "Gingerbread" and applied food carving on burl panel on back. Approximately 9' high × 65" wide. *Private collection.* **$12,000–18,000.**

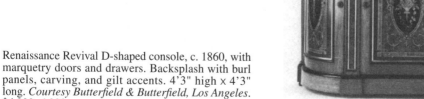

Renaissance Revival D-shaped console, c. 1860, with marquetry doors and drawers. Backsplash with burl panels, carving, and gilt accents. 4'3" high × 4'3" long. *Courtesy Butterfield & Butterfield, Los Angeles.* **$4,000–6,000.**

Walnut Renaissance Revival cabinet, c. 1870, with burl panels, colonettes and incised line decoration. Paneled door with molded medallion and foliate carving. Two side surfaces flank higher central surface for displaying porcelains or statues. Plinth base. 20" deep x 45" wide x 4'8" high. *Courtesy the Howard Collection.* **$3,000–4,500.**

Renaissance Revival music cabinet, c. 1865, with lower shelf. Rouge marble top. Mixed wood, burl veneer and ebonizing. Applied music-motif carving. *Courtesy 19th Century America, Lafayette, La.* **$1,800–2,400.**

Renaissance Revival gilt-mounted display cabinet cum sculpture stand, c. 1870. Breakfront outline, central section pediment with gilt-metal plaque. Cabinet door with cast gilt-metal plaque with dancing satyr, flanked by gilt-incised scrolls, arabesques and carved palmette spandrels. Side cabinets with glazed doors and later-painted interiors. On outset base on bracket feet. 5'7" high x 6'4 1/2" long. *Courtesy Butterfield & Butterfield, Los Angeles.* **$4,000–6,000.**

Walnut Renaissance Revival hallstand, c. 1860, with knobs for hats, two arms to hold umbrellas, painted iron drip pans, applied burl panels, incised line decoration. Incorporating a "table" with marble top and drawer. Crest with stylized foliage. 88" high × 44" wide. *Courtesy Eileen Zambarda, 64 East Antiques, Asheboro, N.C.* **$2,400–3,600.**

A simple c. 1860 Renaissance Revival walnut hallstand with marble-topped table and drawer, drip pans for umbrellas, pegs for coats and hats, mirror. Fanciful shaping typical of hallstands. Original finish. *Courtesy Southampton Antiques, Southampton, Mass.* **$1,500–2,500.**

Small étagère, c. 1860, with three graduated shelves supported by turned uprights. Pierce-carved gallery. 44 1/2" high × 28" wide. *Private collection.* **$300–450.**

Renaissance Revival walnut étagère, c. 1865, with gracefully scrolling fret-carved crest over central mirror flanked by graduated shelves with turned supports and cutout backs. Molded, curving display surfaces. 7' high. *Courtesy The Antique Mail, Hillsborough, N.C.* **$2,500–3,500.**

Renaissance Revival walnut étagère, c. 1860, with many irregularly shaped cutouts, some with mirror backing. Turned uprights. Drawer in base below marble surface. 51" long × 17" deep × 82" high. *Courtesy Byrum Furniture and Antiques, Hertford, N.C.* **$4,000–6,000.**

Walnut Renaissance Revival étagère, c. 1860, possibly by Mitchell and Ramelsberg, Cincinnati, Ohio. Pierced, scrolling crest with fruit carving over domed pediment and more scrolls, over long mirror flanked by graduated shelves supported by brackets and backed by irregularly shaped and molded cutouts with mirrors (lower cutouts without mirrors). Serpentine marble surface over conforming drawer. 7 1/2' high. *Courtesy the Howard Collection.* **$8,000–12,000.**

Renaissance Revival rosewood bookcase, c. 1860, with molded cornice over strapwork- and scroll-decorated frieze above pair of glazed doors. Plinth base. Stiles with acanthus scrolls and molding. 49 1/4" wide x 15" deep x 73 1/2" high. *Courtesy Skinner, Inc., Boston.* **$3,500–4,500.**

Renaissance Revival walnut bookcase cabinet, c. 1860–70. Base with two paneled molded doors over plinth. Paneled sides. Stepped-back top with two glazed doors. Projecting ogee cornice. Applied acanthus decoration. 9' high x 51" wide x 19 1/2" deep (at base). *Private collection.* **$2,400–3,600.**

Unusual Renaissance Revival walnut writing cabinet in two parts, c. 1865. Upper part with mirrored pediment over central metal-inset and ebony-inlaid fall front enclosing compartmented interior, flanked by semicircular inlaid cabinet doors. Lower part with burl walnut surface and rounded corners fitted with velvet-lined wells, flanking central frieze drawer. On pierced trestle supports. Padded footrest. 4' wide x 5'8 1/2" high. *Courtesy Butterfield & Butterfield, Los Angeles.* **$6,000–9,000.**

Renaissance Revival walnut secretary-bookcase, c. 1860–70, with molded domed cornice over two glazed doors flanked by scrolling acanthus decoration. Top sides are flush (not paneled). Burl paneled writing surface slides back to reveal fitted interior, flanked by prone griffins. Double-pedestal base on plinth with two paneled cabinet doors and recessed kneehole. Back and base sides all panel-led. *Courtesy Butte's Antiques, Oxford, N.C.* **$4,000–6,000.**

Renaissance Revival walnut secretary, c. 1860, with burl panels and oval devices-a favorite shape of the period. Paneled sides. Two glazed doors over fall front over drawer over two cabinet doors. On plinth base. Original finish. *Courtesy Southampton Antiques, Southampton, Mass.* **$3,000–5,000.**

Walnut Renaissance Revival two-door wardrobe in three pieces, c. 1860--70. Domed cornice surmounted by carved bust below anthemion-topped pediment. Doors with burl panels and applied roundels. Chamfered corners. Base with one long drawer with heavy burl accents, molded and cut out to show drawer surface. Paneled sides and back. 52" long x 20" deep x 9' high. *Courtesy Butte's Antiques, Oxford, N.C.* **$3,000–4,000.**

Close-up of the bust-carved crest.

Renaissance Revival rosewood wardrobe, c. 1860--70, with arched molded cornice centering heart-shaped urn, with projecting corners. Frieze with rosettes. Glazed door with carved bust of a winged cherub. Chamfered corners with applied carving. One drawer in base over scrolling apron. 51" wide × 23" deep × 98" high. *Courtesy Skinner, Inc., Boston.* **$4,000–5,500.**

Renaissance Revival parcel-gilt, stained and burl maple armoire, c. 1870, with mirrored door over one drawer in plinth base. Paneled sides. Stiles with inlaid "reeding," also found on frieze alternating with rosettes. Topped by scrolling acanthus. 46" wide × 7'9" high. *Courtesy Butterfield & Butterfield, Los Angeles.* **$4,500–6,500.**

Renaissance Revival gilt-incised maple pier mirror by Herter Brothers, c. 1870. Molded cornice over oval medallion gilt-incised with monogram, undulating ribbons and palmettes. Shaped rectangular mirror flanked by two circular platforms with hinged lids, drop finials, and scrolling fluted supports. Base added later. Made for a California residence. 38 1/2" × 7'2" high. *Courtesy Butterfield & Butterfield, Los Angeles.* **$6,000–8,000.**

Walnut Renaissance Revival headboard and footboard, c. 1870. Headpost with shell finial over scroll, foliate and fruit carving, all fitting onto an arched top, with applied scroll and fruit carving, flanked by urn-shaped finials. Footboard with similar decoration. Headboard approximately 55" × 95" high. *Courtesy Frank H. Boos Gallery, Bloomfield Hills, Mich.* **$2,500–4,000.**

Pair of c. 1850-60 Renaissance Revival faux-grained rosewood single beds. Headboards with cartouches, flame-urn finials, applied moldings, supported by square-sectioned standards with applied molding. Wraparound footboards rest on turned trumpet feet. 39" wide × 90" long × 63" high. *Courtesy New Orleans Auction, New Orleans.* **$4,000–6,000** the pair.

Walnut Renaissance Revival dresser, c. 1870, with mirror, the applied carvings and decoration similar to bed on page 117. Arched mirror with two shelves, fitting onto a base with three white marble tops, several short drawers and one long drawer. 56 1/2" wide × 19 1/2" deep × 86 1/2" high. *Courtesy Frank H. Boos Gallery, Bloomfield Hills, Mich.* **$1,800–2,400.** Bed and dresser would sell as a set for **$3,500–5,000.**

A fine c. 1865–75 Renaissance Revival walnut bed with architectural headboard, inlaid reeding, busts of children, burl panels, bronze plaque centered in strapwork-type design. Pediment with palmette and scrolls. Wraparound footboard with beautiful burl panels and bronze plaque. Part of a bedroom suite with following photograph. *Courtesy Morton Goldberg Auction Gallery, New Orleans.*

Dresser with mirror and nightstand from the preceding bedroom suite. **$8,000–12,000** the set.

Renaissance Revival walnut and burl walnut paneled bed, c. 1860, attributed to John Jeliff, Newark, N.J. Central headboard crest bearing carved seated cupid sided by stylized dolphins, caryatids and urns, with three graceful arches enclosing burl panels. Paneled wraparound footboard. 68 1/2" wide x 103" high. *Courtesy New Orleans Auction, New Orleans.* **$8,000–12,000.**

Renaissance Revival inlaid maple and rosewood nightstand or bedside commode, c. 1870, with later faux-marble top. Molded walnut border above fluted and lobed columnar supports over bird's-eye maple platform. Base with cupboard door inlaid with grotesques and lotus bands, raised on turned cylindrical legs on casters. Missing drawer, worn. Made for a California residence by Herter Brothers of New York City. 17" wide x 30 3/4" high. *Courtesy Butterfield & Butterfield, Los Angeles.* **$1,000–1,500** as is. **$2,500–3,500** perfect.

Renaissance Revival walnut bootjack, c. 1870. We don't see many of these today, but they were an optional feature of the standard bedroom suite, which included several pieces for men: the tall chest of drawers, shaving stand and bootjack. Original finish. Note the great needlepoint and owner's mongram. *Courtesy Southampton Antiques, Southampton, Mass.* **$1,200–1,800.**

5

Victorian Ingenuity:
Patents and Progress
1850-1900

By the second half of the 19th century, patenting an idea or a design proved to be a dynamic part of American industry and a highly effective marketing tool. A patented item had the air of being the latest thing-the "new improved" version always had an extra edge in the marketplace. Patents for furniture often involved pieces which could be converted from one function to another (a sofa into a bed), or

movable furniture (folding chairs and tables), or simply improvements on an existing design. Except for the output of a few firms like Wooten and Hunzinger, patents generally did not affect the high-style pieces. The appeal of most of this furniture lies in its novelty and ingenuity, not its elegance. Of course, the "novelty" now seems quaint to us, and this has a charm of its own.

Bed

Patents for sofa beds were issued as early as the 1840s, and the innovation was championed in A. J. Downing's 1850 book *The Architecture of Country Houses.* Downing was always in favor of economy, and sofa beds were an ideal way to provide extra sleeping space in a small cottage or apartment. Other designs included folding beds in the 1850s and wardrobe beds, which developed in the 1860s and went through various permutations until the end of the century. Folding beds were among the innovative pieces on display at the Centennial in 1876 (see Fig. 5-1). The

Fig. 5-1 Patent folding bed displayed at the Centennial Exhibition of 1876 in Philadelphia. From James McCabe's *The Illustrated History of the Centennial Exhibition* (Philadelphia: National Publishing Company,1876)

later examples are sometimes called Murphy beds. Probably the least expensive were the patent lounges, which folded out into beds.

Tables and Chairs

Patents for extension tables also date from the 1840s. This form remained popular until the end of the century and is the dominant configuration for Victorian dining tables. Folding tables date from the 1860s.

The tendency towards specialization in Victorian life led to refinements in manners and furnishings alike and resulted in the development of many new furniture forms created to meet specific needs. For instance, many new types of chairs were introduced. There were window chairs, reception chairs, nursing rockers, porch rockers, platform rockers, folding chairs, reclining chairs, even chairs with perforated backs. There was a corresponding explosion of patents-new techniques led to new forms and vice versa. The Growth of Industrial Art (1892), compiled by the U.S. Commission of Patents, stated that 2,596 patents had been granted in the U.S. for chairs and stools alone.[1]

Obviously, chairs were a major area of experimentation, and there were many designs for folding chairs, the first patent for which was issued in 1855. In the 1860s and '70s many other patents for folding chairs followed until this market slowed down in the 1880s and '90s. E. W. Vaill, in business from 1861 to 1891 in Worcester, Massachusetts, had the largest folding chair factory in the world. There were also patents for reclining and swiveling chairs, which offered new levels of comfort for home and office. Patent platform rockers

developed in the 1860s and increased in popularity through the 1880s.[2]

The Vaill factory was located in an area of Massachusetts that had a concentration of chair factories. Gardner and Company (1863-1888) in nearby Glen Gardner, Massachusetts, specialized in producing plywood chair seats. George Gardner received several patents, the most successful of which was for a plywood perforated chair seat. These popular seats were on display at the firm's Centennial booth (see Fig. 5-2) where they were much admired by visitors. Perforated plywood seats proved to be less expensive and

Fig. 5-2 Perforated veneer seats from Gardner and Company at the Centennial Exhibit. From McCabe's *The Illustrated History of the Centennial Exhibition.*

1. Katherine Grier, *Culture and Comfort* (Amherst: University of Massachusetts Press, 1988), 143.

2. David Hanks, *Innovative Furniture in America 1800 to the Present* (New York: Horizon Press, 1981), 33. 36.

more durable than caned ones for which they were substituted. The perforations could be arranged in pleasing geometric patterns or they could spell out names, thus providing a new venue for advertising.[3]

George J. Hunzinger

Probably the most widely recognized maker of patent seating furniture is George J. Hunzinger. Although his work can be characterized as Renaissance Revival in style, it is so distinctive that it deserves a category of its own. What strikes one the most about his designs is their innovative quality; his work clearly embodies the Victorian love of novelty. Another one of the influential German immigrants, Hunzinger worked in New York City from the 1860s to the end of the century. (After his death, his children carried on the business until the 1920s.) He patented his designs for folding chairs (he called them "camp chairs"), which sometimes used cantilevered construction. The backs and seats of some of his folding chairs were made of woven steel mesh covered in silk or worsted, an idea he patented in 1876.[4] His chairs—whether folding or stationary-have a strong diagonal element, often with a diagonal side brace (see Fig. 5-3). Many of his chairs have distinctive turnings that call attention to joints. Befitting the spirit of the Victorian age, Hunzinger seems to have drawn inspiration from the machines that fascinated the 19th-century imagination and it is interesting to note how much his turned uprights resemble actual machinery.

Hunzinger's was a very successful business, as is evident from the recovery made after the factory was destroyed by fire in 1877. This comeback was due in part to an 1882 patent for a platform

Fig. 5-3 A George Hunzinger walnut side chair, patented 1869 and stamped on the rear leg. This form is more unusual than some of Hunzinger's designs although it incorporates his typical emphatic joints and diagonal uprights. *Courtesy Ioan Bogart, Rockville Centre, N.Y.* **$1,000–1,500.**

rocker with a specific design (Fig. 5-4).[5] Though best known for his patented folding chairs, Hunzinger also made upholstered sofas and chairs that did not fold but still bore traces of his distinctive style. His "lollipop" side chair was patented in 1877.

Wenzel Friedrich

Aside from patent seating furniture, there was also innovation in the types of materials used. Besides wood, there was wicker, cast iron, steel, and even horns from longhorn cattle. One of the best-known makers of unusual chairs was

---

3. Ibid., 59-61.

4. Art and Antiques, ed. *Nineteenth Century Furniture: Innovation, Revival and Reform* (New York: Billboard Publications, 1982), 126.

5. Ibid., 129.

Wenzel Friedrich, a German who emigrated to San Antonio, Texas, around 1853. Trained as a cabinetmaker, he began to manufacture horn furniture in 1880 (see Fig. 5-5). He won awards at the major exhibitions of the day, and his customers included Queen Victoria and the President of France. His chairs, which were made into the 1890s, were often upholstered in animal hides and furs, including fox and American lynx and Jaguar.

Fig. 5-4 "Lollipop" maple platform rocker by George Hunzinger, c. 1885-95. Bearing the original label: "The Hunzinger Duplex Spring Pat. September...1882/One drop of oil (from your sewing machine can) on every joint or hinge will prevent noise." *Courtesy Neal Auction Company, New Orleans, Nicholay & Morgan photographers.* **$1,000–1,500.**

Fig. 5-5 Hat rack by Wenzel Friedrich, San Antonio, Texas. In an 1889 catalog he describes a similar hat rack: "The style and general outline of this hat rack will impress you at once with their striking originality and pleasing effect. It contains 32 horns, all framework is horn veneered, has the best French plate mirror beveled edge, also a drawer." A Texas star is inlaid in ivory on the shelf. It sold for an astounding $250. *Courtesy Witherell Americana Auctions, Elk Grove, Calif.* Dealer estimate: **$20,000–30,000.**

Wooton Desks

Office furniture was another important area for innovative designs during the second half of the 19th century. By far, the most prestigious piece of office furniture was the Wooton desk—officially called "Wooton's Patent Cabinet Office Secretary" (see Fig. 5-6). A symbol of the Victorian belief in progress and prosperity, it epitomized the demand for innovation, organization, and gadgetry. This is a wonderfully functional form, and because of its size and bulk, it also served the honorific function that was so valued in Victorian furniture. Its ownership conveyed importance and power; every successful businessman wanted one. They were, in fact, owned by many of the most powerful men of the day, including John D. Rockefeller, President Ulysses S. Grant, Joseph Pulitzer, Charles Scribner, and Jay Gould.

A period advertisement summed up the virtues of the famous desk:

One hundred and ten compartments, all under one lock and key. A place for everything and everything in its place. Order Reigns Supreme, Confusion Avoided. Time Saved. Vexation Spared. With this Desk one absolutely has no excuse for slovenly habits in the disposal of numerous papers, and a person of method may here realize that pleasure and comfort which is only obtained in the verification of the maxim, "A place for everything, and everything in its place. " Every portion of the desk is immediately before the eye. Nothing in its line con exceed it in usefulness or beauty, and purchasers everywhere express themselves delighted with its manifold conveniences.[6]

Fig. 5-6 Wooten patent desk, c, 1876-1884, probably an extra grade, with bird's-eye maple interior, decorative gallery with applied panels and carving. Also with walnut and burl walnut. 72" high x 43" wide x 35" deep. *Courtesy Leslie Hindman Auctioneers, Chicago.* **$10,000–15,000.** Depending on grade and condition, Wooton desks can go as high as **$75,000.**

---

6. From an advertisement in a British newspaper, May 1884. Cited in Betty Lawson Walters, "The King of Desks: Wooton's Patent Secretary," *Smithsonian Studies in History and Technology* 3 (1969): 1.

William S. Wooton sold his popular desks in countries around the world. In 1875 the company employed 150 men, and in 1876 it produced 150 desks per month. During that same year Wooton desks (rotary models and secretaries) were exhibited at the Centennial.[7]

The Wooton patent desk or secretary was produced in Indianapolis, Indiana, from 1875 to 1884. It came in four grades (ordinary, standard, extra, superior) priced from $90 to $750. Each grade came in three sizes, ranging from 4'7 1/2" to 5'1 1/2" high and from 3'3 1/2" to 3'9 1/2" wide. The form was the same for each, but the standard grade, for example, had veneer panels and better locks than the ordinary grade. The extra grade had incised decoration and a more elaborate pediment than standard, and the superior grade boasted marquetry and a beautifully inlaid interior. When closed, letters could be inserted through the letter slot on some models.

Wooton also manufactured a rotary desk in twelve styles, with single or double pedestal, the pedestals rotating outward to reveal the same kind of vertical slots and cubbyholes found in the Wooton secretary. Some versions had slant tops, others had flat tops or cylinder tops. These varieties were patented around 1876.[8]

Several other manufacturers immediately began copying Wooton's ideas, causing vigorous competition, which may have led to his relatively quick downfall. There were other reasons for the company's demise: by the 1890s typewriters and duplicating machines were in use in business offices, so different office furniture was needed, One central desk would no longer suffice.[9]

Thus the short life of so many patent furniture forms. Epitomizing the Victorian penchant for specialization, many of these oddities have not passed the test of time. What once seemed novel and ingenious now seems quaint at best. But there are many mechanically minded collectors who admire the sheer inventiveness of patent furniture and scour antiques shops seeking out unusual pieces.

---

7. Ibid., 4, 19.

8. Ibid., 12.

9. Ibid., 22.

Eastlake-style walnut and burl walnut Murphy bed, c. 1880. The bedstead mechanically unfolds from a richly veneered and paneled upright cabinet. *Courtesy Neal Auction Company, New Orleans, Nicholoy & Morgan photographers.* **$2,000–3,500.**

Oak patented combination desk/dresser/vanity, c. 1890, with pullout washstand to hold a basin that pulls out from cabinet side. Manufactured by the Eureka Company, Rock Falls, Ill. With Eastlake-type styling, raised panel doors, panelled sides. *Courtesy Pettigrew Auction Gallery, Colorado Springs.* **$900–1,500.**

Murphy bed open.

Oak Murphy bed, c. 1890, incorporating a combination secretary/wardrobe. *Courtesy Pettigrew Auction Gallery, Colorado Springs.* **$1,800–2,400.**

Eastlake-style walnut office armchair on swivel base, c. 1880. Contoured back. Burl panels on apron and crest rail. Spiral-scrolled arms. Bracket-type legs on rollers. Probably "Tyler's Senate Chair" by the Tyler Desk Company of St. Louis. *Private collection.* **$1,000–1,500.**

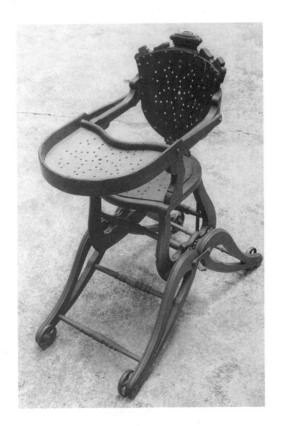

Walnut Renaissance Revival child's high chair, C. 1876, which converts to stroller and rocker. Manufactured by Thompson, Perley and Waite, Boston. With perforated plywood seat, back and tray. Perforated plywood benches and chairs were popular in the 1870s and '80s. 32" high. *Courtesy Whitehall at the Villa, Chapel Hill, N.C.* **$450–650.**

Late 19th-century bentwood table with shaped and molded rosewood top and decorative, scrolling bentwood base. *Courtesy Joan Bogart, Rockville Centre, N.Y.* **$3,000–5,000.**

Late 19th-century leather-upholstered steer-horn chair. A basic design. *Courtesy Butterfield & Butterfield, Los Angeles.* **$1,800–2,400.** Watch out for modern copies!

6

Furniture of Reform: Eastlake and the Aesthetic Movement
1870-1890

The last quarter of the 19th century was marked by reform in furniture design and interior decoration. By the 1870s many had grown tired of the grandness and formality of the Rococo and Renaissance Revivals. What had seemed monumental, heroic and vigorous in the 1850s and '60s came to seem overdone, busy, impractical-even cold. Many decried what they saw as the excesses of revival furniture, especially its emphasis on "showy" ornament, which all too often won out over good principles of design and construction, or what reform writers would refer to as "honest" construction. Above all, "sham" was censured, and "sincerity" was emphasized as a virtue in furniture in popular advertisements and advice books. Ever ready with moral judgments, Victorians invested furniture and interiors with great character-shaping capacities. During the reform era the whole ethos changed, and Americans reinvisioned their homes more as a refuge from the world—a place of sanctuary, comfort and privacy, less a setting for formal public statements. The feeling one wanted to create was more intimate than the grand and formal effect of the revival periods. There was a freer mixing of styles, which added to a feeling of informality. While the Renaissance Revival style continued to be popular for factory output and even dominated the American displays at the Centennial Exhibition in 1876, the real cutting edge was represented by the reform movements.

Why was the country ripe for reform? After the trauma of the Civil War, the country was confronted with a political and economic decline. In the political realm, disillusionment set in with the corruption discovered during Grant's administration from 1868 to 1876. Compounding this was a devasting and severe economic depression that gripped the country beginning in 1873, culminating in the panic of 1893. There were riots in New York City in 1874, a railroad strike in 1877, and many other strikes and riots in the 1880s and '90s. These unsettling events may have contributed to the spirit of reform and the rejection of the highly ornamented, ostentatious styles once so popular.

English Reform, the Aesthetic Movement and Modern Gothic

If America at mid-century had been strongly influenced by French designers, the last quarter of the century brought reform that had its roots several decades before in England. At the time of London's Great Exhibition in 1851, there was general agreement that English design had fallen into a sad state. The historical revivals were bankrupt, and reform was sorely needed. Thus the Aesthetic Movement developed in England during the 1860s. New sources of design provided much-needed alternatives to the overused motifs of the historical revivals. In particular, the 1856 publication of Owen Jones's *The Grammar of Ornament* gave the movement a gold mine of decorative motifs with its catalog of 2,400 different ornamental patterns from all over the world. In another venue, the 1862 International Exhibition in London introduced Japanese goods to the English-speaking world. So different from the dominant western styles, Japanese art proved to be a major inspiration for the Aesthetic Movement. English designers were equally inspired by Gothic designs, and in a surprising twist, found common links between Gothic and Japanese styles. Both were felt to have overall simple, rectilinear form and stylized decoration. Both were felt to embody a kind of purity that was a relief from the hackneyed historical styles.

A romanticized view of English Gothic furniture provided the inspiration for the rectilinear frame and panel furniture of the Aesthetic Movement. Reformers felt that medieval craftsmanship was more honest, sincere and sturdy than that found in the debased revival furniture. And when English designers came in touch with Japanese goods, they saw a connection between the simplicity of Japanese designs and the purity and sincerity they wanted to convey in the decorative arts. The Gothic and the Japanese

styles, as different as they may seem to us today, were felt to express the same spirit and embody a union of the useful and the beautiful in the decorative arts. The publication of Bruce Talbert's book *Gothic Forms Applied to Furniture, Metalwork and Decoration* in 1867 (republished in Boston 1873) was an important contribution on the Gothic side of the reform movement (see Fig. 6-1). The Modern

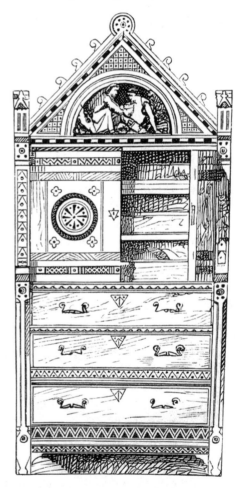

Fig. 6-1 Modern Gothic chest of drawers designed by the Englishman Bruce Talbert and illustrated in his book *Gothic Forms Applied to Furniture* (1867, American edition 1873). His work is very architectural-note the gable with crockets (the little curling pieces) that tops this piece. From *Harper's New Monthly Magazine*, volume 53, 1876, p. 815.

Gothic style owed much to Talbert's work.

Designers like William Morris (1834–1896) and E. W. Godwin (1833–1886) were among those who used obvious construction, functional rectilinear forms and Gothic and Japanese-inspired designs. William Morris placed a premium on handcraftsmanship and the importance of the artisan in crafting fine furniture. This resulted in some stunning furnishings, including fabric and wallpaper, but the products proved too costly for the average person. Godwin's designs, on the other hand, were less predicated on the use of handcraftsmanship and were easily replicated in mass production by English manufacturers. Designs by Morris and Godwin were imported to America during the early 1870s by Daniel Cottier, who had a decorative arts firm in London and a shop in New York City. His firm became an important conduit for the Aesthetic Movement in America.[1]

Charles Eastlake

By far the best-known of the English reformers on American soil was Charles Eastlake. Eastlake subscribed to the branch of the Aesthetic Movement that was devoted to good design without insisting on handcraftsmanship. Eastlake's book *Hints on Household Taste*, although originally published in England in 1868, was far more popular in America, where it was probably the most influential furniture book of its time. The first of several American editions was published in 1872.

The book was not so much a source of specific furniture designs as it was a compendium of advice on how furniture should be made and how homes should be decorated. Eastlake intended the book to teach these principles to a wide audience, not just the elite. As one critic wrote, "Not a marrying couple who read English were to be found without *Hints on Household Taste* in their hands, and all its dicta were accepted as gospel truth. "[2] Eastlake's ideas were further popularized by a score of writers who borrowed freely from him. In that way, his ideas became truly pervasive in America in the 1870s.

Eastlake, like other English reformers, believed that construction should be "honest" and designs functional. Honest construction dictated rectilinear rather than curving forms which were constructively weaker. joints were constructed for strength and not artfully hidden. The emphasis was on sound construction, which determined how the piece would look, rather than the other way around. Fig. 6-2 shows Eastlake's design for a library bookcase that demonstrates several of his ideas.

Eastlake expressed particular disdain for ostentatious "showy" ornament, and furniture that indulged in excessive curving and ornamentation at the expense of sound construction. Perhaps understandably, he reacted against the bountiful curves of the Rococo Revival. He had harsh words for that era:

The tendency of the last age of upholstery was to run into curves. Chairs were inevitably curved in such a manner as to ensure the greatest amount of ugliness with the least possible comfort. The backs of sideboards were curved in the most senseless and extravagant manner;

---

1. Martha Crabill McClaugherty, "Household Art: Creating the Artistic Home, 1863-1893," *Winterthur Portfolio* 18, no. 1 (Spring 1983): 4.

2. Harriet Spofford, Art *Decoration Applied to Furniture* (New York: Harper & Bros., 1878), 147. Quoted in Mary Jean Smith Madigan, "The Influence of Charles Locke Eastlake on American Furniture Manufacture, 1870-90," *Winterthur Portfolio* 10 (1975): 1.

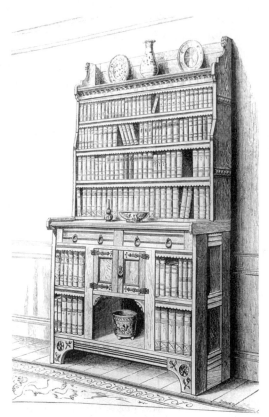

Fig. 6-2 Library bookcase from Charles Eastlake's *Hints on Household Taste* (Plate XX, 1878 edition). This piece displays the features we associate with Eastlake: rectilinear form, reeded molding, panelling, decorative strap hinges, shallow-carved stylized floral designs.

the legs of cabinets were curved, and became in consequence constructively weak; drawing-room tables were curved in every direction,...and were therefore inconvenient to sit at, and always rickety.[3]

As for ornamentation, Eastlake advocated shallow carving and primarily incised line decoration, but never naturalistic carving that was truly representational or lifelike, as was the case with the Rococo Revival era. The exuberant high-relief carving that characterized Rococo Revival furniture and some Renaissance Revival furniture did not have a place in Eastlake's aesthetic. Eastlake believed that "the art of the decorator is to typify, not represent, the works of nature, and it is just this difference between artistic abstraction and pseudo-realism which separates good and noble design from that which is commonplace and bad."[4] Eastlake's decorative motifs tended to be geometric or abstract depictions of nature. Or he might use turned pieces—either as uprights or halved and applied as decoration—to give relief to the overall rectilinear nature of his designs. On fine-quality pieces, he considered marquetry, other forms of inlay and veneering to be suitable.

Eastlake set out to educate the public on points of good design, understanding that mechanization could not be avoided and even made possible the wider availability of better-quality furniture for various budgets. Although he admired the sturdy construction techniques used during the Middle Ages on Gothic furniture, he did not advocate returning to hand work. He knew that mechanization was inevitable in the production of furniture, and he realized that it could make good-quality furniture more affordable for more people. It was not mechanization that Eastlake objected to, but machine-driven designs and the unbridled decoration of furniture that was made possible by factory production. He particularly objected to "wood-mouldings ... by the yard, leaf-brackets by the dozen, and 'scroll-work'...by the pound"—so essential to furniture of the historical revivals.[5]

3. Charles Eastlake, *Hints on Household Taste* (New York: Dover, 1969, a reprint on the 4th edition of 1878), 55-56. Quoted in Madigan, 4.

4. Quoted in Mary Jean Smith Madigan, *Eastlake-Influenced Furniture*: 1870-1890 (Yonkers, N.Y.: Hudson River Museum, 1973), page 2.

5. Ibid., 58. Quoted in Madigan, 3-4.

Factory Eastlake Furniture

Although Eastlake's book was wildly popular in America, the factory-made furniture that bears his name in this country often departs from his dictates. Somewhat unfairly, the term "Eastlake" is often associated with cheap factory furniture of the 1870s and '80s. We call it Eastlake when it is rectilinear and has shallow, incised, stylized decoration, and perhaps spindles-all things he favored. However, factory Eastlake tends to run riot with quantities of applied ornament that would have offended Eastlake himself. In fact, in the 4th British edition of his book, Eastlake made a point of distancing himself from American factory interpretations— what the Americans "are pleased to call 'Eastlake' furniture, with the production of which I have had nothing whatever to do, and for the taste of which I should be very sorry to be considered responsible."[6]

Of the many factories producing Eastlake-style furniture, very few can be associated with particular pieces. Mitchell and Rammelsberg is one of the documented factories that we know produced quantities of Eastlake-inspired furniture. A sizable company, they employed 600 workers by 1870. Their exhibit at the Centennial included Eastlake-type furniture, and they may have been among the trend setters for Eastlake factory furniture. Mitchell and Rammelsberg did not just produce inexpensive Eastlake furniture, however. They also created custom pieces for wealthy clients in their area. This strategy proved so successful that the firm hired an English interior decorator to set up three showrooms in the aesthetic taste, highlighting products made by the firm.[7]

Cabinetmaking Firms

There were also fine cabinetmaking shops in America which created faithful interpretations of Eastlake's ideas. The other strong reform influences show up primarily in the work of fine shops, not factories. For example, the Modern Gothic style, drawing from Bruce Talbert's book, was limited largely to the luxury trade. Strong Gothic motifs did not gain wide popularity with the American public, but we do see fine Modern Gothic furniture produced by a few cabinetmaking firms like Kimbel and Cabus or Pottier and Stymus from about 1875 to 1885. The other component of the reform movement— Japanese design—was also largely limited to elite cabinetmakers, though some Japanese motifs found their way onto factory furniture.

Herter Brothers

Eastlake-inspired designs found their fullest expression in the work of several top-notch firms. The most desirable pieces were made by Herter Brothers, the New York firm which produced furniture for very prosperous Americans on the East Coast and in California as well, including William H. Vanderbilt, J. Pierpont Morgan, Mark Hopkins, Jay Gould, and even the occupants of the White House during the 1870s and '80s.

Gustave and Christian Herter were German immigrants, steeped in European design traditions, which they successfully adapted to American tastes. The firm had its beginnings in the 1850s, when Gustave Herter formed a partnership with August

---

6. Eastlake, xxiv. Quoted in Madigan, 12.

7. Donald C. Peirce, "Mitchell and Rammelsberg: Cincinnati Furniture Manufacturers, 1847-1881," *Winterthur Portfolio* 13 (1979): 219-229.

Pottier for a few years. When Gustave was joined by his half-brother Christian in 1864, the firm's future was assured of great influence in the decorative arts. A very gifted designer, Christian's training in France and travels to England had put him in touch with the latest ideas in Europe, including an early introduction to Japanese design, which was known in Europe about ten years earlier than in America. Japanese influences filtered through the English Aesthetic Movement and became central to Herter's designs of the 1870s.

In 1874 Christian became sole owner of the firm. By this time English reform designs had come into their own, and England and Japan became the principle design sources. Herter visited England in the early 1870s, and from 1875 to the early 1880s the firm's designs followed developments in England. But Herter took the Aesthetic Movement ideas about simple forms and stylized depictions of nature and created designs that were unmistakably his own. His designs often feature stunning marquetry, best displayed in the famous wardrobe he made for the actress Lillian Russell in the early 1880s. With sleek, straight lines, ebonized wood, bold use of empty space and marquetry of gracefully falling chrysanthemums, the piece embodies the principles of the Aesthetic Movement.[8] A table with similar chrysanthemum marquetry is shown in Fig. 6-3.

Because they made furniture for the elite, their marketing habits were not indicative of more ordinary cabinetmakers. They did not exhibit at the 1876 Centennial, for example, nor did they advertise widely. They were able to attract a wealthy clientele simply by their impeccable reputation as one of the leading tastemakers of the 1870s. The firm's show-rooms occupied a prime location in the very fashionable part of Broadway known as the Ladies' Mile, where Tiffany, Lord & Taylor, Sypher & Company, and other prestigious shops were located. In 1874 Christian also built a large factory near Bellvue Hospital.[9]

Publication of the book *Herter Brothers: Furniture and Interiors for a Gilded Age*, by Howe, Frelinghuysen and Voorsanger (Harry N. Abrams, New York, 1994)-—nd the stunning traveling museum exhibition which accompanied publication—will no doubt increase the already avid interest in furniture made by the Herter Brothers. Their consistently fine style and good construction makes Herter Brothers a standout among Victorian furniture makers.

Pottier and Stymus

Perhaps Herter Brothers' closest competitor was the firm of Pottier and Stymus of New York City. Auguste Pottier and William Pierre Stymus worked together from the 1860s through the '70s as one of the most prominent New York cabinet-making and decorating companies. Pottier had been in partnership with Gustave Herter in the early 1850s, but went on to form other highly successful partnerships. Pottier and Stymus joined together in 1859. During the 1860s they were known for highly ornamented Neo-Grec cabinets, but they kept pace with fashion and produced Modern Gothic furniture in the 1870s (see Fig. 6-4). In 1871 they built a large impressive factory, which took up almost an entire city block. With show-rooms on the first floor, this multistoried building also housed the workshops for cabinetmakers, bronzers, upholsterers, interior woodwork, etc. By 1875 the firm did over $1.1 million in annual sales and employed 700 men and 50 women (who

---

8. Katherine S. Howe, Alice Cooney Frelinghuysen and Catherine Hoover Voorsanger, *Herter Brothers: Furniture and Interiors for a Guilded Age* (New York: Harry N. Abrams, 1994), 49-50, 194-95.

9. Ibid., 70.

Fig. 6-3 A fine c. 1870 ebonized Herter writing table from a signed three-piece Herter bedroom set. An amalgam of the Aesthetic Movement, the Japanese taste and Eastlake-with simple rectilinear form, incised decoration, and inlaid panels of stylized chrysanthemums (an Oriental motif). Stretchers with spindles, and central shelf stretcher. On rollers. *Courtesy loan Bogart, Rockville Centre, N.Y.* Dealer estimate with matching bed and nightstand: **$25,000–35,000.** Table above: **$5,000–7,000.**

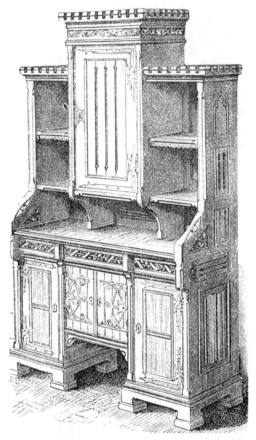

Fig. 6-4 A sideboard by the prestigious New York firm of Pottier and Stymus, another purveyor of the Modern Gothic style. Rectilinear form, with decorative strap hinges, panelling (including linenfold on the side), projecting upper elements, crenelated tops. From *Harper's New Monthly Magazine*, volume 53, 1876, p. 827.

worked with the fine tapestries and upholstery fabrics imported from France).[10]

Although New York furniture manufacturers were relatively slow to harness steam power to their advantage, during the 1870s it became more common. In 1875 Pottier and Stymus boasted a 150-horsepower engine to run their machines.

However, clearly much handwork was still needed, particularly on the high-quality goods, and so the carving was largely done by hand. Carvers were among the most skilled and highly paid of those employed in cabinetmaking shops.[11]

Kimbel and Cabus

The founders of the New York firm of Kimbel and Cabus were also part of the wave of European immigrants from the 1840s. Anton Kimbel (1822-1895), a German whose father was also a furniture maker, studied in Germany, Paris and even Russia before he emigrated to New York City in 1848, where he worked with Charles Baudouine's firm from 1848 to 1851. Kimbel was then financed by his uncle until 1865, at which time he went into a partnership with Joseph Cabus that lasted until 1882.[12] Cabus's background was in cabinetmaking, and he had worked with Alexander Roux.

Kimbel and Cabus produced mainly Renaissance Revival and Modern Gothic furniture. They were strongly influenced by Bruce Talbert's book *Gothic Forms Applied to Furniture, Metalwork and Decoration* (1867). The Modern Gothic style included flying buttresses, crockets and finials, columns, projecting or cantilevered elements (like shelves), coves, incised decoration (gilt or plain), and brass strap hinges. The interpretations by Kimbel and Cabus were marked by ebonized cherrywood, which was incised with gilt highlights and decorated with inset tiles. Kimbel and Cabus were one of the few American firms known for this style which was, however, very popular in England during the 1870s.

The Kimbel and Cabus display at the

---

10. Ibid., 70-74.
11. Ibid., 70-74.
12. Ibid., 26-27.

Centennial included an entire "Modern Gothic" drawing room complete with furniture and wall and ceiling treatments (see Fig. 6-5). This phenomenon of room displays seems to have begun at the Centennial, and it contributed to the notion of interior decoration whereby firms provided not just individual pieces, but an entire look. Kimbel and Cabus also made furniture in the Renaissance Revival style through the 1870s. They generally produced fine furniture in limited stock—in slightly more volume than custom makers like Herter Brothers.

Daniel Pabst

Daniel Pabst, also a German immigrant, arrived in the United States in 1849 and produced his own distinctive brand of Modern Gothic furniture. Around 1854 he set up a cabinetmaker shop in Philadelphia, where he became known as a virtuoso carver. In the 1860s he worked in the Renaissance Revival style and in the 1870s in the Modern Gothic style, obviously influenced by Bruce Talbert's designs. Some of Pabst's work involved executing designs by Philadelphia architect

Fig. 6-5 The Kimbel and Cabus room display at the Centennial Exhibition of 1876, featuring what was called Modern Gothic furniture (it is also in agreement with Eastlake's ideas). Several characteristics which are typical of the style: the mantel with projecting supports, use of decorative spindles, and architectural motifs like the gabled top of the cabinet on the right. From an article by Harriet Prescott Spofford on "Mediaeval Furniture" in *Harper's New Monthly Magazine*, volume 53, 1876, p. 826.

Fig. 6-6 Rosewood library table, c. 1880, with brass and mother-of-pearl inlay. An interesting and unusual mixture of design motifs-with a Louis XVI-shaped top and brass mounts, Renaissance legs and base. The top inlay of a spider in its web, dragonfly and butterflies, was inspired by the Japanese exhibit at the Centennial in 1876. Many details, especially the top, are very similar to work by A. and H. Lejambre of Philadelphia. The mingling of different styles is characteristic of the Aesthetic Movement, although the form is rare. Original finish. *Courtesy Southampton Antiques, Southampton, Mass.* **$4,500–6,500.**

Frank Furness, who may have influenced Pabst to move into the Modern Gothic style (see color section).[13]

Anna and Henry Lejambre

The firm of Anna and Henry Lejambre made a wide range of furniture styles in Philadelphia from 1865 to 1907. Early in their history, the company imported and manufactured French-style furniture and also sold upholstery. Their later pieces reflect the reform styles, including the Japanese taste. The library table illustrated in Fig. 6-6 is closely related to their work.

Japanese Design

Japanese design is another part of the reform movement that impacted smaller firms. Factory-made pieces were largely unaffected by this movement. Japanese-style pieces were only a portion of the output of small cabinet shops and a few factories, never dominating the American market. Americans began to learn about Japan after Commodore Matthew Perry opened relations with that country in 1854. Shortly after that, Japanese goods were exhibited at the 1862 London Exhibition. In America, the craze was fueled by the many Japanese items on display at the Centennial Exhibition in 1876 in Philadelphia, where millions of Ameri-

cans were introduced to Japanese motifs such as cranes, butterflies, cherry blossoms, fans and chrysanthemums. Following the Centennial, Japanese motifs became popular, and Japanese bazaars could be found around America during the 1880s.

There were several firms that were known for their pieces in the Japanese taste and a few companies dealt in bamboo furniture. For example, the Brooklyn, New York, firm of Nimura and Sato imported Japanese bamboo furniture and locally produced faux-bamboo pieces out of maple.[14] The American Bamboo Company of Boston also manufactured faux-bamboo

---

13. Doreen Bolger Burke et al, *In Pursuit of Beauty: Americans and the Aesthetic Movement* (New York: Rizzoli International Publications, 1986), 460.

14. Oscar P. Fitzgerald, *Three Centuries of American Furniture* (Englewood Cliffs, N.J.: Prentice-Hall, 1982). 254.

pieces using maple.[15] A.A. Vantine & Company of New York imported Japanese bamboo furniture, as did J. Lavezzo and Bros. of New York. James E. Wall of Boston imported bamboo and lacquer panels to create Japanese-style furniture during the 1880s.[16] Faux-bamboo bedroom suites are the items most commonly found today (see Fig. 6-7). The light, airy qualities of bamboo were considered health-promoting and conducive to a res-t-ful atmosphere—ideal for bedrooms.

Fig. 6-7 Maple faux-bamboo bed, c. 1880, Japanese inspired but with Renaissance-style raised panel arches (outlined in "bamboo" moldings). Shallow-carved bamboo and fan motifs on headboard and footboard. 59 1/2" wide × 72 1/2" long. Some veneer damage. *Courtesy Skinner, Inc., Boston.* **$2,500–3,500.**

---

15. William Hosley, *The Japan Idea: Ail and Life in Victorian America* (Hartford, Conn.: Wadsworth Atheneum, 1990), 142.

16. Burke et al, 479.

The Household Art Movement

The concept of "home" went through the cultural shift prevalent from mid-century to late century. Home became a retreat from the hectic pace of modern life. Before the Civil War Americans celebrated technological progress with unabashed pride, but by the 1880s, they sought a respite from the fast pace of mechanized life. To defend against the less-positive aspects of modern life, writers (many of them women) sought to emphasize the centrality-we could even say the sanctity-of the home. Home was no longer a place for ostentatious display of one's wealth, but a moral-even spiritual-force directed against a rapidly changing and often disturbing world.

Eastlake and others of the reform movement believed in the power of one's surroundings to act as a moral force that could influence one for the better. Beauty and usefulness and morality were all bound up together. The reformers looked back on the revival furniture of midcentury and saw not just over-ornamentation, but "sham" and dishonesty—harsh words for furniture. Eastlake and others used words like "sincere," "honest," and "truthful" to describe the furniture they admired.

This concern with the character-shaping effects of interior design was part of the Household Art Movement—interior design with lofty aims, reaching beyond mere decoration. The Household Art Movement was America's answer to the Aesthetic Movement in England. In America, concerns had less to do with idealistic goals of handcraftsmanship and more to do with the moral benefits of beauty—the character-shaping qualities of home furnishings. A spokeswoman for the movement wrote:

Its study is as important, in some respects, as the study of politics; for the private home is at the foundation of the public state...The art of furnishing comprehends much more than the knack of putting pictures and tables and chairs into a suitable co-relation; it comprehends a large part of making the home attractive and shaping the family with the gentle-manners that make life easier to one and pleasing to all.[17]

This type of "art furniture" included the best of Eastlake and Aesthetic Movement pieces-furniture that was dominated by straight lines, with surface ornament, and spindles for decoration.

The interior spaces of houses began to change, reflecting more emphasis on comfort and informality. Configuration of interior spaces moved to a more open floor plan, with less of the rigid separation of spheres that had marked the earlier styles. In this same era the interior decorators first came into their own. Until around 1870, convention associated certain styles with certain rooms, and regardless of the style, it was felt that the furniture should match or be closely related. The reform movement discarded the idea that matching suites provided the basis for a room. A more informal atmosphere was sought—one that was warm and sincere, not cold and formal. An eclectic mixing of styles became the order of the day. Since rooms were no longer limited to one style, a new principle was needed to order a home (it was more complicated). For wealthy clients, the major cabinetmakers began serving as interior designers to bring overall unity to rooms and to the entire home. The large furniture firms—including Herter Brothers, Kimbel and Cabus, Marcotte & Company, Pottier and Stymus, Roux and Company, Cottier and Com-

---

17. Spofford, 232. Quoted in McClaugherty, 6.

pany, and Sypher and Company—added interior design services.[18] For the middle class, advice books were full of hints on the subject.

Household spaces evolved to meet the new informal atmosphere. The hall, once a space for formal presentation and furnished for symbolic impact, became a more inviting space and was often open to the living room. The hallstand was replaced by less imposing furniture. The area once strictly known as the parlor took on new names, which conveyed the growing desire for cordial hospitality. "Parlor" changed to "Living room" or the British terms "drawing room" or "morning room" might be used.

In the living room, the symmetrical arrangement of a matched suite around a marble-topped table was replaced with a more eclectic arrangement. Furniture was placed in small groups conducive to intimate conversation. These easy groupings might allow for an Inglenook, a "Moorish alcove" or a "Turkish corner"—tucked away, intimate corners that included cosy comfort.

In this more relaxed mood, the matched parlor suite was scorned—at least by the well to do—partly because it smacked of machine production, which these elitists wanted to deny. Although no longer fashionable with the upper class, people of more modest means still bought parlor suites that were turned out by Midwestern factories in a steady stream up until the end of the century. During the 1870s, the seven-piece parlor suite was a vital part of factory production. By the late 1870s competition between the large factories led to innovation and a demand for new pieces like corner chairs and window seats. By the 1880s the criteria for the par-

lor suite evolved to reflect the fact that it was no longer a requirement in wealthy homes.

The market was strong for inexpensive sets, and a simple way to reduce costs was to reduce the number of pieces. By the 1880s the factory parlor suite was downsized to a five-piece suite. Sometimes a rocker (usually a platform rocker) replaced the lady's armchair.[19] Other changes to suites helped lower costs. The lounge, with a straight back and one raised end, sometimes replaced the sofa—the lounge being less expensive to produce because of simpler designs that required less upholstery.[20] By the 1890s inexpensive factory parlor sets were often produced in a threesome—sofa, armchair and rocker. This inclusion of the rocker was another indication of the move away from the formality that had dominated the parlor for most of the Victorian era.

In this late Victorian atmosphere, the marble-topped center table was no longer welcome, as the overall effect was less formal and any suggestion of coldness was avoided. The use of marble generally fell from favor. The marble mantels and fireplace surrounds were replaced by wood mantels with tiers of shelves for display.

The mantel became a more important focus in the room. Reform mantels were often topped with mirrors flanked by display shelves (see Fig. 6-8). Mantels practically became miniature personal museums. A collection of beautiful objects was thought to add harmony to the home. An attractive Oriental vase placed on the mantel was seen as beneficial to one's character. Bric-a-brac, that wonderful Victorian term for clutter, was not a dust catcher but a way to shape character. Hanging shelves, mantels with shelves

---

18. Burke et al, 116.
19. Grier, 209-10.
20. Grier, 219-20.

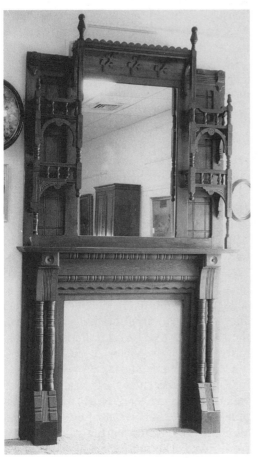

Fig. 6-8 Oak Eastlake mantel, c. 1880, with turned and incised decoration. The upper section with shelves and spindled galleries provided display space for art and collectibles—the bric-a-brac so loved by Victorians. Mantels became another focus in the living room (as opposed to the traditional center table) and another place for the display of personal collections, a vital part of the late Victorian living room. 61" wide × 9'3" high. *Courtesy Butte's Antiques, Oxford, N.C.* **$1,200–1,800.**

and drawers, wall pockets and wall brackets could all serve to display collections that expressed one's cultivation.

In affluent homes, new rooms evolved during the 1870s and 1880s: the conservatory, which was devoted to culture and natural history; the billiard room and the smoking room—the preserves of men intent on relaxation. The smoking room was something of an American adaptation of Turkish pleasures seen for the first time at the Centennial of 1876. There Turkish bazaars boasted "hookahs" for smoking, comfortable pillows to sit upon, lovely tapestries, and beautiful serving women. Americans were introduced to new ideas about relaxation and luxury.[21] Overstuffed upholstery became popular and was called "Turkish" because it was associated with comfort and relaxation, in contrast to the formality of the tight, buttoned upholstery of the Rococo and Renaissance Revivals. The Turkish fad gained strength with the Columbian Exposition in 1893, where there was an entire Turkish village that featured rooms, a mosque, bazaar and 40 booths selling furniture.[22] In this more cosy setting, the furniture of the last quarter of the 19th century also tended to be less grand and imposing than the Revival styles had been. Yet, as vital as the reform movement was in America, it is important to realize that the broad public continued to have an appetite for richness and ornament, as can be seen in the fad for "Turkish" things. No matter what the opinion of Eastlake or any other reform-minded designer, much of America demanded the lavishly ornamented factory furniture in the Renaissance Revival style (and enhanced Eastlake, as well) into the 1880s. By the 1890s oak fantasies were taking over, with even more carving. The furniture of restraint did exist for a brief time in 19th-century America, but the lure of ornament was never far away!

21. Burke et al., 112.
22. Grier, 193.

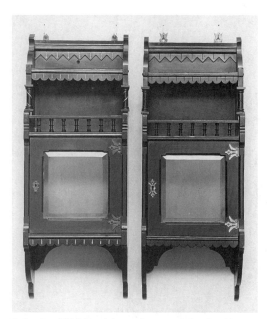

Pair of c. 1880 Eastlake-style carved ebonized hanging cabinets, with bevelled glass cabinet doors. One with gilt accents. 12 1/2" wide × 7 1/4" deep × 31 1/2" high. *Courtesy Neal Auction Company, New Orleans, La., Nicolay & Morgan photographers.* **$800–1,200** the pair.

Aesthetic Movement ebonized hanging shelf, c. 1880, with stylized geometric incised decoration, including many motifs—houndstooth check, beading, sunburst, pierced stars, strap hinges and pierced Gothic quatrefoil. The Aesthetic Movement in America combined many styles—Gothic, geometric designs and exotic looks such as Moorish or Japanese. This is an appealing factory-made hodgepodge. *Courtesy Morton Goldberg Auctioneers, New Orleans, La.* **$800–1,200.**

Aesthetic Movement ebonized print rack and stand, c. 1880. Hinged folio panels finely carved with circular panels of floral urns in the Aesthetic taste, with two lower shelves. 22" wide × 35" high. *Courtesy Neal Auction Company, New Orleans, La., Nicolay & Morgan photographers.* **$1,800–2,400.**

Aesthetic Movement stands and screen, c. 1880. Mahoganized, factory-made. With typical incised lines, stylized floral patterns, "reeding" on uprights. Screen with pierced decoration; perhaps influenced by the Moorish craze. Stand on right with Japanese influence in treatment of the gallery and bamboo-like leaves. Left: **$800–1,200.** Center: **$600–900.** Right: **$600–900.** *Courtesy Morton Goldberg Auction Gallery, New Orleans.*

Pair of c. 1875 Modern Gothic hall or reception chairs with lift seats to accommodate fans, gloves,etc. Walnut and burl walnut, with ash secondary. *Collection of Dr. Marla Neiman, photo courtesy of 19th Century America, Lafayette, La.* **$2,000–3,000.**

One of a set of 6 walnut Renaissance Revival-Eastlake transitional dining chairs with caned seats, c. 1870s. Chair back with molded stiles, crest rail and splat with applied burl panels. Bracket arms. Turned front legs and double stretchers. While the overall appearance of these chairs is Renaissance Revival, the detailed incised lines and the simplified turnings are Eastlake. *Courtesy Crabtree & Company, Cameron, N.C.* **$900–1,200** the set.

Aesthetic Movement–influenced walnut side chair, c. 1880, with stylized sunflower in back splat and connecting chair rail to high front stretcher. The high stretcher is typical of Aesthetic-influenced chairs, as is the sunflower motif. This is a factory product and much simpler than the custom-made chairs also illustrated in this chapter. The original caned seat is now set with a board and "flat" upholstery. *Courtesy Merrywood Antiques, Richmond, Va.* **$100–175.**

Three of a set of 10 Aesthetic Movement mahogany dining chairs, c. 1880. Repeated spindles were a popular motif with Eastlake and the Aesthetic Movement. Note the high front, side and rear stretchers. Reeded stiles ending in scrolls; similar scrolls complete the armrests. Interesting turned front legs. On casters. Original finish. Two arm chairs, eight side chairs. *Courtesy New Orleans Auction Company, New Orleans.* **$4,500–6,500** the set.

Two of a set of 12 Modern Gothic walnut dining chairs, c. 1880, (two armchairs and ten side chairs). "Modern Gothic" was the name given to pieces that were rectilinear in form, similar to Eastlake but with obvious Gothic motifs, such as the cutout trefoils, quatrefoils and arches here. This was a later stylistic development than the Gothic Revival of the 1830s and '40s; the Eastlake elements like the shallow, incised carving seen here indicate a date of about 1880. Kimbel and Cabus was one firm known for "Modern Gothic" work-their room display at the Centennial featured the style. *Courtesy Grogan & Company, Boston.* **$8,000–12,000** the set.

An unusual late Aesthetic Movement side chair, c. 1885–90, of chestnut, mahogany and brass. With mother-of-pearl inlay on crest and seat rail. Crest rail curves up and around in the shape of animal heads. Back splat of three vertical pieces. Delicate well-turned front legs. Fine attention to detail, especially in the inlays. With a Moorish feeling that was popular with the Aesthetic Movement. A mate to this chair is at the High Museum in Atlanta, Ga. *Courtesy Joan Bogart, Rockville, Centre, N.Y.* Dealer estimate: **$7,000–12,000** (or you might find one in an ordinary "antiques-junk" shop for $300!)

Pair of ebonized Aesthetic Movement side chairs, c. 1880, related to the following example (a similar crane centers the back splats). Overall rectilinear design, with complex backs broken up by geometric patterns. Reeded stiles topped by stylized sunflowers that create an unusual silhouette for the crest rail—one that is found on other Aesthetic chairs. Overstuffed seats with reeded rails, high stretcher and fretwork. Turned front legs, on casters. *Courtesy Turner Antiques, New York City.* **$1,600–2,400** the pair.

A fine c. 1880 ebonized Aesthetic Movement chair of generous proportions. Back with oval enclosing a crane (a motif borrowed from the Japanese, a major design source for the Aesthetic Movement) and cattails, surrounded by cutout stylized flowering vines. Stiles and rails with repetitive geometric motifs. Front legs turned and with incised decoration, on casters, Brackets connecting legs to seat rail. *Courtesy Turner Antiques, New York City.* **$1,000–1,500.**

Walnut Eastlake-inspired corner chair, c. 1880–90. This rather quaint corner form was introduced late in the period as a novelty item to perk up the standard parlor suite. Arms with stylized floral carving, seat rail with burl panels, dropped apron with incised decoration, turned legs, on rollers. 24 1/2" x 24 1/2" x 29 1/2" high. *Courtesy Eileen Zambarda, 64 East Antiques, Asheboro, N.C.* **$600–900**.

Eastlake sewing or nursing rocker, c. 1870–80, with turned front legs and stretcher, caned seat and back, reeded elbows, stiles and crest, spindles. Private collection. **$175–275.**

Walnut Eastlake platform rocker, c. 1870. Stiles, crest and seat rail with incised reeding-basic to most American factory-made Eastlake furniture. *Courtesy Depot Antiques, Hillsborough, N.C.* **$275–425.**

Eastlake-Aesthetic Movement armchair, c. 1870–80, with incised molding and stylized floral decoration. Short "trumpet" legs. *Courtesy the Antiques Emporium, Raleigh, N.C.* **$400–600.**

Walnut Eastlake side chair, c. 1880–90, with decorative crest featuring spindles, fan-shaped pieces, incised stylized flower. With "elbows," turned front legs. 18" deep x 18" wide x 36" high. *Courtesy Carolina Antique Mall, Raleigh, N.C.* **$175–275.**

Eastlake-Aesthetic armchair, c. 1880. Ebonized wood with gilt incised decoration, "reeding," stylized flowers. Crest rail with spindles. Turned legs. 39" high. *Courtesy Butte's Antiques, Oxford, N.C.* **$400–600.**

Drawing room chair featured in Eastlake's *Hints on Household Taste* (1878 edition). With rectilinear form, spindles, incised geometric designs—similar in feeling to the preceding chair.

Eastlake-type library chair, c. 1870, in leather (as is).Back (:anted to a comfortable angle and flanked by reeded stiles. Padded arms terminate in roundels and curving burl panels. Trumpet feet, on white porcelain casters. *Courtesy Whitehall at the Villa, Chapel Hill, N.C.* **$1,200–1,800.**

Aesthetic Movement marquetry armchair, c, 1880. Reeded and studded stiles, side rails with repetitive, stylized inlay. Interesting treatment of arms, with "Melting" Romanesque columns with lions' faces, acanthus feet, on rollers. Reflecting the Aesthetic taste for the exotic. *Courtesy Pettigrew Auction, Colorado Springs.* **$1,200–1,800.**

Walnut factory-Eastlake settee, c. 1870-80, with shaped upholstered arms, back with incised reeded stiles enclosing two upholstered panels centering a wooden decorative piece. Crest features stylized floral decoration. Turned legs, on rollers. With two side chairs. 53" long x 39" high. *Courtesy Crabtree & Company Antiques, Cameron, N.C.* **$800–1,200** the set.

Walnut Eastlake loveseat, c. 1870, with incised arm and crest rail decoration. Applied and raised burl walnut panel on skirt, uprights and crest rail. Refinished and reupholstered. Typical factory interpretation of Eastlake (who would not have curved the arms). 54" wide × 21 1/2" deep × 36" high. *Private collection.* **$400–600.**

Walnut factory loveseat, c. 1890, with two-part back divided by wooden scrolling designs that overflow onto crest rail. Also with some Eastlake motifs: reeding, incised decoration, dropped apron. On rollers. *Courtesy Depot Antiques, Hillsborough, N.C.* **$450–650.**

Modern Gothic walnut octagonal table, c. 1880. Inset tooled leather top with leaf-carved border above a conforming apron pierced with quatrefoils and raised on four canted incised legs joined with a cross stretcher. 36" wide × 27 1/2" high. *Courtesy Neal Auction Company, New Orleans, Nicholay & Morgan photographers.* **$800–1,200.**

Walnut Eastlake parlor table, c. 1880, with marble top. Frieze with incised lines (all machine-executed), drop finials. Base with four central legs joined by X-stretchers, extending to four bracket-type feet. 16' × 20" × 28 1/2" high. *Private collection.* **$375–475.**

Walnut Eastlake table, c. 1870-80. Marble top, reeded frieze with drop finials. Base with four clustered legs centering urn finial and flaring out and downward. Applied stylized foliage and incised decoration on legs. On rollers. 30' high × 27" × 20'. *Private collection.* **$500–750.**

Eastlake walnut table, c. 1880, with rouge marble top. Frieze with dropped decoration. Four centered legs, each joined to central turned shaft by incised floral panels, and flaring outward. On casters. 31" long × 22" deep × 30" high. *Courtesy Butte's Antiques, Oxford, N.C.* **$600–800.**

Eastlake walnut side table, c. 1880, with white marble top. Legs arranged in X-formation around central shaft and joined by cutout panels. Bracket-type feet on casters, with incised line decoration. 18 1/2" wide × 27 1/2" deep × 30" high. *Courtesy Carolina Antique Mail, Raleigh, N.C.* **$375–475.**

Eastlake-style walnut library table, c. 1880, made by Herter Brothers (among those who took Eastlake's principles to their fullest expression in America). Rectangular top with leather inset and reeded edge. Two frieze drawers with reeding. Legs are reeded and turned and joined by stretchers that pass through the legs, emphasizing the joint (a concept favored by Eastlake, who believed that construction should be honest). Spindles (another Eastlake favorite) link stretchers to frieze and add decorative interest. Pull-out slide. Shelf stretcher. On casters. *Courtesy Turner Antiques, New York City.* **$5,000–7,500.**

Renaissance Revival-Eastlake oval marble top parlor table, c. 1870. White marble top above shaped incised carved skirt, supported by four galleried legs around a central turned column. 28" high × 25 1/2" wide × 19 1/2" deep. The oval top is very non-Eastlake. *Courtesy Neal Auction Company, New Orleans, Nicolay & Morgan, photographers.* **$450–650.**

An important Aesthetic Movement music cabinet by Herter Brothers of New York City. Parcel gilt, painted, inlaid and ebonized cherrywood. Frieze drawers inlaid with stylized flower heads and pierced cast handles over two bevelled glazed lift-up doors enclosing sliding baize-lined sheet music shelves flanked by carved gilt-incised cupboard doors with fielded panels painted with seated muses-Terpsichore and Calliope. Over carved and spindle-set apron on square feet. Back is stamped "HERTER BROS." 8'6" wide × 34" deep × 42 1/2" high. Commissioned for a California residence, c. 1880. *Courtesy Butterfield & Butterfield, Los Angeles.* **$25,000–35,000.**

Walnut Eastlake-type dining table, c. 1880, with reeded frieze. Legs in X-formation around central 8-sided pedestal, joined by fret-carved panels, with vasiform uprights and bracket-type feet. With two more leaves. 48" x 48" x 28 1/2" high. *Courtesy Butte's Antiques, Oxford, N.C.* **$1800–2,400.**

Eastlake cherry chest of drawers, c. 1870–80. Three over two drawers with incised molding flanked by sides with incised decoration. Panelled sides. On rollers. Original pulls, replaced escutcheons. *Courtesy Antiques Emporium, Raleigh, N.C.* **$400–600.** The same piece in walnut with marble top: **$600–900.**

A well-designed, Eastlake cherry dressing table, c. 1875–80. Rectangular mirror frame set between a pair of drawers resting on lower case having central drawer above an open section fitted with half-shelf and between pedestal ends, each with narrow drawer above cupboard door mounted with strap-work hinges. 49" wide × 21" deep × 60" high. *Courtesy Neal Auction Company, New Orleans, Nicolay & Morgan photographers.* **$800–1,200.**

Walnut factory-Eastlake dresser, c. 1870-80, with two glove drawers flanking inset marble top. Three drawers with incised molding and burl panels. Panelled sides. Mirror flanked by candle brackets, with incised molding, and topped by repeated stylized flower motif and crenelations. "Button and scallop" dovetails, made by the Knapp dovetailing machine which was invented in 1868. 30" wide × 61" high. *Courtesy Depot Antiques, Hillsborough, N.C.* **$600–900.** With marble tops: **$750–1,200.**

Eastlake/Renaissance Revival walnut washstand, c. 1870. with one long drawer over two drawers beside a cabinet—all with reeding and burl panels. Case with reeding and incised decoration. Marble top, backsplash with two candlestands, Renaissance-type shaping and crest. 33" wide × 20" deep × 48" high. This is a marriage—the original backsplash was marble. We often naively believe that Victorian pieces are so "new" that they have not suffered the indignities that befall many 18th-century pieces. Not so! Marriages, divorces, splitting of sets, stylistic additions and alterations are all found in abundance. *Private collection.* **$600–900.**

Marble washstand in the Japanese taste, c. 1880, with marble top. Backsplash with Japanese crest over painted panel. A combination of Eastlake-type reeding and Japanese lines—for instance, on the sides, the cabinet doors centering carved panels of birds, and the fretwork below the cabinets. Central cutout shelf stretcher. Made by Mitchell and Rammelsberg, Cincinnati, Ohio, a major factory and producer of well-designed Eastlake, Modern Gothic, and Japanese-inspired pieces. 38" wide x 19" deep x 39" high. *Courtesy Turner Antiques, New York City.* **$2,500–3,500.**

Eastlake walnut side-lock tall chest, c. 1870. Drawers accented with applied burl panels. Plinth base. Top with one drawer and gallery with raised central section, decorated with applied "crenelations." Drawers with Knapp dovetails. 49" wide x 20" deep x 63" high. *Courtesy Butte's Antiques, Oxford, N.C.* **$1,800–3,000.**

Eastlake walnut sideboard, c. 1870-80, with many different types of decoration: marquetry panels of game birds, reeding, molding, rows of repeated incised and cutout geometric designs, spindles and burl panels. Typical of Eastlake is the rectilinear form and stepped-back upper section. Eastlake would not have approved of the birds, however. He would have rendered them in a more, stylized, less lifelike manner. Original finish. *Courtesy Southampton Antiques, Southampton, Mass.* **$2,400—3,600.**

Sideboard, c. 1880, from a design by Charles Locke Eastlake, featured in *Hints on Household Taste.* Walnut and tulipwood, original finish. Base on saw-tooth-carved feet with panelled sides, panelled doors with prominent decorative hardware. Central open area framed by an arch, with drawers above. Three shelves above with "bamboo"-turned supports. With painted Minton-Hollis tiles. 76 1/2" high × 54" wide × 27" deep. The number of pieces that are Eastlake style or influenced by Eastlake is vastly greater than the number of pieces copied directly from his own designs. This is a handsome piece and a relative rarity; it will be quickly snatched up by a collector. *Courtesy Turner Antiques, New York City.* **$10,000–15,000.**

Charles Hastlake's design for a dining room sideboard. Plate XI, from the 1878 edition of *Hints on Household Taste*——compare to the previous example.

"Modern Gothic" secretary of ebonized cherrvwood, c. 1875, attributed to Kimbel and Cabus, New York City. Gabled cornice with gilt-incised decoration opening to reveal a storage compartment above a marquetry-border bookcase door containing a petit point and Berlin-work needlepoint portrait of a maiden and flanked by a pair of galleried marquetry drawers, resting on a lower case fitted with a fold-out adjustable writing surface above a pair of recessed doors decorated with elaborate pierced brass hinges, and panelled sides outlined with gilt-incised fish scales. The whole raised on a canted chamfered trestle-form base. 36 1/2" wide × 22" deep × 65" high. *Courtesy Neal Auction Company, New Orleans, Nicolay & Morgan photographers.* **$3,000–4,500.**

Ebonized cabinet attributed to Kimbel and Cabus, New York City, c. 1880. Strongly influenced by designs from the Aesthetic Movement and especially Bruce Talbert. This piece is also in agreement with Eastlake's ideas, in its rectilinear form, trestle base borrowed from medieval furniture, incised line decoration, inset ceramic tiles, and spindle-decorated gallery. *Courtesy Joan Bogart, Rockville Centre, N.Y.* Dealer estimate: **$6,000–10,000.**

A fine c. 1870–80 Eastlake walnut fall-front secretary or secretaire a abattant. Panelled fall front and drawer fronts with egg-and-dart borders. Plinth base. Fall front engineered in balanced cantilever fashion. Interior with secret drawer (spring loaded). Well-turned colonettes topped by stylized leaf carving, fish scale carving below. Panelled sides and back. Cherry drawer sides and bottoms. Brass pulls with owl and duck motif. 36' wide × 20' deep × 5'2" high. *Courtesy Rudy's Antiques, Virginia Beach, Va.* **$3,000–4,500.**

Eastlake walnut cylinder (rolltop) desk, c. 1870–90—a popular Victorian desk form. Spindled gallery (typical of the Eastlake style) and reeding are the only decorations on this simple masculine form. Original finish and rough condition. *Courtesy Southampton Antiques, Southampton, Mass.* As is: **$800–1,200.** Restored: **$1,800–2,400.**

Walnut Eastlake cylinder secretary/bookcase, c. 1870–80, with burl panels, reeding, stylized floral motif, panelled sides. Poplar interior, with a yellow wash (typical of Victorian interiors). Original condition. 39" wide × 22" deep × 7'2" high. *Courtesy Rudy's Antiques, Virginia Beach, Va.* **$3,600–4,800.**

Eastlake walnut cylinder secretary, c. 1870–90, with burl panels. The cornice reflects the American tendency to embellish Eastlake's simple forms. Refinished *Courtesy Southampton Antiques, Southampton, Mass.* **$3,000–4,200.**

Eastlake walnut bookcase, c. 1870–80, with one drawer below stepped-back bookcase. Incised molding, crenelations. Original ring polls. May originally have had a gallery. Although this certainly is Eastlake style in terms of overall rectilinear design and decorative motifs, Eastlake actually had specific ideas about bookcases. He felt that they should not have glass doors; instead, books could be protected from dust by curtains or by a narrow decorative leather flap. 30" wide × 16" deep × 5' high. *Courtesy Depot Antiques, Hillsborough, N.C.* **$800–1,200.**

Eastlake cylinder desk with attached bookcases, c. 1880–90. Walnut, with incised line decoration, burl panels, crenelations, reeding. Desk with beveled mirror, cylinder top, drawer and cabinet door. Bookcases each with drawer in base and stepped-back glazed door, egg-and-dart-type cornice. Panelled sides. 67" wide × 25" deep × 5'10" high. *Courtesy Butte's Antiques, Oxford, N.C.* **$4,000–6,000.**

Eastlake bookcase/cabinet of faux-grained soft wood, c. 1880. With a crenelated cornice. Two glazed doors over three graduated drawers. Applied roundels. Plinth base. *Courtesy Whitehall at the Villa, Chapel Hill, N.C.* **$1,800–2,500.**

Eastlake-style walnut writing desk, c. 1880. Floral-carved geometric pediment above a rectangular bevelled glass mirror flanked on either side by two small cabinets, recessed behind a lift-top writing surface with inset leather opening to reveal a leather interior with fitted compartment of drawers and cubby-holes, raised on a trestle-type base with recessed shelf. 30 1/2" wide × 21 1/4" deep × 53" high. *Courtesy Frank H. Boos Gallery, Bloomfield Hills, Mich.* **$1,200–1,600.**

Cherry or mahoganized maple chiffonier, c. 1880–1900, with attached bevelled mirror with simple acanthus decorations, roundels and Eastlake-type reeded molding. Original finish. On casters. This was a new form during this period, being a variation on the tall chest. Late in the Victorian age a taste developed for whimsical design, with new asymmetrical arrangements of cabinets and drawers. This Configuration was taken to its most extreme in the many side-by-sides from that period. *Courtesy Southampton Antiques, Southampton, Mass.* **$500–750.**

Aesthetic-influenced factory-made mahogany side cabinet, c. 1890. Elliptical top with one long rectangular shelf with a pierced fan-carved ball and spindle-carved backsplash above an elliptical beveled glass mirror behind two small shelves with ball-and-spool supports. Rectangular top above a frieze of one long drawer above two long doors with carved leaf-and-ribbon decoration, raised on exaggerated cabriole legs. 15" deep x 17 1/2" wide x 55 1/2" high. *Courtesy Frank H. Boos Auction Gallery, Bloomfield, Hills, Mich.* **$800–1,200.**

Walnut Fort Wayne Organ Company Packard Organ with windpipes, c. 1880. Eastlake incised decoration, Renaissance fretwork. 49" long x 23" deep x 70 1/2" high. *Courtesy Frank H. Boos Gallery, Bloomfield Hills, Mich.* In good working order, **$1,000–1,500.**

Factory-made pine bedstead and dresser with inset tiles, c. 1880, bringing together several styles, which is typical of late 19th-century factory production. Herringbone effect, tiles, incised stylized floral decoration, turned uprights, drop finials, urn finials, stiffly carved crest. Probably English, but similar to some American examples. *Courtesy Morton Goldberg Auctions, New Orleans.* **$2,400–3,600** the set.

Bed from Egyptian Revival ebonized cherrywood and gilt-incised two-piece bedroom suite, c. 1876. Architectural headboard inset with polychromed and gilt plaque depicting Egyptians, and with panelled section and baluster-turned stiles. Low fact-board incised with papyrus blossoms and pseudo-hiero-glyphics. Made in New York. Original condition. The Egyptian Revival shows up occasionally from the Renaissance Revival period to the end of the century, grafting onto the current styles—in this case an East-lake or Aesthetic look. 62" wide × 89" deep × 82" high. *Courtesy Neal Auction Company, New Orleans, Nicholay & Morgan photographers.* (Priced as set with following photograph.)

Dresser matching bed at bottom of page, opposite. Tall cheval mirror topped by polychromed and gilt plaque depicting Egyptians watering a garden. Resting on double marble-topped cabinet bases fitted with four drawers each. Original condition. 83" wide × 23" deep × 90" high. *Courtesy Neal Auction Company, New Orleans, Nicholay & Morgan photographers.* **$10,000–15,000** the set.

Eastlake walnut and burl walnut double bed, c. 1880, with some Neo-Grec touches (such as the anthemion crest rail, columns flanking central burl panel, and drops above columns). The horizontal panels of this bed are typical of Eastlake beds. 74" long × 52" wide × 95" high. *Courtesy New Orleans Auction Gallery, New Orleans.* **$1,200–1,800.**

Faux-bamboo Japanese-style chest of drawers, c. 1880. Two over three graduated drawers with decorative frieze which matches gallery tops of other pieces from the set (mirror shown, hanging above chest). Marble top with splash, doubling piece as a washstand. *Courtesy Butterfield & Butterfield, Los Angeles.* Chest: **$2,400–3,600.** Mirror: **$800–1,200.** Note on suites or sets: Complete bedroom sets should bring more than the separate pieces, but often don't! Therefore dealers and auction houses frequently separate them to maximize profit. Sets consist of as many as seven pieces.

Faux-bamboo wardrobe, c. 1880, with single mirrored door and single drawer. Galleried top. (Note following photo of mirror and chest from same set).*Courtesy Butterfield & Butterfield, Los Angeles.* Wardrobe: **$3,600–4,800.** Double wardrobe: **$4,500–6,500.**

Factory-made dresser and wardrobe from a c. 1890 bedroom suite. To call this Eastlake is a stretch—the base of the dresser is factory Eastlake, but the crests have the exuberant carving of the 1890s opulent period. Characteristic of 1890s factory furniture is the real mishmash of styles—Eastlake; spiral turnings from the Renaissance; the crest treatment, headboard and footboard inspired by the rococo. *Courtesy Flomaton Antique - Auction, Flomaton, Ala.* Dresser: **$1,200–1,800.** Wardrobe: **$1,200–1,800.**

7

Mail-Order Opulence: 1890-1900

In many ways golden oak furniture was a natural outgrowth of the popular factory-Eastlake furniture of the 1880s. Eastlake furniture, with its straight lines and incremental add-on decoration, was easily adapted to factory production. Of course, even in the 1880s factory designers were more generous with ornament than Mr. Eastlake himself would have found tasteful. But by the end of the 1880s, factory styles became even more ornate. Only remnants of the Eastlake idea survived when this extremely eclectic style of decoration and carving began to dominate factory production. This mass-produced furniture was made primarily for middle-class customers, and it needed to be attractive and inexpensive at the same time. The new Midwestern factories with their mechanized production made this dream possible for a large number of Americans.

Many of the factories making golden oak furniture were founded in the Midwest in the 1870s and 1880s. From the start they were equipped with steam to power new woodworking machines. Grand Rapids, Michigan, was probably the most concentrated area for golden oak, although there were also manufacturing centers in Ohio, Illinois, Indiana, New York and Virginia. These factories made huge quantities of furniture, and many of them contracted with the emerging mail-order firms to provide cheap furniture for millions of Americans.

From the 1880s on, this furniture was available through department store catalogs, and especially from Montgomery Ward and Company and Sears, Roebuck and Company from 1893 on. As railroads penetrated more and more of the country, and post offices opened up following the tracks, mail order became a popular way to sell to rural America. As late as 1880, about 70% of America's population was still rural. This was a huge customer base eager for affordable furniture, and mail order proved to be the best way to reach them. Much to the distress of the general stores, Chicago-based companies like Sears, Roebuck and Montgomery Ward began making steady inroads into the rural market. Chicago had its own burgeoning furniture industry with a full range of large factories and high-quality custom shops. Its central location was a key advantage to the great mail-order houses as they set out to create millions of loyal customers all over the country. Extravagant sales copy aside, those companies provided inexpensive furniture. Sears, Roebuck originally purchased furniture from the large factories nearby, but soon after the turn of the century, they actually owned a range of factories, including an upholstered-furniture plant in Chicago.

Another popular variation on catalog sales was golden oak furniture offered as premiums by the Larkin Soap Company of Buffalo, New York—which sold household goods, food, toiletries, notions, and soap. Premiums were used as incentives to purchase Larkin products. The company issued a premium catalog twice a year. One of their most popular premiums was the Larkin desk with slant front and open shelves.

Rural Free Delivery, which began in 1896, and Parcel Post, after 1912, helped make mail-order furniture an option.[1]

From Golden Oak to Fake Oak

By the 1880s the supply of walnut, the favored wood for Renaissance Revival furniture, had been seriously depleted. Manufacturers turned to oak, which was readily available in the Midwest, particularly in southern Illinois and Indiana. Great stands of red oak and white oak were harvested and shipped to factories to be made into golden oak furniture. Oak was strong and durable, but not as easily carved as walnut and mahogany. Mail-order firms wanted strong, sturdy furniture, for which oak was a perfect choice. Often the components were made and shipped to the retailer for final assembly, or parts were crated and shipped directly to the customer.

During this period, oak was treated (finished) in several different ways and was used in solid and veneer forms. Quartersawn oak was very desirable because it produced boards with an attractive patterning of rays. Because the boards were cut to show the most pattern, some timber was wasted, resulting in a more expensive product. Besides its attractive look, quartersawn wood tends to shrink less than other cuts, making a more durable piece of furniture.

One of the drawbacks to oak was its lack of color. The whole Victorian era favored dark woods—rosewood, mahogany, black walnut—so darkened oak must have seemed an obvious improvement to designers in the 1880s and '90s. Various experiments were conducted to come up with attractive finishes. Noticing the effects of tobacco juice on the factory floors, one designer in Grand Rapids tried nicotine stains on oak. This darkly stained oak was called "mud oak" by its detractors, but it proved a strong seller nonetheless.[2]

Fumed oak was the result of exposing unfinished oak to ammonia fumes. Since the fumes penetrate deep into the wood, it is difficult to undo this type of treatment-in fact, it can be a losing battle. Weathered oak, another finish, has a silvery gray look which was produced by using fumes or by simple exposure to the elements. "Antique" oak has a nut-brown finish or contrasting highlights and darker areas achieved by spraying. Golden oak, the most desired finish today, was attained by a hard, orange shellac finish.

While oak was the most desirable wood, furniture made from stained maple or other stained woods—fake oak—was often sold at the low end of the market. Ash, chestnut, elm and hickory all look similar to oak and were frequent substitutes. Inexpensive hotel furniture was of-

---

1. Mail-order golden oak furniture continued to be popular well past 1900, the end date for our book. Golden oak was one of the remnants of the Victorian age that carried over into the 20th century, but after 1900 the Colonial Revival and other styles replaced the Victorian mentality, at least on the cutting edge of fashion. Thus we have chosen to end our coverage of golden oak at 1900, a date which most agree signals a new design era. Our book *Colonial Revival Furniture* (Wallace-Homestead, 1993) covers the new design era.

2. Frank Edward Ransom, *The City Built on Wood* (Ann Arbor, Michigan: Edwards Brothers, 1955), 27.

ten made of various woods and stained to look like the favored oak. Sears, Roebuck and other mail-order kings also sold great quantities of fake oak advertised as having an antique oak finish. Even if you are not an expert in wood types, it is fairly easy to unmask fake oak. When you look at the underside of a table or the inside of a door, for example, the patterns on the outside or top should also be found underneath. If not, you have fake oak.

Settings and Furniture Forms

Through mail order, a family could furnish the parlor in one purchase. By this time the seven-piece suite had evolved into a more affordable three-piece suite, usually consisting of a settee, armchair and rocker. Indeed, the rocker came into its own during this era, with platform rockers leading the way. Once relegated to private areas of the house, the informality of rockers was gradually allowed into the parlor as the century wore on and manners compromised with comfort. Of course, parlors in the countryside always had a character that was different from the formal rooms in sophisticated city settings. Rural parlors might fall prey to a kind of formality that made them unusable except for the milestones of life—like weddings and funerals—or they might be more like living rooms that were comfortable and full of personal touches.

Matching suites were a big seller, not only for the parlor but also for the dining room and bedroom. The basic chamber (bedroom) suite consisted of a bedstead, dresser, and washstand (usually with towel rack). Dining rooms almost always centered around an extension table—either of pedestal form or with legs at the corners. China closets were made by the millions (see Fig. 7-1), and press-backed chairs and sideboards were other dining room furnishings. Ice boxes—usually found in the kitchen—were also common in this era. They were often made of elm or elm veneered in oak.

Practical, sturdy office furniture in oak and other woods, often was made by companies specializing in office furniture. Side-by-sides and Larkin desks may be

Fig. 7-1 Golden oak tripartite china closet, c. 1900, with four paw feet, applied acanthus carving, and scrolling crest. Central convex glass door flanked by two columns with capitals. Upper section with bevelled glass in circle and teardrop design. Oak and oak veneer. The golden oak china closet is another one of those forms that is found in many, many variations. just about everyone's grandmother seems to have had one! This one is a nice example. 6' high. *Courtesy Butte's Antiques, Oxford, N.C.* **$3,000–5,000.**

quaint and appealing, but the panelled flat-top desks and the rolltop desks are truly practical. Perhaps because of their relative simplicity, attractive style, and usefulness, they are sought by today's consumers as well.

Mass-produced mail-order furniture (oak or otherwise) was one area of furniture manufacturing that took advantage of new steam-driven technologies. The ubiquitous pressed-back chairs (see Fig. 7-2) were, of course, not hand-carved but rather decorated with an embossing machine that was introduced in the late 1880s. The depth of cut was limited to about one inch, and the embossing machine was not capable of undercutting or fine detail. Embossed designs were sometimes cut away from the wood stock and then applied to furniture—a method commonly used on mail-order furniture as an alternative to more expensive carved ornaments.[3]

We might criticize factory production for the weak design, but the freedom apparent in shapes and motifs is really what gives many pieces their charm. One can easily say that these pieces do not make organic wholes. Often the designer simply used whatever carved pieces were available and had workers apply them to any number of forms, rather than planning the decoration around the form and function of a particular piece. This said, however, there is often an exuberance in the decoration that customers clearly loved and that appeals to collectors today. Again, this furniture reminds us that the Victorians loved novelty, variety, and visual surprises—which could take the form of asymmetrical arrangements, irregular shapes, and a great variety of applied carving. Side-by-sides, a good example of this

Fig. 7-2 Simple pressed back oak side chair, c. 1900. 17-3/4" wide x 39-1/4" high. *Courtesy Carolina Antique Mall, Raleigh, N.C.* **$125–225.**

aesthetic, are often a tour de force of applied carving, turned pieces and bevelled or stained glass set in eccentric shapes (see Fig. 7-3).

3. Michael J. Ettema, "Technological Innovation and Design Economics in Furniture Manufacture, "*Winter" Portfolio* 16 (1981): 221-23.

Grand Rapids

Grand Rapids was a center of mass-produced furniture during this time. However, its output was not limited to the low-end market. Most successful firms had a high-end line which they produced in smaller quantities, using better-quality materials and more hand work. During the 1880s Grand Rapids factories began using mahogany again, generally for their more expensive suites. Demand was strong enough for the Honduras Lumber Company to establish an office there in 1886. A Nelson and Matter mahogany bedroom suite furnished the White House during the administration of President Arthur[4]—surely a testament to the quality of some of the work. During the 1880s original designs were emphasized—as we can see from the whimsical, fanciful pieces illustrated on pages 179–191. Along with the mass-produced items designed to be crated and shipped and made under contract for mail-order companies or other buyers, most factories also produced a line of better goods with which to secure their reputation. These higher-quality pieces might use mahogany or oak and exhibit profuse carving. A newspaper article from Detroit in 1877 commented on the carving:

Each establishment has its own staff of designers and they are busy the whole year round planning articles for furniture as comfortable, unique, and beautiful as the art of man can compass. The designing and execution are alike perfect. The wood carving departments are a wonder in their way. Some of the wood carvers came from Glasgow, having learned their business on the Clyde, carving figureheads, stem and stern adornments and cabin decorations for the mercantile, naval, racing, and pleasure craft of the world. This apprenticeship stood them in good stead. There is no style of carving too intricate for their deft chisels.... It is an interesting sight to behold a force of thirty to forty of these handcraftsmen employed in one large room, and to inspect the wonderful variety of work executed there.[5]

Along with the skilled carvers on staff in Grand Rapids factories, there were also firms specializing in turned and carved wood ornaments. Power-driven spindle

Fig. 7-3 Mahoganized hardwood side-by-side, c. 1890, exhibiting the pastiche of decorative elements on factory-made pieces of that era: grotesque masks and swirling acanthus, rope-turned corners, irregularly shaped bevelled mirror, bowfront drawers under the slant front, curving glass on the china cabinet door, scalloped apron. A tour de force of whimsical design. 6' high. *Courtesy The Antique Mall, Hillsborough, N.C.* **$1,800–2,800.**

4. Ransom, 24.

5. Ibid., 27.

carvers, capable only of crude carving, were introduced in the late 1880s. Hand carvers were still needed to bring out the details and to do more intricate work on better-quality pieces. Some companies sought out carvers in Europe, as did the Berkey and Gay firm, which procured skilled carvers from Italy.[6]

Custom Furniture

Not all of the furniture from this period was factory-produced. There were also custom shops that made huge, extravagantly carved furniture, sometimes out of oak, but also using the scarcer mahogany and walnut. (Mahogany had begun to make a comeback in the 1880s after almost 30 years of limited use.) Massive is the best word to describe these pieces. Impressive size is one of the hallmarks of Victorian furniture as a whole and it remained true in this last phase as well. Size carried symbolic weight and, clearly, bigger was better. These pieces were meant to convey the owner's economic and social status. Like so much Victorian furniture, the opulent furniture of the 1890s is assertive. The size and extensive carving can be almost overwhelming.

One of the best known of the custom shops was the firm of R. J. Horner of New York City. He worked around the turn of the century in a variety of styles, but is best known for his opulently carved oak pieces (see Figs. 7-4 through 7-7). His work is truly massive and positively encrusted with high-relief imaginative carving of putti, mythical beasts like griffins, dolphins and satyrs. The subject matter is different, but the level of detail approaches the great naturalistic carving of the Rococo Revival period. The figures are not stylized—they are as realistic as such fantastic figures could be. When the carving is executed in oak, it is somewhat coarser than carving in other woods, simply due to the properties of oak. The overall feeling is robust with Renaissance-inspired motifs such as bust carving, scrolling foliate carving, gadrooning and putti holding scrolls and swags.

The wealthy at midcentury had brought the bounty of nature and its carnage into their dining rooms on massive sideboards. It was an idealized view of nature clearly mastered by man. By the end of the century, the wealthy again were filling their dining rooms with assertive carved figures, but now taken from mythology rather than nature.

In these finer pieces made by custom shops, one will find bevelled glass, designs created from stained glass, and extensive carving—in oak, mahogany or walnut. Although Empire can be seen as the base style for much factory-made golden oak, this is not nearly as prominent in the products of custom shops, whose overall look owes more to the incredible, fanciful, high-relief carving that could only be executed by hand. Hairy paw feet from Empire designs were certainly a mainstay of factory furniture, but the ferocious-animal motif was more fully embodied on custom pieces in the form of satyrs, dragons, griffins, and other mythical beasts.

---

6. Ibid., 34.

Fig. 7-4 A remarkable c. 1880 11-piece oak dining room suite (Figs. 7-4 through 7-7), consisting of six side chairs, two armchairs, dining table, sideboard, and server. The suite's provenance indicates that it was purchased directly from R. J. Horner in New York City in the 1880s. Horner's work often blurs the distinction between sculpture and furniture. Chairs (two pictured) with acanthus-carved stiles topped off by bust carving, crests with scrolling acanthus. Scrolling arms with flat acanthus carving. Plain seat rails with dropped scrolling decoration. Cabriole legs with knee carving and paw feet, joined by curving H-stretcher. On casters. *Courtesy Morton Goldberg Auction Gallery, New Orleans.* Set of eight chairs alone: **$6,000–8,000.**

Fig. 7-5 Oak server from the suite. Panelled gallery with cupid and cabochon crest. Gadrooned and shaped serving area over frieze carved with fantastic mythical beasts and gadrooned urn, flanked by high-relief masks. Supported by bearded-male forms entwined with rams and fruit and terminating in prominent human feet (an unusual touch). Panelled back and shaped, molded shelf over mask/paw feet. Server alone: **$3,000–4,500.**

Fig. 7-6 Oak dining table from the suite. Gadrooned edge over profusely carved frieze with Renaissance-type scrolls, vines, ribbons and masks. Supported by massive acanthus-carved pedestal and four winged-female figures with acanthus skirts and large paw feet. With several leaves to enlarge this grand table. Table alone: **$8,000–12,000.**

Fig. 7-7 Oak sideboard from the suite. The base uses motifs from the server, with the male/ram columns, paw/mask feet, gadrooned top edge, and projecting masks. Two cabinet doors with putti, masks, ribbons and Renaissance scrolls. Drawers similarly carved. Top with mirrored back flanked by mythical beast supporting complex crest of entwined scrolls, putti and satyrs centering cabochon and plumes. Sideboard alone: **$8,000–12,000.** The set: **$25,000–35,000.**

Pressed oak side chair, c. 1900, with elaborate well-turned spindle back and turned-spindle front stretchers, caned seat. Note also the twist-turning on uprights of the back and a scalloped front apron. Such points put the quality of these chairs far above the average. *Courtesy The Antique Emporium, Raleigh, N.C.* **$1,600–2,400** set of eight.

One of a pair of walnut pressed-back chairs, c. 1890, with pretty rococo-type pressed decoration and burl panels, spindles, turned front stretchers and legs. 41 1/2" high x 16 1/2" deep x 17-1/2" wide. Such chairs in walnut are extremely rare. *Courtesy Blair Hotel Antiques, Pittsboro, N.C.* **$450–600** the pair.

Oak sculpted-back dining chair from a set of twelve, c. 1890, with caned seat, turned spindles and legs, crest rail with carrying cutout. Refinished. 33" high. *Private collection.* **$1,500–2,400** set of twelve.

Oak potty armchair, c. 1890, with pressed decoration, turned spindles. *Courtesy Depot Antiques, Hillsborough, N.C.* **$100–175.**

Left: Oak rocker with lion's-head arms, c. 1890. **$300–450.** Back: Flame oak and straight-grain oak lady's fall-front desk, c. 1890, with drawer raised on shaped legs. **$500–750.** Center: Oak library table, c. 1890, with spiral turning, paw feet. **$1,200–1,800.** Right: Lion-carved oak armchair, c. 1890. **$800–1,200.** *Courtesy Pettigrew Auction Gallery, Colorado Springs.*

Oak couch with back that folds down to create a bed, c. 1890. The late 19th century produced many versions of sofas that converted into beds. This would have been a relatively affordable model, and one probably available through mail order. *Courtesy Eileen Zambarda, 64 East Antiques, Asheboro, N.C.* **$600–900.**

Oak pedestal dining table, c. 1900, with four original leaves (not shown). Solid oak top over pedestal with four massive paw feet. The massive pedestal table is found in a multitude of variations. 54" diameter. *Courtesy Southampton Antiques, Southampton, Mass.* **$1,200–1,800** as shown. Note that this table can become elaborate but can be simpler as well. Tables with no carved feet, only an Empire Revival scroll, were very common—especially via mail order—and sell for $600–900, depending on leaves, conditions, etc. Slightly more elaborate variations may have a lion's head at the top of the legs near the pedestal and sell for $2,400 or more. Use this example as a benchmark to judge both more simple and more complex examples.

Heavily carved oak dining table, c. 1890, with griffin base, carved frieze, pedestal and base for griffins. If not expandable with leaves, such tables were used in libraries. Attributed to R. J. Horner, New York City. Obviously a high-style example for an opulent era. *Courtesy Witherell Americana Auctions, Elk Grove, Calif.* **$6,000–9,000.**

Carved mahogany partner's desk, c. 1890, with griffin base. Top with gadrooned edge over heavily scroll-carved frieze with three over two drawers. Attributed to R. J. Horner, New York City. *Courtesy Witherell Americana Auctions, Elk Grove, Calif.* Dealer estimate: **$6,000–9,000.**

Carved oak partner's desk, c. 1890. The four corners having relief-carved Jenny Lind-type busts of women, the panelled drawers with carved pulls. Acanthus-carved knees and paw feet. 55" wide × 38" deep × 30' high. *Courtesy James D. Julia, Inc., Fairfield, Maine.* **$4,000–6,000.**

Oak office furniture , c. 1900: Three-drawer file cabinet. **$800–1,200.** Bookcase with ten glass doors over four panelled drawers. **$1,800–2,400.** S-scroll rolltop desk of plain style with panelled sides. **$1,000–1,500.** Swivel desk chair. **$375–600.** *Courtesy Pettigrew Auction Gallery, Colorado Springs.*

Another simple and widely found piece-the golden oak Larkin desk, c. 1890. With applied stylized acanthus carving on back and slant front. Interior with cubbyholes. 5' high. *Courtesy Depot Antiques, Hillsborough, N.C.* **$600–900.**

Oak D-shaped china closet, c. 1895, with curved glass sides flanking central door. Resting on paw feet. Old, dark finish. 4-1/2' high. *Private collection.* **$650–950.**

Oak secretary of simple form, c. 1890. Incised decoration, raised-panel slant front with fitted interior, over four drawers with molded edges. 27" wide × 16-1/2" deep × 5'2" high. *Courtesy Blair Hotel Antiques, Pittsboro, N.C.* **$800–1,200.**

Oak china closet with curved glass sides, c. 1890. Central serpentine door. Columns headed by lions. Paw feet. Scroll-carved cornice. *Courtesy Pettigrew Auction Gallery, Colorado Springs.* **$2,000–4,000.**

Ebonized Empire Revival bookcase, c. 1890, with bevelled glass door flanked by columns ending in paw feet and topped with corinthian capitals. Breakfronted cornice. Replaced plywood back. 40" wide x 64" high. *Courtesy Eileen Zumbarda, 64 East Antiques, Asheboro, N.C.* **$1,200–1,800.**

Mahogany side cabinet, c. 1890. Base resting on six paw feet. Two bevelled-glass doors centering two smaller doors over central open recessed area. Top with mirrored back and attenuated columns supporting two pagoda-like "roofs," centering open area for display with upper shelf and fret-carved gallery. With lots of delicate applied carving and fret carving, there is a fineness to the detail that makes this piece different from the massive oak pieces also popular at the time. This model retains its original "diamond dust" mirrors and cast-iron latticework details at the juncture of the feet and base. In original, mint condition. *Courtesy 19th Century America, Lafayette, La.* Dealer estimate: **$5,000–7,500.**

Oak sideboard, c. 1890, with mirrored backsplash topped by fabulous mythical beasts with scrolling manes. Marble surface above three over two drawers over two cabinet doors with Renaissance-inspired carving, divided by fluted pilasters. Panelled sides. 54" long x 23" deep x 5'5" high. *Courtesy L & L Antiques, Hickory, N.C.* **$2,400–3,600.**

Opulent-period mahogany sideboard by R. J. Horner, New York City, c. 1880-1900. Much of his work shows this profuse Renaissance-inspired carving including mythical beasts, like the "dolphins" on the canted corners. Base on scroll feet with four cabinet doors and one drawer below three frieze drawers, all profusely carved. Serving area backed by large bevelled mirror. Carved columns support the massive scrolling pediment. Also with two display shelves. *Courtesy Southampton Antiques, Southampton, Mass.* **$8,000–12,000.**

Oak hallstand, c. 1890, with hooks, bevelled mirror, seat with lift lid for storage. Typical simple 1890s form that was standard issue from catalog firms. With applied scrolling acanthus and rolling pin-type decoration. 74" high. *Courtesy Blair Hotel Antiques, Pittsboro, N.C.* **$1,000–1,600.**

Opulent oak hall bench, c. 1890, absolutely encrusted with carving. Arms supported by winged lions. Seat lifts for storage. Base with scrolling foliage and mask carving. Paw feet. 65" wide x 47" high. *Courtesy Pettigrew Auction Gallery, Colorado Springs.* **$3,000–4,800.**

Golden oak bedroom suite, c. 1890. In general, golden oak furniture uses modified heavy Empire forms and employs figured oak veneer in the same way flame mahogany veneer was used on Empire furniture-the wood grain itself supplies the decorative interest. This type of cornice is limited to golden oak furniture-with cigarlike bar surmounted by scrolls. *Courtesy Morton Goldberg Auction Gallery, New Orleans.* Dresser: **$900–1,500.** Washstand: **$600–900.**

Golden oak dresser, c. 1890 with applied acanthus and scroll carving. oak and oak veneer. Slightly bowed drawers. Bevelled mirror. 40" side × 76" high. *Courtesy Calico Quilt, Goldston, N.C.* **$450–700.**

Wardrobe from the suite. Base with configuration similar to dressers, with stepped-back upper section. Two mirrored doors, upper edges framed in scrolling acanthus, flanked by columns and divided by panel with applied carving. Cornice similar to those on dressers. Panelled sides. *Courtesy Morton Goldberg Auction Gallery, New Orleans.* **$1,500–2,400.**

Mail-order-type tall chest with mirrors, c. 1900–1920. Left: With serpentine-fronted drawers. Mahoganized maple or cherry. **$400–600.** Middle: Oak with applied scrolled carving on drawer faces. **$450–650.** Right: Narrow chest with panelled sides. Original finish. **$450–650.** These forms take us to the end of the Victorian period; we are now moving into the era dominated by factory-produced Colonial Revival furniture, represented in this photo by the chair (for extensive reference, see our book *Colonial Revival Furniture with Prices*). *Courtesy Pettigrew Auction Gallery, Colorado Springs.*

Panelled bedstead from the suite. Footboard with applied acanthus carving and rolling pin-type crest. Headboard similarly decorated. The table is Eastlake and was not part of the original suite. *Courtesy Morton Goldberg Auction Gallery, New Orleans.* **$900–1,500.**

BIBLIOGRAPHY

Ames, Kenneth L., ed. *Victorian Furniture: Essays from a Victorian Society Autumn Symposium.* Philadelphia: Victorian Society in America, 1983. Published as *Nineteenth Century* 8, nos. 3–4 (1982).

———. *Death in the Dining Room and Other Tales of Victorian Culture.* Philadelphia: Temple University Press, 1992.

———. "Designed in France: Notes on the Transmission of French Styles to America." *Winterthur Portfolio* 12 (1977): 103–14.

———. "Grand Rapids Furniture at the Time of the Centennial." *Winterthur Portfolio* 10 (1975): 23–50.

———. "The Rocking Chair in 19th Century America." *The Magazine Antiques* 103 (1973): 322–327.

———. "Sitting in (Néo-Grec) Style." *Nineteenth Century* 2, nos. 3–4 (Autumn 1976): 50–58.

———. "What is the Néo-Grec?" *Nineteenth Century* 2, no. 2 (Summer 1976): 12–21.

Art and Antiques, ed. *Nineteenth Century Furniture: Innovation, Revival and Reform.* Introduction by Mary Jean Madigan. New York: Billboard Publications, an Art and Antiques Book, 1982.

Aslin, Elizabeth. *The Aesthetic Movement: Prelude to Art Nouveau.* New York: A. Praeger, 1969.

Bates, Elizabeth Bidwell and Jonathan L. Fairbanks. *American Furniture, 1620 to the Present.* New York: Richard Marek Publishers, 1981.

Bishop, Robert and Patricia Coblentz. *The World of Antiques, Art, and Architecture in Victorian America.* New York: E. P. Dutton, 1979.

Blundell, Peter S. *Market Place Guide to Oak Furniture—Styles and Values.* Paducah, Ky.: Collector Books, 1980.

Burke, Doreen Bolger, et al. *In Pursuit of Beauty: Americans and the Aesthetic Movement.* New York: Rizzoli International Publications in association with the Metropolitan Museum of Art, 1986.

Butler, Joseph T. *American Antiques 1800–1900.* New York: The Odyssey Press, 1969.

Cook, Clarence. *The House Beautiful: Essays on Beds, Tables, Stools, and Candlesticks.* New York: Scribner, Armstrong and Company, 1878. Reprint, Croton-on-Hudson, N.Y.: North River Press, 1980.

Darling, Sharon. *Chicago Furniture: Art, Craft and Industry, 1833–1983.* New York: W. W. Norton, 1984.

Dietz, Ulysses G. *Century of Revivals: 19th-Century American Furniture from the Collection of the Newark Museum.* Newark, N.J.: Newark Museum of Art, 1983.

Downing, Andrew Jackson. *The Architecture of Country Houses Including Designs for Cottages, and Farm-Houses, and Villas, with Remarks on Interiors, Furniture, and the Best Modes of*

Warming and Ventilating. New York: D. Appleton, 1850; reprint, New York: Dover Publications, 1969.

Dubrow, Eileen and Richard. *American Furniture of the Nineteenth Century, 1840–1880.* Exton, Penna: Schiffer Publishing, Ltd., 1983.

———. *Made in America 1875–1905.* West Chester, Penna.: Schiffer Publishing, Ltd., 1982.

Eastlake, Charles. *Hints on Household Taste in Furniture, Upholstery, and Other Details.* London: Longmans, Green & Co., 1868. 2nd edition 1869. 3rd edition 1872. 4th revised edition 1878 (this edition reprinted by Dover Publications, New York, 1969). In America, 1st edition 1872, 2nd edition 1874. 3rd edition 1875. 4th edition 1876. 5th edition 1877.

Ettema, Michael J. "Technological Innovation and Design Economics in Furniture Manufacture." *Winterthur Portfolio* 16, nos. 2/3 (Summer/Autumn 1981): 197–233.

Fitzgerald, Oscar P. *Three Centuries of American Furniture.* Englewood Cliffs, N.J.: Prentice-Hall, 1982.

Garrett, Wendell. *Victorian America: Classical Romanticism to Guilded Opulence.* New York: Rizzoli International Publications, 1993.

Gloag, John. *Victorian Comfort: A Social History of Design from 1830–1900.* New York: Macmillan Company, 1961.

Grier, Katherine. *Culture and Comfort: People, Parlors, and Upholstery, 1850–1930.* Amherst: University of Massachusetts Press, 1988.

Grover, Kathryn, ed. *Dining in America, 1850–1900.* Amherst: University of Massachusetts Press, 1987.

Hanks, David. *Innovative Furniture in America 1800 to the Present.* New York: Horizon Press, 1981.

Hauserman, Diane D. "Alexander Roux and His 'Plain and Artistic Furniture'."

The Magazine Antiques 93, no. 2 (February 1968): 210–217.

Hosley, William. *The Japan Idea: Art and Life in Victorian America.* Hartford, Conn.: Wadsworth Atheneum, 1990.

Howe, D. W., ed. *Victorian America.* Philadelphia: University of Pennsylvania Press, 1976.

Howe, Katherine S. and David B. Warren. *The Gothic Revival Style in America, 1830–1870.* Houston: Museum of Fine Arts, 1976.

Howe, Katherine S., Alice Cooney Frelinghuysen and Catherine Hoover Voorsanger. *Herter Brothers: Furniture and Interiors for a Gilded Age.* New York: Harry N. Abrams, Inc., 1994.

Johnson, J. Stewart. "John Jelliff, Cabinetmaker." *The Magazine Antiques* 206 (August 1972): 256–260.

MacKay, James. *Turn of the Century Antiques.* New York: Dutton, 1974.

Madigan, Mary Jean Smith. *Eastlake-Influenced American Furniture 1870–1890.* Yonkers, N.Y.: Hudson River Museum, 1973.

———. "The Influence of Charles Locke Eastlake on American Furniture Manufacture, 1870–90." *Winterthur Portfolio* 10 (1975): 1–22.

McClaugherty, Martha Crabill. "Household Art: Creating the Artistic Home, 1868–1893." *Winterthur Portfolio* 18, no. 1 (Spring 1983): 1–26.

Meeks, Carroll L. V. *The Railroad Station.* New Haven: Yale University Press, 1956.

Nineteenth-Century America: Furniture and Other Decorative Arts. Introduction by Berry B. Tracy. New York: Metropolitan Museum of Art, 1970.

Ormsbee, Thomas H. *Field Guide to American Victorian Furniture.* Boston and Toronto: Little, Brown and Company, 1952.

Otto, Cecelia Jackson. *American Furniture of the Nineteenth Century.* New York: The Viking Press, 1965.

———. "Pillar and Scroll: Greek Revival Furniture of the 1830s." *The Magazine Antiques* 81 (May 1962): 504–507.

Pearce, John N. and Lorraine W. Pearce. "More on the Meeks Cabinetmakers." *The Magazine Antiques* 90 (July 1966): 69–73.

Pearce, John N., Lorraine W. Pearce, and Robert C. Smith. "The Meeks Family of Cabinetmakers." *The Magazine Antiques* 85 (April 1964): 414–420.

Peirce, Donald C. "Mitchell and Rammelsberg: Cincinnati Furniture Manufacturers, 1847–1881." *Winterthur Portfolio* 13 (1979): 209–29.

Ransom, Frank Edward. *The City Built on Wood: The History of the Furniture Industry in Grand Rapids, Michigan 1850–1950.* Ann Arbor, Mich.: Edwards Brothers, 1955.

Schwartz, Marvin D., Edward J. Stanek, and Douglas K. True. *The Furniture of John Henry Belter and the Rococo Revival: An Inquiry into Nineteenth-Century Furniture Design through a Study of the Gloria and Richard Manney Collection.* New York: E. P. Dutton, 1981.

Smith, Robert C. "Gothic and Elizabethan Revival Furniture, 1800–1850." *The Magazine Antiques* 75 (March 1959): 272–276.

Spofford, Harriet. *Art Decoration Applied to Furniture.* New York: Harper and Brothers, 1878.

Stevenson, Louise. *The Victorian Homefront: American Thought and Culture, 1860–1880.* Boston: Twayne, 1991.

Strickland, Peter L. L. "Furniture by the Lejambre Family of Philadelphia." *The Magazine Antiques* 113, no. 3 (March 1978): 600–613.

Walters, Betty Lawson. "The King of Desks: Wooton's Patent Secretary." *Smithsonian Studies in History and Technology* No. 3 (1969): 1–22.

Weidman, Gregory R. *Furniture in Maryland, 1740–1940.* Baltimore: Maryland Historical Society, 1984.

Winkler, Gail and Roger W. Moss. *Victorian Interior Decoration: American Interiors 1830–1900.* New York: Holt, 1986.

CONTRIBUTORS

The Antique Mall, Inc.
387 Ja-Max Drive
Hillsborough, NC 27278
(919) 732-8882

Antiques Emporium
Cameron Village
2060 Clark Avenue
Raleigh, NC 27605
(919) 834-7250

Blair Hotel Antiques
11 Hillsboro Street
Pittsboro, NC 27312
(919) 542-1141

Joan Bogart
Box 265
Rockville Centre, NY 11571
(516) 764-5286

Frank H. Boos Gallery
420 Enterprise Court
Bloomfield Hills, MI 48301
(810) 332-1500

Butterfield & Butterfield
7601 Sunset Boulevard
Los Angeles, CA 90046
(213) 850-7500

The Butterfly—Fine Antiques
Durham, NC

Butte's Antiques
Oxford, NC

Byrum Furniture and Antiques
117 Morris Street
Hertford, NC 27944
(919) 426-7478

Calico Quilt
PO Box 249
Goldston, NC 27252
(919) 898-4998

Carolina Antique Mall
Cameron Village
2060 Clark Avenue
Raleigh, NC 27605
(919) 833-8227

Crabtree & Company Antiques
Carthage Street
Cameron, NC
(910) 245-3163

Depot Antiques
Daniel Boone Village
Hillsborough, NC 27278
(919) 732-9796

Leighton Adair Butts
1900 Carolina Dr.
Tryon, NC 28782
(704) 856-6849

Edwards Antiques and Collectibles
302 Hillsboro Street
Pittsboro, NC 27312
(919) 542-5649

Flomaton Antique Auction
207 Palafox Street
Flomaton, AL 36441
(334) 296-3059

Frederick Craddock III Antiques
Lynchburg, VA

The Flying Eagle Galleries
Durham, NC

Freeman\Fine Arts
1808-10 Chestnut Street
Philadelphia, PA 19103
(215) 563-9275

Morton Goldberg Auction Galleries
New Orleans, LA

Grogan & Company
890 Commonwealth Ave.
Boston, MA 02215
(617) 566-4100

Heritage House Antiques
PO Box 245
Bland, VA 24315
(703) 688-3755

Leslie Hindman Auctioneers
Chicago, IL

James D. Julia, Inc.
PO Box 830
Fairfield, ME 04937
(207) 453-7125

L & L Antiques
4025 Hwy. 70 S.W.
Hickory, NC 28601
(704) 328-9373

Merrywood Antiques
5608 Patterson Ave.
Richmond, VA 23226
(804) 288-9309

Neal Auction Company
4038 Magazine Street
New Orleans, LA 70115
(504) 899-5329

New Orleans Auction Gallery, Inc.
801 Magazine Street
New Orleans, LA 70130
(504) 566-1849

19th Century America
3603 Johnston Street
Lafayette, LA 70501
(318) 988-1020

Pettigrew Auction Gallery
1645 South Tejon Street
Colorado Springs, CO 80906
(719) 633-7963

Rudy's Antiques
3324 Virginia Beach Boulevard
Virginia Beach, VA 23452
(804) 340-2079

64 East Antiques and Collectibles
4660 U.S. Hwy. 64 East
Franklinville, NC 27248
(910) 824-1542

Skinner, Inc.
Auctioneers and Appraisers of Fine Art
63 Park Plaza
Boston, MA 02116
(617) 350-5400

Kimball M. Sterling
125 W. Market Street
Johnson City, TN 37601
(615) 928-1471

Southampton Antiques
172 College Highway (Route 10)
Southampton, MA 01073
(413) 527-1022

Turner Antiques, Ltd.
Madison Avenue Antiques Center #6
760 Madison Avenue
New York, NY 10021

Whitehall at the Villa
David Lindquist; Elizabeth Lindquist
   Mann
1213 East Franklin Street
Chapel Hill, NC 27514
(919) 942-3179

Witherell Americana Auctions
3620 West Island Court
Elk Grove, CA 95758
(916) 683-3266

Woodbine Antiques
213 College Street
Oxford, NC 27565
(919) 693-2973

INDEX